Abortion and Infanticide

ABORTION AND INFANTICIDE

MICHAEL TOOLEY

CLARENDON PRESS · OXFORD

Oxford University Press, Walton Street, Oxford OX2 6DP

Oxford New York Toronto
Delhi Bombay Calcutta Madras Karachi
Kuala Lumpur Singapore Hong Kong Tokyo
Nairobi Dar es Salaam Cape Town
Melbourne Auckland

and associated companies in
Beirut Berlin Ibadan Mexico City Nicosia

Oxford is a trade mark of Oxford University Press

Published in the United States by
Oxford University Press, New York

© Michael Tooley 1983

First published 1983
Reprinted 1985
New as Paperback 1985

British Library Cataloguing in Publication Data
Tooley, Michael
Abortion and infanticide.
1. Abortion
I. Title
179'.7 HQ767
ISBN 0 19 824674 9
ISBN 0 19 824916 0 (paperback)

Library of Congress Cataloging in Publication Data
Tooley, Michael, 1941–
Abortion and infanticide.
Bibliography: p.
Includes index.
1. Abortion—Moral and ethical aspects. 2. Infan-
ticide—Moral and ethical aspects. I. Title.
[DNLM: 1. Abortion, Induced—Psychology. 2. In-
fanticide—Psychology. HG 767 T671a]
HQ767.3.T66 1983 363.4'6 83 6261
ISBN 0 19 824674 9
ISBN 0 19 824916 0 (paperback)

Printed in Great Britain
at the University Press, Oxford
by David Stanford
Printer to the University

To my aunts,
Dell and Madeline Tooley
and to the memory of my grandparents,
Olive and Jim Tooley

Preface

All the research for this book, and most of the writing, were carried out during my appointment as a Research Fellow, and later as a Senior Research Fellow, in the Department of Philosophy in the Research School of Social Sciences of the Australian National University. This appointment provided me with the opportunity to pursue a number of research projects in a setting that was relaxed and congenial. I am very grateful indeed for having had this opportunity, especially as I found the Australian philosophical community a very stimulating one in which to work.

I am deeply indebted to a number of people for helpful comments and criticisms: Professor Antony Flew, who read all of an earlier draft, and had many valuable suggestions; Professor Emeritus Archibald McIntyre, former Head of the Department of Physiology at Monash University, who scrutinized very carefully the sections dealing with the scientific evidence concerning human development; and Dr William Godfrey-Smith, who commented in detail on the discussion in Chapter 7. My greatest debt, however, is to the two readers for Oxford University Press—Derek Parfit and Jeff McMahan. This book is much stronger as a result of their excellent and extraordinarily detailed criticisms and suggestions.

MICHAEL TOOLEY

Contents

Introduction

In recent years, the moral issues raised by abortion and, to a much lesser extent, by infanticide, have been the subject of vigorous and sustained discussion in philosophical circles. This book is addressed, however, not merely to philosophers, but to everyone who is seriously interested in the difficult moral questions raised by abortion, and who would like to see how the issues can be sharpened and clarified, and the discussion advanced, by a philosophically informed approach.

Philosophy is, for many people, an unfamiliar subject. The book begins, therefore, with a brief account of the nature of philosophy in general, and of ethics in particular. This is followed by a discussion of some important techniques that philosophers frequently employ in thinking about ethical issues. The thrust of later discussions and arguments will be more easily grasped, I believe, given an appreciation of the nature of philosophy, together with an understanding of some of the underlying techniques and strategies that play a central role in philosophical thinking.

The first part of the book also contains a brief discussion of some relevant, but unresolved issues in meta-ethics. Section 1.4 is concerned with the problem of whether moral principles can be objectively justified, and if so, how, while section 1.5 deals with the question of the role that appeal to moral intuitions may appropriately play in an evaluation of ethical views.

The second part of the book focuses upon abortion. The discussion here has two main aspects. First, it is necessary to determine what the basic, underlying issues are. This task is much less straightforward than it might seem to those unfamiliar with philosophical discussions in this area. We shall come to see, in fact, that virtually all public debate on the question of the morality of abortion fails to grapple with the fundamental moral issues.

The crucial questions having been isolated, the next step is to consider alternative answers that might be advanced, together with the most important considerations that can be offered for and against each. We shall see that some of the issues are philosophically very difficult, and that it is by no means obvious what the correct view is. None the less, I believe that when alternative possibilities are subjected to close critical scrutiny, it can be shown that there is at most a very limited range of answers that are intellectually acceptable.

Most current discussions of abortion tend to treat it in isolation from the question of the morality of infanticide. One of the central contentions to be advanced here is that it is very difficult indeed to arrive at a defensible position on abortion unless one is prepared to come to terms with the difficult issue of the moral status of infanticide. The third part of the book, therefore, deals with infanticide. Here I attempt to do three main things. First, I argue that the question of the morality of infanticide cannot be settled by appealing to moral intuitions, contrary to what many contemporary philosophers appear to believe. Second, I survey the historical and anthropological background, in order to put the question in a slightly different perspective, and one which will, I hope, facilitate a more dispassionate approach to the question. Finally, I consider the most important arguments bearing upon the issue of the morality of infanticide. One of the conclusions that I attempt to establish is that this issue cannot be resolved without taking a very careful look at human development, and I therefore go on to offer a fairly detailed summary of what is currently known about relevant aspects of human development, both before and after birth.

The final part of the book contains a brief summary of the main conclusions, a general survey of some of the important methodological considerations that have guided the discussion, and an indication of those areas where further examination appears to be needed before there can be a completely satisfactory resolution of some of the problems discussed here.

PART I
PHILOSOPHICAL BACKGROUND

1
Ethics, Meta-ethics, and Philosophical Thinking

1.1 The Nature of Philosophy

What is philosophy? What are its goals and methods? How is it related to other disciplines, such as science? Philosophers offer somewhat different answers to these questions. For our present purposes, however, such disagreements are not especially important, and it will suffice to offer a conception of philosophy that is at least broad enough to include most of the activities thought of as falling within the scope of philosophy.

Philosophy may be viewed as having three main aspects. First, it is concerned with analysing fundamental concepts, and with clarifying the relations between them. Among the basic concepts with which philosophers are concerned are the concepts of space, time, causality, laws, probability, justification, sense experience, rightness, wrongness, justice, equality, inference, validity, possibility, necessity, identity. One of the primary goals of philosophy is to offer illuminating analyses of these fundamental concepts, where this is a matter of finding simpler, and in some sense more basic concepts, in terms of which the same ideas can be expressed.

Second, philosophy is concerned with the justification of important and basic human beliefs. Among such beliefs are the beliefs in the existence of other minds, and in the existence of an independently real, external world, beliefs about the past and about the future, and beliefs about what is right or wrong, good or bad. One of the primary tasks of philosophy is to determine whether, and to what extent, such beliefs are reasonable, and if they are reasonable, precisely what account is to be given of their justification.

A third main task of philosophy is that of providing a unified and comprehensive general account of the nature of reality. Our beliefs about the world derive from many sources —such as everyday experience, scientific experimentation and theorizing, religion, and tradition. Sometimes there seem to be tensions, or apparent conflicts, between different beliefs. For example, if one believes that the laws of physics are ultimately deterministic, does that leave room for belief in minds, conceived of as immaterial things that interact with the bodies with which they are associated? Or for belief in God, thought of as a person who intervenes in human history? Or for belief in human freedom of action? Philosophers are interested in exploring such tensions, and in examining the relations between beliefs in different areas, in order to ascertain whether some of those beliefs may have to be changed if one is to have a consistent and unified picture of the world. The ultimate aim is a synoptic vision of reality.

So understood, philosophy may be approached either as a technical discipline, or as a Socratic enterprise. In the former case, philosophy presents one with a collection of intriguing and challenging problems—problems which are exciting independently of any relation to one's own life and the lives of others, and with which, in many cases, philosophers have grappled for well over 2,000 years.

Alternatively, one may start out from the Socratic dictum that the unexamined life is not worth living, and one may view philosophy as an enterprise in which one's own most basic beliefs and values are to be subjected to searching critical scrutiny.

Viewed in the latter way, it is easy to see why there is a widespread fear and distrust of philosophical thinking. Most people have not, after all, arrived at their fundamental beliefs and values on the basis of a careful consideration of the alternatives, and of what can be said for and against each. Many of their most basic beliefs and values are ones that they have come to hold simply because they were raised in an environment in which those beliefs and values were accepted without question. Raised in a different society, or by rather different parents, many of their most fundamental beliefs and values would be likely to have been quite different. As a consequence, when one subjects one's beliefs and values to critical examination, when one asks what reasons there are for believing one thing rather than another, for accepting one set of values, moral principles, or way of life, rather than others, the outcome may very well be that some change in one's beliefs and values is called for. In a sense, then, philosophy is a subversive discipline, and profoundly so. But the object is not to tear down and to destroy. It is to find a more plausible and more defensible set of beliefs and values, and thereby, a more satisfactory view of the world, and of man's place in it.

Philosophy as a technical discipline and philosophy as a Socratic enterprise are thus not utterly different things. The difference is one of emphasis and orientation, a function of the bearing of the problems considered upon human life in general, and upon one's own life in particular. The same method of philosophical thinking lies at the heart of both.

1.2 Ethics

The questions we shall be concerned with here fall within the branch of philosophy known as ethics. A brief general survey of this area of philosophy will, I believe, help the reader to place subsequent discussions in their proper settings.

The three aspects of philosophy mentioned above are all encountered within the field of ethics. First, analysis. Philosophers working in ethics have devoted considerable attention to questions of analysis. Such questions can be seen as falling into two main groups. First, there are questions concerning the analysis of specific ethical terms. What does it mean to say that an action is *right*, or that it is *wrong*? That one *ought*, or ought not, do something? What does it mean to say that some state of affairs is *good*? Or that it is *valuable*, or *desirable*? What does it mean to say that someone has a *right* to something? Can such terms be analysed? If some of them can be analysed, what will the analysis involve? Will it be in terms of other ethical expressions, or is it possible to offer an analysis that is free of ethical terms?

Second, and also within the general area of analysis, there are questions concerning the meaning of ethical *statements*. What sort of meaning do ethical statements have? How do they function? Does an ethical statement, such as 'It is wrong to cause suffering', serve to put forward some claim about the nature of the world, or about some transcendent realm of values? Does it, in short, say something which is either true or false? Or does it have some very different sort of function?

Many philosophers maintain that ethical statements say something which is either true or false—that their primary function, at least, is to describe certain states of affairs, to formulate propositions expressing moral facts. Many other philosophers, however, think that this view is mistaken, and a variety of alternative positions have been advanced concerning the meaning of ethical statements. One view, known as emotivism, suggests that moral statements function to express one's feelings or attitudes towards acts of the sort in question.[1] To say that murder is wrong, on this view, is just to express a certain negative attitude towards acts of murder.

Another view, known as prescriptivism, maintains that ethical statements are, in effect, universalized imperatives—imperatives directed not at any particular person, but at people in general.[2] On this view, a statement such as 'Euthanasia is wrong' is, as a first approximation, to be analysed as equivalent to 'Everyone, refrain from euthanasia.'

What is the significance of these two areas of ethical analysis for the discussion that follows? As regards the analysis of particular ethical terms, this assumes importance only in one place—section 5.2. There I shall be considering the question of the conditions that something must satisfy in order to have a right to life, and I shall be advancing an argument in which the question of the correct analysis of the concept of a right is quite crucial.

The analysis of the meaning of ethical statements, in contrast, has no bearing upon specific arguments. On the other hand, the fact that this question has not been satisfactorily resolved has important implications for the justification of

---

[1] A brief statement of an emotivist view of ethical language can be found in chapter 6 of A. J. Ayer's *Language, Truth and Logic*, 1936. A more detailed statement and defence is contained in Charles L. Stevenson's *Ethics and Language*, 1944.

[2] For a lucid defence of a prescriptivist approach to the analysis of ethical language, see R. M. Hare's *The Language of Morals*, 1952.

ethical principles, and this in turn raises some critical questions about the appropriate method for the discussion of ethical issues. Some of these questions will be considered in the next three sections.

Let us now turn to the second aspect of philosophy—that of justification. In the field of ethics, this involves two main tasks. One of these is concerned with general issues of justification within ethics. Are some ethical statements correct, and others incorrect? Can ethical statements be justified, or criticized? Can one give reasons either for accepting some ethical statements, or for rejecting others? If so, how can this be done?

The answers one offers to these questions will depend, among other things, upon the account that one accepts of the meaning of ethical statements. If ethical statements possess factual meaning, then to say that an ethical statement is justified will, presumably, just be to say that the available evidence makes it likely that it is true. The really serious questions, of course, remain. Is it possible for one to know that some ethical statements are true, and others false? Is it possible for there to be evidence that would make some ethical statements reasonable and others not? If so, what sort of evidence is relevant?

The situation is, none the less, very different if ethical statements are neither true nor false, if they do not function to make assertions. Then it is, to say the least, much less clear what could be meant by saying that some moral principles are correct, or justified, and others not. Most philosophers, in fact, tend to assume that if ethical statements do not possess factual meaning, it makes no sense to speak of some as justified and others not.

This inference may seem very plausible. I want to urge, however, that it not be embraced too quickly. It rests upon the assumption that it cannot be appropriate to speak of ethical principles as being capable of objective justification unless it is possible for there to be grounds that can make it likely that an ethical principle is true. But perhaps there is some other acceptable model of objective justification that may be applicable to ethical statements even if they are not such as can be either true or false? This possibility will be considered in section 1.4.

The other main undertaking in ethics that is connected with the problem of justification is that of formulating, and subjecting to critical scrutiny, competing sets of general ethical principles that will, ideally, provide a comprehensive account of when actions are right or wrong, and of when states of affairs are good or bad. How this task is to be viewed will depend upon the general question of the justifiability of ethical statements. If objective justification is possible, then one should be aiming at a comprehensive set of general principles that are objectively justified. But suppose, on the other hand, that it should turn out that ethical principles are not susceptible to any sort of objective justification. What implications would this have for the philosophical discussion of the merits of competing ethical systems? Would it imply, in particular, that rational discussion of ethical issues was impossible, and that what passes for rational discussion in this area must be nothing more than an exercise in propaganda, an attempt to persuade others to adopt one's views through the use of various emotional appeals?

It is important to see that the impossibility of any sort of objective justification would not have such implications. The reason is that objective *criticism* of ethical systems is possible even if objective justification is not. In the first place, an ethical system can be criticized on purely *logical* grounds, since it may incorporate principles that are, possibly in quite subtle ways, mutually inconsistent. Second, as will become clear shortly, most actual ethical systems involve moral principles some of which rest upon *non-ethical* claims. A demonstration that some of those non-ethical claims are implausible may thus provide a person with a good reason for abandoning the ethical principles that presuppose them.

These possibilities will be explored more fully in the next section. The important point here is merely that there are types of criticism that can be brought to bear upon ethical systems regardless of whether it is possible to offer any sort of objective justification for ethical claims. The enterprise of comparing and evaluating ethical systems thus remains a sound and valuable undertaking—albeit a more limited one— even if moral scepticism should turn out to be the correct view to take on the question of the possibility of an objective justification of ethical claims.

Let us turn, now, to the final philosophical undertaking—that of setting out a synoptic vision of reality, of offering a general account of what there is. The relevance of ethics to this enterprise is connected with the question of the meaning of ethical statements. If ethical statements function to make assertions, if they say something which is either true or false, this may have implications with respect to what sorts of things there are.

The reason is this. Suppose that some ethical statements, such as 'It is wrong to cause suffering', are true. What account is to be offered of the truth of such statements? The answer will depend upon how the concept of truth is to be analysed in general. But consider a view that many would accept, to the effect that a statement (or proposition) is true in virtue of its standing in some appropriate relation to some corresponding fact, or state of affairs. If this view is adopted, the question becomes one of what the truth-maker is for the statement, 'It is wrong to cause suffering.' Again, different answers are possible. One view, however, is that the state of affairs that makes this statement true involves what have been referred to as *non-natural* properties or relations—where a non-natural property or relation is one that cannot be reduced to, or analysed in terms of, the physical and psychological properties (and relations) which characterize entities, including people, in the natural world. If this view is adopted, the resulting picture of reality is quite different from what it would otherwise be. It is clear, then, that the questions, first, of whether ethical statements are such as are either true or false, and, if so, what account is to be given of their truth, raise issues that have an important bearing upon the philosophical task of constructing a comprehensive and unified picture of the world.

1.3 The Clarification and Evaluation of Ethical Positions

There are a variety of techniques that philosophers typically employ in examining systems of ethical principles. The discussion in this section will be confined to those techniques whose employment does not presuppose that ethical statements can be objectively justified.

The examination of an ethical position usually involves two aspects: clarification and evaluation. Let us begin by considering some techniques of clarification. The first two aspects of clarification are connected with ways in which individual ethical statements may be unclear. One obvious way is that a statement may contain terms that are *vague or ambiguous*. An important illustration of this in the present context is afforded by principles that contain the expression 'human being'. We shall see later that this expression is often used in significantly different senses by people debating the morality of abortion. When this ambiguity goes unnoticed, as it usually does, the result is a discussion in which people talk past one another, generating considerable heat, but very little illumination. In approaching moral questions philosophically it is important to be sensitive to such ambiguity, and to attempt to make explicit the different possible meanings of crucial terms. When this is done, fruitful discussion becomes possible.

The second reason that individual ethical statements often stand in need of clarification is that the moral principles that people advance often involve *tacit restrictions of scope*. If, for example, someone says that killing is wrong, it is unlikely that he intends that statement to be interpreted in an unrestricted way. First, because he probably does not object to the killing of non-human animals, let alone to the killing of plants. Second, because he may very well not even think that the killing of humans is always wrong. He may hold, for example, that there is nothing wrong with capital punishment, or with killing in self-defence. Thus, one of the first tasks, when confronted with a statement such as 'Killing is wrong', is to determine precisely what is being affirmed. The result will be a somewhat more complex statement, in which the scope restrictions implicit in the original statement are made explicit.

Two other important techniques of clarification are concerned not with individual ethical statements, but with the over-all structure of the moral principles that underlie an individual's moral point of view. Many such principles can be arrived at in a very direct fashion. In the first place, people are usually prepared to advance a number of general principles that they believe represent their moral outlook. Second, one can propose other general principles, and see whether the individual is prepared to accept them. There are, however, two other, less direct methods of eliciting general principles. The first of these turns upon the fact that, in addition to feelings about the correctness or incorrectness of general moral principles, individuals also have feelings about what is right or wrong in a number of concrete situations. In many cases, these feelings about particular cases will be explicable by reference to general principles that the person himself would advance, or immediately assent to once they were proposed. But in other cases, these feelings may point to restrictions upon the individual's general moral principles, or even to other general moral principles that the individual might be hesitant about accepting when first proposed, but that seem to underlie the person's moral judgements in a wide range of concrete cases.

The second less direct method involves the application of a similar procedure in order to discover moral principles of greater generality that seem to underlie a number of the individual's less general principles. Thus, just as one can ask an individual who says that an action of a certain type is right in one concrete situation but wrong in another, what the difference is, so also if it is held that all actions of one type are right, and all actions of another type wrong, one can ask what the morally relevant difference is between the two types of actions. And the answer will be provided by another general moral principle, albeit of a deeper sort, since it will serve to explain the general moral principles which assert that actions of the one type are right, and actions of the other type wrong. We shall see later that this technique of searching for deeper general principles is a very important one.

But must it always be possible to formulate general moral principles? May one not have to be content with moral judgements that arise in concrete situations—as some existentialists have urged—at least some of the time? Is there any reason for supposing that there must be general moral principles that could in principle be discovered? Most philosophers think that there is. If a judgement is to be a moral judgement, rather than merely an expression of one's momentary likes and dislikes, enthusiasms or revulsions, it must be based upon features of the situation. One cannot justifiably advance different moral judgements in two situations unless one is prepared to hold that there is some morally relevant feature, present in the one case and not in the other. It may be difficult, of course, to say precisely what that feature is. But the mere fact that there must be such a feature, if one's differing moral judgements are to be justified, means that it must be in principle possible to formulate general moral principles that will capture what it is that is different about the two situations.

The second main technique for clarifying the overall structure of an individual's ethical position turns upon an important distinction between moral principles that are *basic for an individual* and those that are *derived*.[3] This distinction can be explained as follows. Consider, for example, the claim that adultery is wrong. To say that this is a derived moral principle for a certain individual is to say that the reason that that person accepts it is that he thinks it follows from some other ethical principle that he accepts, together with some factual claim of a *non-ethical* sort. Suppose, for example, that a person believes that adultery is wrong because, and only because, he believes that God forbids adultery, and that what God forbids is wrong. The claim that adultery is wrong then represents a derived moral principle for the person in question. Similarly, it would be a derived principle for a person who accepts it because he believes that adultery causes unhappiness, and that what causes unhappiness is wrong. In contrast, a person might hold that adultery is wrong without thinking that the principle can be derived from some other moral principle together with some factual belief of a non-ethical sort. In that case the principle would be a basic one for that person.

This distinction between moral principles that are basic for a given individual, and those that are derived, points immediately to an important way in which the underlying

[3] This distinction was set out by Amartya K. Sen in his article, 'The Nature and Classes of Prescriptive Judgments', *Philosophical Quarterly*, Volume 17, Number 66, 1967, pp. 46–62. See pp. 50–1.

structure of a person's moral outlook can be clarified. It will involve determining, first, which of a person's moral principles are basic for him, and which are derived, and second, in the case of those principles that are derived, what the derivation is. The latter will involve the specification of relevant basic moral principles, and relevant factual claims of a non-ethical sort, together with some argument which is thought to lead from those claims to the derived moral principle in question.

To sum up, then, the principal techniques of clarification are as follows. First, there is the detection, and elimination, of any crucial vagueness or ambiguity. Second, there is the technique of making explicit any tacit scope restrictions involved in individual statements. Third, there is the eliciting of general ethical claims that underlie less general ones. Finally, there is the technique of distinguishing between moral principles that are basic for the person, and those that are derived, and of determining what underlying assumptions and arguments the individual believes provide the grounds for the derived moral principles.

Let us now consider methods that can be used to evaluate ethical positions, and whose application does not presuppose that ethical principles can be objectively justified. At bottom, there are really only two such methods. The one involves showing that a certain ethical position is logically inconsistent in some respect. The other involves showing that there is good reason for rejecting one or more of the factual claims of a non-ethical sort that underlie some of the person's derived moral principles.

The first method can, however, take somewhat different forms, which it may be helpful to distinguish. One of the more important is the method of *counter-examples*. Suppose that a person holds that all actions of a certain type are wrong. A counter-example would consist of some situation involving an action of the relevant type, but which the individual would not judge to be wrong. Confronted with such a situation, the person will need to revise some aspect of his over-all ethical outlook. Either he will have to hold that his judgement about the particular case is mistaken, or he will have to modify, or abandon completely, the general moral claim that actions of the relevant type are wrong.

This is straightforward. However there is an aspect of the method of counter-examples that sometimes evokes suspicion. This is the use of purely hypothetical, or imaginary counter-examples—a practice that is quite common in philosophical discussions of ethical questions. What is the rationale underlying such counter-examples? After all, if a person claims that all swans are white, it is no refutation to say that one can imagine a black swan. One must be able to point to an actual case of a non-white swan. How then can purely imaginary cases provide any reason for rejecting general ethical principles?

The key to understanding what is going on in the use of hypothetical counter-examples lies in the distinction, set out above, between moral principles that are basic for an individual and those that are derived. When a moral principle is a derived one for an individual, appeals to what would be right or wrong in purely hypothetical situations may very well not provide any reason for questioning the principle. For it may be that the apparent conflict between the hypothetical case and the general moral principle is due to the fact that certain factual beliefs of a non-ethical sort, which are in fact true, would not be true in the hypothetical situation being considered. If any of those beliefs are used by the individual in his derivation of the moral principle in question, the hypothetical case will provide no ground for rejecting the derived moral principle, any more than it would give one reason for questioning the underlying non-ethical beliefs.

Suppose, for example, that Mary holds that it is wrong to pull cats' tails, and that she does so because she believes that it is wrong to cause pain, and that pulling cats' tails causes them pain. One will not provide Mary with any reason for giving up her derived moral belief that it is wrong to pull cats' tails by asking her to consider a world in which cats enjoy having their tails pulled.

When the moral principle is a basic one for the individual, the situation is quite different. Here purely hypothetical cases are relevant. For when the principle is a basic one, it does not rest upon any non-ethical beliefs about the nature of the world. The principle should thus be applicable not merely to the world as it actually is, but to any world that one can imagine. So if one can specify some *conceivable* situation that falls under a principle that is basic for a given individual, and where the individual's moral feelings are not what they ought to be given the moral principle in question, some revision in the individual's moral outlook is in order. One possibility is for the person to cease regarding the principle as basic, and to view it instead as a derived principle that rests upon some other moral principle or principles, together with some non-ethical, purely factual assumptions about the nature of the world. A second possibility is for the individual to abandon the general principle completely. The final possibility is for him to retain the general principle as a basic one, and to hold that his moral feelings about the hypothetical case are somehow mistaken, and that they ought to be rejected, rather than the general ethical principle.

To sum up, the crucial point is this. Moral principles that are basic for an individual, in contrast to those that are derived, do not rest upon any non-ethical beliefs about what the world is like. As a consequence, moral principles that are basic for an individual function to pick out those features of situations or actions that the individual judges to be morally relevant regardless of what is the case. This means that an appeal to hypothetical counter-examples is perfectly in order when one is examining moral principles that are basic for an individual. This deserves to be emphasized, since the use of hypothetical counter-examples is both quite common, and very important, in philosophical thinking.

The strategy of searching for counter-examples is an important one in examining a person's ethical position. Another technique that is also very useful involves carefully working out the consequences of a given position. In the case of some very simple ethical positions, it will be quite obvious what principles follow from those that are explicitly stated. Often, however, a person's ethical outlook may be quite complex, either because it involves a large number of independent principles, or because some of the principles are complicated ones. It may then be quite difficult to see precisely what one is committed to in accepting the position. The construction of carefully formulated deductive arguments will enable one to determine the precise implications of the explicitly stated principles.

This, in turn, may enable one to see that the person's over-all ethical outlook is inconsistent in some respect. For example, it may be possible to deduce contradictory conclusions from the position in question, thereby showing that it is implicitly inconsistent. A second possibility is that, although the position does not entail contradictory conclusions, it does entail some consequence that the individual cannot accept. This means that the person's over-all ethical outlook, of which the explicitly formulated position is only a part, is logically inconsistent.

Let us now turn to the second way in which ethical positions can be criticized even if it turns out that ethical claims cannot be objectively justified. This second method arises out of the distinction between principles that are basic for an individual, and those that are derived. When a moral principle is a derived one, the person in question accepts it only because he thinks that it follows from some other moral principle together with some non-ethical beliefs about the world. As a consequence, there are two questions that can be raised about any derived moral belief. The first concerns the argument to which the person is appealing to get from the more basic ethical principle and the non-ethical belief to the derived moral principle: Is the argument valid? The second concerns the non-ethical belief involved in the derivation: Is this belief a reasonable one? If the answer to either question is no, the person has a good reason for abandoning the derived moral principle in question.

This second method of criticizing an ethical position has, I believe, considerable scope, owing to two factors. On the one hand, most people accept many ethical principles that they are unable to view as basic moral principles, since they are not such as they would accept no matter what changes in the world one envisages. But on the other hand, the justifications that they propose for those principles are often extremely shaky—either because they involve bad arguments, or, more commonly, because they rest upon some highly speculative non-ethical claims about the world that will not really stand up under critical scrutiny.

1.4 The Problem of Objective Justification

In the previous section we saw that ethical positions can be subject to rational criticism even if ethical principles cannot be objectively justified. First, because some of the ethical principles that a person accepts may be mutually inconsistent. And second, because some of the derivations upon which the individual's acceptance of some of his ethical principles rests may in fact be unsound, either owing to faulty logic, or owing to non-ethical beliefs that are not supported by the available evidence.

Philosophical reflection can show, then, that many moral positions are untenable. This will still leave one, however, with many possible sets of moral principles that do not suffer from either of the above two defects. How is one to choose among these alternatives? Is it ultimately just a matter of taste, or can there be objective grounds for ruling out at least some of the alternatives, and perhaps even for viewing one moral system as the correct one?

The issue of whether ethical principles can be objectively justified is very difficult. Essentially, there are three main alternatives. The first, which I shall refer to as the view that ethical principles can be *epistemically justified*, involves three claims—a semantical claim, an ontological claim, and an epistemological claim. The semantical claim concerns the sort of meaning possessed by ethical statements. The contention is that such statements do function to describe reality; they say something which is either true or false. The ontological claim is that there are, in reality, states of affairs that serve to make at least some 'positive' ethical statements true. Finally, the epistemological claim is that it is possible for humans to know that some 'positive' ethical statements are true, or at least, for them to have rationally justified ethical beliefs.

The claim that moral principles can be epistemically justified has both been accepted, and rejected, by many philosophers. Most of those who reject it adopt the position often referred to as *moral scepticism*. This is the view that ethical claims cannot be objectively justified at all, whether epistemically or otherwise.

Moral scepticism takes somewhat different forms. Most

commonly, perhaps, it rests upon the contention that ethical statements do not function descriptively. This claim that ethical statements are neither true nor false may strike many as very implausible, given that most people certainly believe that some ethical statements are true, and others false. This claim is, however, by no means groundless, and a variety of considerations have been advanced in support of it. Of these, one of the most important concerns an apparent conceptual connection between accepting moral claims and being motivated to act in certain corresponding ways. Could a person, for example, believe that it was prima facie wrong not to keep one's promises, and yet be completely indifferent as to whether he or any other people ever kept their promises? Wouldn't one be tempted to say that such a person did not really believe that it was wrong to break one's promises? Yet how could there possibly be such a conceptual connection if ethical statements functioned descriptively? For to believe that some state of affairs is the case is not necessarily to be motivated to act in any particular way. A person who learns that he is drinking contaminated water will usually stop, but this is because he will usually have a desire not to get sick. Beliefs, unaccompanied by relevant desires, do not, it would seem, affect what one is likely to do. Therefore, if ethical beliefs *necessarily* imply the presence of an inclination to act in certain ways, or to encourage others to do so, it would seem that an ethical belief cannot be a matter, or at least not simply a matter, of believing that something is the case.

Some philosophers who are moral sceptics do not, however, appeal to the view that ethical statements are neither true nor false. Rather than challenging the semantical claim involved in the view that ethical judgements can be epistemically justified, they challenge either the ontological claim or the epistemological one. The result is what John Mackie has referred to as an 'error theory'.[4] According to this theory, ethical statements are such as are either true or false. However, every ethical statement that could possibly be used in

---

[4] The error theory was originally set out by John L. Mackie in his article, 'A Refutation of Morals', the *Australasian Journal of Philosophy*, Volume 24, 1946, pp. 77–90. For a more detailed discussion, see John L. Mackie, *Ethics—Inventing Right and Wrong*, 1977, chapter 1.

formulating a moral outlook is, as a matter of fact, either false, or at least such as one has no reason to believe it true. For statements such as 'One should not cause suffering', or 'Pain is a bad thing', can only be true if there are objective values, in a broad sense, somewhere in reality, and according to the error theory, either there are no objective values, or, if there are, at least we have no reason at all to believe that this is so.

Why might one adopt the error theory of morality? Mackie mentions a number of supporting considerations. One is connected with the relativity of values[5]—the fact that individuals accept quite different moral principles, and, moreover, that the principles that individuals accept tend to be very closely related to those accepted by their parents or society. If there were objective values, and if it were possible for people to be aware of them, would one expect there to be this sort of relativity of values?

Second, there is the ontological peculiarity of objective values.[6] Suppose that there are moral standards that are somehow written into reality. Confronted with such standards, wouldn't it always be possible to wonder whether there was any reason for accepting those standards, rather than some others? And might it not be the case that one found oneself in no way motivated to act in accordance with those standards? Yet the concept of objective values appears, in contrast, to be the concept of entities that both provide one with good reasons for accepting certain moral principles, and that tend to motivate one to act in accordance with those principles. It is not easy to grasp how there could be states of affairs with these unusual properties.

Another aspect of the ontological peculiarity is this. If there is some state of affairs that makes it wrong to cause suffering, then that state of affairs must presumably involve, on the one hand, the property of being an action that causes suffering, and, on the other, some moral property—such as the property of being wrong. How are we to conceive of the relation between these properties? Could it be thought of as a matter of one property having another property: the

[5] Mackie, *Ethics*, pp. 36–8.   [6] Ibid., pp. 39–40.

first-order property of being an action that causes suffering
has a certain second-order property, namely, that of being a
wrong-making property? But this takes us only part of the
way. The crucial point is that the relation between the two
properties must somehow be a *necessary* one: if it is prima
facie wrong to cause suffering, it is wrong not merely in this
world, but in every conceivable world. How are we to make
sense of this necessity? What account of it can be offered? As
yet, no halfway satisfactory answer to this question has been
advanced.

These problems, of course, may turn out not to be insur-
mountable. But they do pose serious difficulties for the view
that ethical statements can be epistemically justified, and it is
easy to understand why many philosophers feel that moral
scepticism is correct. But one needs to ask, at this point,
whether there are just the two alternatives. Is one forced to
hold either that ethical statements can be epistemically justified, or that they cannot be objectively justified at all? Might
there not be some third alternative? In particular, might it
not be the case that there are grounds that make it reasonable
to choose some ethical systems over others, even if ethical
statements are neither true nor false, or even if there are no
objective values?

But what might such grounds be? One possibility is some
relation to the interests of people living together in society.
It seems true, for example, that most systems of morality,
though they usually involve some rules that appear to impair
the interests of people in general, do, on the whole, result in
societies that most people would find preferable to societies
with no moral rules at all. One can therefore say that, given
the desires that people normally have, they have a reason for
preferring a society with moral rules to one without. Similarly, it seems true that systems of moral rules vary considerably with respect to the impact they have upon the
interests of people in general. If so, then people have a reason
for preferring some systems of moral rules to others. And as
this is quite independent of the question of whether any
ethical statements are true, it suggests that there may be a
way in which systems of morality can be rationally compared
even if it is the case either that moral statements do not

function to make assertions, or that there are not, as a matter of fact, any objective values.

A very clear exposition of this general approach to the justification of moral principles can be found in Michael Scriven's book, *Primary Philosophy*:

> Roughly, then, it will be argued that there is a particular conception of morality which can be shown to be an extension of rationality. This conception is relevant to many decisions about actions and attitudes that affect more than one person, and where it is relevant, we shall see that immorality can be said to be irrational. This does not mean that any immoral act by any person is irrational in terms of that person's current goals; it means that having moral goals is rationally preferable to not having them.[7]

The basic idea, then, is that it may be possible to justify ethical principles by showing that it is *rational* to accept them. Rational, however, not in the sense that there is evidence that makes it likely that they are true, but in the sense that it is in the interest of people in general to accept them. In short, ethical principles may be such as can be *non-epistemically* justified, even if they cannot be epistemically justified.

This approach avoids virtually all of the difficulties that the other response to moral scepticism encounters. It does so, however, at a cost. Perhaps the most important point in this respect is that it is not really possible to show that certain ethical principles are non-epistemically justified *simpliciter*. The reason is that it need not be in absolutely everyone's interest to have moral goals. A person with unlimited power, certainly, would have no reason for accepting moral principles. The most that can be shown, then, is that certain moral principles are non-epistemically reasonable for appropriately specified sorts of societies. The idea of objective moral rules that are universally binding must, in a sense, be set aside.

Some philosophers feel that this is a serious defect in a non-epistemic approach to the justification of morality. Others, such as Scriven, argue that it is not, on the ground

---

[7] Michael Scriven, *Primary Philosophy*, 1966, p. 230.

that a non-epistemic justification can be offered for any group of individuals that is likely to exist:

Morality, Nietzsche said, is for the weak. This is true enough, but in the relevant sense we are all weak. To be precise, we are all less powerful than any significantly probable opposing combination of human and natural forces, and for that reason there is great advantage in the moral compromise for every human being.[8]

Where does this leave us? Should we adopt the view that ethical claims can be epistemically justified? Or the view that they can be non-epistemically justified? Or should we be moral sceptics? The position that I am inclined to accept is that ethical principles can be non-epistemically justified, and I shall, from time to time, indicate points at which acceptance of a non-epistemic approach to the justification of morality would provide additional support for some specific ethical claim that I am advancing. On the other hand, it seems to me that the issues raised by the question of the objective justifiability of ethical claims are puzzling indeed, and that, as a consequence, it would be foolish to rest anything of importance in the discussion that follows upon the adoption of a particular view on the foundations of morality. The meta-ethical stance adopted will thus be, in effect, one of neutrality.

1.5 Moral Intuitions and the Problem of Method in Ethics

A crucial methodological issue concerns the role that appeal to moral feelings or intuitions should play in ethical discussion. Opinions differ widely on this matter. Some philosophers treat moral intuitions as the touchstone of moral truth. Other philosophers think an appeal to moral feelings is worthless, and that the way to approach moral questions is by appealing to some general ethical theory that has been established independently of any reference to moral feelings. In this section I shall explain my own attitude towards this issue.

Why do some philosophers feel that moral feelings or intuitions are of no value in determining which ethical principles should be accepted? The main reason is probably a matter, first, of the variability of moral intuitions both from one society to another, and from one individual to another within a given society, and second, of the fact that a person's ethical intuitions seem to depend very heavily upon what ethical principles were accepted by his parents, or by the society in which he was raised. But precisely why should this variability and dependence be thought damaging? Doesn't one encounter similar phenomena in other areas? Ordinary beliefs about the external world vary both from one society to another, and within a given society. Moreover, what beliefs a person accepts about the external world obviously depend very much upon the beliefs of his parents, or upon those of his society. So why should such facts provide grounds for holding that moral feelings and intuitions are of no value?

This is an important response, but it can be seen to be unsatisfactory. The reason is this. What is being argued is that the variability, and the dependence upon certain social factors, of moral feelings, intuitions, or experiences means that they cannot provide an acceptable evidential basis for ethical principles. The analogous argument in the case of the external world would involve the claim that the comparable variability, and dependence upon certain social factors, of *sensory experiences*, means that they cannot provide an acceptable evidential basis for beliefs about the external world. But now the problem with the response is apparent. One does not have a comparable variation in sensory experiences either within a society or from one society to another. Nor is it the case that a person's capacities to make sensory discriminations depend upon the beliefs of his parents, or upon those of his society. If there were such variation, and such dependence, then there would be an excellent reason for holding that sensory experience cannot be evidence for conclusions about the nature of the external world. But there is not.

Where does this leave one? Many philosophers feel that the correct conclusion to draw is that any appeal to moral intuitions should be completely abandoned, and that one should attempt instead to find some other, more satisfactory basis for a general moral theory. This ideal of constructing an ethical theory on some basis very different from moral feelings is one that I find very appealing. But on the other hand, the actual attempts that have been made to carry through this programme do not seem especially convincing. This leads me to ask whether it may not be possible to embrace the ideal, while still appealing to moral feelings as a sort of stop-gap measure.

One thing seems clear. If this combination of views is to make any sense, one cannot hold that moral feelings are absolutely worthless. One must maintain that agreement with the moral feelings of people makes it at least somewhat more likely that a given moral principle is correct, and does so *even though* moral feelings do not have ultimate or basic evidential significance.

What rationale might be offered for this view? The one that I have in mind is as follows. Let us assume that the fact that an individual, on his own, comes to have a certain moral feeling (or to accept a certain moral belief), provides no reason at all for thinking the relevant moral principle is correct. But let us also assume that moral principles can somehow be objectively justified. We saw in the preceding section that there are two alternatives here: epistemic justification and non-epistemic justification. Both possibilities need to be considered.

Suppose, then, that moral principles can be epistemically justified, so that there is some way of arriving at ethical knowledge, or at least, at epistemically reasonable ethical beliefs. If the knowledge or justified beliefs thus arrived at can be communicated from one generation to another, then it seems reasonable to believe that over a period of time people will gradually arrive at systems of ethical beliefs that are more and more reasonable, and so will have moral feelings or intuitions that are better and better indicators of what ethical principles it is reasonable to accept.

A similar sort of argument can be advanced if one assumes that moral principles can be non-epistemically justified. Initially, the moral principles that people accept may have only a very tenuous relation to what is in the interest of people in general. The moral feelings and intuitions that people have at that time, therefore, will not be reliable indicators of what the correct moral principles are. With the passage of time, however, moral rules will change, and it seems plausible that a major factor that will influence the direction of change, if ethical principles are neither true nor false, is the effect that acceptance of various principles has upon the interests of people in general. There will be a tendency, then, for societies to adopt moral principles that stand in a closer and closer relation to the interests of people. As a result, moral feelings will gradually become more reliable indicators of what ethical principles ought to be accepted.

In short, the argument is this. If ethical knowledge is possible, then it seems reasonable to expect that people will gradually arrive at moral beliefs that are epistemically justified. If, on the other hand, ethical principles are neither true nor false, but can be non-epistemically justified, then there is reason to believe that people will gradually arrive at ethical principles that are non-epistemically justified. In either case, then, even if moral feelings or intuitions are not initially good grounds for accepting certain ethical principles, over a period of time there will come to be a closer and closer correlation between moral feelings and objectively justified moral principles.

If this argument is right, then one can plausibly adopt the position suggested above. That is to say, one can hold that agreement with the moral feelings of people makes it at least somewhat more likely, other things being equal, that a given moral principle is correct, while denying that moral feelings have any ultimate or basic evidential significance.

How much weight is to be assigned to a particular moral feeling or intuition will depend, however, upon a number of factors. If the appeal to moral feelings or intuitions is to be a reflective and critical one, these factors need to be taken into account.

One obviously relevant factor is the extent to which a given moral feeling is shared, not merely by one's contemporaries in one's own society, but by people of other times and other cultures. The more nearly universal a particular moral judgement is, the more likely it is that it corresponds to an objectively justified principle.

A second important factor concerns the way any moral agreement on a given issue has arisen. On the one hand, similar moral feelings may develop in quite diverse societies, and they may be adopted by other people simply because of their intrinsic appeal, and not because of accompanying promises of gain or threats of loss. A very different situation exists, however, when moral principles are regarded as an essential part of some total world view. Individuals who might not be at all inclined to accept certain moral principles on their own may very well come to accept them if they are attracted to a certain total view of the world that cannot be adopted without also accepting the moral principles in question. When this sort of significance obtains, the moral feelings that come into existence deserve to be discounted, unless there is a good reason to believe that the corresponding moral principles would have been accepted just as readily even if they had not been part of a 'package deal'.

Both points can be illustrated by the familiar example of sexual morality in Western society. Until quite recently, most people felt that pre-marital sex was morally wrong. I am suggesting that such intuitions should have been discounted in any discussions of the moral question, and for two reasons. First, those moral feelings were by no means universally shared, even within Western society. Second, the moral view in question was an essential part of Christianity. Jesus had believed that fornication was something that defiled a person, and this view was vigorously advanced by the Christian churches. The widespread acceptance of the Christian religion thus resulted in societies in which most people had very strong intuitions that pre-marital sex was morally wrong, and seriously so. Some who accepted Christianity undoubtedly found the Christian view of sex plausible in its own right. But at the same time, it can hardly be doubted that many accepted the moral views in question only because this was necessary if they were to become Christians.

Many present-day philosophers fail to take these factors into account when they appeal to moral intuitions. Thus, they often treat the moral intuitions of their own society—and very often, their own personal moral feelings—as perfectly good reasons for accepting various moral principles. They rarely seem to ask to what extent those moral feelings are shared by other people in their own society, let alone by members of other societies, past or present. Nor do they commonly reflect upon the fact that certain moral views may have come to be accepted only because they were part of some very general world view—and one that they themselves, perhaps, can no longer accept.

There is a final factor that needs to be taken into account in any reflective and critical appeal to moral intuitions. It arises out of the distinction between ethical principles that are basic for an individual, and those that are derived. What I want to maintain is that when one appeals to moral feelings or intuitions, such appeal should in general be confined to intuitions concerning *basic* moral principles.

Two considerations can be offered in support of this methodological contention. In the first place, when one is dealing with a moral belief that is a derived one for the individual in question, that person's feeling that the belief is correct has no independent standing. It arises out of his feelings that some other, more basic moral belief is correct, together with his conviction that some relevant factual claim of a non-ethical sort is true. What one needs to do, then, is to examine what can be said for and against those underlying judgements. If either claim proves faulty, the intuition concerning the derived moral principle should be totally discounted, since, by definition, the individual himself will abandon the derived moral principle once he is convinced that it rests upon an indefensible claim.

This first point applies regardless of which account one adopts of the objective justification of ethical principles. The second point, in contrast, seems to have force mainly, or perhaps only, if one holds that moral intuitions have basic epistemic value. It can be put as follows. Assume that there is a faculty by which one intuits moral truths. Will such truths be basic or derived? It seems rather unlikely that they will be derived, for in that case the faculty would also involve an implicit recognition of the relevant non-ethical truths. If there is a faculty of moral intuition, then, it would seem that it should deal only with moral beliefs that are not derived on the basis of factual beliefs of a non-ethical sort.

To sum up, my over-all attitude towards an appeal to intuitions in doing moral philosophy is as follows. First of all, I believe that there are good reasons for not ascribing any ultimate or basic epistemic significance to moral feelings or intuitions. If ethical principles are to be objectively justified, it should be in some other way. Unfortunately, however, there do not appear to be any really satisfactory, independently grounded ethical theories presently available. This led us to consider whether it might not be possible to ascribe some sort of limited, and derived, significance to moral feelings. I attempted to show that plausible support can be offered for such a view. Finally, I urged that it was very important that any appeal to moral feelings be a reflective and critical one, and I mentioned three factors that seem especially important in this regard.

PART II
ABORTION

2

Abortion – Introductory Remarks

Views on the morality of abortion are of three main types, which I shall refer to as the conservative, or anti-abortionist position, the moderate position, and the liberal, or pro-abortionist position. The conservative, or anti-abortionist view is that abortion, at any time from conception onward, is always wrong, and indeed, seriously so, with the possible exception of some cases where it is necessary in order to save the woman's life. At the other extreme is the liberal position, according to which abortion is never wrong, or at least not seriously so. Finally, there are a number of moderate positions, according to which abortion is sometimes morally wrong, and sometimes not. These differ with respect to the considerations thought to be morally relevant. Some advocates of a moderate position hold that the time at which the abortion occurs is important, it being morally permissible up to a certain point in the foetus's development, but prima facie wrong thereafter. Another factor frequently appealed to is the probable condition of the resulting child: if it will be badly deformed, or mentally impaired, then abortion is not wrong. A third ground often advanced by moderates as justifying abortion concerns the effect upon the woman of not terminating the pregnancy. If her physical or psychological health is likely to be damaged, abortion may be morally permissible. Another possible factor is the likely effect upon the family. Many moderates hold that if an additional child will place considerable strain upon other members of the family, then abortion is justified. A final consideration concerns the circumstances surrounding conception. It is often maintained, for example, that abortion is morally permissible in cases of rape or incest.

To decide among these alternative views on the morality of abortion, one must first isolate the fundamental issues. This is more difficult than one might think. For example, it is often believed, especially in public debate on abortion, that the crucial issue is whether the foetus is a human being. Yet we shall see, in due course, that this whole approach is radically misconceived.

Another common approach to the question of the morality of abortion, which I also wish to reject, involves viewing the situation as one in which there is a conflict of rights. On the one hand, there is the foetus's right to life. On the other, the woman's right to exercise control over what happens in and to her body. From this perspective, the crucial issue is which of these prima-facie rights should prevail in this situation.

These first two approaches to the morality of abortion will be examined in the next two chapters. I shall then go on to discuss the questions that I believe lie at the heart of the problem:

(1) What makes something a person?

(2) Is it intrinsically wrong to destroy potential persons?

(3) At what point in its development is a human being a person, and not merely a potential person?

A satisfactory understanding of these three questions will require an explanation of the precise meanings to be assigned to the two key expressions, 'person' and 'potential person'. For the moment, however, a rough, first approximation will suffice. Let us begin, then, by assuming that some entities possess a right to life. If this is so, it seems very plausible to hold that *at least some* of them do so in virtue of properties that they now have, rather than in virtue of properties that they will later come to possess. It is possible, of course, that *all* entities that have a right to life do so in virtue of properties they now have. On the other hand, it is certainly conceivable that some entities possess a right to life not in virtue of their present properties, but in virtue of properties they will later come to have. But while this second possibility deserves to be taken very seriously, it is also very important to have some term that refers only to beings of the first sort—that is, to entities that have a right to life, and do so in virtue of their present properties, rather than in virtue of their potentialities. The term 'person' will here be understood in such a way that it applies to all and only entities of this sort.

How should the term 'person' be defined in order to achieve

this result? The simplest way of doing this would be to say that a person is, *by definition*, an entity that has a right to life, not because of properties it will come to possess, but because of properties that it now possesses. It can be objected, however, that this definition is potentially misleading, since it assigns to the term 'person' quite a different sort of meaning from its ordinary one. For as defined above, to say that something is a person entails that the entity has a right to life. The term 'person' is therefore functioning as an evaluative term—specifically, a term with moral content. In contrast, the term 'person', as ordinarily interpreted, appears to be a purely descriptive term—as is illustrated by the fact that even philosophers who reject the whole idea of rights, such as utilitarians, apply the term 'person' to normal adult human beings.

I think that it is right both that the term 'person', as ordinarily used, is generally a descriptive term, and that it is potentially misleading to define it instead in such a way that it is changed into an evaluative term.[1] At the same time, however, I believe that the assignment of descriptive content to the term 'person' is ordinarily guided by moral considerations. This suggests the following approach. Instead of defining a person as an entity that possesses a right to life, and that does so in virtue of its present properties, rather than in virtue of its potentialities, one can first determine what properties, other than potentialities, suffice to endow an entity with a right to life. Then one can define the term 'person' as applying to all and only those things that have at least one of the relevant properties. Suppose, for example, that it is the property of having the capacity for thought that gives something a right to life. Then to say that something is a person will just be to say that it has the capacity for thought. Or suppose that both self-consciousness and rationality suffice to give something a right to life. Then to say that something is a person will just be to say that it possesses either rationality or self-consciousness.

When this approach is adopted, the term 'person' functions

---

[1] I am indebted to Derek Parfit and Jefferson McMahan for pointing out some confusions that are apt to arise if one assigns evaluative, rather than descriptive content, to the term 'person'.

—as I believe it ordinarily does—as a purely descriptive term. The fact that something is a person does not by itself, therefore, imply any ethical conclusions. In particular, it does not follow from the fact that something is a person that it has a right to life. The fact that the descriptive content of the term 'person' has been selected with certain moral considerations in mind does mean, however, that if one's moral views are in fact correct, then it will be the case that an entity is a person if and only if it has a right to life, and does so in virtue of its present properties, rather than in virtue of its potentialities.

Given the term 'person', it is a relatively straightforward matter to provide a rough indication of the meaning to be assigned to the expression 'potential person'. Thus, as an approximation that will be satisfactory for the moment, one can define a potential person as something that will, in the 'normal' course of affairs, develop into a person.

Given these accounts of the expressions 'person' and 'potential person', it would *seem* that most human organisms, though not all, are at least potential persons from conception onward.[2] Thus if it is intrinsically wrong to destroy potential persons, there will be a prima-facie case for the view that abortion is generally wrong. The strength of the case would depend, of course, upon *how* wrong it was to destroy potential persons. If, as some people believe, the wrongness of destroying potential persons were comparable to that of destroying persons, the case would be very strong indeed. Many have thought, in fact, that it would serve to establish the correctness of the conservative view on abortion. We shall see, however, that the latter conclusion is mistaken.

What if it turns out that the destruction of potential persons, rather than being morally on a par with the destruction of persons, is not intrinsically wrong at all? In that case the third question mentioned above will become crucial. That question will not, however, be examined in the present part of this book. The reason is that the question of when a human being first becomes a person is also central to the

---

[2] When we examine the notion of a potential person more closely, however, we shall see that whether this is so depends upon the precise interpretation assigned to the expression, 'potential person'.

question of the morality of infanticide, and it will simplify matters, and eliminate duplication, if the third question is postponed until the discussion of infanticide in Part III. The core of Part II, accordingly, will be concerned with what it is that makes something a person, and with whether it is intrinsically wrong to destroy potential persons.

Discussion of these central questions will force us to consider a number of deeper issues, some of which may be briefly mentioned here. The first concerns the relation between obligations *with respect to* something and obligations *to* something. John, for example, may have an obligation with respect to a certain car—namely, not to destroy it— because it belongs to Mary. John's obligation with respect to the car therefore derives from an obligation that he has to Mary. This naturally leads one to ask whether this is true in general, whether all obligations with respect to an entity are based upon obligations to some entity.

The importance of this question may not be immediately evident, but it will emerge if we turn to a second issue—that of the *basis* of obligations to individuals. Must an entity possess certain properties before anyone can have any obligations to it? I think that most people would hold that this is so. For there would be very wide agreement, surely, that while one can have obligations with respect to non-living things, one cannot have any obligations to them. I also think that there would be very general agreement as to the reason why this is so—namely, that one cannot have any obligations to something that is not capable of any mental life whatever.

If there is this general connection between an entity's capacity for some sort of mental life and the possibility of obligations to it, it is natural to ask whether there may not be other, more specific connections. Perhaps the *types* of obligations that one can have to an entity are a function of the types of mental states it is capable of having. Or perhaps the *strengths* of some obligations depend upon what sorts of mental states are present. Some such view appears to be accepted by very many people, since, on the one hand, they appear to hold that one has some obligations to animals, and not merely with respect to them—such as an obligation not to inflict unnecessary pain upon them—and, on the other hand, they rarely believe that one's obligations to non-human animals are on a par with one's obligations to normal adult human beings.

The significance of the first issue can now be made clear. An obligation not to destroy a particular foetus might derive from an obligation one has to some other individual. Perhaps the foetus is Mary's and she does not want it to be destroyed. Or perhaps one has an obligation to other members of society to help increase the population to an acceptable level. Or perhaps there is a deity who wants as many people as possible to enjoy the great banquet of life, and one is under an obligation to obey that deity. But suppose that there are no obligations of these sorts. Another possibility is that one's obligation not to destroy the foetus is an obligation to the foetus itself. If, however, obligations to entities presuppose that entities have certain characteristics, it may be the case that human foetuses, at least in the early stages of development, do not possess those properties. If this were so, the only possibility that would remain would be an obligation not to destroy the foetus which did not derive from an obligation *to* anything—either the foetus, or its parents, or society, or a deity. But this, of course, will not be a genuine possibility if all obligations with respect to anything must derive from obligations to some entity. The latter issue, therefore, has an important bearing upon the grounds that might be offered for holding that abortion is morally wrong.

A third, very important underlying issue concerns the *types* of properties that are the basis of obligations to entities. Potentialities aside, there is a difficult question whether obligations to an entity rest upon its occurrent properties, or upon its capacities or dispositions, or upon some combination. Suppose, for example, that the obligation to something not to destroy it is based upon a certain sort of mental life. Is it enough that the entity is at present capable of having a mental life of the sort in question, or is it also necessary that it has at some time actually had a mental life of that sort?

A final underlying issue concerns the relative moral seriousness of acts and omissions that have the same consequences. This question is obviously very important in connection with voluntary euthanasia, where much stress has often been laid upon the distinction between active and passive euthanasia, between acting so as to terminate life and merely allowing someone to die. It is perhaps surprising that it is also very important in connection with abortion. We shall see, however, that the view that one takes as to the relative seriousness of acts and omissions has considerable bearing upon the crucial issue of the morality of destroying potential persons.

Two issues that are certainly very relevant to the question of the morality of abortion will not be discussed in this part. One has already been mentioned, namely the extent to which a human organism at different stages in its development has acquired those characteristics that make something a person. The other concerns what might be called consequentialist objections to abortion. The thrust of such objections is that even if abortion is not intrinsically wrong, it is none the less wrong all things considered, since it has consequences that are morally undesirable. Discussion of this contention will also be left until Part III. Since such consequentialist objections are at least as forceful when directed against infanticide, repetition can be avoided, and they can be confronted in their most forceful form, by taking them up in the context of the question of infanticide.

3
The Relevance of the
Moral Status of the Foetus

Until comparatively recently, the general philosophical opinion was that if a human foetus had a right to life, abortion must be seriously wrong, except perhaps to save the woman's life. This view has, however, been very seriously challenged by Judith Jarvis Thomson in her much discussed article, 'A Defense of Abortion'.[1] This chapter will be concerned with her line of argument, and with subsequent attempts to rebut it.

Thomson does not believe that a human foetus has a right to life from conception onward. But she suggests that we grant this assumption, for the sake of argument, and then consider what follows from it. In particular, she is interested in evaluating the following central argument. A human foetus has a right to life. A woman has a right to decide what happens in and to her body. The latter right, however, is not as serious as the right to life. If there is a conflict, then, between the foetus's right to life and the woman's right to exercise control over her body, the former takes precedence. Aborttion, when it results in the death of the foetus, is therefore morally wrong, unless the alternative would involve the woman's death.

At the heart of Thomson's attack upon this argument is her observation that people do not normally view an individual's right to life as imposing obligations upon others to provide whatever is necessary for his survival. She illustrates this with her case of the violinist:

You wake up in the morning and find yourself back to back in bed with an unconscious violinist. A famous unconscious violinist. He has been

[1] Judith Jarvis Thomson, 'A Defense of Abortion', *Philosophy & Public Affairs*, Volume 1, Number 1, 1971, pp. 47-66.

found to have a fatal kidney ailment, and the Society of Music Lovers has canvassed all the available medical records and found that you alone have the right blood type to help. They have therefore kidnapped you, and last night the violinist's circulatory system was plugged into yours, so that your kidneys can be used to extract poisons from his blood as well as your own. The director of the hospital now tells you, 'Look, we're sorry the Society of Music Lovers did this to you—we would never have permitted it if we had known. But still, they did it, and the violinist is now plugged into you. To unplug you would be to kill him. But never mind, it's only for nine months. By then he will have recovered from his ailment, and can safely be unplugged from you.' Is it morally incumbent on you to accede to this situation? No doubt it would be very nice of you if you did, a great kindness. But do you *have* to accede to it? What if it were not nine months, but nine years? Or longer still? What if the director of the hospital says, 'Tough luck, I agree, but you've now got to stay in bed, with the violinist plugged into you, for the rest of your life. Because remember this. All persons have a right to life, and violinists are persons. Granted you have a right to decide what happens in and to your body, but a person's right to life outweighs your right to decide what happens in and to your body. So you cannot ever be unplugged from him.' I imagine you would regard this as outrageous, which suggests that something really is wrong with that plausible-sounding argument I mentioned a moment ago.[2]

But if this is correct, if it is morally permissible for a person to disconnect himself from the violinist, even when he knows that the inevitable result will be the death of the violinist, how can abortion be wrong even if human foetuses have a right to life? What is the morally significant difference between these two cases?

Various answers have been proposed, most of them anticipated and discussed by Thomson in her original article. In the main, they involve variations on two themes. The first concerns different ways one can be responsible for another's death. One version of this first theme appeals to the distinction between actively killing and merely refraining from saving. Thus Baruch Brody, in his book *Abortion and the Sanctity of Human Life: A Philosophical View*, holds that it is morally permissible to deny someone the use of one's body provided that in doing so one is not killing him, but merely allowing him to die.[3] Brody then claims that in denying the

[2] Ibid., pp. 48-9.
[3] Baruch Brody, *Abortion and the Sanctity of Human Life: A Philosophical View*, 1975. For Brody's discussion of Thomson, see pp. 27-30.

foetus the continued use of her body by means of abortion, the woman is killing the foetus, not merely allowing it to die, and hence that abortion cannot be justified by appealing to a woman's right to control what happens in and to her body.

It is not clear precisely what Brody's criticism of Thomson is. There are two possibilities. On the one hand, he may be claiming that there is a morally significant difference between the case of abortion and Thomson's case of the violinist, in that the former involves killing, and the latter merely letting die. There are two problems with this line. First, it is unclear that the violinist case is properly classified as a case of letting die, rather than as one of killing. The paradigm case of letting die is one where the death of another results from one's refraining from acting. In Thomson's example, the violinist will survive if the woman does nothing; he dies only if she unplugs him. It is also true, of course, that the case is rather different from paradigm cases of killing, such as running over with a steam-roller. But if the killing/letting die distinction is to be a specific instance of the more general acting/refraining from acting distinction, unplugging the violinist must be classified as a case of killing, not as one of letting die.

Second, and more important, if one does interpret the killing/letting die distinction in such a way that unplugging the violinist is viewed as a case of letting die, it will no longer be true that abortion, in general, involves killing. Cutting up the foetus, and removing the parts from the uterus, will certainly be a case of killing. But abortion by means of drugs that induce miscarriage or premature birth will not. Such cases of abortion will be like that of the violinist: a human is disconnected from a life-support system, in a situation in which it will die as a result. So if Brody holds that the violinist's death is merely a case of letting die, he will have to say the same thing about abortion performed in certain ways. If it is permissible to disconnect oneself from the violinist, it will, presumably, also be permissible to have an abortion, provided that one is careful to choose the right method.

The second possibility is that Brody really wants to construe 'letting die' strictly—that is, as a case of refraining from doing something that will save someone's life. If he does, then it will be true that abortion is always a case of killing, never one of merely letting die. But equally, unplugging the violinist will be a case of killing. If Brody wants to take this line, then, he must hold that it is not morally permissible to disconnect oneself from the violinist.

Commenting on an earlier article by Brody, Thomson points out that 'Brody . . . does not say you may unplug the violinist. On the other hand, he does not explicitly say you may not. All he explicitly says on the matter is that my "account of the violinist" is "very problematic".'[4] One might have expected that this observation would have encouraged Brody to make it clear what his view of the violinist case is. Unfortunately, it did not have this effect, and in the discussion of Thomson in his book the issue is once again evaded. Perhaps, then, Brody really wants to hold that it is morally wrong to unplug oneself from the violinist, and that abortion is wrong for the same reason. If so, he has been rather far from forthright about the matter and, as a result, fails to offer any grounds at all for rejecting Thomson's contention that 'it is not morally required of anyone that he give long stretches of his life—nine years or nine months—to sustaining the life of a person who has no special right . . . to demand it'.[5]

A second variation on the first theme appeals to a distinction between 'direct' and 'indirect' killing. As used in this context, 'direct' has a special, technical meaning. Interpretations vary with different defenders of the distinction, but what it usually amounts to is roughly this. A killing is said to be direct if the death is either one's desired end, or else a means to one's end. If the killing is only a foreseen consequence of one's action, and neither desired in itself nor a means to something which is, then the killing is said to be indirect.

This distinction is appealed to by John Finnis in his article, 'The Rights and Wrongs of Abortion: A Reply to Judith Thomson'.[6] Finnis holds that while indirect killing of the innocent is sometimes justified, direct killing never is, and

[4] Judith Jarvis Thomson, 'Rights and Deaths', *Philosophy & Public Affairs*, Volume 2, Number 2, 1973, pp. 146–59. See p. 157.

[5] 'A Defense of Abortion', p. 63.

[6] *Philosophy & Public Affairs*, Volume 2, Number 2, 1973, pp. 117–45.

that abortion differs from the unplugging of the violinist in that the former is a case of direct killing, while the latter is only indirect. So one can grant that it is morally permissible to unplug oneself from the violinist, while holding abortion to be morally wrong.

Two comments are in order. First, if one's case against abortion rests upon the distinction between direct and indirect killing, will one be able to argue that abortion is in general wrong? Those who favour this approach appear to think that one will be able to do this, since they hold that abortion is itself always a case of direct killing. But it is not easy to see how the latter view can be correct. For one way of performing abortions is by inducing premature labour. The foetus, born too early, will be incapable of surviving. In such cases, the resulting death of the foetus need not be either a desired end nor a means to any end. So it would certainly seem that not all abortions involve a direct killing of the foetus. If one rests one's case against abortion upon the distinction between direct and indirect killing, it would seem that one can show at most that abortion is morally wrong if it is carried out in certain ways.

Second, there is the question of whether the distinction between direct and indirect killing can bear the moral weight being placed upon it here. Thomson, in common with the vast majority of present-day moral philosophers, believes that it cannot, and in her reply to Finnis she makes out a very persuasive case against the view that the distinction is morally significant.[7] I believe that Thomson is right on this matter; however it would take us too far afield to examine that issue here.

In any case, it appears that Thomson's argument probably cannot be rebutted by appealing to some distinction between different ways in which one can be responsible for someone's death. So let us turn to the second line of criticism, which is, I believe, rather more promising.

Thomson, by means of the violinist analogy, attempted to show that a successful anti-abortion argument could not rest upon the claim that the right to life is stronger than the right

[7] 'Rights and Deaths', pp. 149-55.

to control what happens in and to one's body. The first line of criticism attempted, unsuccessfully, to show that Thomson was mistaken about this. The second line of criticism does not. It attempts, instead, to show that there is a slightly different anti-abortion argument that escapes Thomson's objection.

The second line of argument turns upon the fact that there is a possibly crucial difference between the situation of the violinist and that of the foetus. Both need the use of a certain person's body if they are to survive. But in the case of the violinist, the relevant person is in no way responsible for the violinist's being in need of assistance, whereas in the case of the foetus it can be said that the woman is among those who are at least partially responsible, in some sense, for the foetus's being in need of a life-support system—assuming that the pregnancy did not result from rape. Thus one might be asked to consider the following situation. There is a pleasurable activity that I like to engage in. I know that in some cases this activity will have the unhappy side effect of destroying someone's food supply. This will not cause the person any discomfort, provided that I supply him with food, which I can do, albeit at considerable trouble and expense. Now it seems to me that even if I arrange things so that the probability that the activity will have the unfortunate effect is as small as possible, I am still responsible for the person's being in the situation of needing food on those few occasions when things go wrong, and thus am under an obligation to supply him with what he needs.

If this is right, the anti-abortionist can argue that although people in general may be under no moral obligation to allow others the use of their bodies, even when it is necessary if the other individual is to survive, a pregnant woman is, in general, under a moral obligation to allow the foetus the use of her body, since she is morally responsible for there being a foetus that stands in need of a life-support system.[8]

---

[8] Compare Mary Anne Warren's discussion in her article, 'On the Moral and Legal Status of Abortion', *Monist*, Volume 57, Number 1, 1973, pp. 48–52, and Leonard S. Carrier's in his paper, 'Abortion and the Right to Life', *Social Theory and Practice*, Volume 3, Number 4, pp. 398–9.

Thomson raises this objection herself. She believes that it is not convincing:

Again, suppose it were like this: people-seeds drift about in the air like pollen, and if you open your windows, one may drift in and take root in your carpets or upholstery. You don't want children, so you fix up your windows with fine mesh screens, the very best you can buy. As can happen, however, and on very, very rare occasions does happen, one of the screens is defective; and a seed drifts in and takes root. Does the person-plant who now develops have a right to the use of your house? Surely not—despite the fact that you voluntarily opened your windows, you knowingly kept carpets and upholstered furniture, and you knew that screens were sometimes defective. Someone may argue that you are responsible for its rooting, that it does have a right to your house, because after all you *could* have lived out your life with bare floors and furniture, or with sealed windows and doors. But this won't do—for by the same token anyone can avoid a pregnancy due to rape by having a hysterectomy, or anyway by never leaving home without a (reliable!) army.[9]

This attempt to bridge the apparent gulf between rape and voluntary intercourse is certainly interesting. It is tempting to dismiss it very quickly, on the ground that people are not morally responsible for consequences of their actions that depend upon immoral actions of other people, in the way that they are responsible for consequences not thus dependent. However the claim that one is not responsible for what will result from one's actions if other people choose to act immorally is not as unproblematic as may at first appear. If I live in a world that is full of people who would often choose to shoot someone if only they had a gun, and if I know that this is the case, then surely I am morally blameworthy if I leave loaded guns lying around for trivial reasons. So it seems to me that it is not in general true that one has no responsibility for consequences of one's actions that are dependent upon the immoral actions of others.

I find it difficult to formulate a satisfactory account of one's responsibility for consequences of actions that depend upon the foreseeable immoral actions of others. However I think that the force of the present objection is not diminished by the absence of such an account. The reason will become clear if we consider the structure of Thomson's argument.

[9] 'A Defense of Abortion', p. 59.

First, she has offered an argument that lends support to the view that abortion is justified at least in the case of rape. Second, she has pointed out that one cannot drive a wedge between rape and other cases simply by appealing to the fact that in other cases the woman is responsible for there being a foetus that needs assistance, since the woman is also to some extent responsible in cases of rape. But if a wedge cannot be driven between rape and other cases in this way, isn't one forced to admit that abortion is morally permissible in at least some cases where intercourse is voluntary?

One who objects to this argument can try attacking it in either of two ways. First, one might challenge the second step, by arguing that one is not responsible for consequences of one's actions that depend upon immoral actions of others, and hence that the woman's responsibility for the well-being of the foetus differs when pregnancy results from voluntary intercourse rather than from rape. Alternatively, one might accept the second step, and try running the argument in the other direction, contending that since the woman is clearly responsible in the voluntary intercourse case, we now see that she is also to some extent responsible in the rape case.

The choice between these two objections turns upon the account one offers of one's responsibilities for consequences of one's actions that depend upon the actions of others. I believe that it is not an easy matter to set out a plausible account of one's responsibilities for such consequences, and so it is unclear to me which response is correct. Many other philosophers, in contrast, would find the choice a clear-cut one, since they have very definite views as to whether one is responsible for consequences of one's actions that depend upon the immoral actions of others. But it is not necessary to resolve this issue; it suffices that Thomson's argument is open to objection whichever way it is resolved.

For consider the situation where one leaves loaded guns lying around, knowing that there are would-be murderers about. Reflection upon such a case, if it leads anywhere, can only lead to one's *extending* the range of situations in which one judges a person morally responsible for some outcome. It cannot lead to the conclusion that people are not morally responsible even for foreseeable consequences of their actions that are not dependent upon the immoral actions of others. Or consider again the destruction of food case, and alter it slightly so that some innocent action of mine will lead to the destruction of some individual's food supply only if someone else acts immorally. If someone does act immorally, and the individual's food supply gets destroyed, am I under an obligation to provide him with food? The answer is perhaps unclear. Some would answer yes, and others no. But surely what one cannot do is to answer no and then take that as grounds for holding that one is also not responsible in the case where the destruction of the food results from one's own action in a way not dependent upon the action of anyone else.

Summing up, then, the situation is this. Thomson attempts to extend her earlier conclusion concerning abortion in cases of rape to cases where intercourse is voluntary, by appealing to the fact that in both cases the woman could have acted so as to have avoided becoming pregnant. This attempt to assimilate the two cases is not especially plausible. The crucial point, however, is that if it were granted, the result would be that one would have to adopt, not a more liberal position on abortion in cases where pregnancy results from voluntary intercourse, but a less liberal position on abortion in cases of rape.

There is another important objection to Thomson's line of argument, which is rarely noticed. It arises from the following disanalogy between the people-seed case and that of pregnancy resulting from voluntary intercourse. In the people-seed case, there are only two sorts of alternatives. Either one exposes oneself to the danger of people-seeds taking root in one's house, or one reconciles oneself to a somewhat dreary existence in rooms that are stuffy and uncarpeted. In contrast, it does not seem that one is thus limited in the real life case; the choice is not confined to chastity on the one hand, and the risk of pregnancy on the other. Yet it is curious how, when the topic is abortion or contraception, rather than sexual morality *per se*, people lose sight of the fact that there are delightfully unchaste alternatives to normal intercourse. Of course many may prefer the latter, and even very strongly so. But unless one is prepared to argue that only procreative sex is morally acceptable, and that expressive and recreational sex are out, there may be good reasons for holding that people might very well re-examine their preferences, and even expend some effort in broadening their tastes somewhat. Certainly, if abortion involves the death of individuals possessing a serious right to life, people who want to enjoy sex without producing children will have one of the best possible reasons for developing a liking for alternatives to normal intercourse.

The upshot seems to be this. Judith Thomson is certainly right that the assumption that human foetuses have a serious right to life will not serve defenders of a conservative position on abortion in the simple way they have commonly thought that it would. On the other hand, it does seem to be the case that if one knowingly takes the risk that one may bring it about that some other person stands in need of assistance, one thereby places oneself under a serious obligation to provide that assistance—an obligation that people in general presumably are not under. Now if one could avoid bringing it about that someone else needed assistance only by great personal sacrifice, it might be possible to argue that in such a situation one was not under any special obligation to the person adversely affected. But we have seen that this line of argument is not available here, since it is possible for people to avoid bringing about the existence of individuals who will be dependent upon them without any great personal sacrifice with respect to the emotional or sensual quality of their lives. Consequently, if human foetuses do have a serious right to life, there would seem to be a very strong argument in support of the contention that abortion is, with very few exceptions, morally wrong, and seriously so. The question of whether human foetuses do have a right to life—or, more generally, the issue of their moral status—is, then, the crucial issue it initially appeared to be. The problem of the morality of abortion cannot be resolved until one has a plausible account of the moral status of human foetuses.

4

Persons and Human Beings

4.1 The Distinction and its Importance

The distinction between persons and human beings is of central importance in connection with topics such as abortion and euthanasia. As the relevant expressions are used in a variety of ways, I need to explain how they will be understood here. First, the expression 'human being'. This is usually, though not invariably, used in such a way that something is not classified as a human being unless it belongs to a specific biological species—*Homo sapiens*—with the species, in turn, being characterized in terms of certain physical properties, either genetic ones, or ones that relate to physiological form and function. Often, the expression 'human being' is employed in such a way that any organism belonging to the species *Homo sapiens* is classified as a human being. Sometimes, however, the expression is so interpreted that being a member of the species *Homo sapiens*, while necessary, is not sufficient to make one a human being. Certain other properties are also required. These are usually properties of a *psychological* sort, such as, for example, having the capacity for rational thought.

In the present discussion the expression 'human being' will be taken as synonymous with the expression 'member of the biological species, *Homo sapiens*'. There are two reasons for this. First, I think this is the usual interpretation of the expression 'human being'. Second, and more important, we shall be concerned here with the moral relevance of certain biological characteristics, and this makes it convenient to use the expression 'human being' to attribute only characteristics of that sort. Sometimes, however, I shall employ the clumsier expression, 'member of the species *Homo sapiens*', especially at crucial points, to emphasize precisely what is being asserted.

Next, the term 'person'. Chapter 2 contained some preliminary discussion of the meaning to be assigned to this term. Two points that emerged were these. In the first place, it seems advisable to treat the term 'person' as a purely descriptive term, rather than as one whose definition involves moral concepts. For this appears to be the way the term 'person' is ordinarily construed. Second, however, it seems desirable that the descriptive content assigned to the term 'person' be guided by moral considerations, in order to have a term that can play a certain, very important role, in the discussion of moral issues.

This leads to the question of precisely what the moral considerations are that are to serve to determine the descriptive content assigned to the term 'person'. The preliminary suggestion advanced in chapter 2 was that the definition of the term 'person' should be guided by consideration of the properties that give something a right to life. One first determines what properties suffice to endow something with a right to life. Next, one asks which of those properties are potentialities, and which are not. Those properties that are not potentialities may be referred to as 'person-making' characteristics, and a person is then defined as an entity that possesses at least one of the characteristics in question.

Suppose, for example, that self-consciousness and rationality are the only characteristics—potentialities aside—that suffice to give something a right to life. Then the concept of a person will be construed, purely descriptively, as the concept of an entity that possesses either self-consciousness or rationality.

The result will be an interpretation of the term 'person' such that, on the one hand, its meaning will be very close to the meanings typically assigned to the term in ordinary discourse, and, on the other, one will have a term that will play a very useful role in moral discussion. The type of account just suggested does, however, have certain drawbacks. These arise from the fact that the moral consideration that is to guide the assigning of descriptive content involves the concept of a *right*. This seems unfortunate for at least two reasons. First, not all moral theories countenance talk about rights. One would like, if possible, to characterize the moral considerations that are to guide the definition of the term 'person' in a way that makes some sense within the context of theories, such as utilitarianism, that eschew the language of rights. Second, as Hare remarks, our understanding of the concept of a right does not seem as satisfactory as our understanding of what it means to say that someone ought to do something, or to say that some action is right, or some action wrong—a comment that is certainly well confirmed by current discussions of how the concept of a right is to be analysed.[1] For this reason, too, it would be best if the guiding consideration could be formulated in a way that avoided talk about rights in favour of more fundamental ethical language.

Let us attempt, then, to formulate the guiding moral consideration in a way that does not involve the concept of a right. A natural approach is to talk instead about the properties that suffice to make the destruction of something intrinsically wrong. However, just as in the case of the formulation in terms of the concept of a right to life, it may not be the case that all of the properties that suffice to make the destruction of something intrinsically wrong should enter into the definition of the term 'person'. The reason is this. Suppose, for example, that it is intrinsically wrong to destroy anything with the capacity for self-consciousness. It might, then, also be intrinsically wrong to destroy anything with the potentiality for self-consciousness—anything that would, in the normal course of affairs, come to have the capacity for self-consciousness. But if this were so, it would not follow that reference to both properties should enter into the characterization of the concept of a person. For if one said that something was a person if it either possessed the capacity for self-consciousness, or had the potentiality for that capacity, it would no longer be possible to classify some entities as things that, though not yet persons, will become persons. And so one would be assigning a very different meaning to the term 'person' than it ordinarily has.

In general, then, a distinction may have to be drawn within the class of properties whose possession makes it intrinsically

[1] Compare R. M. Hare's remarks in his article, 'Abortion and the Golden Rule', *Philosophy & Public Affairs*, Volume 4, Number 3, 1975, pp. 202-4.

wrong to destroy something—between properties that are not
potentialities, and properties that are. Only the former
should enter into the characterization of the concept of a
person.

The present suggestion, then, is that the decision as to the
precise descriptive content to be assigned to the term 'person'
should be guided by consideration of the non-potential
properties that make the destruction of something intrinsically wrong. It can be shown, however, that this suggestion
needs to be refined somewhat, in at least two respects, if one
is to have a concept that can play the same role in moral
discourse as the everyday concept of a person. The first point
is that the class of objects whose destruction is intrinsically
wrong, and is so in virtue of non-potential properties, may be
a rather disparate class, depending upon one's substantive
moral theory. Most moral theories imply that the destruction
of normal adult human beings is intrinsically wrong. But some
moral theories imply that it is also intrinsically wrong to
destroy such things as plant and animal species, and great
works of art.[2] If such a theory turned out to be correct, it
would imply, given the above suggestion as to the moral
consideration that is to guide the assignment of descriptive
content to the term 'person', that great works of art are persons. This shows that the above suggestion requires some
modification.

A natural move at this point is to introduce the notion of
being intrinsically valuable, and then to draw a distinction
between entities that it is intrinsically wrong to destroy
because they are intrinsically valuable, and entities that it is
intrinsically wrong to destroy, but not for that reason. The
descriptive content to be assigned to the term 'person' will
then be guided by consideration of those non-potential
properties that make it intrinsically wrong to destroy something, and do so independently of the thing's intrinsic value.

This modification seems satisfactory. For in the first place,

---

[2] Stanley Benn attempts to support the view that the destruction of great
works of art is intrinsically wrong in his paper, 'Personal Freedom and Environmental Ethics: The Moral Inequality of Species', in *Equality and Freedom; International Comparative Jurisprudence*, Volume II edited by Dorsey Grey, 1977,
pp. 401-24. See pp. 413-14.

I believe that philosophers who maintain that the destruction of great works of art is intrinsically wrong do so because they hold that great works of art are intrinsically valuable. Second, I think that even those who maintain that individual human beings are intrinsically valuable would not want to say that this is the *only* reason why it is intrinsically wrong to kill normal adult human beings. For the people in question do not maintain that failing to create additional human beings is also wrong, and to the same degree. Yet this is what they would have to hold if they believed that the wrongness of killing humans beings derived solely from the fact that they are intrinsically valuable.

There is, however, an alternative way of attempting to make the desired modification. It arises from the fact that in addition to the concept of an obligation to perform a certain action, there is also the concept of an obligation *to* an individual, and in addition to the concept of an action's being wrong, there is also the concept of an action's *wronging* someone, of doing wrong *to* some individual. Now it might seem that one could make use of these additional ethical concepts in order to capture the desired modification. In particular, cannot one say that the assignment of descriptive content to the term 'person' should be guided by consideration of the non-potential properties that make the destruction of an entity an action that is not merely intrinsically wrong but one that wrongs the entity in question—one that violates an obligation *to* the individual destroyed?

This approach certainly seems promising, since whatever appeal there may be to the claim that the destruction of great works of art is intrinsically wrong hardly carries over to the idea that one has an obligation to great works of art not to destroy them. But there is a problem. If one is to appeal to the distinction between a duty to do something and a duty to some individual to do something, one needs to provide an account of the latter notion.

How is the notion of an obligation to an individual to be analysed? There appear to be two main types of analysis.[3] The first treats obligations to individuals and rights as

---

[3] I am indebted to Frank Share for some helpful discussion of this point.

correlative. Thus a duty to an individual is analysed along the following lines:

X has a duty to individual Y to perform action A

means the same as:

Y has some right R that X perform action A.

This analysis is plausible enough. But if it is employed in the present context, we are simply back to the idea of employing the concept of a right in formulating the moral consideration that is to guide the assignment of descriptive content to the term 'person'.

The other main type of analysis of the notion of having an obligation to an individual introduces the notion of an individual's interest:

X has a duty to individual Y to perform action A

means the same as:

X has a duty to perform action A, and A is in Y's interest.

As it stands, this analysis is exposed to various objections. One is this. Suppose that Mary promises John that she will look after his cat. She then has an obligation to do something that is in the cat's interest. But, contrary to what is entailed by the above analysis, she has an obligation only to John, and not to his cat.

Let us assume, however, that the analysis can be revised to overcome this and other problems. Even granting this, it would seem that the resulting account of the moral consideration that is to determine the descriptive content assigned to the term 'person' will not be satisfactory. The reason is this. Suppose that the reason it is wrong to destroy normal adult human beings is that they possess both consciousness and the capacity for rational thought. Suppose, further, that it is conceivable that there might be beings with these characteristics, but which were devoid of all desires and preferences. If the moral position in question were correct, we would certainly want such beings to fall within the class of persons. But if the above account were accepted, they could not possibly be persons, since the analysis entails that one cannot have an obligation to an individual unless it is a subject of interests.

The upshot is this. If one attempts to formulate the required modification by appealing to the notion of an obligation to an individual, one needs to go on to give some account of the latter notion. If one explains it in terms of the concept of a right, one is simply back with the first account that was offered of the moral consideration that is to guide the assignment of descriptive content to the term 'person'. On the other hand, if one explains it in terms of the concept of an individual's interest, it seems that one is no longer putting forward a morally neutral account of the considerations that are to guide the determination of the descriptive content of the term 'person'. For the view that the class of persons might contain some entities that are not subjects of interests appears to be a possible one, but would be ruled out by the account in question. It would seem, then, that the concept of an obligation to an individual cannot provide us with an account that is both morally neutral and distinct from the accounts already considered.

The second refinement that is needed is suggested by the following reflection. Some people believe that if a person is suffering from some incurable illness, then it is not wrong for him to commit suicide, or for him to have someone else take active steps to end his life. If this view turned out to be correct, and if one adopted the suggestion that the descriptive content of the term 'person' should be determined by a consideration of what non-potential properties make it intrinsically wrong to destroy something, and do so independently of its value, then it would not do, for example, to define a person as something possessing self-consciousness and rationality. For this would imply that it was intrinsically wrong for a self-conscious, rational being to commit suicide. What one would have to do, instead, is to define a person as a self-conscious being that has the capacity for thought, and that does not have a rational desire to end its own life. But such an account is very different from our ordinary concept of a person, since it entails that something ceases to be a person once it is in a situation that makes it reasonable for it to desire its own death.

The point, in short, is this. On the one hand, our ordinary classification of things as persons seems to depend only upon relatively enduring properties of entities. On the other hand, whether it is intrinsically wrong to destroy something will, if certain moral views are correct, also depend upon less permanent facts about the individual in question. In specifying the moral considerations that are to guide the assignment of descriptive content to the term 'person', this distinction between those properties that are relatively permanent and those that are not needs to be taken into account if one is to have a concept of a person that does not diverge quite radically from our ordinary one.

The distinction between properties that are relatively enduring and those that are not is not, of course, an especially precise distinction. I think, however, that it is sufficiently clear for our purposes here. If we do employ this distinction, the revised account can be put as follows. The descriptive content of the term 'person' is to be determined by those relatively permanent, non-potential properties of an entity that, possibly in conjunction with other, less permanent features, make it intrinsically wrong to destroy something, and that do so independently of its intrinsic value.

The upshot is that there are at least two fairly appealing choices with respect to the moral consideration that is to guide the assignment of descriptive content to the term 'person'. The one option involves asking what non-potential properties suffice to give something a right to life, and then defining a person as an entity that possesses at least one of those properties. The other alternative involves asking what relatively permanent, non-potential properties, possibly in conjunction with other, less permanent features of an entity, make it intrinsically wrong to destroy an entity, and do so independently of its intrinsic value. A person can then be defined as an entity that possesses at least one of those enduring properties.

The first alternative is quite a natural one, especially in the present context, since arguments advanced by anti-abortionists usually involve the contention that human foetuses have a right to life. But as noted above, there are also some disadvantages associated with this approach. One is that it is a very controversial matter precisely how the concept of a right is to be analysed. The other is that there are important ethical positions—such as classical utilitarianism—that deny that there are rights. If the first alternative were adopted, advocates of such positions would have to be described as denying that there are any persons. As this consequence seems needlessly paradoxical, I now think it best, on the whole, to adopt the second alternative.

Fortunately, the choice between these two alternatives is not, ultimately, a very serious matter in the present context. What is crucial is rather that, whatever account one adopts of the moral considerations that are to guide the assigning of descriptive content to the term 'person', there is a radical difference between classifying something as a human being and classifying it as a person. Unfortunately, this crucial difference often gets obscured in discussions of abortion, owing to two fairly widespread tendencies. The one involves using expressions such as 'human being' in such a way that to classify something as a human being entails either that it is a person, or that it has a right to life. This first tendency is found in some discussions by Baruch Brody. Thus, for example, in an article on abortion, Brody refers to the difficulty of determining 'whether destroying the foetus constitutes the taking of a human life', and suggests that it is very plausible that 'the taking of a human life is an action that has bad consequences for him whose life is being taken'.[4] When Brody speaks here of something as having a human life, he apparently construes this as entailing that the entity in question is a person, or that it has a right to life. Otherwise it would be very puzzling why he should think that there was a difficulty about determining whether a foetus developing inside a human mother was itself a human being.

This conclusion is confirmed by Brody's discussion in a later book on this subject, where he is rather more explicit with regard to his use of the expression 'human being':

The final point is terminological. When, in this book, I use the phrase 'human being', I mean 'a member of the species Homo sapiens

[4] Baruch A. Brody, 'Abortion and the Law', *Journal of Philosophy*, Volume 68, Number 12, 1971, pp. 357-69. See pp. 357-8.

who has a right to life similar to the right to life had by you, me, and so on.' My initial assumption that the fetus is a human being is an assumption about its rights, and not merely about the species to which it belongs.[5]

The second, and closely related tendency, involves using the expressions 'human being' and 'person' interchangeably. This tendency is illustrated by the opening sentence of Judith Jarvis Thomson's article: 'Most opposition to abortion relies on the premise that the fetus is a human being, a person, from the moment of conception.'[6] Another illustration is provided by Roger Wertheimer, who explicitly says: 'First off I should note that the expressions "a human life", "a human being", "a person" are virtually interchangeable in this context.'[7]

Both tendencies are unfortunate. For one thing, they tend to lend an undeserved appearance of plausibility to anti-abortion viewpoints. For if either usage is adopted, a defender of a liberal view of abortion can be described as maintaining that foetuses developing inside human mothers are not human beings. If one keeps firmly in mind how the expression 'human being' is being employed, there is no problem. But the usage is not the common one, and it is easy to lose sight of this fact, with the result that the liberal view will appear quite implausible.

The danger of misinterpretation is especially great given the heated atmosphere of much discussion of the morality of abortion. But even philosophers, in cool moments, can be led astray by uses of the expression 'human being' that imply either that something has a right to life, or that it is a person. Wertheimer, for example, says that 'except for monstrosities, every member of our species is indubitably a person, a human being, at the very latest at birth'.[8] Is it really *indubitable* that new-born babies are persons? We shall see later that the claim that new-born babies are persons is, in fact, profoundly problematic, and I would suggest that at least part of the

[5] Baruch Brody, *Abortion and the Sanctity of Human Life*, p. 3.
[6] Thomson, 'A Defense of Abortion', p. 47.
[7] Roger Wertheimer, 'Understanding the Abortion Argument', *Philosophy & Public Affairs*, Volume 1, Number 1, pp. 67–95. See p. 69.
[8] Ibid.

reason why Wertheimer puts it forward as indubitable is that he is falling prey to the confusion naturally engendered by the practice of using 'person' and 'human being' interchangeably.

Another illustration is provided by Thomson:

I am inclined to think also that we shall probably have to agree that the fetus has already become a human person well before birth. Indeed, it comes as a surprise when one first learns how early in its life it begins to acquire human characteristics. By the tenth week, for example, it already has a face, arms and legs, fingers and toes; it has internal organs, and brain activity is detectable.[9]

But what do such physiological characteristics have to do with the question of whether the organism is a person? Thomson, partly, I think, because of the unfortunate use of terminology, does not even raise this question. As a result, she virtually takes it for granted that there are some cases in which abortion is 'positively indecent'.[10]

There is a second reason why the above two tendencies are philosophically unhappy. If one says that the dispute between pro-abortionists and anti-abortionists centres on whether the foetus is a human, it is natural to conclude that it is essentially a disagreement about certain non-moral facts, a disagreement about what non-moral properties a foetus possesses. Thus Wertheimer says that 'if one insists on using that raggy fact-value distinction, then one ought to say that the dispute is over a matter of fact in the sense in which it is a fact that the Negro slaves were human beings'.[11] I believe that the two cases are not parallel, and that Wertheimer is once again being misled by his use of the expression 'human being'. For I believe that it will become clear, in what follows, that most disagreement about the morality of abortion derives from disagreement about basic moral principles, not from disagreement about the facts of the case. It is true that some people who accept an anti-abortionist view do so because of certain factual beliefs of a theological or metaphysical nature, such as the belief that all members of the species *Homo sapiens* have immaterial souls. But what usually separates the conservative on abortion from the liberal is not disagreement

---

[9] Thomson, 'A Defense of Abortion', pp. 47–8.
[10] Ibid., p. 65.   [11] Wertheimer, op. cit., p. 78.

about theological or metaphysical matters, let alone disagreement about the biological facts concerning human development. It is, instead, moral disagreement, either about the properties that should enter into the concept of a person, or about whether it is wrong to destroy potential persons.

Finally, the third, and most important reason for not using the expression 'human being' in such a way that it either entails that something is a person, or that it has a right to life, is this. One of the crucial questions involved in the issue of the morality of abortion is that of the moral significance of purely *biological* facts, such as the foetus's belonging to a certain species. When 'person' and 'human being' are used interchangeably, or when 'human being' is used in such a way that it either entails that something is a person, or that it has a right to life, then it is natural to suppose that belonging to a particular biological species is morally relevant—an assumption almost universally embraced by popular anti-abortion movements, where great stress is placed upon the genetic and physiological characteristics of embryos and foetuses developing inside human mothers. A terminology that encourages people simply to assume that biological facts are morally relevant is very unsatisfactory, given that one of the things most needed, if there is to be an appreciation of the underlying moral issues, is critical reflection upon the claim that membership of a particular species— *Homo sapiens*— endows one with a certain moral status.

4.2 The Moral Irrelevance of Species Membership

Among opponents of abortion, the most popular argument turns upon the humanity of the foetus. The argument is usually formulated in terms of the foetus's right to life. The most direct formulation, however, runs as follows:

(1) An embryo or foetus developing inside a human mother is itself a human being, and an innocent one, from conception onwards.

(2) It is seriously wrong to kill an innocent human being.

(3) Abortion involves killing an embryo or foetus developing inside a human mother.

Therefore:

(4) Abortion is seriously wrong.

This argument raises a number of issues. The most important, however, concerns the acceptability of the second premise—the claim that the killing of innocent human beings is seriously wrong.

This claim can be interpreted in different ways, depending, among other things, upon the meaning assigned to the expression 'human being'. In this chapter we shall be concerned only with the acceptability of the principle when 'human being' is interpreted as meaning: member of the species *Homo sapiens.* This is, I believe, the most common interpretation of the principle, at least in the context of anti-abortion arguments. Other interpretations will be considered later, in chapters 6 and 11.

There is a further restriction upon the scope of the present discussion: we shall be concerned only with whether the claim, that the killing of innocent human beings is wrong, is acceptable as a *basic* moral principle, rather than as a *derived* one.

The distinction between basic moral principles and derived ones is very closely related to a distinction set out in chapter 1, namely, that between moral principles that are basic *for* a given individual and those that are derived *for* that individual. The latter distinction can be employed even if it turns out that moral scepticism is true, and that no objective justification can be provided for moral principles. The distinction between basic and derived moral principles, in contrast, presupposes that some moral principles are true, or objectively correct, while others are not.

Consider the following two moral principles:

(i) It is wrong to inflict pain upon organisms.
(ii) It is wrong to pull cats' tails.

Most people would think that, if moral scepticism is false, then both of these principles are objectively correct. Yet they seem to differ in status. The first appears to be in some sense more basic than the second. But what exactly does this come to? Apparently to this. There is a *non-moral* claim about the world, namely:

(iii) Pulling cats' tails causes them to experience pain,

which, together with (i), entails (ii). Principle (ii) can, then, be derived from another moral claim together with some non-moral fact about the world. In view of this, one might suspect that the objective acceptability of moral claim (ii) depends upon what the world is like in a way that (i) does not. And that does seem to be the case. If cats were to evolve so that, rather than being a source of pain, having their tails pulled was a pleasurable experience, one would surely cease to view (ii) as a correct moral principle.

In brief, then, a moral principle is *basic* if its acceptability is not dependent upon any non-moral facts. It is a *derived* moral principle if it is acceptable only because it is entailed by one or more basic moral principles together with propositions expressing some non-moral facts.

This distinction can also be expressed in terms of the notions of right-making and wrong-making characteristics. Basic moral principles state, of some characteristic, either that it is a right-making characteristic or that it is a wrong-making characteristic. Derived moral principles, in contrast, do not specify right-making and wrong-making characteristics. Rather, they specify characteristics that are, in some way, associated with right-making or with wrong-making characteristics. The association may be simply a matter of two characteristics being frequently found together, or there may be a much tighter relation, involving some natural law.

Consider, then, the claim that it is wrong to kill innocent members of the species *Homo sapiens*. A person who accepts this principle may view it either as a basic moral principle or as a derived one. When it is viewed as derived, one needs to determine what the derivation is, and then examine the proposed basic moral principle, together with the non-moral factual claim, upon which the principle rests. Possible derivations of the principle that it is wrong to kill innocent human beings will be considered in later chapters. The discussion in the present chapter will be confined to the claim that it is a basic moral principle that it is wrong to kill innocent human beings.

How might one attempt to show that the property of

being an action of killing an innocent human being is not in itself a wrong-making characteristic? One approach is the method of direct counter-example: one attempts to describe a case of killing an innocent human being in which the action does not appear to be wrong. Of course, it is often the case that an action is not wrong, all things considered, even though it does possess some wrong-making characteristic, either because it possesses more significant right-making characteristics, or because the alternatives available have even more serious wrong-making characteristics. A successful counter-example, by contrast, would be a situation that does not involve conflicting moral considerations, but where it is nevertheless not wrong to kill an innocent human being.

Are there such counter-examples? A number of philosophers hold that there are. The most widely accepted one seems to be this. Some human beings have suffered brain damage that, while so extensive as to destroy completely the neurological basis of consciousness, memory, personality, thinking, and all of the higher mental functions, has left the brain stem intact and functioning. As the brain stem controls basic bodily functions such as circulation, respiration, digestion, etc., such a human can remain alive, even without artificial life-support systems. Now if the damage is irreparable, not merely at the present stage of technology, but in principle, it seems plausible to hold that although a human organism lingers on, the conscious individual once associated with that body no longer exists, and hence that it is not even prima facie wrong to kill the human organism that remains.[12] If this is right, the property of being an action of killing a member of the species *Homo sapiens* cannot itself be a wrong-making characteristic of actions.[13]

Another possible counter-example involves the closely related case in which the brain of some human has been completely destroyed—including the brain stem—but where life processes are artificially maintained. I would hold that it

[12] In section 11.42 we shall see that some philosophers would dissent from this claim, on the ground that as long as an organism is able to maintain its own life processes, without artificial help, a rational soul must be present.

[13] This argument is advanced by R. B. Brandt in his article, 'The Morality of Abortion', *Monist*, Volume 56, Number 4, 1972, pp. 503-26. See pp. 509-10.

is not even prima facie wrong to turn off a respirator in such a case, even though one is thereby killing a human organism.

Many philosophers would view this as an unsatisfactory counter-example. For while they would generally agree that it is not even prima facie wrong to turn off the respirator, they would argue that if the whole brain has been destroyed, the human in question is already dead, so that in turning off the respirator one is not killing any human being.

I believe that it can be shown that this view of the matter rests upon a confusion—specifically, that between the death of an organism, and what might be called the death of a person—and that while the destruction of the whole brain is certainly a sufficient condition for the death of a human person, it is not an acceptable criterion for the death of a human organism.

What is my reason for thinking that destruction of the whole brain is not an acceptable criterion of the death of a human organism? The underlying line of thought, in brief, is as follows. The concept of being a *living* thing is a *general* biological concept, applicable to all species, both plant and animal. The concept of death, however, is simply the concept of the cessation of life. So just as the concept of being a living thing is a general concept that applies to individuals belonging to all species, the same must be true of the concept of death. But this means that if those processes, such as growth, and repair and reproduction of parts, which characterize living things in general, are still going on in a human organism, then that organism cannot properly be characterized as dead, *unless* it can be argued that it is not enough that such processes go on: they must also be sustained by the organism without artificial assistance. But it seems clear that this cannot be plausibly maintained, since it would imply, for example, that humans who are otherwise normal, but who cannot survive without artificial help, are not alive. If this line of argument is right, then it would seem that when one turns off a respirator that is maintaining life processes in a human being whose brain has been completely destroyed, one is killing a living human being. So the second counter-example can be sustained.

The above two counter-examples show, not merely that it

is not a basic moral principle that killing human beings is wrong, but that it is not a correct principle, either basic or derived. The next two arguments, in contrast, do not challenge the correctness of the principle, but only the view that it is a basic principle.

The second line of argument is this. Suppose that a disease arises that alters the genetic make-up of human beings, so that all future offspring, rather than having the sort of mental life and skills possessed by normal adult human beings today, enjoy a mental life comparable to that of chickens. If, at some point in time, all present and future humans were of this sort, would it still be seriously wrong for any non-human persons who happen to exist to kill human beings? It seems to me that it would not.

An objection to this second argument is that if there were the genetic change envisaged above, the resulting animals would not belong to the species *Homo sapiens*. That might be the case, but need not be so. For it is conceivable that the resulting animals could interbreed with any previous human beings still alive, and thus that they would, according to the ordinary understanding of species membership, belong to the same species, and hence would be *Homo sapiens*. So if it would not be wrong to kill such beings, the property of being an action that kills an innocent human being cannot be a wrong-making characteristic.

This brings me to the third argument. The fundamental strategy underlying this argument can perhaps best be grasped if we begin by considering its application to other issues. Consider, first, the claim that it is wrong to enslave white human beings. Is this a basic moral principle? If it is, what is to be said about the enslaving of black human beings? It does not fall under the principle in question, so either it is not wrong, or there must be some other principle under which it falls. But surely one wants to say that the reason it is wrong to enslave white human beings is *the same reason* that it is wrong to enslave black ones, and this implies that there must be some underlying principle covering both types of actions. A first attempt at an underlying principle would be that it is wrong to enslave human beings. This is clearly a move in the right direction, since it is a more general principle from which the other two principles can be derived, and it is free of the morally irrelevant reference to skin colour.

Consider again the wrongness of pulling a cat's tail. A person interested only in cats might conceivably think that it was a basic moral principle that it was wrong to pull cats' tails. If this view were right, then being a cat would be a morally relevant property, since it would enter, in an essential way, into a wrong-making characteristic of actions of tail-pulling. However a person with wider sympathies, if asked to consider a broader class of actions, including pullings of dogs' tails, would surely say that the principle that it is wrong to pull cats' tails is not a basic principle, and that there is some more general principle involved which also makes it wrong to pull dogs' tails. One attempt at formulating the broader principle would be that it is wrong to pull tails in general. A more plausible attempt would be that it is wrong to inflict pain.

The underlying strategy, then, is this. Confronted with a claim that a certain principle is basic, one attempts to find some class of actions not falling under the principle, but that seem to be wrong for the same sort of reason. If there is such a class, there must be some more basic moral principle that explains why actions in both classes are wrong.

Let us now return to the claim that it is a basic moral principle that the killing of innocent human beings is wrong. Can one find some other class of actions that seem to be wrong in the same way? Surely one can. There might exist on some other planet, such as Mars, non-human animals that speak languages, have highly developed cultures, that have advanced further scientifically, technologically, and aesthetically than humans have, and that both enjoy sensations, thoughts, feelings, beliefs, and desires, and attribute such mental states both to us and to themselves. Would it not be wrong to kill such Martians? And wrong for precisely the same reason that it is wrong to kill normal adult human beings?

The appeal here is to a type of situation that may very well be purely imaginary, and, as was noted in section 1.3, such appeals are sometimes thought to be objectionable. If one insists upon not considering hypothetical situations, one can attempt to make the same point by appealing to animals such as dolphins, or chimpanzees that have learned a language. But such cases are at best less clear-cut, and the proper approach is to appeal to the purely hypothetical case. For as was argued earlier, the refusal to admit hypothetical cases is not methodologically justified, and generally reflects a failure to grasp the concept of a *basic* moral principle.

The thrust of the argument, then, is that there must be some principle that covers both the killing of normal adult human beings and the killing of other animals with comparable capacities and similar mental states. We need not consider here what the principle is. The relevant point is simply that it will be free of reference to particular species.

Let us now consider some possible objections. The first objection is that the argument has not really established the conclusion in question, since it is always possible to get a more general principle by a union of the species in question: 'It is wrong to kill something if it is either an innocent human being or an innocent Martian.' But this response won't do. One wants to know why it is seriously wrong to kill innocent human beings or innocent Martians, but not wrong to kill carrots or earthworms. One needs to be given what no mere list of species can provide: an *explanation* of why it is wrong to kill members of some species, but not members of others. Such an explanation will be provided by some principle that refers, not to particular species, but to some characteristic that members of the species in question typically possess.

A second objection is this. Consideration of the case of Martians may show that there must be a reason for not killing that applies equally to humans and to Martians. But does it really show that there cannot also be a reason for not killing that applies only to the killing of humans by other humans, and not to the killing of Martians by humans? For consider the following. Most people believe that it is wrong to kill humans, but they also believe that it is more wrong to kill one's parents. If this view is right, why may it not also be more wrong for humans to kill other humans, than for humans to kill Martians? In short, even if there are general moral principles, concerning killing, that do not refer to particular species, why can there not be other principles as well, that do involve reference to species, and that supply what might be referred to as *agent-relative* reasons for not killing.[14]

This possibility of additional, agent-relative reasons for not killing, that would apply to the killing of humans by other humans, but not to the killing of Martians by humans, can, I believe, be admitted without damaging the present argument. It is my view, however, that biological considerations, such as membership in the same species, do not constitute acceptable agent-relative considerations. It might be thought that this view conflicts with the intuitions of most people, in view of the widespread feeling that it is more wrong to kill members of one's own family than those who are not. However it is important to ask precisely what the basis of this feeling is. I suggest that when this is done, it turns out that what is relevant, at least for most people, is not some biological relation, but shared experiences and social interaction over an extended period of time. Consider, for example, a case of artificial insemination by donor. Would most people really feel that it is more wrong to kill one's biological father, in such a case, than to kill some other individual? It seems to me that they would not.

In conclusion, then, there appear to be excellent reasons for holding that basic ethical principles should be free of reference to individual species, and that, in particular, it cannot be a basic moral principle that killing innocent human beings is wrong. This in itself, however, is not quite tantamount to showing that species membership is morally irrelevant. For even if basic moral principles should not contain any expressions that refer to particular species, perhaps they can quite properly contain variables that range over species, with the result that species membership will be morally relevant, albeit in a slightly oblique way. The possibility that I have in mind here can be made clear by an example. Jean Beer Blumenfeld, in an article, 'Abortion and the Human Brain', advances the following principle: 'It is morally wrong to intentionally kill an innocent individual belonging to a species whose members typically are rational beings, unless at least one of the following

---

[14] The possibility of agent-relative considerations was pointed out to me by Jefferson McMahan and Derek Parfit.

conditions obtains: . . .'[15] As this principle does not refer to any particular species, the arguments offered above do not preclude its being a basic moral principle. And if it is a basic moral principle, species membership is, to some extent, morally significant.

There are, however, good reasons for holding that the principle proposed by Blumenfeld cannot be a basic moral principle. In the first place, Blumenfeld's principle is an instance of a much more general principle:

> It is morally wrong to intentionally kill an innocent individual belonging to any *class* whose members typically are rational beings, unless at least one of the following conditions obtains: . . .

Another instance of this more general principle is:

> It is morally wrong to intentionally kill an innocent individual belonging to any class of featherless things with *n* legs whose members typically are rational beings, unless at least one of the following conditions obtains: . . .

Suppose it is true that most featherless bipeds are human beings possessing the capacity for rationality. There will then be a class falling under the principle just stated. If that principle is true, we will be forced to conclude that it is wrong to destroy any featherless biped, human or otherwise. If we reject this conclusion, as most would, we must agree that not all instances of the more general principle stated above are acceptable. The question then is why the instance proposed by Blumenfeld should be accepted. *Why* should the concept of a class of things capable of interbreeding be thought to be morally significant in a way that other concepts, such as that of a class of featherless things with the same number of feet, are not?

The most plausible attempt to answer this question has already been mentioned, namely, the suggestion that since kinship connections seem to have a bearing upon one's obligations, perhaps membership in the same species also does. I

---

[15] Jean Beer Blumenfeld, 'Abortion and the Human Brain', *Philosophical Studies*, Volume 32, 1977, pp. 251-68. See p. 268.

have urged, however, that if kinship connections are morally relevant, they are so in virtue of social relations, rather than in virtue of biological ones. If this is the right view of the matter, there is no reason to hold that the relation of belonging to the same species is morally significant in itself.

A second consideration is this. Let John and Mary be two individuals that are not rational beings, and that belong to different species, but which are indistinguishable with respect to their psychological capacities and their mental lives. It is possible that John belongs to a species 99 per cent of which are rational beings, while Mary belongs to a species of which only 1 per cent are rational beings. If species membership is morally relevant in the way that Blumenfeld thinks, it will be wrong to kill John, but may very well not be wrong to kill Mary, in spite of the fact that John and Mary do not differ with respect to any psychological properties, either actual or potential.

A third reason for holding that Blumenfeld's principle cannot be a basic moral principle is this. Suppose that there is some species, typical members of which are rational beings, and that this species is divided into two groups that, as a matter of fact, never interbreed, though they are certainly capable of doing so. Let John be an individual belonging to the smaller of the two groups. If the situation is as stated, and if Blumenfeld's principle is correct, it will be wrong to kill John even if John is not a rational being. Now imagine the world changed in the following way. A long time before John is born, a disease strikes the other group, causing a genetic change which destroys the rationality of all members of that group, and of all their descendants. Such a change is compatible with the two groups still being capable of interbreeding. If this had happened, it would no longer be true that the majority of individuals belonging to the species were rational beings, since the individuals belonging to the larger group would no longer be rational. Consequently, Blumenfeld's principle would not apply, and there would no longer be any reason to refrain from killing John. Hence, if the principle espoused by Blumenfeld were a basic moral principle, one would be confronted by the consequence that whether it is intrinsically wrong to kill a particular individual depends upon facts about the world that are independent of the individual. This is surely not a view to be accepted unless supported by very strong arguments. Blumenfeld offers none at all.

It is important to emphasize that these arguments are directed against the claim that the principle is a basic one. For if it were a derived one, it could not of course be attacked by appealing to hypothetical cases. Blumenfeld does not indicate what status the principle is supposed to have, and it is possible that she views it as merely a derived principle.

There are at least two sorts of considerations that might be advanced in support of the contention that it is an acceptable derived principle. The first appeals to consequentialist considerations. Assume that some members of our own species are not rational animals. It may be the case that if people were allowed to destroy such humans for trivial reasons, general respect for the lives of all humans would be weakened. If so, then there is a reason for prohibiting the killing of any human being.

A second defence focuses upon underlying properties. Perhaps it is not only rational beings that it is wrong to kill. Perhaps it is also wrong to destroy any being possessing some sort of potentiality for rationality. Further, may it not be the case that if typical members of a species are rational, all other members will have at least a certain potentiality for rationality? If so, it will be a derived moral principle that it is wrong to kill individuals belonging to species, typical members of which are rational beings.

These possibilities will be considered later, primarily in chapters 6 and 11. They have not been ruled out by the present arguments. If either of them is sound, there will be a sense in which species membership is morally significant—namely, it will be connected, factually, with other properties that are morally significant in themselves. The question in this section, however, has been a different one: whether the concept of species membership enters into *basic* moral principles, and hence whether species membership is morally significant *in itself*. The arguments advanced above provide strong support, I believe, for the contention that species membership is not morally significant in itself—which is to say, basic moral principles will contain neither singular terms that refer to particular species, nor general terms that involve the concept of species membership.

This conclusion would, I think, be very widely accepted by contemporary philosophers. Still, some recent writers appear to take issue with it, and at least one writer has attacked it in very strong terms indeed. The latter critique is best left to the next section. Here I shall confine myself to commenting briefly on some philosophers who have expressed disagreement with the above conclusion, but who have not attempted to mount a sustained and detailed case against it. One such person is James Humber, who contends that '. . . the right to life is ordinarily spoken of as a *human* right, i.e., it is not a personal right, nor is it a right which one possesses by virtue of his being a member of a special group or class of humans. To hold otherwise not only makes a mockery of ordinary language, it also undercuts morals completely, potentially justifying all sorts of horrors.'[16] Humber may be making either of two claims here. On the one hand, he may be asserting that the property of belonging to the species *Homo sapiens* will enter into basic moral principles dealing with what beings have a right to life. If this is his claim, he has offered no argument at all for it, either in the passage quoted or elsewhere in his article. Alternatively, he may be contending only that all human beings should be viewed as having a right to life. For this contention is at least supported by the allusion to the familiar argument that unless all humans are held to have a right to life, moral horrors will ensue. But if this is his contention, he is not advancing a claim that conflicts with the view, defended here, that basic moral principles will not involve reference to species membership.

Another writer who appears, at least initially, to be challenging the view that species membership is not morally significant in itself is Richard Werner: 'It is my contention that there is a basic prima facie moral obligation against the

---

[16] James M. Humber, 'Abortion: The Avoidable Moral Dilemma', *Journal of Value Inquiry*, Volume 9, Number 4, 1975, pp. 282–302. See p. 292. In this article, which is full of emotive language, Humber contends that 'the arguments of the pro-abortionists are all so poor that they should not be accepted at face value, but rather should be seen as after-the-fact rationalizations for beliefs held to be true on other grounds'. (282–3.) It is not surprising, then, that Humber chooses simply to ignore the most important arguments against the view which he favours.

taking of innocent human life.' Werner goes on to offer the following explanation of what he is claiming here: 'In more familiar terms, I am claiming that an innocent human life is intrinsically valuable and can only be taken in the direst of circumstances.'[17]

Unfortunately, this explanation fails to discriminate between two quite different possibilities. To say that things of type T are intrinsically valuable is to say at least that, leaving aside all causal consequences of the existence of things of type T, the world is a better place if it contains some things of that type, and it may also be to say that the more things of type T the world contains, the better. But this leaves open what it is about things of type T that makes it intrinsically good for the world to contain such things. It may be property T itself, or it may be some other property S that all things of type T either happen to possess, or must possess in virtue of certain natural laws. Thus Werner's statement that human life is intrinsically valuable does not discriminate between the claim, on the one hand, that the existence of humans is intrinsically valuable because the property of being a member of a certain biological species is itself one whose instantiation is intrinsically valuable, and, on the other, the claim that the existence of humans is intrinsically valuable because humans possess some other property whose instantiation is intrinsically valuable.

The argument that Werner offers turns upon the contention that future generations that have the 'capacity' to exist also have a right to exist.[18] We shall see later that this line of argument is unacceptable. What is relevant here, however, is that even if Werner's claim were granted, it would lend no support to the view that the existence of human beings is intrinsically valuable *because* the property of being a human is one whose instantiation is intrinsically valuable. For one might hold that a future generation's right to exist is based, not upon the fact that it will belong to a certain biological species, but upon the fact that it will consist of individuals possessing rationality.

[17] Richard Werner, 'Abortion: The Moral Status of the Unborn', *Social Theory and Practice*, Volume 3, Number 2, 1974, pp. 201-22. See pp. 209-10.
[18] Ibid., pp. 217-18.

Another philosopher who wants to challenge the conclusion advanced here is Francis Wade. Commenting on my remark that 'difference in species is not per se a morally relevant difference', he says: 'It is not the *difference* in species that sets up distinct moral relations but it is membership in *Homo sapiens* that makes a being a man and his being a member of this species *is* morally relevant.'[19] His attempted rejection of my view is, however, only apparent. This emerges in his discussion of a somewhat related statement by Engelhardt to the effect that 'purely biological facts, as such, have no implications concerning psychological or personal reality.'[20] Wade says:

The only truth this statement has depends on its being taken in the restrictive sense where it applies only to knowledge and not to things. When applied to things that biological statements deal with, it does not hold up. Engelhardt himself argues that developed brains (a biological fact) are necessary (imply concrete potentiality) for conscious life. Moreover, the difference between a kitten and an infant I take to be a biological difference, yet this fact determines (implicates) the morality of my dealings with the two beings: drowning a kitten is not morally the same as drowning an infant.[21]

Wade is being grossly unfair to Engelhardt. The whole point of talking about the implications of biological facts *as such* is to make it clear that one is making a claim about what biological statements logically entail. Wade shifts to a different sense of 'implies', according to which what a statement implies is a matter of *nomological* connections, as well as logical ones—where nomological connections are ones that exist in virtue of laws of nature. The upshot is that Wade is not really asserting that biological properties are morally relevant *per se*, i.e. that they enter into the formulation of basic moral principles. He is claiming only that there are other properties that are morally significant in themselves, and which are connected, by natural laws, with biological properties. Thus Wade is not really disagreeing with my con-

---

[19] Francis C. Wade, 'Potentiality in the Abortion Discussion', *Review of Metaphysics*, Volume 29, Number 2, 1975, pp. 239–55. See p. 251.

[20] H. T. Engelhardt, 'The Ontology of Abortion', *Ethics*, Volume 84, 1974, pp. 217–34. The quote is from p. 226.

[21] Wade, op. cit., p. 251.

tention that species membership is not morally significant in itself. He believes that he is disagreeing, but this is because he chooses to ignore expressions such as *'per se'* and 'in itself', which makes it clear precisely what is, and what is not, being asserted.

A final writer who thinks he is rejecting the position defended here is William May. In his article, 'Abortion and Man's Moral Being', May says:

Common to the thought of Fletcher, Tooley and those who would agree with them is the belief that 'membership in a species is of no moral significance.' This belief is warranted *only* if one is capable of showing that man's significance as a *moral* being (for this is one crucial way in which he differs from other animals) is ultimately explicable fully and adequately in terms of a difference in the degree of development of man (or some men) over the development that has taken place in other animals and is *not* rooted in man's being a different *kind* of animal from all other animals. My position is that our belief that a human being is a moral being and thus the subject of moral rights is based on a belief that human beings differ radically in kind from other animals: men are moral beings not because of something they achieve or do but because of what they are.[22]

May's argument is simply irrelevant to the issue being considered. Assume, for illustration, and for the sake of discussion, that humans differ from other animals in that they alone have immaterial minds, and that it is because of this that humans have rights. This is perfectly compatible with the claim that basic moral principles will not involve the concept of species membership. May has apparently failed to understand what is being claimed in the passage to which he refers—a failure facilitated by very serious misquotation. For the original passage reads: 'But they have overlooked the point that this cannot be an acceptable *basic* moral principle, since difference in species is not in itself a morally relevant difference.'[23] The omission of the first half of the sentence is unfortunate in itself, containing as it does the explicit and emphasized reference to basic moral principles. But May's casual rendering of the part that he does 'quote' is even more

[22] William E. May, 'Abortion and Man's Moral Being', in *Abortion: Pro and Con*, edited by Robert L. Perkins, 1974, pp. 13-35. See p. 23.
[23] Michael Tooley, 'Abortion and Infanticide', *Philosophy & Public Affairs*, Volume 2, Number 1, 1972, pp. 37-65. See p. 55.

striking, especially the unacknowledged omission of the crucial phrase 'in itself'.

To briefly sum up this section. I have tried to show, first, that there are good reasons for accepting the claim that membership in a biological species is not morally significant *in itself*, i.e. that *basic* moral principles will not involve the concept of species membership, nor terms referring to particular species. I have argued, further, that this claim is, when properly understood, quite uncontroversial, and that philosophers who contend that it is mistaken generally do so because they fail to distinguish between basic moral principles and derived ones, and hence between the claim that membership in a species is morally significant in itself, and the claim that it is morally significant either in itself or in virtue of its relation to other properties that are morally significant in themselves.

4.3 The Appeal to Essentialism

There is, however, at least one present-day philosopher who *seems* to have attempted to mount a reasonably sustained defence of the view that basic moral principles may properly incorporate reference to particular biological species, such as *Homo sapiens*: Roger Wertheimer, in his essay, 'Philosophy on Humanity'. I say 'seems' advisedly. Wertheimer's article is, unfortunately, quite emotional—polemic being offered where precision is sorely needed. In particular, Wertheimer does not draw any explicit distinction between basic moral principles and derived ones, with the result that there is room for considerable doubt as to exactly what thesis he is defending. Moreover, there are times when he does not seem to be operating with such a distinction, even implicitly. For some of the claims he makes stand in need of support very different from what he offers, *if* they are claims about basic moral principles. Finally, some of the things he says toward the end of his paper appear to be inconsistent with the view that being a member of the species *Homo sapiens* is morally significant in itself.

But on the other hand, there are passages where he definitely seems to be embracing, and passionately so, the view that species membership is morally significant in itself. I am inclined to think that this is his view, and that passages that seem to conflict with it reflect, on the one hand, genuine difficulties with that position, and, on the other, the carelessly argued and highly emotive style of Wertheimer's piece. In any case, one can glean from the essay two possible arguments for the view that species membership is morally relevant in itself. These arguments are worth considering, regardless of whether the view in question is in fact Wertheimer's.

Wertheimer begins by describing what he refers to as the 'Standard Belief':

Let us call the kind of moral status most people ascribe to human beings *human* (*moral*) *status*. The term refers to a kind of independent and superior consideration to be accorded an entity, not to the kind of entity to be accorded the consideration, so it is not a definitional truth that human beings have human status. But most people believe that being human has *moral cachet*: viz., a human being has human status in virtue of being a human being (and thus each human being has human status). Call this the *Standard Belief*. That most people accept it is an empirical fact.[24]

There are two expressions in this passage that produce uncertainty as to exactly what Wertheimer takes the Standard Belief to be: 'human being', and 'in virtue of'. Given only this passage, it would be natural to construe 'human being' as meaning the same as 'member of the species *Homo sapiens*'. And it would be natural to interpret 'in virtue of' as indicating that the property of being a human being was morally significant in itself. In which case the Standard Belief would be the belief that the property of being a member of the species *Homo sapiens* is one that enters into basic moral principles. Two things, however, stand in the way of this natural interpretation, both suggested by the following passage:

While people may disagree about what overriding considerations may legitimize killing a human being, most people believe that killing a

[24] Roger Wertheimer, 'Philosophy on Humanity', in Robert Perkins, op. cit., pp. 107-28. See pp. 107-8.

human being is in principle wrong and that, if a fetus is a full-fledged human being, it may be destroyed only for those reasons that justify destroying any other human being. The very structure of this familiar controversy evidences a shared assumption: the Standard Belief.[25]

In the first place, if Wertheimer were using 'human being' to mean 'member of the biological species *Homo sapiens*,' it would, surely, be far from obvious that most people believe that it is in principle wrong to kill a human being, since there is reason to believe that most people do not hold that killing a human that has suffered irreparable brain damage resulting in permanent unconsciousness is wrong, at least in the way that killing a normal adult human being is. So it appears that Wertheimer may be interpreting 'human being' in such a way that membership of the species *Homo sapiens* is a necessary, but not a sufficient condition, for being a human being.

Second, the facts in question do not support any claim about what *basic* moral principles people accept. An individual may believe that it is in principle wrong to kill human beings, not because they have the property of being human, but because of some other property possessed by all humans —perhaps as a matter of biological necessity—such that it is wrong to kill things possessing that property. So if the Standard Belief is a belief about basic moral principles, the facts referred to by Wertheimer do not show that anyone accepts it, let alone that most people do.

So it might appear that the Standard Belief is not what it initially seemed. But before jumping to this conclusion, let us pursue further Wertheimer's line of thought. He goes on to discuss rationality, and he introduces what he refers to as the Factunorm Principle. It states that 'what and how we do think is evidence for the principles of rationality, what and how we ought to think'.[26] He then remarks that: 'All this, the Factunorm Principle, and the rest, plus more that could be said, is but an elaboration of two "assumptions"; we are rational and it is rational to believe what is believed by rational persons.'[27] Wertheimer says that although not all philosophers accept the Factunorm Principle, many do,

[25] Ibid., p. 108.   [26] Ibid., p. 110.   [27] Ibid., p. 112.

'particularly those intent on developing a substantive moral theory':

By their conscious practice and often by explicit statement, most such philosophers acknowledge that a reason for thinking that some moral belief implied by a theory is true (false) is that the belief is accepted (rejected) by most people. Certainly for most of the most important moral philosophers, conformity with common belief is a test and a touchstone if not the bedrock of moral theory. That is an empirical fact easily established; the texts are public and unequivocal.

That fact, taken with the fact that the Standard Belief is a common belief, might suggest that most if not all philosophers accept the Standard Belief. Yet the fact is they all reject it.[28]

This passage is important for two reasons. First, it presents one of Wertheimer's two arguments in support of the Standard Belief. The Factunorm Principle apparently implies that what most people believe is, other things being equal, likely to be true. The Standard Belief is accepted by most people. Therefore it is likely to be true.

Second, the above passage seems to throw some light on what is meant by the Standard Belief. For Wertheimer says that the Standard Belief is a belief that is rejected by *all* philosophers (save one). This strongly suggests that the Standard Belief cannot be a *derived* moral belief that it is wrong to treat innocent human beings in certain ways. For most Roman Catholic philosophers, for example, would hold that it is at least a correct derived moral principle that it is wrong to kill innocent human beings. If the Standard Belief is to be a moral claim rejected by virtually all philosophers it must, it would seem, be a *basic* moral claim.

The other problematic point concerns how Wertheimer is employing the expression 'human being'. This must, I fear, remain obscure. On the one hand, Wertheimer says: 'The term "human being" is correctly applied to all and only members of our biological species.' This seems as forthright as one could wish. Unfortunately, he immediately goes on to remark that 'that specification is informative but incomplete without criteria for species membership'; and, in the same paragraph, he says that 'the abortion argument supplies

---

[28] Ibid., pp. 112–13. In a footnote, Wertheimer qualifies the last statement: 'Anyway, all (save one) that I know of.'

sufficient evidence that no neat set of necessary and sufficient conditions for being human is generally agreed upon—
which is to say that there is no such set'.[29] I find these
remarks very puzzling. The notion of species membership is,
after all, a biological notion, and any fuzziness that may exist
about some obscure cases surely does not raise any doubts
about the biological species to which normal embryos
developing inside a human mother belong.

My suspicion is that Wertheimer, contrary to what he
explicitly says in the passage just quoted, does not use the
expression 'human being' to mean: member of the species
Homo sapiens. It seems to me more likely that he uses it,
instead, to mean something like: *mature*, or *fully developed*
member of the species *Homo sapiens*. Recall, for example,
the statement quoted earlier to the effect that 'if a fetus is
a full-fledged human being, it may be destroyed only for
those reasons that justify destroying any other human
being'.[30] This seems to support the interpretation just
suggested.

The result is that there would seem to be two different
claims that Wertheimer may have in mind when he speaks of
the Standard Belief. On the one hand, there is the claim that
the property of being a member of the species *Homo sapiens*
is one that enters into basic moral principles dealing, inter
alia, with the morality of destroying things. On the other
hand, there is the claim that being a 'full-fledged' member of
the species *Homo sapiens* is one that enters into certain
basic moral principles. I am not at all confident as to which
of these is supposed to be the Standard Belief. I am inclined
to think it is probably the second of these claims. The difficulty is that this interpretation is inconsistent with Wertheimer's explicit statement that 'the term "human being" is
correctly applied to all and only members of our biological
species.'[31] Fortunately, however, the choice between these
interpretations is not crucial in the present context. What is
crucial is that the belief in question must be one concerning
basic moral principles. For otherwise the Standard Belief
would not be one that is rejected by virtually all philosophers,

[29] Ibid., p. 114.   [30] Ibid., p. 108.   [31] Ibid., p. 114.

nor would it be relevant to the contention that is being defended in the present discussion.

Wertheimer offers two arguments in support of the Standard Belief. The first, mentioned above, can be put as follows. The Factunorm Principle is true, and it implies that, other things being equal, what most people believe is likely to be true. The Standard Belief is accepted by most people. Therefore it is likely to be true.

The major premiss of this argument, to the effect that, other things being equal, what most people believe is likely to be true, is far from unproblematic. But even if it is granted for the sake of discussion, the argument seems unacceptable. In the first place, what is one to say about a belief that, though shared by most people, is also rejected by most people who are knowledgeable about the subject area in question? Surely this is not a case where other things are equal. And in such a case where the views of most people are not shared by those who have been trained to think about the relevant issues, and who have spent considerable time doing so, is it not more likely that it is the majority that have mistaken beliefs? In view of the fact, then, that virtually all philosophers reject the Standard Belief, it is surely unjustified to view this as a situation where other things are equal, and hence as one in which one is justified in concluding that what most people believe is likely to be true.

In the second place, it is far from clear that most people accept the Standard Belief. Certainly it would require a very careful study to show that this was so, since one would need to provide people with an understanding of the philosophical distinction between basic moral principles and derived ones. And my own, admittedly very limited experience has been that, when people do acquire an understanding of the distinction between basic moral principles and derived ones, most of them turn out *not* to accept the Standard Belief.

Wertheimer's second argument in support of the Standard Belief is contained in the following, rather difficult passage:

Our reasons for identifying ourselves as human beings are our reasons for accepting the Standard Belief.

As a step toward understanding this, let us take as a rough statement of the notion of human status the dictum, G: You₁ are to do unto others$_a$ as you$_2$ would have others$_b$ do unto you$_3$. The dictum is addressed to you$_1$, any rational agent, because, like any rational principle, G is addressed and applies to all and only those who can listen and apply it, rational agents. So too, the others$_b$ are all the other rational agents, and when G is addressed to any of them, you$_1$ are one of the other others$_b$. However, while you$_1$ = you$_2$ = you$_3$, neither you$_2$ nor you$_3$ need be rational agents; you$_2$ need only be what might be called a subjunctively rational creature. So too, the others$_a$ need not be rational agents; they include all but not necessarily only the others$_b$. The others$_a$ comprise the class of those with human status; or rather, they plus yourself$_3$ comprise that class. The question of what has moral cachet is the question of how the others$_a$ are to be identified. To ask it is to ask what it would be rational for you$_2$ to identify yourself$_3$ as so that you$_3$ are among the others$_a$ when G is addressed to any of the others$_b$. That is, it would be rational for you$_1$ to accept and act upon G only if you$_2$ filled in G by identifying the others$_a$ in such a way that you$_3$ could not be excluded from the others$_a$ when the others$_b$ act upon G. And for that very reason it would be irrational for you$_1$ to accept any of the philosophical alternatives to the Standard Belief, because, although you$_1$ are rational, you$_1$ are not necessarily rational and so you$_3$ could become or have been nonrational. Any of your$_1$ cognitive or affective capacities could become or could have been different without altering your$_1$ identity, so the individual whose interests are your$_1$ own could remain constant while those principles would not require the consideration of his (= your$_3$) interests. By contrast, being human is an essential property of anything possessing it. You$_1$ could not be or have been other than a human being and still be identifiable as you$_3$. The Standard Belief is a common belief because it enables all and only those known creatures to whom G can be addressed to rationally accept G, for it ensures that each and every one of them has a rational claim to the consideration of his or her interests throughout his or her lifetime.[32]

This is, at least, an interesting attempt to justify the Standard Belief. It fails, however, for at least two important reasons. The first is that it is not logically necessary that the individual human persons who now exist will always be individuals belonging to the species *Homo sapiens*. Kafka's description in his *Metamorphosis* of the transformation of Gregor from an individual with a human body into one with the body of an insect makes plausible, in an intuitive way, the idea that an individual at one time might belong to one species, and later belong to another. Kafka's tale, however, does leave the causal aspects of the transformation obscure,

[32] Ibid., pp. 119–20.

and this makes it possible for one to hold that Gregor may not have survived the transformation. Perhaps what one has is simply a psychological replica of Gregor? I believe, however, that causal descriptions could be incorporated that would ensure that it was Gregor, and not a psychological replica, that existed at the end of the transformation. This is perhaps somewhat easier to do if one holds the view that the mind is an immaterial substance, than if one holds, for example, that the mind is identical with the brain, but I believe that it can be done in the latter case as well. If this is right, it cannot be a *logically necessary* property of individual human beings that they will never become non-human individuals. It appears that Wertheimer is mistaken, then, when he contends that the Standard Belief will ensure that one's interests will be protected throughout one's lifetime.

Second, Wertheimer claims that no alternative to the Standard Belief will ensure that one will not at some time be in a position in which G does not prohibit people from acting in ways that disadvantage one. This claim is also false. For consider the following alternative to the Standard Belief: the property of being a member of the species *Homo sapiens* that has not suffered irreparable brain damage destroying completely any capacity for consciousness is a property that has moral cachet. It is true that this is not a very 'philosophical' alternative, involving as it does reference to a particular species. But if one is to defend the Standard Belief, one must show that there are no tenable alternatives. And it seems clear that the alternative mentioned is at least as acceptable as the Standard Belief. Since there is no reason for me to care what happens to what was my body once my brain has suffered irreparable damage that renders impossible any experience or mental activity, it cannot be irrational for me to reject the Standard Belief in favour of the more restricted alternative.

There are, of course, alternatives that are clearly superior to both. One is that 'others$_a$' should be construed as including both rational individuals and subjunctively rational individuals—where an individual who has enjoyed rationality and consciousness in the past may be said to be a subjunctively rational individual if it is logically possible for that individual to enjoy rationality and consciousness again at some time in the future. The crucial reason for preferring this alternative is that while it is not a necessary property of me that I shall always be a human being, it is a necessary property of me that I shall always be at least a subjunctively rational individual. For when it becomes logically impossible for there ever to be a conscious, rational individual who stands in certain appropriate causal relations to that temporal part of me that now exists, *I* will no longer exist, though of course my body may continue to exist, either as a mindless human organism, or, conceivably, as the body of some other human individual.

The above two considerations show that Wertheimer's argument does not provide a satisfactory justification for the Standard Belief. Let us now consider another important way in which his approach is defective. It concerns the membership in the class of others$_a$ that results if one adopts Wertheimer's approach. The objection can be put as follows. The class of others$_a$ contains the class of others$_b$, which in turn is the class of all rational agents, but it also includes all human beings. In short, an individual belongs to the class of others$_a$ if and only if he is either a rational agent or a human being. It is clear that the moral outlook that results is not acceptable. Consider again the Martians. Moral principle G will prohibit the mistreatment of any Martians currently enjoying rationality, since they fall within the class of others$_a$. But what of any who happen to be in a coma, and thus who are merely subjunctively rational? They will not fall within the class of others$_a$. So given Wertheimer's approach, there is no rule prohibiting us from killing them. This is surely unacceptable. If there are reasons for not treating subjunctively rational members of our own species in certain ways, those reasons should apply equally to subjunctively rational members of other species.

A closely related point is this. If Wertheimer's approach were correct, it would be wrong for humans to kill subjunctively rational humans, but not for Martians to do so. For an important class of cases, then, the morality of killing would rest completely upon *agent-relative* considerations: whether it is wrong to kill a subjunctively rational individual

will depend upon whether one belongs to the same species as
that individual. This result is also, I suggest, quite unacceptable: the morality of killing should not be agent-relative in
this way.

To sum up. Wertheimer attempts to defend the view that
membership in the species *Homo sapiens* is morally relevant
by means of an argument that rests upon the claim that it is a
necessary property of human beings that they will never
become members of other species. This argument is defective
in a number of ways. In the first place, it is not a necessary
property of any human being that he will always belong to
the species *Homo sapiens*. If one is looking for some property
that all human persons necessarily possess, the property of
being at least subjunctively rational is a much more plausible
candidate. In the second place, the property of belonging to
the species *Homo sapiens* picks out a class of individuals that
is too wide in some respects, and too narrow in others. Too
wide, because there would seem to be at least some members
of *Homo sapiens*—namely, individuals that have suffered
irreparable brain damage that makes consciousness impossible—whose destruction is not at all comparable to the
killing of normal adult human beings. And too narrow,
because it excludes relevant members of other species, and
does so even when it is combined with the class of rational
individuals. The property of being at least subjunctively
rational, in contrast, is free of both these defects.

The conclusion of this chapter, then, is essentially negative:
basic moral principles should involve reference neither to
particular species nor to the general concept of species membership. How, then, should basic moral principles dealing
with the morality of killing be formulated? It turns out that
there are several plausible alternatives for a species-free
formulation of such principles. The choice among these
alternatives will be explored in the following chapters.

5

The Concept of a Person

5.1 Introductory Remarks

This chapter is concerned with what properties should enter into the concept of a person. A variety of answers will be canvassed, together with arguments for and against. The objective, as explained in section 4.1, is to formulate a concept of a person that is itself purely descriptive, and free of all moral and evaluative elements. The choice of content is to be determined, however, by moral considerations. In particular, it is to be guided by the answer to the following question:

> What relatively permanent, non-potential properties, possibly in conjunction with other, less permanent features of an entity, make it intrinsically wrong to destroy an entity, and do so independently of its intrinsic value?

A person is to be defined as an entity that possesses at least one of those enduring, non-potential properties.

The question of the properties that should enter into the definition of the concept of a person, thus understood, is closely related to the question of when it is intrinsically wrong to *kill* something; however they differ in certain respects. To kill something is, by definition, to destroy a biological organism, whereas persons may be destroyed without doing this. First, because there is nothing incoherent in the notion of a non-biological person. Perhaps complex computers with certain capabilities which may exist some day should be classified as persons. Or perhaps there are non-embodied persons, such as ghosts and gods. Second, as will be discussed shortly, there are ways of destroying human persons that do not involve the killing of any biological organism. So the question of the morality of killing is in these respects narrower than that of what properties should enter into the definition of a person. But it is also a wider one. Some biological organisms that, it would seem, are not yet persons, will develop into persons if not interfered with. A full account of the morality of killing must specify whether the destruction of such potential persons is intrinsically wrong.

None the less, to set out and defend an account of the properties that should enter into the definition of a person is to provide answers to many of the central issues involved in the morality of killing. An adequate account of the morality of killing, for example, must explain such things as the scope of the prohibition against killing, the exceptions with respect to things falling within the scope, and the stringency of the obligation not to kill. Any defence of a particular view as to the properties that should enter into the definition of a person will go a long way towards doing these things. In the first place, the specification of person-making characteristics will provide at least a partial account of the types of things that it is intrinsically wrong to destroy, and hence of the obligations not to kill. How complete the account is will depend mainly upon the moral status of potential persons. Second, it seems likely that any defence of a particular view as to the properties that should enter into the definition of a person will also provide a basis for holding that if certain other things are true of a given person—such as that he is suffering terribly from some terminal illness and would like to end his own life—then it is not wrong to kill such an individual, even though normally it would be. Third, if the rationale offered in defence of a certain account of what properties should enter into the definition of a person involves reference to considerations that bear upon obligations other than the obligation not to kill, it will probably provide one with some explanation of the stringency of that obligation, some account of why the obligation not to kill is so much stronger than most other obligations.

What properties, then, should enter into the definition of the concept of a person? Many answers have been proposed. A natural starting-point, however, accepted by virtually all of them, is the idea that for something to be a person it must, at the very least, be capable of consciousness. But this apparent agreement is in fact deceptive, since the term 'consciousness' may be construed differently, depending upon one's general views in philosophy of mind. Philosophers who are logical behaviourists, or central state materialists, will be inclined to analyse consciousness in terms either of a general capacity on the part of the individual to acquire information about events, both external and internal, or, more narrowly, in terms of a capacity to acquire information about one's own present mental states. A dualist, in contrast, will be inclined to offer an analysis of consciousness according to which states of consciousness are private and non-physical in nature. These differing accounts of consciousness do not affect our ordinary ethical decisions, since behaviourists, identity theorists, and dualists generally agree about what things are conscious and what things are not. But this agreement with respect to everyday moral decisions should not blind one to the underlying disagreement concerning fundamental moral principles—disagreement that in the not too distant future may well lead to very serious moral disagreements about everyday matters. Consider, for example, the possibility of robots that possess various of the intellectual capabilities of normal adult human beings. Imagine, in fact, one whose 'psychological' behaviour and 'intellectual' capacities were indistinguishable from those of human beings. What would be the moral status of such a being? Would it be just a complex, inanimate object that one could destroy at will, and otherwise treat as one pleased? Or would it possess consciousness? Would it have sensations, thoughts, and feelings? If its behaviour were indistinguishable from human behaviour, a behaviourist would have to say that such a robot enjoyed all the mental states that humans enjoy. A central state materialist would, I think, be forced to take the same view. A dualist, on the other hand, would probably say that the fact that the robot's behaviour was exactly like human behaviour would not provide sufficient reason for holding that it enjoyed states of consciousness, conceived of as states that are non-physical and private. The upshot is that the logical behaviourist and the central state materialist would classify the robot as a person, while the dualist probably would not.

As a result, it appears to be impossible to settle certain

absolutely fundamental issues in ethics without at the same time taking a stand on certain equally fundamental questions in philosophy of mind. This is an important fact, which deserves to be stressed. For while there has been some awareness of it among those working in philosophy of mind—for example, in discussions of what it is about pain that makes it so unappealing—moral philosophers have given very little attention to it. Until it is attended to, there is little hope of setting out a satisfactory set of basic moral principles.

If, for the moment, we ignore this disagreement about how 'consciousness' is to be construed in the statement of moral principles, we can say that there is very general agreement that something is not a person unless it is, in some sense, capable of consciousness. One can then ask what, if anything, must be added to consciousness in order for something to be a person. Some people, including many Oriental thinkers, hold that nothing need be added, that sentience itself is sufficient to make it wrong to destroy something. Many people, however, feel that mere consciousness it not itself sufficient to make something a person, and several proposals have been advanced as to what additional properties are required. Among the more important suggestions are the following:

(1) the capacity to experience pleasure and/or pain;

(2) the capacity for having desires;

(3) the capacity for remembering past events;

(4) the capacity for having expectations with respect to future events;

(5) an awareness of the passage of time;

(6) the property of being a continuing, conscious self, or subject of mental states, construed, in a minimal way, as nothing more than a construct out of appropriately related mental states;

(7) the property of being a continuing, conscious self, construed as a pure ego, that is, as an entity that is distinct from the experiences and other mental states that it has;

(8) the capacity for self-consciousness, that is, for awareness of the fact that one is a continuing, conscious subject of mental states;

(9) the property of having mental states that involve propositional attitudes, such as beliefs and desires;

(10) the capacity for having thought episodes, that is, states of consciousness involving intentionality;

(11) the capacity for reasoning;

(12) problem solving ability;

(13) the property of being autonomous, that is, of having the capacity for making decisions based upon an evaluation of relevant considerations;

(14) the capacity for using language;

(15) the ability to interact socially with others.

These alternatives, and various combinations of them, provide one with quite a bewildering selection of candidates for the properties that should enter into the definition of the concept of a person. Most philosophers, on the whole, have generally been content simply to indicate their own preferred choices—usually rationality, autonomy, or self-consciousness. Rarely have they attempted to develop any sort of persuasive argument either in support of their own view, or against the more important alternatives. From a certain point of view, this is understandable. Most of our interaction is with human beings, who by and large either possess *all* of those properties, or will come to do so with the passage of time. As a result, the question which of these properties are the morally significant ones has not seemed pressing.

But there are a variety of reasons why it *is* a pressing question. In the first place, normal adult human beings do not, in their development, acquire all of the above properties at the same time. If the fact that one would later acquire a given property had moral significance comparable to the actual possession of that property, this would make no difference. But it is clear that many people do not believe that potentialities have that sort of significance, since otherwise one could make no sense of their lack of compunction about the destruction of fertilized human egg cells. Such people are confronted with the problem of distinguishing morally between different stages in the development of a human being. How this is done will depend upon when the foetus acquires the morally crucial property or properties, and this in turn will depend upon which of the above properties, or combinations of them, are the properties that should enter into the definition of a person.

A second reason concerns the moral status of non-human animals. Western society, in part because of its religious tradition, has been very casual about assuming that the destruction of non-human animals is not morally wrong. Recently, this attitude has been seriously called into question, in some cases with regard to particular species, such as dolphins and chimpanzees, and in other cases with regard to all sentient beings.[1] It is clear that a re-examination of the traditional Western outlook is in order. For while it may be that no non-human animals that we are presently acquainted with possess all of the properties listed above, some do possess most of them. It is, therefore, crucial to determine precisely what properties suffice to make something a person.

Some writers are rather pessimistic about the chance of success for such an enterprise. Jane English, for example, argues as follows:

These approaches are typical: foes of abortion propose sufficient conditions for personhood which fetuses satisfy, while friends of abortion counter with necessary conditions for personhood which fetuses lack. But these both presuppose that the concept of a person can be captured in a strait jacket of necessary and/or sufficient conditions. Rather, 'person' is a cluster of features, of which rationality, having a self concept, and being conceived of humans are only part.

What is typical of persons? Within our concept of a person we include, first, certain biological factors: descended from humans, having a certain genetic make-up, having a head, hands, arms, eyes, capable of locomotion, breathing, eating, sleeping. There are psychological factors: sentience, perception, having a concept of self and of one's own interests and desires, the ability to use tools, the ability to use language or symbol systems, the ability to joke, to be angry, to doubt. There are rationality factors: the ability to reason and draw conclusions, the ability to generalize and to learn from past experience, the ability to sacrifice present interests for greater gains in the future. There are social factors: the ability to work in groups and respond to peer pressures, the ability to recognize and consider as valuable the interests of others, seeing oneself as one among 'other minds,' the ability to sympathize, encourage, love, the ability to evoke from others the responses of sympathy, encouragement, love, the ability to work with others for

---

[1] For some helpful discussion of the moral status of animals, see Leonard Nelson's 'Duties to Animals', and Roslind Godlovitch's 'Animals and Morals', both available in *Animals, Men, and Morals*, edited by Stanley and Roslind Godlovitch, 1972, and Peter Singer's 'Animals and the Value of Life', in *Matters of Life and Death*, edited by Tom Regan, 1980.

mutual advantage. Then there are legal factors: being subject to the law and protected by it, having the ability to sue and enter contracts, being counted in the census, having a name and citizenship, the ability to own property, inherit, and so forth.

Now the point is not that this list is incomplete, or that you can find counterinstances to each of its points. People typically exhibit rationality, for instance, but someone who was irrational would not thereby fail to qualify as a person. On the other hand, something could exhibit the majority of these features and still fail to be a person, as an advanced robot might. There is no single core of necessary and sufficient features which we can draw upon with the assurance that they constitute what really makes a person; there are only features that are more or less typical.[2]

Granted that there are many properties, falling into several diverse groups, that persons *typically* possess, how does this entail any conclusion about the possibility of isolating those properties that are in themselves morally significant with respect to what beings it is wrong to destroy? It seems that Jane English has not really offered any argument here. Moreover, if one considers some of the properties mentioned as typical of persons, it is certainly possible to offer reasons why they are not morally significant in themselves. First, the grounds outlined in the previous chapter for not viewing species membership as morally significant in itself are applicable to biological factors in general. Second, one can surely set aside legal factors. An entity's legal properties and capabilities are a function of the institutions of the particular society to which it happens to belong. The wrongness of destroying something, surely, is not dependent upon such facts. Third, I believe that social factors can also be set aside. Consider a rational individual possessing the psychological attributes of normal adult human beings, but who is unable to co-operate with others, or to empathize with them, or to evoke any positive responses from them. Not an especially appealing sort of individual, perhaps, but I doubt that many would wish to say that there would be no serious moral objection to killing him. This issue deserves more serious consideration, of course, but there does seem to be at least a good prima-facie

[2] Jane English, 'Abortion and the Concept of a Person', *Canadian Journal of Philosophy*, Volume 5, Number 2, 1975, pp. 233-43. See pp. 234-5. A similar point is made by Jonathan Glover in his book, *Causing Deaths and Saving Lives*, 1977, p. 127.

case for the view that social factors do not enter into our moral judgements about the wrongness of killing.

If this line of thought is right, most of the properties mentioned by English can be set aside, and one is left with those that she labels psychological factors and rationality factors. Perhaps English would maintain that even if one is justified in setting aside biological, legal, and social factors, there is no hope of selecting a single core of psychological and rationality factors that will provide necessary and sufficient conditions for something's being a person. But why should this be so? If many of the properties that persons typically have can be set aside as morally irrelevant, why should it not be possible to carry this process further, until one has a 'single core' that specifies what makes something a person?

There is this difference, which may underlie what English is saying. To exclude biological factors, one has to do little more than make explicit certain distinctions, and then ask people their moral judgements about certain possible situations. In a sense, then, the irrelevance of biological factors is implicit in ordinary moral thinking. I feel that the same is true with regard to legal factors, and social factors. The situation seems very different with regard to the psychological and/or rationality factors that make something a person. Here I do not believe that there is any single view that is implicit in the ordinary moral thinking of most people. If this is right, then the sort of argument that one can offer for excluding biological, legal, and social factors cannot be used to determine which of the psychological and/or rationality factors are the important ones.

So perhaps what underlies English's pessimism is a belief that no appeal to ordinary moral intuitions, however refined and reflective, can result in a generally shared view about what it is that makes something a person. But such a belief need not lead to pessimism unless one holds that moral intuitions are the ultimate court of appeal with respect to the acceptability of fundamental moral principles. I have already offered reasons for rejecting this view. All that I would add here is that the inability to determine, through an appeal to intuitions, what properties should enter into the definition of the concept of a person, is a further, and very important reason, for abandoning the appeal to intuitions. The question of what beings it is seriously wrong to destroy is one of the central questions of ethics. One should not rest content with an approach that is unable to provide an answer to this question.

The discussion in succeeding sections of the present chapter is devoted to an examination of a variety of attempts to determine what properties should enter into the definition of a person. Possible connections between the concept of a person and such notions as rights, interests, and capacities will be explored. An account of what it is that makes something a person will be set out, and reasons for accepting it will be advanced.

5.2 Persons and Rights

In discussing how the term person was to be interpreted, I mentioned the possibility of its descriptive content being determined by reference to those properties that give something a right to continued existence. However an alternative proposal was adopted, according to which the content of the term 'person' is to be determined instead by a consideration of what relatively enduring, non-potential properties make it intrinsically wrong to destroy something, and do so independently of its intrinsic value. There were two reasons for adopting this alternative. First, some ethical theories eschew talk of rights entirely. Second, the concept of a right is in some respects less clear than other basic ethical notions—for reasons that will emerge, in part, in this section.

Nevertheless, there is a very close relation between these two ways of specifying the descriptive content of the term person. For if potentialities are set aside, it may be that the only reasons why it is ever intrinsically wrong to destroy things of a given type is that things of that type are intrinsically valuable, or that things of that type possess a right not to be destroyed. Since I think that most people would, in fact, accept this view, it may be helpful to approach the issue of what it is that makes something a person by trying to get clear about the conditions under which something has a given right, and, in particular, a right not to be destroyed. This approach is also very natural in the context of a discussion of abortion, given that much of the argument pro and con revolves about the question whether human foetuses have a right to life.

How is one to determine whether a given entity has a certain right? An approach that I believe is very promising, especially in the present context, starts out from the observation that there appear to be two radically different sorts of reasons why an entity may lack a certain right. Compare, for example, the following two claims:

(1) A child does not have a right to smoke;
(2) A newspaper does not have a right not to be torn up.

The first claim raises a substantive moral issue. People might well disagree about it, and support their conflicting views by appealing to different moral theories. The second claim, in contrast, seems an unlikely candidate for moral dispute. It is natural to say that newspapers just are not the sort of things that can have any rights at all, including a right not to be torn up. So there is no need to appeal to a substantive moral theory to resolve the question whether a newspaper has a right not to be torn up.

One way of characterizing this difference, albeit one that will not especially commend itself to philosophers of a Quinean bent, is to say that the second claim, unlike the first, is true by virtue of a certain *conceptual* connection, and that is why no moral theory is needed in order to see that it is true. The explanation, then, of why it is that a newspaper does not have a right not to be torn up, is that there is some property P such that first, newspapers lack property P, and second, it is a conceptual truth that only things with property P can be possessors of rights.

What might property P be? A plausible answer is set out and defended by Joel Feinberg in his stimulating paper, 'The Rights of Animals and Unborn Generations'. It takes the form of what he refers to as the *interest principle*: '. . . the sorts of beings who *can* have rights are precisely those who have (or can have) interests'.[3] Then, since 'interests must be

---

[3] Joel Feinberg, 'The Rights of Animals and Unborn Generations', in *Philosophy and Environmental Crisis*, edited by William T. Blackstone, 1974, pp. 43–68. See p. 51.

compounded somehow out of conations',[4] it follows that things devoid of desires, such as newspapers, can have neither interests nor rights. Here, then, is one account of the difference in status between judgements such as (1) and (2) above.

One would like, however, some defence of the interest principle. Since the interest principle is supposed to express a conceptual connection between rights and interests, such a defence will presumably involve showing how the interest principle can be derived, in a straightforward logical way, from analyses of the concepts of a right and of an interest.

First, however, let us consider the bearing of the interest principle upon the question what it is that makes something a person. If we assume for the moment that the class of persons either coincides with, or is a subset of, the class of things possessing a right not to be destroyed, the interest principle tells us that an entity cannot be a person unless it is capable of having interests. This in itself may be a conclusion of considerable importance. Consider, for example, a fertilized human egg cell. Some day it will come to have desires and interests. Qua zygote, however, it does not even have the *capacity* for having desires. What about interests? This depends upon the account one offers of the relation between desires and interests. It seems to me that a zygote cannot properly be spoken of as a subject of interests. This question needs, however, to be examined very carefully. But if it does turn out that a zygote cannot have interests, it would follow, in view of the interest principle together with the above assumption that the class of persons is contained in the class of things possessing a right to continued existence, that zygotes are not persons.

The interest principle can support, then, a thesis about necessary conditions for being a person that may bear in an important way upon moral decisions. Yet many significant questions will not be answered by it. In particular, it provides no help with the question of the moral status of human organisms once they have developed to the point where they do have desires, and thus are capable of having interests. The

4 Ibid., pp. 49-50.

interest principle states that they *can* have rights. It does not state whether they *do* have rights—including, in particular, a right not to be destroyed.

It is possible, however, that the interest principle does not exhaust the conceptual connections between rights and interests. It formulates only a very general connection: a thing cannot have any right at all unless it is capable of having at least some interest. May there not be more specific connections, between particular rights and particular sorts of interests? The following line of thought lends plausibility to this suggestion. Consider animals such as cats. Some philosophers, such as Benn and McCloskey, are inclined to hold that entities such as cats do not have any rights at all.[5] But let us assume, for the moment, that cats do have some rights, such as a right not to be tortured, and consider the following claim:

(3) A cat does not have a right to a university education.

How is this statement to be regarded? In particular, is it comparable in status to the claim that children do not have a right to smoke, or, instead, to the claim that newspapers do not have a right not to be torn up? To the latter, I should have thought. It is hard to imagine (3) being a matter of serious moral dispute. Just as a newspaper is not the sort of thing that can have any rights at all, including a right not to be destroyed, so one is inclined to say that a cat, though it may have some rights, such as a right not to be tortured, is not the sort of thing that can possibly have a right to a university education.

This intuitive judgement about the status of claims such as (3) is reinforced, moreover, if one turns to the question of the grounds of the interest principle. Consider, for example, the account offered by Feinberg, which he summarizes as follows:

Now we can extract from our discussion of animal rights a crucial principle for tentative use in the resolution of the other riddles about the

---

[5] See Stanley Benn's 'Personal Freedom and Environmental Ethics: The Moral Inequality of Species', in *Equality and Freedom: International Comparative Jurisprudence*, Volume II, edited by Dorsey Grey, New York and London, 1977, pp. 401-24, especially pp. 405-8; and pp. 410-14 of H. J McCloskey's 'The Right to Life', *Mind*, Volume 84, Number 335, 1975, pp. 403-25. In asserting that lower animals have no rights, Benn and McCloskey are not denying that there are ways of treating lower animals which are morally wrong.

applicability of the concept of a right, namely, that the sorts of beings who *can* have rights are precisely those who have (or can have) interests. I have come to this tentative conclusion for two reasons: (1) because a right holder must be capable of being represented and it is impossible to represent a being that has no interests, and (2) because a right holder must be capable of being a beneficiary in his own person, and a being without interests is a being that is incapable of being harmed or benefitted, having no good or 'sake' of its own. Thus, a being without interests has no 'behalf' to act in, and no 'sake' to act for.[6]

If this justification of the interest principle is sound, it can also be employed to support principles connecting particular rights with specific sorts of interests. Just as one cannot represent a being that has no interests at all, so one cannot, in demanding a university education for a cat, be representing the cat unless one is thereby representing some interest that the cat has, and that would be served by its receiving a university education. Similarly, one cannot be acting for the sake of a cat in arguing that it should receive a university education unless the cat has some interest that will thereby be furthered. If Feinberg's defence of the interest principle is sound, other, more specific principles must also be correct. These more specific principles can be summed up, albeit somewhat vaguely, by the following, *particular-interests principle*:

> It is a conceptual truth that an entity cannot have a particular right R unless it is at least capable of having some interest I which is furthered by its having right R.

Given this particular-interests principle, certain familiar facts, whose importance has not often been appreciated, become comprehensible. Compare an act of killing a normal adult human being with an act of torturing one for five minutes. Though both acts are seriously wrong, they are not equally so. Here, as in most cases, to violate an individual's right to life is more seriously wrong than to violate his right not to have pain inflicted upon him. Consider, however, the corresponding actions in the case of a new-born kitten. Most people feel it is seriously wrong to torture a kitten for five minutes, but not so to kill it painlessly. How is this difference

[6] Feinberg, op. cit., p. 51.

in the moral ordering of the two types of acts, between the
human case and the kitten case, to be explained? One answer
is that while normal adult human beings have both a right to
life and a right not to be tortured, a kitten has only the
latter. But why should this be so? The particular-interests
principle suggests a possible explanation. Though kittens have
some interests, including, in particular, an interest in not
being tortured, which derives from their capacity to feel pain,
they do not have an interest in continued existence, and
hence do not have a right not to be destroyed. This answer
contains, of course, a large promissory element. One needs a
defence of the view that kittens have no interest in continued
existence. This will be considered shortly. The point here is
simply that there is an important question about the rationale
underlying the moral ordering of certain sorts of acts, and that
the particular-interests principle points to a possible answer.

Feinberg's defence of the interest principle involves an
appeal to certain facts about rights, to the effect that 'a right
holder must be capable of being represented', and 'a right
holder must be capable of being a beneficiary in his own
person.'[7] If his argument is to be sound, these must in turn
be conceptual truths. Perhaps they are. However, it seems
that the argument should not rest with claims of this sort.
What one would like is an argument based on an analysis of
the fundamental notion of a right, and it is to such a line of
argument that I now wish to turn.

How is the concept of a right to be analysed? A number
of different accounts have been proposed. Among the most
common, however, are those that view rights as related to
conditional obligations. On such a view, to say that A has a
right to X is to say, roughly, that if certain conditions are
satisfied, then others are under a prima-facie obligation to
refrain from actions that would deprive A of X. Stanley Benn
and Richard Peters advanced an analysis of this sort: 'To say
that X has a right to £5 is to imply that there is a rule which,
when applied to the case of X and some other person Y,
imposes on Y a duty to pay X £5 if X so chooses.'[8] In a

---

[7] Ibid., p. 51.
[8] S. I. Benn and R. S. Peters, *The Principles of Political Thought*, 1965, p. 101.

similar vein, Richard Brandt has suggested that: 'We can say, roughly, that to have a moral right to something is for *someone else to be morally obligated* (in the objective sense) to act or refrain from acting in some way in respect to the thing to which I am said to have the right, if I want him to.'[9]

On these accounts, the obligation is conditional upon what the person with the right chooses or wants. One alternative to this would be an account in which the obligation is dependent not upon what a person wants, but upon what is in his interest. Another possible view is that the obligation is conditional upon the individual's not having waived the right in question.

We shall consider these alternatives shortly. Let us begin, however, with the suggestion that 'A has a right to X' is to be analysed as equivalent in meaning to 'If A wants X, others are under a prima-facie obligation to refrain from actions that would deprive him of it.' An immediate difficulty with this account is as follows. Suppose that Puss is a cat. It might be argued that there is a sense in which it is true that if Puss wants to go on living, then others are under a prima-facie obligation not to prevent her from doing so. Thus it will follow, from the analysis just set out, that Puss has a right to life—a view of cats that most people would reject.

The problem arises through unclarity regarding the truth conditions of the ordinary 'if . . . then . . .' conditional. In particular, it is not clear whether a conditional such as 'If Puss has a desire to go on living, then others are under a prima-facie obligation not to prevent her from doing so' implies, for example, that Puss is capable of having such a desire. It seems best, then, to revise the analysis as follows, in order to make explicit precisely what is being asserted:

A has a right to X

means the same as

A is capable of wanting X, and if A does want X, others are under a prima-facie obligation to refrain from actions that would deprive him of it.

[9] Richard R. Brandt, *Ethical Theory*, 1959, p. 436. Brandt immediately goes on to point out that this account is 'not *quite* right', and that 'it needs to be complicated in some ways.'

Thus revised, it will no longer follow from the analysis alone that things such as cats—let alone stones—have a right to life.

The analysis is, none the less, still open to serious objections. Before considering these, however, let us see how the argument proceeds. We were interested in the idea of deriving the interest principle, and the particular-interests version of it, from an analysis of the concept of a right. The present analysis does entail principles that, though not identical with the interest principles, are obviously closely related. The particular-interests principle states that an individual cannot have a particular right R unless it is capable of having a certain sort of corresponding interest I. The analysis of rights just set out does not quite entail this, but it does entail that an individual cannot have a right to X unless it is capable of having the corresponding desire for X. Let us refer to this related principle as the *modified particular-interests principle*. If the above account of rights is correct, then we at least have a derivation of a principle that can do the sort of thing that the particular-interests principle was introduced to do, namely, provide necessary conditions upon the types of beings that can have specific rights.

For the moment, then, let us operate with the modified particular-interests principle. What conclusions follow from it regarding the conditions that something must satisfy in order to be a person? Again, we are assuming, tentatively, that the class of persons either coincides with, or is a subclass of, the class of things possessing a right to life. Or, more precisely, we are assuming that the class of persons either coincides with, or is a subclass of, the class of things with *a right to continued existence*. The reason that things should be put in terms of a right to continued existence, rather than in terms of a right to life, is twofold. In the first place, one may want to attribute a right completely analogous to the right to life to a variety of non-biological individuals, such as certain very advanced computers of the future, and non-embodied minds. In the second place, it would seem possible to violate a biological person's 'right to life' without killing any biological organism. Suppose, for example, that there are technological developments that allow the brain of an adult human to be completely reprogrammed, so that the organism winds up with memories (or rather, apparent memories), beliefs, attitudes, and personality traits completely different from those associated with it before it was subjected to reprogramming. (The pope is reprogrammed, say, on the model of David Hume.) In such a case, however beneficial the change might be, most people would surely want to say that *someone* had been destroyed, that an adult human being's 'right to life' had been violated, even though no biological organism had been killed.[10]

Applying the modified particular-interests principle to the right to continue to exist leads to the conclusion that something cannot have a right to continued existence unless it is capable of having a desire to continue to exist. But what is involved in having this capacity? To answer this question, we need to ask what is involved in having the desire to continue to exist. We can then go on to consider what is required if something is to have the capacity of having that desire.

Two points about desires are relevant here. The first is that desires can be attributed only to things that have experiences. Consider, for example, a rather simple machine that is so designed that when its batteries run down, it 'searches' for an electrical outlet from which to get recharged. Such a machine exhibits behaviour analogous to that which animals exhibit when they want something. It is true that the behaviour exhibited by animals is typically both more complex, and suggestive of a much wider range of desires. However, one can easily imagine machines, gradually more complex, which would also act as if they were searching for a variety of objects. This greater complexity would not in itself, it would seem, lead one to attribute genuine desires to a machine. It is only when one comes to feel that one should attribute *consciousness* to a machine that one will want to attribute desires to it, in other than a metaphorical sense.

It is perhaps important to emphasize that this point does not rest upon an assumption that logical behaviourism, for example, cannot provide a satisfactory account of mental concepts. That is to say, the point here does not turn upon a

[10] Some philosophers would, however, reject this view of the matter. See, for example, Bernard Williams's discussion in his article, 'The Self and the Future', pp. 126-41 in *The Philosophy of Mind*, edited by Jonathan Glover, 1976.

dualistic construal of talk about experiences. What I am saying is that however one analyses such concepts as experience, consciousness, and desire, any satisfactory analysis of the latter concept will imply that only things that have experiences, only things that are conscious, can have desires.

The second point is that desires involve what many philosophers refer to as propositional attitudes. The fundamental way of describing a desire is as a desire that a certain proposition, or a certain sentence, be true. It is easy not to notice this, since in everyday life one often speaks of desiring things, such as an apple or a newspaper. Such talk, however, is elliptical, the context together with one's ordinary beliefs serving to make it clear that one wants to eat the apple and read the newspaper. It is sentences such as 'John wants it to be the case that he is eating an apple in the next few minutes' that provide an explicit and context-free description of an individual's desires.

This is important if one is interested in getting clear about precisely what is involved in having a given desire. Its significance in the present context is this. If desires involve propositional attitudes, an individual cannot have a desire unless he understands the proposition that he desires true. Understanding a proposition, in turn, presupposes possession of the concepts involved in it. To have desires, then, one must possess the related concepts.

Consider now the desire to continue to exist. In view of the first point about desires, anything that has this desire will have to be a subject of experiences. And in view of the second, it will have to understand a certain proposition. Part of what is involved in that proposition is the concept of something's continuing to exist. This idea, in turn, involves the concept of a temporal ordering of events, together with the idea of a thing existing at one time being identical with a thing existing at another, later time. In order to have a desire that anything continue to exist, then, one must possess these concepts. Here, however, we are concerned with a desire that a subject of experiences continue to exist, and continue to exist *as* a subject of experiences. One must therefore have the concept of a continuing subject of experiences. Finally, the desire is not a desire that just any subject of experiences continue to exist: it is a desire that *this* subject of experiences continue to exist. And it would seem that, in order to have this desire, one must be in some sense aware of the subject of experiences in question. To sum up, then, to have a desire for one's own continued existence presupposes that one possesses the concept of a continuing subject of experiences, and that one is aware of oneself as a subject of experiences.

The term 'self-consciousness' can be interpreted in different ways. One very natural interpretation, however, is that something possesses self-consciousness if and only if it is a subject of experiences, and is aware of itself as a subject of experiences. So construed, one conclusion of the above argument is that something cannot have a desire to continue to exist unless it possesses self-consciousness.

A word of explanation is in order, however, regarding the interpretation of talk about awareness of oneself as a subject of experiences. Otherwise there is a danger that the above conclusions will be misinterpreted. To some philosophers, talk about awareness of oneself as a subject of experiences will suggest the idea that one is aware of some entity, often referred to as a pure ego, that stands behind experiences, and has them, and which is in no way reducible to the experiences themselves and their interrelations. Other philosophers will tend to a very different interpretation, according to which talk about awareness of oneself as a subject of experiences is just a way of referring to an awareness of certain relations among experiences, and not to anything over and above the experiences. It is this latter, reductionist view of self-consciousness that I myself am inclined to adopt. In the context of the present argument, however, I do not think that it matters which of these views is correct. Accordingly, expressions such as 'awareness of oneself as a subject of experiences' should be interpreted in a way that is neutral with respect to these different possibilities.

So far we have been considering what must be the case if something is to have a desire to continue to exist. We now need to ask what must be the case if something is to have the *capacity* for having such a desire. One thing that certainly follows from the previous conclusion is that something cannot have the capacity for having a desire for continued existence *unless* it is capable of possessing the concepts mentioned above, and also is capable of possessing self-consciousness. But I believe that a stronger conclusion is justified, namely, that whatever concepts are necessary if one is to have a desire for continued existence are also necessary if one is to be capable of having such a desire. Some philosophers have felt that this conclusion is unjustified. Robert Howell has put the point very clearly:

> As we saw, Tooley argues—I think correctly—that to desire to live on as a subject of continuing experiences one must have the concept of a subject of such experiences. But why does Tooley take this conclusion to show that to be *capable* of desiring to live on one must have the concept of such a subject? Why is it not the proper conclusion merely that the capability for this desire requires the capability of having this concept?[11]

The objection is a natural one, but I believe it is mistaken. It seems to me that once one knows that a person presently lacks certain concepts, one is in a position to know not merely that he does not have certain desires, but that he is not now capable of having those desires. The desires that a thing is capable of having *at a given time* are limited by the concepts it possesses at that time. What leads Howell astray, I think, is a certain imprecision in everyday talk about capacities. Suppose that someone asks whether Mary is capable of running a six-minute mile. One person might say: 'Certainly, she's capable of running a six-minute mile, but she would have to get back into serious training for a few weeks.' What he is saying might equally well be put: 'No, she's not capable of running a six-minute mile at present, but she would be if she went back into serious training for a few weeks.' The moral is that when we speak about what someone is capable of, we may, as the first sentence illustrates, be talking, not about what they are presently capable of, but about what they could become capable of in a reasonably short period of time.

Ordinary talk about capacities and capabilities is therefore somewhat imprecise. One must distinguish between capacities

---

[11] Robert Howell, 'Correspondence', *Philosophy & Public Affairs*, Volume 2, Number 4, 1973, pp. 407-10. See p. 408.

in a narrower and stricter sense, and capacities in a broader sense that includes potentialities for acquiring capacities in the narrower sense. Howell, I believe, is using 'capability' in the broader sense. When it is used in that way, it is true that the capability for a given desire requires only the capability for having the corresponding concepts. However it is very important, in the present context, not to confuse capacities and potentialities, and in the argument I have advanced, 'capacity' is accordingly to be taken in the narrower and stricter sense. When 'capacity' is employed in this way, Howell's objection is mistaken. If one does not now possess a certain concept, one does not *now* have the capacity for having certain corresponding desires.

Given this clarification, the basic structure of the argument is more or less complete. We now need to go on to consider, in some detail, the crucial premiss in the argument, viz., the claim that there is a certain conceptual connection between rights and corresponding desires. Before doing that, however, I think it may be useful to set out a brief summary of the argument:

(1) The concept of a right is such that an individual cannot have a right that p be the case unless the individual is capable of desiring that p be the case.
(2) An individual cannot at time t have the capacity, in the strict sense, of desiring that p be the case unless that individual possesses at time t the concepts involved in the proposition that p.
(3) The proposition that an individual desires true when he desires to continue to exist involves the concept of a subject of experiences, the concept of a temporal order, and the concept of identity of things over time.

Hence:

(4) An individual cannot have a right to continued existence unless he possesses the concept of a subject of experiences, the concept of a temporal order, and the concept of identity of things over time.

Moreover:

(5) The proposition that an individual desires true when he desires to continue to exist is not merely the proposition that some subject of experiences or other continue to exist, but the proposition that *this* subject of experiences continue to exist.

(6) In order to have a desire about an individual picked out by an expression such as 'this subject of experiences', one must in some sense be aware of the individual in question.

Hence:

(7) An individual cannot have a right to continued existence unless he has the capacity of being aware of himself as a subject of experiences.

The most problematic assumption in this argument would seem to be the very first one, viz., the claim that the concept of a right is such that an individual cannot have a right that p unless the individual is capable of desiring that p be the case. The justification offered in support of this premiss was the following analysis of the concept of a right:

A has a right to X

means the same as

A is capable of wanting X, and if A does want X, others are under a prima facie obligation to refrain from actions that would deprive him of it.

The time has come to consider some objections to this proposed analysis.

If the above analysis were correct, it would follow that all of the obligations that arise on account of some individual's right to something are obligations that exist only if the individual in question has the appropriate, corresponding *desire*. There are at least two reasons for thinking that this cannot be right. In the first place, there are a number of counter-examples to the proposed analysis that seem to show that, at least in some cases, an individual's having a certain right may place obligations upon others not by virtue of what the individual actually wants at the time in question, but by virtue of what is *in his interest*. In the second place, there are cases that seem to show that the obligations to which rights give rise may, in at least some cases, derive not from the fact that an individual wants something, nor even from the fact that having it is in his interest, but simply from the fact that he has *not waived* his right to the thing in question.

First, then, some cases that seem to support the view that rights give rise to obligations that are conditional not upon what an individual desires, but upon what is in his interest. One very simple case, frequently mentioned in this context, is that of an individual who is asleep. The suggestion is that a sleeping individual does not, while asleep, have any desires at all, so that, if the analysis of rights proposed above were correct, there would be no obligations to a sleeping individual arising out of his rights. The analysis entails, therefore, that someone can take your car, or even kill you, while you are asleep, without violating your rights. In contrast, if rights can give rise to obligations that are conditional upon what is an individual's interests, rather than merely upon what he desires, it will still make sense to say that one has obligations to sleeping individuals, based upon their rights.

Is it true that a sleeping individual has no desires? It is certainly true that one can, and does, ascribe desires to sleeping persons. However I think that the proponent of the above objection would argue that when one talks about the desires of someone who is asleep, the sense is not the same as when one ascribes desires to a fully conscious individual. Statements about the desires of someone who is asleep, it might be suggested, are best regarded as a philosophically somewhat misleading way of referring to the desires the individual *would* now have were he not asleep.

In response, it might be argued that a desire is closer to a disposition than the above objection allows. For is it not true that each of us, at times when we are fully conscious, has any number of desires that are not, at the time in question, present as conscious states? And given that this is so, why cannot one equally have desires, in precisely the same sense, while one is asleep?

There is certainly something in this response, and perhaps it is satisfactory. It is, however, not entirely unproblematic, even in the case of the sleeping person, and its plausibility appears to become less if one considers, not a person who is asleep, but one who is in a coma. We need not pursue this question, however, since the above analysis of rights is exposed to other counter-examples that cannot be handled in this way.

Consider, for example, the following case. A somewhat puritanical religious sect that admires male soprano voices advocates that appropriate minor surgery be performed on new-born males. The operation is a painless one, and the infants voice no objection. Yet one is surely tempted to say that individuals' rights are being violated.

Here, as in the case of the unconscious individual, no problem arises if one adopts the view that rights can also give rise to obligations that are conditional, not upon desires, but upon interests. For while the infants do not have, at the time of the operation, any desire that it not be performed, it is contrary to their long-term interests.

It might be suggested, however, that rather than introducing reference to what is in an individual's interest, one should simply formulate a slightly more complex account of the way in which rights can give rise to obligations that are conditional upon desires. It is true that the infants have no desire that the operation not be performed, *at the time of the operation*— due to the fact that they are incapable, at that time, of having such a desire. But later, when they are capable of having such a desire, they will wish that the operation had not been performed. So why can one not say that it is this future desire which, in view of the relevant right, places an obligation upon others not to perform the operation in question?

It is certainly possible to proceed in this way. But there are, I believe, at least two reasons for not doing so. The first is that the resulting account of rights will be very complex. The second is that it may not be clear when one has arrived at a complete analysis.

To illustrate the first point, consider the problem of revising the analysis offered above in order to cover the case just discussed. Apparently one will need something like the following:

A has a right to X

means the same as

> A is a type of entity that is capable, at least sometimes, of having a desire for X, and if either of the following conditions obtains, then, by virtue of that fact alone, other individuals will be under a prima facie obligation to refrain from actions that would deprive A of X:
>
> (a) A wants X;
>
> (b) A does not want X at the time in question, either because A is incapable of having such a desire at that time, or because there is some relevant information that A lacks, but there will be a later time at which A will exist, when A will have an informed desire for X.

This is already becoming somewhat involved. The complications, however, do not end here. In the first place, one will need another clause to deal with the case of the individual in a temporary coma:

> (c) Although A does not desire X at the time in question, because A is temporarily in a coma, and therefore incapable of having such a desire at that time, there is an immediately earlier time interval during which A did want X, and there will be a later time at which A will exist, provided that no one performs an action that deprives him of X, and at which time A will, if he exists, have a desire for X.

Secondly, there are still other cases that must be allowed for, and that will require the introduction of further, even more complicated clauses. One such case is familiar from discussions of women's liberation. Suppose one conditions an individual so that she will be satisfied with being a dependent helpmate, and will never have any interest in, for example, intellectually challenging activities to which humans not thus conditioned are naturally attracted. Doesn't this violate her rights? Yet if clauses (a), (b), and (c) together provided an adequate account, one would be forced to say that such conditioning violates a woman's rights only if she later comes to wish that she had not been subjected to such conditioning. As long as the conditioning were completely successful, one would be forced to say that her rights had not been violated.

It is clear that this is a substantive moral view, and hence not such as can properly be entailed by any mere analysis of the concept of a right. Therefore another clause must be added to the analysis, in order to allow for the possibility of this sort of violation of one's rights.

The second reason for not proceeding in this way should now be apparent. The method followed has been to propose an analysis, and then to modify it in the face of successive counter-examples. The problem with this approach is that one does not really know when the process is complete. What guarantee is there that more subtle counter-examples, necessitating still further revision, and hence greater complexity, will not be forthcoming?

The answer, surely, is that there is no guarantee. The situation would be different if one could point to some single, underlying problem that is giving rise to the various counter-examples. For then it might be possible to show, at some point, that the clauses added to the original account were adequate to block not merely the counter-examples considered, but all possible ones that might arise from the underlying difficulty in question.

Let us ask, then, whether the counter-examples considered above all have a single source. Is there any feature that is common to all those cases of violations of someone's rights? It seems clear that there is, and that it is precisely the factor mentioned earlier, namely, that the actions in question, though they do not violate a desire that the individual has at the time of the action, are *contrary to that individual's interest*. It is in the interest of the comatose person not to be killed. It is in the interest of the children not to be operated on. It is in the interest of women not to be educated in such a way that they have no desires to engage in intellectually challenging activities.

The situation, in short, appears to be this. Given an account of rights according to which rights are obligations that are conditional, in a complex way, upon desires, one needs to make use of the concept of an individual's interest in order to determine whether the account is sufficiently comprehensive. But if the notion of actions that are contrary to an individual's interest is crucial in this way, it seems more sensible to introduce it at the beginning, thereby offering an account of rights according to which they involve obligations that are conditional upon an individual's interest, rather than upon his desires. The result will be a much less complex account, and one whose underlying rationale is clear.

What form should such an analysis take? One very simple formulation is this:

A has a right to X

means the same as:

> A is such that it can be in A's interest to have X, and if it is in A's interest to have X, then, by virtue of that fact alone, others are under a prima-facie obligation to refrain from actions that would deprive him of X.

Thus formulated, however, the analysis is open to an objection advanced by B. C. Postow in her article, 'Rights and Obligations'. Postow contends that no account of rights according to which the obligations that rights impose are conditional simply upon what the individual wants, or upon what is in his interest, can be satisfactory. She offers two cases in support of this contention, of which the most forceful is the following:

One such sort of case is that where the right-holder fails to inform the obligated party of the fact that he no longer desires that to which he has a right. Suppose, for example, that Hilda borrows $500 from Tom, with the promise to deposit a like sum in his bank account on June 1. Tom has a moral right to have this done, and Hilda a moral obligation to do it. On June 1, Tom is in a monastery in Tibet, desiring to cease the accumulation of material possessions and wealth. We may even assume that he has conceived this desire after careful consideration of his true interests. He is unable, however, to communicate his new wishes to Hilda. Yet he still has a right to have the money deposited in the bank, and Hilda still has an obligation to deposit it.[12]

This objection does seem to show that the obligations to which rights give rise cannot be conditional simply upon the right-holder's desires, or upon what is in his interest. The analysis must, apparently, incorporate the concept of the *waiving* of a right.

[12] B. C. Postow, 'Rights and Obligations', *Philosophical Studies*, Volume 32, 1977, pp. 217–32. See p. 218.

If this is correct, what form should the analysis take? One possibility is an account that drops all reference to desires and to what is in an individual's interest, and that construes rights in terms of obligations that are conditional simply upon an individual's not having waived the right in question:

A has a right to X

means the same as

Unless A has given an individual his permission to deprive him of X, that individual is under a prima facie obligation to refrain from actions that would deprive A of X.

One problem with this analysis is that it does not account for the difference, mentioned at the beginning of this section, between claims such as that a child does not have a right to smoke, and that a newspaper does not have a right not to be torn up. Nothing follows from the analysis regarding the sorts of beings that *can* have rights. However this difficulty can be surmounted by an obvious modification:

A has a right to X

means the same as

A is the sort of being that is capable of giving another individual permission to deprive him of X, and unless A has given an individual permission to deprive him of X, that individual is under a prima-facie obligation to refrain from actions that would deprive A of X.

There are, however, a number of reasons for rejecting this general sort of analysis. First, concerning the rights of non-human animals: most non-human animals are incapable of giving other individuals permission to do anything, so that on the view in question, such animals could not possess any rights.

Second, if something must be capable of waiving a right if it is to be a right-holder, it would seem to follow that there could be individuals whose mental life was comparable to that of normal adult human beings, but to whom one could not attribute any rights. For there does not appear to be anything incoherent in the idea of an individual who was capable of the thoughts, feelings, and experiences we are capable of, but who totally lacked the ability to communicate his thoughts and feelings to other individuals. Such an individual would be incapable of giving others permission to do anything, and hence could not, on the above view, possess any rights. This conclusion is not very appealing, since it is very natural to think that two beings should not differ with respect to basic rights unless they differ with respect to the mental lives they enjoy, or are capable of enjoying.

Third, consider the attribution of rights to minors. In many cases the obligations that arise from those rights do not lapse simply because the minor has given someone permission to deprive him of the thing in question.

Cases such as these seem to show that the obligations to which rights give rise cannot be viewed as conditional *simply* upon the individual's not having waived the right in question. Any adequate account of rights needs to involve *both* the concept of the waiving of a right and the concept of something's being in an individual's interest.

If this is correct, the following would seem to be a very natural view. In the first place, if an individual has a right to something, and if it is in his interest not to be deprived of it, then, other things being equal, others are under a prima-facie obligation not to deprive him of it. But second, if such an individual is capable of making an informed and rational choice to give others permission to deprive him of the thing in question, then others are under a prima-facie obligation if and only if he has not given them permission to deprive him of it. So we have something like the following analysis:

A has a right to X

means the same as

A is such that it can be in A's interest to have X, and *either* (1) A is not capable of making an informed and rational choice whether to grant others permission to deprive him of X, in which case, if it is in A's interest not to be deprived of X, then, by that fact alone, others are under a prima facie obligation not to deprive A of X, *or* (2) A is capable of making an informed and rational choice whether to grant others permission to deprive him of X, in which case others are under a prima-facie obligation not to deprive A of X if and only if A has not granted them permission to do so.

Details aside, there are two main ways in which this account of rights differs from the initial account. First, the reference to the capacity for having a desire for X has been replaced by reference to the property of being such that it can be in one's interest not to be deprived of X. Second, the concept of granting others permission to deprive one of X has been introduced. How do these two changes affect the argument, offered above, dealing with necessary conditions something must satisfy if it is to have a right to continued existence?

The second modification does not appear to affect the argument. The reason is that one cannot grant someone permission to do something unless one understands what it is one is permitting the other person to do. This means, in particular, that an individual cannot grant someone permission to bring it about that he does not continue to exist unless he possesses the concept of continued existence, and conceives of himself as the sort of being that could continue to exist. An individual must, then, possess certain concepts if he is to be capable of waiving his right to continued existence.

The first modification, on the other hand, does affect the argument, and in a serious way. Recall the first two steps in the argument:

(1) The concept of a right is such that an individual cannot have a right that p be the case unless the individual is capable of desiring that p be the case.

(2) An individual cannot at time t have the capacity, in the strict sense, of desiring that p be the case unless that individual possesses, at time t, the concepts involved in the proposition that p.

Given the revised account of rights, (1) will have to be replaced by:

(1*) The concept of a right is such that an individual cannot have a right that p be the case unless the individual is such that it can be in its interest that p be the case;

(2), in turn, will have to undergo a similar modification, with the reference to a desire replaced by reference to what is in the individual's interest:

> (2*) An individual cannot, at time t, be such that it is in that individual's interest that p be the case unless the individual possesses, at time t, the concepts involved in the proposition that p.

But (2*), in contrast with (2), appears to be clearly false. It is, for example, in my interest now to consume adequate amounts of various nutrients. Yet I need not possess any concepts of the relevant substances, nor even the concept of an essential nutrient.

This difficulty shows that a more radical revision of the argument is in order. The place to begin, I think, is with the question of the relation between interests and desires. In the first place, then, does an individual have to have desires at a given time in order for it to be the case that some things are in its interest? The answer would seem to be no. For suppose that there were a disease that completely eradicated all desires in normal adult human beings, but only for a time. If John has contracted the disease, and is now in a desireless state, but will return to normal, and will then enjoy a life that he deems worth living, one surely wants to say that John's continued existence is in his interest. So individuals can have interests at a given time without having any desires at that time.

Is it possible for something to have interests without having desires at *any* time? Certainly, there is a sense of the term 'interest' in which this is so. A plant, for example, may be spoken of as having an interest in getting enough water. But something that was capable of interests only in this attenuated sense could not be a right-holder. To be a subject of rights one needs to be capable of having interests in the sense that involves the capacity for having desires.

Interests in the morally relevant sense, then, presuppose desires, albeit not necessarily desires existing at the same time. The next question is whether specific interests presuppose the presence of corresponding desires. If this were the case, the original argument would require only relatively minor revision. But we have already seen, in effect, that this cannot be the case. It may very well be in my interest to consume adequate quantities of calcium, even if at no time do I have any desire to do so.

One cannot appeal, then, to any general relation between specific interests and corresponding desires. This being so, it would seem that the only way of attempting to recast the original argument is by considering, not interests in general, but the interest in continuing to exist, and by asking whether there are any conditions that something must satisfy in order to have this particular interest—conditions akin to those advanced above.

What must be the case if the continued existence of something is to be in its interest? It will help to focus our thinking, I believe, if we consider a crucial case raised by Derek Parfit. Imagine a human baby that has developed to the point of being sentient, and of having simple desires, but that is not yet capable of having any desire for continued existence. Suppose, further, that the baby will later enjoy a happy life, and will be glad that it was not destroyed. Can we or can we not say that it is in the baby's interest not to be destroyed.

To approach this case, let us consider a closely related one, namely that of a human embryo that has not developed sufficiently far to have any desires, or even any states of consciousness at all, but that will develop into an individual who will enjoy a happy life, and who will be glad that his mother did not have an abortion. Can we or can we not say that it is in the embryo's interest not to be destroyed?

I want to urge, very strongly, that the claim that it is in the embryo's interest not to be destroyed cannot be correct. The reason is as follows. Let Mary be an individual who enjoys a happy life. Then, although some philosophers have expressed doubts about this, it might very well be said that it was certainly in Mary's interest that a certain embryo was not destroyed several years earlier. This claim, together with the tendency to use expressions such as 'Mary before she was born' to refer to the embryo in question, may lead one to think that it was in the embryo's interest not to be destroyed. But this way of thinking involves conceptual confusion. A subject of interests, in the relevant sense of 'interest', must necessarily be a subject of conscious states, including experiences and desires. This means that in identifying Mary with the embryo, and attributing to it her interest in its earlier non-destruction, one is treating the embryo as if it were itself a subject of consciousness. But by hypothesis, the embryo being considered here has not developed to the point where there is any subject of consciousness associated with it. It cannot, therefore, have any interests at all, and *a fortiori*, it cannot have any interest in its own continued existence.

Let us now return to the first case—that of a human baby that is sentient, and which has simple desires, but which is not yet capable of having more complex desires, such as a desire for its own continued existence. Given that it will develop into an individual who will lead a happy life, and who will be glad that the baby was not destroyed, does one want to say that the baby's not being destroyed is in the baby's own interest?

Again, the following line of thought may seem initially tempting. If Mary is the resulting individual, then it was in Mary's interest that the baby not have been destroyed. But the baby just *is* Mary when she was young. So it must have been in the baby's interest that it not have been destroyed.

Indeed, this argument is considerably more tempting in the present case than in the former, since here there is something that is a subject of consciousness, and which it is natural to identify with Mary. I suggest, however, that if one reflects upon the case, it becomes clear that such an identification is justified only if certain further things are the case. Thus, on the one hand, suppose that Mary is able to remember quite clearly some of the experiences that the baby enjoyed. Given that sort of causal and psychological connection, it would seem perfectly reasonable to hold that Mary and the baby are one and the same subject of consciousness, and thus, that if it is in Mary's interest that the baby not have been destroyed, then this must also have been in the baby's interest. On the other hand, suppose that not only does Mary, at a much later time, not remember any of the baby's experiences, but the experiences in question are not psychologically linked, either by memory or in any other way, to mental states enjoyed by the human organism in question at *any* later time. Here it seems to me clearly incorrect to say that Mary and the baby are one and the same subject of consciousness, and therefore it cannot be correct to transfer, from Mary to the baby, Mary's interest in the baby's not having been destroyed.

Let us now return to the question of what must be the case if the continued existence of something is to be in its own interest. The picture that emerges from the two cases just discussed, together with earlier reflections, is this. In the first place, nothing at all can be in an entity's interest unless it has desires at some time or other. But more than this is required if the continued existence of the entity is to be in its own interest. One possibility, which will generally be sufficient, is that the individual have, at the time in question, a desire for its own continued existence. Yet it also seems clear that an individual's continued existence can be in its own interest even when this is not the case. What is needed, apparently, is that the continued existence of the individual will make possible the satisfaction of some desires existing at other times. But not just any desires existing at other times will do. Indeed, as is illustrated by the case of the baby just discussed, and by the earlier deprogramming/reprogramming example, it is not even sufficient that they be desires associated with the same physical organism. It is crucial that they be desires that belong to one and the same subject of consciousness.

The critical question, then, concerns the conditions under which desires existing at different times can be correctly attributed to a single, continuing subject of consciousness. This difficult question will be discussed, at some length, in the next section. The view that I shall there attempt to defend has the following consequence, which is important in the present context:

Desires existing at different times can belong to a single, continuing subject of consciousness only if that subject of consciousness possesses, at some time, the concept of a continuing self or mental substance.

If this claim is correct, it becomes possible, given the

revised analysis of the concept of a right, to offer the following reformulation of the argument outlined earlier:

(1) The concept of a right is such that an individual cannot have a right at time t to continued existence unless the individual is such that it can be in its interest at time t that it continue to exist.

(2) The continued existence of a given subject of consciousness cannot be in that individual's interest at time t unless *either* that individual has a desire, at time t, to continue to exist as a subject of consciousness, *or* that individual can have desires at other times.

(3) An individual cannot have a desire to continue to exist as a subject of consciousness unless it possesses the concept of a continuing self or mental substance.

(4) An individual existing at one time cannot have desires at other times unless there is at least one time at which it possesses the concept of a continuing self or mental substance.

Therefore:

(5) An individual cannot have a right to continued existence unless there is at least one time at which it possesses the concept of a continuing self or mental substance.

This conclusion is an important one. The reason emerges if one asks what relation, if any, there is between the development of the human brain and the development of the human mind. There are, of course, very different views on this matter. Some philosophers, as we shall see in chapter 11, hold that there is no relation at all. They believe that the mind, with all its mature capacities, is present in a human from conception onward, and hence is there before the brain has even begun to develop. Most philosophers, however, reject this view. Some hold that the mind is in fact identical with the brain. Others that the mind is distinct from the brain, but causally dependent upon it. In either case, the result is a view according to which the development of the brain and the development of the mind are necessarily closely tied to one another.

The empirical evidence certainly points very strongly

toward some theory of the latter sort. Consider, for example, what is known about how human mental capabilities proceed in step with brain development, or what is known about how damage to different parts of the brain can affect, in different ways, an individual's intellectual capacities.

Why, then, do some philosophers reject the view that there is a very intimate relationship between the development of the mind and the development of the brain? The answer is that they do not appeal to empirical evidence. They believe that their position can be established by means of a purely philosophical argument. I shall argue, however, in section 11.42, that the metaphysical argument in question involves a number of untenable philosophical claims.

Let us tentatively assume, then, that the human mind is, at the very least, such as develops hand in hand with the development of the brain. This, together with completely uncontroversial facts about the biological development of human beings, implies that not all individuals belonging to the species *Homo sapiens* are subjects of consciousness. But if there is no subject of consciousness at all associated, for example, with a human zygote, then, *a fortiori*, there cannot be a subject of consciousness, associated with a human zygote, which is such that that subject of consciousness either possesses, or will possess at some later time, the concept of a continuing self or mental substance. Consequently, if the argument set out above is correct, at least some human beings do not have a right to continued existence, and what is perhaps the central anti-abortion contention must be rejected as incorrect.

But is the argument correct? The argument involves three crucial claims. First, there is the contention that it follows from a sound analysis of rights that there is a conceptual connection between specific rights and the capacities for specific interests. Second, there is the claim that interests presuppose desires. Third, there is the claim that the unification of mental states existing at different times, including desires, into a single, continuing subject of consciousness, requires that the individual possesses, at some time, the concept of a continuing self or mental substance. The first two contentions have been discussed in the present section. The third will be examined in the section which follows.

5.3 Interests, Rationality, Agency, and Self-consciousness

How should the term 'person' be defined? In this section I shall consider four of the most plausible answers to that question:

(1) A person is a subject of non-momentary interests;
(2) A person is an entity that possesses rationality;
(3) A person is an entity that is capable of action;
(4) A person is an entity that possesses self-consciousness.

An important issue, which will not be considered in this section, is whether a certain *capacity* is sufficient by itself to make something a person, or whether the exercise of that capacity, at some time, is also required. This question is taken up in section 5.4.

Let us begin with the concept of a subject of non-momentary interests. This is, very roughly, the concept of an entity that is capable of having a variety of desires, both at a given time and at other times, all of which are interrelated, or 'unified', in certain ways. A much more precise account of this concept of a subject of non-momentary interests is, of course, necessary. To set out such an account, we need to take a close look, first, at the relevant notion of a desire, and, second, at the relations that must exist between desires if there is to be an appropriate unification of them.

What is the relevant concept of a desire? The important point here is that desires, if they are to be morally significant, cannot be viewed simply as states of an organism that explain its behaviour in certain ways. They must be thought of as states that stand in some relation to consciousness, however the latter may be conceived.

Consider, for example, a missile that scans its environment, looking for warm objects, and then moves towards the hottest one. Such a device might be said, speaking metaphorically, to have a desire to be near the warmest object in its environment. Such 'desires' share many properties with the corresponding states of persons. Thus, for example, the missile's 'desires', like ordinary desires, possess the property of intentionality. Just as a person may want something that does not exist, so the missile may engage in 'activity' directed at finding a hot object even when no such object exists. Or the missile may 'want' to be near the hottest object in its environment and it may be true, as a matter of fact, that the hottest object is also the reddest object, without its following that the missile 'wants' to be near the reddest object. For the missile's behaviour may be causally affected by the temperature of the object, but not by its colour.

These similarities, however, would not seem to be morally significant. The fact that a given action frustrates the missile's 'desire' surely constitutes no reason at all for refraining from the action. What, then, is the morally significant difference between an individual's desires and the missile's 'desires'? The most plausible answer, I suggest, is that the former, but not the latter, stand in some relation to certain states of consciousness.

What might that relation be? One view is that the morally relevant feature is some sort of representation, in consciousness, of the desire. A person who wants to be near something warm is disposed not only to act in certain ways, but to have certain thoughts, such as the thought that he would like to be near something warm. Why not take this to be the morally relevant feature of desires?

I think this feature is morally relevant. There is, however, an objection to the view that it is *the* property by virtue of which desires are morally significant. Consider pain. Whatever else one wants to say about pain, it is surely true that if a sensation is painful, it must be such that, considered in itself, its absence is desired. What, then, is one to say about lower animals? If a state could not be a desire unless it involved a disposition to have certain thoughts, lower animals would, presumably, not have desires. In their case, then, pains would not be states whose absence they desire. And this would leave one with a serious problem: What is it about pain that makes its experience by lower animals a bad thing?

One response is that the badness of pain in general needs to be explained in some other way, and cannot be viewed as based solely upon the fact that a desire that a certain state be absent is being frustrated. Perhaps this is right; the issue is a difficult one. There is, however, an alternative account of desire that seems plausible, and that has the merit of not leading to difficulties in the case of lower animals. This alternative view is that what must be added to states of the type enjoyed by the missile in order to have desires is some, at least potentially conscious 'representation' of the object desired. If what is liked or disliked is itself a present state of consciousness, it can be viewed as 'representing' itself. If what is liked or disliked is an object presently being perceived, the perception can be taken as 'representing' the object. If what is liked or disliked is neither a present state of consciousness nor something presently perceived, then something else, which does involve consciousness, will be needed to 'represent' the object desired. Thoughts, or dispositions to have thoughts, will be needed in this case, if the state is to be a morally significant one.

The reasonableness of this requirement emerges, I believe, if one considers the case of a human with two heads, so that one has two centres of consciousness associated with a single body. What would determine to which of the two minds a given action should be attributed? The natural answer is that it is a matter of the relations between the thoughts in each mind and the actions taking place. If there is in one mind, but not in the other, a thought that expresses either a decision to perform an action of the sort in question, or a desire that the action can be viewed as attempting to satisfy, then there is a ground for attributing the action to the mind that has the thought, or that is disposed to have it.

The argument, in short, is this. If 'actions', and the 'desires' that underlie them, are to be assignable to one subject of consciousness, rather than to another, or none at all, one of two things must be the case. Either the object at which the 'action' and the underlying 'desire' are directed must itself be a present state of consciousness, or the 'action', or the underlying 'desire', must be at least potentially represented by states of consciousness belonging to the subject in question. The difference between desires and 'desires' is that the former are assignable to subjects of consciousness while the latter are not, and it is this, I am suggesting, that makes desires morally significant in a way that 'desires' are not.

An entity that has desires must, therefore, also be an entity that has experiences. It must be a subject of consciousness. One can, therefore, assign all the desires existing at a given time to different sets, based upon whether or not they belong to the same subject of consciousness.

But is this way of dividing up desires morally significant? Can it make a moral difference whether or not two desires existing at a given time belong to the same subject of consciousness? That is to say, does this relation among desires enter into the formulation of basic moral principles?

This is, of course, a special case of a more general question, which can be put as follows. Consider all the desires that exist at some time or other. There are many ways of dividing them up into groups. Are some of these ways morally more significant than others? And is there perhaps some one way of assigning them to different groups that plays a crucial role in the formulation of basic moral principles?

Moral theories differ strongly on this matter. Some imply that the assignment of desires to different sets on the basis of various interrelations among them has no moral significance. Consider, for example, the version of utilitarianism that affirms that the right action is always the one that will result in the greatest total satisfaction of desires. If this view is right, then no assignment of desires to different sets can be morally significant in itself. For the division of desires into different sets in no way affects the sum total of satisfaction associated with any given action.

In contrast, a number of other ethical theories assign a crucial role to the division of desires into groups. For example, theories that involve notions such as equality and desert require some concept of an individual, and whether or not a given action furthers equality, or gives individuals what they deserve, will depend upon how desires are assigned to individuals. Some methods of grouping desires may result in there being some groups that contain only desires that get satisfied, while other groups contain only desires that never get satisfied. If a method with this outcome is correct, then the distribution of satisfactions over individuals is very unequal. Other ways of dividing up precisely the same desires will result in groups containing roughly the same proportion of satisfied and unsatisfied desires. Judged by these methods, the distribution of satisfactions over individuals is very equitable. Ethical theories involving notions such as equality or desert therefore require some account of the correct way of dividing desires up into morally relevant groups—of assigning them to different individuals.

Which sort of moral theory is correct? The type that attributes some ultimate moral significance to the assignment of desires to different individuals, or the type that does not? If commonly held moral intuitions were the touchstone of truth in such matters, the answer would be clear, since notions that presuppose an assignment of desires to individuals—such as equality and desert—play a crucial role in the moral thinking of most people. On the other hand, for those who either completely reject moral intuitions, or hold that they have no ultimate epistemic significance, the answer is very far from being clear. Indeed, it seems to me that the choice between these two radically different types of ethical theories raises one of the deeper and more difficult questions in meta-ethics. Therefore, while I shall, throughout this book, proceed on the assumption that the dividing up of desires into groups on the basis of interrelations among them is of *crucial* moral significance, I do not, at present, see how one would even begin to justify this contention.

Let us assume, then, that there are some relations among desires that serve to unify them into morally significant groups. Since, as we have seen, desires must belong to subjects of consciousness, the unification of desires into morally significant groups will also result in the construction of some sort of enduring subjects of mental states out of the momentary subjects of consciousness to which particular desires belong. I shall refer to the individuals that result from such a morally significant unification of desires into groups as subjects of non-momentary interests.

In explaining how the expression, 'subject of non-momentary interests', is to be used, I have employed moral language. Is the expression then an evaluative one? The answer is that the situation here is the same as in the case of the term 'person'. That is to say, on the one hand, the assignment of meaning to the expression, 'subject of non-momentary interests', is to be guided by moral considerations, but, on the other, the meaning assigned is to be purely descriptive. Thus, in order to arrive at a definition of this expression, one will ask what relationships among desires serve to unify them into morally significant groups. The relations thus specified, however, will be purely descriptive ones, and it is these that will be used in assigning meaning to the expression, 'subject of non-momentary interests'.

Let us now consider some alternative accounts of the relations among desires that serve to unify them into a non-momentary interest. One possible view is that desires are to be assigned to distinct, morally significant groups on the basis of whether they belong to the same mental substance. What is meant by 'same mental substance'? The way this expression will be construed here is as follows. Consider what it means to say that two temporal parts, P_1 and P_2, existing at different times, t_1 and t_2, are in fact temporal parts of one and the same physical object. A standard account of the unity relation that must hold between P_1 and P_2 if they are to be temporal parts of the same thing is this. P_1 and P_2 stand in the unity relation if and only if there is some continuous space-time line linking up P_1 at time t_1 with P_2 at time t_2 such that the sequence of temporal parts located along that space-time line does not involve any discontinuous change. Given this account of the unity relation for temporal parts of a physical object, there would be a serious question whether one could make sense of the notion of the same mental substance by simply transferring the unity relation from physical states to mental states. For it seems at least possible that mental states are not located in space. However I think it can be shown that the account in question is not the right one. Imagine a world very similar to our own, except that physical objects sometimes disappear without a trace. Whenever this happens, however, an object qualitatively indistinguishable from the one that disappeared appears precisely one second later, in a position one centimetre further away from the centre of gravity of the universe. Assume, moreover, that an object pops into existence only when a qualitatively indistinguishable object, standing in the appropriate relation, has just disappeared. I suggest that if the world were like this, one would not speak of one object disappearing and another appearing. One would instead think of the first object as having moved, discontinuously, from one space-time point to another one centimetre and one second away.

What this shows, I believe, is that spatio-temporal continuity is only a sort of rough criterion that one employs for judging when two physical states existing at different times are temporal parts of the same thing. It is not part of the *concept* of the unity relation. What is involved in the latter then? The answer suggested by the above example is: certain *causal* relations. The reason one is inclined to say that the table that has just popped into existence is the same table as the one that disappeared one second and one centimetre away is that one believes that the latter temporal slice of a table is causally dependent upon the earlier in a certain way.

A more complete account of the unity relation would involve some complications. The details need not detain us here however, since what is important in the present context is that when one shifts from an account involving spatio-temporal continuity to one based upon causal dependence, there is no longer any bar to applying the account to mental substances as well as physical ones.

Let us now return to the question of the relations among desires that serve to unify them into morally significant groupings. The first suggestion is that desires existing at different times are to be assigned to distinct, morally significant groups on the basis of whether they belong to different mental substances. In view of the above discussion, this comes down to saying that desires are to be viewed as belonging to a single, morally significant group if and only if they belong to mental states that stand in certain relations of causal dependence.

Is this view acceptable? Recall the deprogramming/reprogramming possibility discussed earlier, and suppose, in particular, that Billy Graham is reprogrammed to be a person like Bertrand Russell. The first question is whether the satisfaction of desires associated with the individual who exists after the reprogramming is in any way in Billy Graham's interest. Most people would hold, I believe, that it is not. The second question, then, is whether the desires before and after reprogramming belong to the same mental substance—in the sense just explained. If they do, one will have a reason for rejecting the contention that desires are interrelated in morally significant ways if they belong to the same mental substance. The case we are considering, however, does not appear clearcut. It might be argued, with at least some plausibility, that it is not clear that the appropriate relations of causal dependence are present, and hence that it is not clear that the desires present before and after reprogramming belong to the same mental substance.

I believe that this objection can be avoided, however, by slightly altering the case. Imagine a world in which it is a law that people of the Billy Graham sort always undergo a radical transformation at a certain age, losing all their memories, beliefs, desires, attitudes, personality traits, and so on, and acquiring those beliefs, attitudes, personality traits, etc., typically associated with Bertrand Russell. Assume further that this change is not caused by anything physical, either external to the individual or within his own brain. I suggest that in such a case it is reasonable to believe that the relevant relations of causal dependence are present, and thus that it would be true, given the sense of 'same mental substance' explained above, that the desires present before and after reprogramming would belong to the same mental substance. Therefore it cannot be the relation of belonging to the same mental substance which serves to tie desires together in the morally significant way we are considering here.

If sameness of the underlying mental substance is not sufficient, what must be added to it? There are a number of possibilities. One answer, suggested by many discussions of personal identity, is that what must be added is the presence of *memory links* between desires existing at different times, or, alternatively, between the momentary, total states of consciousness with which the desires are associated.

But what exactly is involved in memory? Let us assume that memory involves beliefs about the past, and not merely images that correspond to certain past events or experiences.

We are still left with serious options as to the types of beliefs involved. Is it enough, for example, that one has beliefs that certain sorts of experiences existed in the past? Or does one also have to believe that those experiences belonged to the same mental substance as certain present states of consciousness? In the former case, it would be possible for desires to be unified without any associated sense of the existence of a continuing mental substance, while in the latter case this would not be possible: the unification of desires would presuppose self-consciousness.

It is far from clear how one is to decide between these two possibilities. But it is also unclear that either is acceptable, as is shown by a variation on the case just discussed. Imagine a world in which the causal laws relating earlier and later states of a mental substance are such that, apart from memory beliefs, there is virtually no similarity from one moment to another. General beliefs, attitudes, desires, and personality traits all change in bewildering, albeit law-governed fashion. At one moment there is a person like Bertrand Russell; at the next, one like Adolf Hitler; then one like Socrates, followed by one resembling Pius XII. These different temporal 'person-slices' are linked together by causal relations and by memory, where the latter is to be taken as involving a belief that the mental states that are remembered belong to the same mental substance as do the present memories—that is to say, a belief that there is a certain relation of causal dependence between the momentary subject that has the memories and the momentary subject that had the experiences that are now being remembered. In a case of this sort, would one view all of the desires as belonging to a single, morally significant grouping? I believe that most people would not.

In ordinary life, when an individual does change in a dramatic fashion, even if only over a long period of time, one sometimes says that it is no longer the same person. It is tempting to dismiss this as merely a loose, metaphorical way of speaking. The example just considered suggests that there may be a point behind it, that certain changes in the properties of a continuing mental substance are such that one no longer views desires existing at different times, and associated with a continuing mental substance, as capable of being treated as belonging to a single, unified, morally significant grouping.

It appears, therefore, that some *psychological continuity* is required. This may, however, be compatible with quite radical changes. What seems to matter is that later stages of a mental substance 'flow' from earlier ones in a way that involves more than mere causal dependence of later stages upon earlier ones. There must also be some relation between the contents of the beliefs, desires, and attitudes at different times. The changes that the individual undergoes must, apparently, be ones that would be expected in an individual with the experiences and psychological attributes in question.

Does this sort of psychological continuity suffice by itself to tie desires together in the morally relevant way? Once again, it is not at all clear how the issue is ultimately to be argued. One can say, however, that an affirmative answer to this question would necessitate some major changes in some of our moral attitudes. In particular, it would be necessary to view most animals as subjects of non-momentary interests, given that they presumably exhibit continuity with respect to general beliefs, desires, and personality traits. This in turn would mean that if an animal is such that its desires are, on the whole, likely to be satisfied if it continues to exist, it will have a non-momentary interest in its own continued existence —an interest that would be violated by its destruction.

My own inclination is to say that such continuity, though necessary, is not sufficient. If desires are to be interrelated in a morally significant way, there must also be *recognition of the continuity* by the enduring mental substance in question. Later mental states must be seen both as causally dependent upon, and as 'flowing from', earlier mental states.

If this is right, we have one way in which desires existing at different times can be interrelated in a morally significant way: they can be desires belonging to an enduring mental substance that exhibits a certain psychological continuity in the alteration of its properties over time, and where the mental substance is aware, via memory, of both the causal dependence and the psychological continuity linking earlier and later stages.

But may there not be other ways in which desires can be

interrelated in a morally significant way? Is it clear, for example, that memory is essential? What is one to say about a mental substance in which there is psychological continuity between attributes at different times, and where there is, at any given time, a desire that the mental substance continue to exist, and that it have desires that stand in certain relations to present desires? If the mental substance does come to have desires of the sort desired at an earlier time, isn't it natural to view the earlier and later desires as interrelated in a morally significant way?

The backward-looking unification of desires into interests involves beliefs. The forward-looking unification, in contrast, involves desires. What about the possibility of a forward-looking unification based upon beliefs? In particular, what is one to say about the case of an enduring mental substance that has neither any memory of the past, nor any desire about the future, but that exhibits psychological continuity, and that has a belief that it will continue to exist and will display traits that flow from its present ones? Is such a mental substance to be viewed as a subject of non-momentary interest?

My own inclination, again, is to ascribe non-momentary interests both to an entity that has desires about future states of itself, and to an entity that has beliefs, but no desires, about such states. Yet I find it very hard to see what sort of argument could be offered in support of this view. The whole issue of the conditions under which desires existing at different times are to be regarded as unified in a morally significant way, and hence as constituting an enduring interest, seems to me deeply puzzling.

It would be nice if one could dismiss this problem as unimportant. But, some crucial exceptions aside, this is not the case for the vast majority of ethical theories, since they involve notions such as justice, equality, punishment, and desert—notions that presuppose some account of the conditions under which desires existing at different times can be ascribed to a single, enduring, appropriately constituted subject of experiences.

A brief summary of the preceding discussion may be helpful. We have been considering one possible answer to the question of what it is that makes something a person—the view, namely, that persons are to be identified with entities that have desires that are interrelated in such a way that the entities can be viewed as subjects of non-momentary interests. But what conditions must something satisfy in order to be this sort of entity? An answer to this question involves, as we have seen, the resolution of two important issues. First, what is the relevant concept of a desire (or preference) in this context? Second, what are the appropriate interrelations among desires?

With regard to the first issue, I argued that the relevant concept of a desire cannot be simply that of a state that underlies and explains behaviour in a certain way. It must also be the concept of a state that is either potentially represented in consciousness, or directed at some state of consciousness. This claim, I believe, is very plausible.

The answer to the second question is much more problematic. The view that I have tentatively advanced is this. First, sameness of mental substance plus psychological continuity is a necessary, but not a sufficient condition, for desires existing at different times to be viewed as part of a single, unified non-momentary interest. Second, there are at least three other conditions that, taken together with sameness of mental substance plus psychological continuity, are sufficient:

(1) The desires are linked together by memory beliefs concerning the existence of earlier desires associated with the same mental substance;
(2) Earlier desires are accompanied by beliefs that there will be later desires belonging to the same mental substance;
(3) Earlier desires are accompanied by desires for the existence of later desires belonging to the same mental substance.

Let us now turn to the second of the four views set out at the beginning of this section, to the effect that it is the possession of rationality that makes something a person. The term 'rational' is sometimes used in such a way that it would apply to a complex machine that was capable, for example, of proving mathematical theorems, of constructing scientific hypotheses, of deriving consequences from those hypotheses, and then of modifying the hypotheses in the light of its 'sensory' input, regardless of whether the machine possessed consciousness. In considering the present suggestion, however, I shall assume that the term is being used in such a way that something cannot be said to be rational unless it possesses consciousness—and indeed, consciousness of a certain sort: to be rational, a being must be capable of enjoying thought-episodes—where a thought-episode is, roughly, a structured state of consciousness involving a representation of some proposition.

Can rationality be equated with the capacity for having thought-episodes? Most people, I think, would say not, on the ground, for example, that an enduring mental substance that had no thoughts other than ones directly caused by its immediate perceptual environment would not count as rational. What more, then, is required? There are, I think, three main views. One type of interpretation connects rationality with various reasoning capacities. Sometimes the capacity for thinking deductively is held to be sufficient, and sometimes it is maintained that non-deductive reasoning is also essential, or possibly even certain types of non-deductive reasoning beyond that of simple instantial generalization. A second interpretation of the term 'rationality'—developed by Jonathan Bennett in his book, *Rationality*—analyses it as involving the capacity to have thoughts about the past and the future, together with the capacity to have thoughts which involve generalizations.[13] A third interpretation of rationality relates it to action concepts. To be rational is to be capable of acting on the basis of reasons, arrived at by a process of deliberation in which competing considerations are weighed against one another.

To be rational in the third sense is just to be what many philosophers would refer to as an agent. So let us set this

[13] Jonathan Bennett, *Rationality*, 1964. Bennett insists that linguistic behaviour is crucial, on the ground that *'only linguistic behaviour can be appropriate or inappropriate to that which is not both particular and present'*. (p. 87.) I do not find Bennett's arguments convincing on this matter. As far as rationality goes, I do not see why the internalized expression of propositions in thought-episodes cannot serve just as well as the externalized expression of propositions in language.

third interpretation of 'rationality' aside until we turn to consider the suggestion that it is being an agent that makes something a person.

Does the possession of rationality, in either of the first two senses, make something a person? As regards the first sense of rationality, I am inclined to think that it is neither necessary nor sufficient for something to possess it in order to be a person. Imagine that the mental life of cows is in fact as follows. They do have thoughts, some of which express memory-beliefs to the effect that the individual having the present thought is identical with the individual that was eating the grass in the pasture a bit earlier, and others of which express beliefs about the future—such as a belief that this individual will be out in the pasture again tomorrow. Suppose further that cows have desires not only about their present states, but about some future states. Perhaps the cow in question is looking forward with anticipation to eating some tasty grass. If the mental life of a cow really were like this, I suggest that it would be difficult not to regard its destruction as intrinsically wrong. Yet I cannot see why something might not enjoy a mental life of this sort, while lacking completely any capacity for deductive reasoning, let alone for inductive reasoning or scientific theorizing. So it does not seem plausible that possession of a capacity for reasoning is a necessary condition for being a person.

Next, consider something all of whose thoughts deal with proofs of difficult mathematical theorems, and that is very successful in discovering original arguments. Would it be wrong to destroy such an entity? Certainly, such an entity might be very valuable, either instrumentally or in itself, and it might be wrong to destroy it for that reason. But to be a person, it must be wrong to destroy it independently of such considerations.

Is this the case? In answering this question, one needs to be careful that one is not attributing additional properties to the entity in question. Thus, when one thinks of a great, conscious theorem-prover, it is very natural to attribute various feelings to it—for example, to think of it as enjoying the activity of working out a new proof, or as taking pleasure in an especially elegant result. But the possession of rationality in the sense we are considering here, even when accompanied by consciousness, does not entail the presence of mental states such as desires and emotions. And I want to suggest that when such states are explicitly excluded, and one considers an entity that possesses only rationality in the first sense (plus consciousness), one is no longer tempted by the view that such an entity is a person. If this is right, then rationality, in the first sense, cannot be a sufficient condition of something's being a person.

At this point it might be asked, however, whether rationality, plus consciousness, *plus rudimentary desires*, might not be sufficient to make something a person. What is one to say about a conscious theorem-prover that can experience pleasure and pain? This is a more difficult issue. Perhaps it will help if we compare the case of such a theorem-prover with that of the cow looking forward to tomorrow's adventures. Suppose that one is somehow able to produce both cows and theorem-provers quickly and effortlessly. How does the action of destroying such a cow, and replacing it with another, compare with the action of destroying such a theorem-proving mental substance, and replacing it by another? In the case of the cow, such destruction may be contrary to some desire it has, and it will certainly mean the end of a particular series of states of consciousness that are linked, not merely causally, but psychologically as well. The situation is very different in the case of the conscious theorem-prover that has rudimentary desires, but no conscious memories of its past states of consciousness, and neither any beliefs nor any desires about its future states of consciousness. For the destruction of such an entity—provided that it were done painlessly—would not violate any desire that it had. Nor would it even mean the termination of some series of psychologically linked states of consciousness. Are these differences crucial? I want to suggest that they are, and that as a result, the destruction of the cows we are imagining is morally problematic, while the destruction of the theorem-provers is not. If this is right, then rationality, in the sense involving capacities for reasoning, even when accompanied by consciousness together with rudimentary desires, cannot be a sufficient condition of something's being a person.

What about rationality in the second sense—which involves the ability to have thoughts about the past and future, and thoughts that involve general propositions? On the one hand, some conception of time certainly seems necessary. But on the other, it is not at all clear why the ability to entertain general beliefs should be necessary. No capacity for making general judgements was attributed to the cow considered above, and it is hard to see how any inconsistency would arise if one explicitly said that the cow lacked the capacity for entertaining general beliefs. Hence there would not seem to be any reason for holding that a necessary condition for being a person is that one be able to entertain and affirm general propositions.

Is rationality in this second sense sufficient to make something a person? Consider a mental substance that records observations, constructs scientific theories on the basis of those observations, and that is capable of having thoughts about past observations, and about the theories and generalizations it has arrived at. Is there any more reason for viewing such a conscious, scientific theorizer, and recorder of past events as a person than there is in the case of the conscious theorem-prover? It is hard to see that there is. The conscious theorizer and recorder might very well lack the concept of a continuing mental substance, and therefore might have neither memory-beliefs that certain states of consciousness belonged to it, nor any desires or beliefs about future states of consciousness belonging to it. As a consequence, an action of destroying such an entity, and replacing it by a comparable one, would not violate any desire that the entity had. Nor would it mean the termination of any psychologically linked series of states of consciousness. It seems plausible, then, to assign the same moral status to the conscious theorizer and recorder as to the conscious theorem-prover. If this is right, then rationality, in the sense of the capacity for having thoughts involving either temporal or general propositions, or both, cannot suffice to make something a person.

This brings us to the third suggestion, to the effect that it is being an agent that makes something a person. The term 'agent', like 'rationality', can be construed in different ways. Sometimes all that is meant in calling something an agent is that some of its behaviour can best be understood as resulting from beliefs and desires that the entity has. But this sense is, presumably, too broad, since any organism that reacts to pleasure and pain can be viewed as engaging in behaviour which results from certain beliefs and desires. The sense of agency that is appropriate here is a narrower one—namely, that suggested in connection with the third possible interpretation of rationality: an agent is a continuing mental substance that is capable of acting on the basis of reasons, arrived at by a process of deliberation in which competing considerations are weighed against one another.

Two philosophers who have adopted this general view of what it is that makes something a person are Stanley Benn and John McCloskey. Benn, for example, says:

I characterize a natural person as someone aware of himself, not just as process or happening, but as agent, as having the capacity to make decisions that make a difference to the way the world goes, as creatively initiating changes designed to make things 'better'; he is conscious of himself as capable of having projects that constitute certain existing or possible states 'important' or 'unimportant', and in relation to which he can assess his own performances as successful or unsuccessful. And, as a kind of meta-project, he has the overarching enterprise of making of himself something he can esteem.[14]

In a similar vein, McCloskey says:

I suggest, therefore, that it cannot be solely on the basis of the possession of excellences such as sentience, rationality, emotionality, that rights, entitlements, be possessed and grounded, and the right to life in particular be defended, for example, on behalf of animals. It is when the notion of choice, possible or actual choice, enters the picture that the idea of a right possessed by the holder of the right gets some sort of grip. When there is evidence of the possibility of choice and of the making of rational choices including moral choices, and more so, when there is evidence of a language used to express thoughts, decisions, wishes, choices, we move from the idea of duties *concerning the being* to the idea of the being *as a possessor* or potential or possible possessor of rights.[15]

---

[14] Stanley I. Benn, 'Personal Freedom and Environmental Ethics: The Moral Inequality of Species', p. 406. For a briefer formulation of the same view, see pp. 99-100 of Benn's 'Abortion, Infanticide, and Respect for Persons', in *The Problem of Abortion*, edited by Joel Feinberg, 1973.

[15] H. J. McCloskey, 'The Right to Life', *Mind*, Volume 84, 1975, pp. 403-25. See p. 413.

Why is the property of being an agent, thus construed, important in this way? McCloskey says:

. . . we need to consider why choice and decision, including moral choice and decision, are so basic and important. The reason seems to lie in part in the idea of the immense worth of free existence, in part in the idea that the decider's life and development are his to determine, if and because he can determine them.[16]

McCloskey's emphasis here upon the agent's capacity for self-determination is also present in Benn's account, according to which a natural person is aware of himself as something with the capacity for initiating creative changes in the world and in himself, and hence as no mere 'process or happening'.

What is the relation between being an agent, in the above sense, and being a person? Is being an agent sufficient to ensure that one is a person? And is it possible to be a person without being an agent?

There are philosophers who would reject the claim that being an agent is sufficient to make one a person. The usual reason for doing so, however, is the belief that there is no relatively enduring, non-potential property that, together with other features, makes it intrinsically wrong to destroy something, and does so independently of the value of the entity. Being an agent cannot suffice to make something a person, because nothing can do that.

In the context of the present discussion, however, we can set aside this view, and confine our attention to those who think that there are properties that make something a person. When this is done, I believe that it turns out that there is relatively little disagreement with the claim that being an agent is *sufficient* to make something a person. The crucial question is whether it is also *necessary*.

One reason that might be advanced for holding that it cannot be is that, in view of the connection between being an agent and having the capacity for free self-determination —which both McCloskey and Benn insist upon—it would follow, if it were a necessary condition, that even normal adult human beings will not be persons if the thesis of universal

[16] Ibid., p. 414.

determinism turns out to be true. And isn't this objectionable? For its being the case that everything, including all states and activities of human beings, is determined by causally prior events, surely would not be a reason for concluding that the killing of normal adult human beings was not morally wrong.

This objection assumes, however, that both Benn and Mc-Closkey are interpreting notions such as self-determination and decision-making in a way that involves free will in a libertarian sense—that is, in a sense in which the existence of free will is incompatible with its being the case that absolutely all events are causally determined. The articles in question are not explicit on this matter. It turns out that McCloskey does have in mind an incompatibilist interpretation of freedom and self-determination, while Benn does not. So the objection tells against McCloskey, but not against Benn.

If, with Stanley Benn, one takes the view that agency does not presuppose libertarian free will, what is it that makes something an agent? Presumably, an agent must have non-momentary interests. But is anything more required? It appears that both McCloskey and Benn want it to be part of their concept of an agent that one be capable of decisions, of rational choices—where this involves being able to weigh conflicting considerations, in order to arrive at a decision about what to do. Why should this be thought necessary if an entity is to be a person? Consider a continuing mental substance that has memory-thoughts about past mental states that belonged to the same mental substance, that believes that there will be, in the future, a mental substance identical with it, that has desires about the future of that mental substance, and whose personality traits do not alter radically with the passage of time. Suppose, finally, that this entity has no capacity for deliberation. It has desires, which it is aware of, and finds itself acting upon, but it never has any sense of considering different possibilities, of weighing conflicting considerations and, thereby, of deciding to do one thing rather than another. If Benn and McCloskey are right, such a being would not have a right to life. It is possible that they are right in thinking that the capacity for choice and delibera-tion is essential if one is to be a subject of rights. I suspect, however, that the moral intuitions of most people go the opposite way on this matter. In my view, of course, that does not decide the issue. But it does point to the desirability of a supporting argument if one holds that the property of being a subject of non-momentary interests does not suffice to make one a person, that one must also possess the capacity for deliberation and rational choice.

When choice is viewed as involving libertarian free will, one can see why someone might hold that the capacity for choice is crucial, in spite of the difficulty mentioned above. But if deliberation can be a purely deterministic process, in which conflicting considerations of various strengths combine to produce a decision to perform one action rather than another, it is much harder to see why the presence of the capacity to undergo such decision processes should serve to distinguish between those things that have a right to continued existence and those that do not. My own inclination is to say that if something can recall some of its past states, can envisage a future for itself, and have desires about that, and if its personality traits do not alter in too drastic a fashion over short periods of time, then it is intrinsically wrong to destroy it, and it is irrelevant whether some of its desires have arisen through a process in which conflicting considerations are weighed against one another.

The conclusion I am suggesting, then, is this. Provided that it is granted that there are persons, the claim that the property of being an agent is sufficient to make something a person appears very plausible. On the other hand, the claim that this property is necessary does not seem very plausible, unless the notion of an agent is interpreted in a somewhat attenuated sense, according to which an agent is anything that possesses a non-momentary interest. Usually something more is required if an individual is to be an agent. Sometimes free will, or a capacity for contra-causal action is required. Sometimes it is the presence of the capacity for deliberation and rational choice. I have urged that neither of these should be treated as a necessary condition for something's being a person.

This brings us to the fourth suggestion, to the effect that it is self-consciousness that makes something a person. The expression 'self-consciousness', like the terms 'rationality' and 'agent', can be construed in a number of rather different ways, depending upon how the component terms—'self' and 'consciousness'—are interpreted. In the case of the first term, there are three main possibilities. First, there is the pure ego interpretation. According to this view, the term 'self' should be taken as applying to something that has experiences and that is in the various mental states, and that cannot be identified with any of those mental states, or with any collection of them. Second, there is the logical construction analysis. According to this view, the concept of a self is not the concept of some entity that stands behind experiences, but simply the concept of a collection of experiences that exhibit a certain sort of unity—that stand in certain relations, especially causal ones. Finally, there is what might be called the neutral analysis. According to this third view, statements about the self are, in general, competely non-committal regarding whether, if there are selves, those entities are pure egos, or merely certain complex relations among experiences.

In the case of the term 'consciousness', there are a number of possible interpretations that vary greatly in strength: (1) direct awareness, or knowledge by acquaintance; (2) knowledge, either direct or indirect; (3) justified, true belief; (4) justified belief; (5) belief, whether justified or not.

Let us now consider the claim that something cannot be a person unless it possesses self-consciousness. What objections this claim is exposed to depends upon how 'self-consciousness' is interpreted. When it is taken as involving direct awareness of a pure ego, it can be objected that it is far from clear that most, or even any human beings enjoy any direct awareness of a pure ego. The force of this objection is, however, unclear, since a number of philosophers maintain that normal adult human beings are directly aware of a pure ego, and the issue is by no means a simple one. Fortunately, we need not pursue it here. For if it is true either that the notion of a direct awareness of a pure ego is incoherent, or at least that many normal adults do not enjoy such awareness, the conclusion that one need draw in the present context is merely that the term 'self-consciousness' has to be interpreted in a different way if possession of self-consciousness is plausibly to be viewed as being a necessary condition for being a person. One will either have to adopt a reductionist view of the nature of the self, and thus hold that self-consciousness involves a direct awareness only of certain interrelations among mental states, or else interpret 'consciousness' in a weaker sense, so that self-consciousness requires, perhaps, only knowledge, either inferential or non-inferential, of an underlying pure ego.

There is, however, at least one very general objection to the claim that self-consciousness is necessary if something is to be a person, which appears to be applicable regardless of how the term 'self-consciousness' is interpreted. This objection derives from the earlier discussion of the unification of desires into non-momentary interests. In the case where the desires are unified by memory-beliefs to the effect that certain desires belong to the same mental substance as that to which these present ones belong, there is no problem. The individual does have knowledge of a continuing mental substance—which may be conceived of either as an underlying pure ego, or as merely a construct out of experiences and their interrelations. But what of the case in which an individual has no memory of the past, yet believes that he is a continuing mental substance, and has various hopes about his future states? Such a person is aware of a continuing mental substance, but he is not aware of it *qua* continuing mental substance. He believes, and hopes, that that is what he is, but he does not know that it is the case. So if 'self-consciousness' is interpreted in a way that implies knowledge of a continuing self, it seems that there could be something that had non-momentary interests, but that lacked self-consciousness.

It seems, moreover, that even if one construes 'self-consciousness' in a very weak sense that requires only that the individual believe that he is a continuing mental substance, it is not necessary for something to possess self-consciousness in order to be a subject with non-momentary interests. For consider the case of the individual just mentioned, with no memory of the past, but with beliefs and hopes about the future. Would it make a morally significant difference if that individual, rather than believing that he was a continuing self, merely hoped that he was?

If this is right, and if being a subject of non-momentary interests is sufficient to make something a person, then self-consciousness cannot be necessary. Given the ways in which desires can apparently be unified into non-momentary interests, it will be essential for something to possess the concept of a continuing self. It will also, apparently, be necessary for the individual to exercise that concept in certain ways with regard to itself. But this exercise need not involve cognitive states: certain conative states will do as well.

Finally, let us consider whether self-consciousness is sufficient to make something a person. Consider a continuing mental substance that has memory knowledge of past experiences as experiences belonging to the same mental substance, and that knows that there will be future experiences belonging to the same mental substance, provided that it is not destroyed. There appears to be nothing incoherent in the idea that such a being might neither have any desires at any time, nor even be structurally capable of doing so. Such an entity would possess self-consciousness, but it would not be a subject of interests, either continuing or momentary. What is one to say about the morality of destroying such a being?

This question is one that is quite crucial for moral theory. Many people, I believe, would be strongly inclined to say that it would be wrong to destroy such a being and that, moreover, the wrongness cannot be explained by reference to its value. Thus, if the world were somewhat over-populated with beings of this sort, that would be a good reason for not bringing more into existence; it would not be a good reason for destroying some that already existed. If this is right, beings devoid of desires, but possessing self-consciousness, must be regarded as persons.

Is there any reason to resist this conclusion? A very serious one, I think. In the first place, the notion of interest plays an absolutely crucial role in most present-day moral theories. Various forms of act and rule utilitarianism, contract theories, ideal observer theories, Hare's universal prescriptivism, and other theories, much though they disagree on a variety of issues, are united in the attempt to somehow relate the content of correct moral rules to the interests of individuals.

Second, while moral theory is hardly without its fads and fashions, I do not think that the above fact can be lightly dismissed in that way. The attempt to connect morality to interests is very deep-rooted indeed, owing in large part, I think, to the fact that establishing some connection between morality and interest appears to be one of the most promising ways of attempting to make sense of morality, of showing that the institution of morality is, after all, a rational one.

Where does this leave us? I began this section by asking which of the following things make something a person: (1) having a non-momentary interest; (2) rationality; (3) being an agent; (4) self-consciousness. The conclusions that I have urged, some tentatively, others not, are these. First, the having of a non-momentary interest is sufficient to make something a person. Whether it is also necessary is, as we have just seen, much less clear. Second, rationality by itself is not sufficient to make something a person, and, unless it is interpreted in a weak sense, in which nothing more than the capacity to have thoughts, or the capacity for temporal judgements, is involved, it does not appear to be necessary either. Third, being an agent appears to be sufficient to make something a person, since something cannot be an agent unless it has a non-momentary interest. It does not, however, seem necessary for something to possess either libertarian free will, or the capacity for deliberation and rational choice, in order to be a person. Finally, self-consciousness, however interpreted, does not appear necessary if something is to be a person, although the possession, and some relevant exercise of the concept of a continuing mental substance, apparently is. The difficult question is whether self-consciousness is sufficient to make something a person, even in the absence of interests. The answer to this question may depend upon whether an epistemic or a non-epistemic approach to the justification of basic moral principles is correct. If the latter approach is correct, then it would seem to follow that self-consciousness, in the absence of all interests, cannot suffice to make something a person. This conclusion seems, moreover, to be in agreement with most current ethical theories.

5.4 The Question of Capacities

What is it that makes something a person? Various answers were considered in the preceding section. All the accounts, however, were non-committal with respect to whether it is a certain capacity that makes something a person, or a certain capacity together with the exercise of that capacity at some relevant time. The present section will be concerned with this issue.

Some philosophers have taken the view that it is the mere capacity, exercised or unexercised, that is morally decisive. This seems to be Brody's view: 'What is essential for being human is the possession of the potential for human activities that comes with having the structures required for a functioning brain.'[17] As the expression, 'the structures required for a functioning brain', suggests, and as he elsewhere makes clear, it is a certain capacity that Brody is referring to here, rather than a mere potentiality—his use of the term 'potentiality' notwithstanding. What is not clear, however, is precisely what capacity he takes to be morally relevant. If it is merely the capacity of a functioning brain, most animals will have to be viewed as persons. If it is the capacity of a functioning *human* brain, Brody is exposed to the objection, defended at length in chapter 4, that reference to the property of belonging to a particular biological species cannot enter into basic moral principles. If it is the capacity for activities of a certain sort—a sort of which most humans are eventually capable— Brody is left with the task of specifying which ones. It also seems very likely that any such specification will imply that Brody's own views on abortion are untenable.

Brody does ultimately acknowledge, in a footnote, that there are serious problems here for his own position:

Saying this raises, of course, a fundamental problem about the rights of animals, especially their right to life. Unless one is prepared to require what might be called advanced abilities from the brain in question— and that would be likely to exclude infants and brain-damaged or severely retarded adults, as well as fetuses, from the class of human beings—the crucial difference between us, who have a strong right to life, and animals, who are commonly regarded as having a far weaker one, is the species to which they belong. Can that difference in species support the difference in rights, especially when we recognize in animals the very property essential for being human?

[17] Brody, *Abortion and the Sanctity of Human Life*, p. 114.

On this difficult question, see my 'Morality and Religion Reconsidered', in *Philosophy of Religion: The Analytic Approach* (Englewood Cliffs, N. J.: Prentice-Hall, 1974).[18]

Given how crucial these questions are, it is rather surprising that Brody chooses not to pursue them at all, or even to indicate what his views are. Why does Brody instead refer the reader to an article in another book? The answer will emerge if we consider a crucial section of that article, in which Brody is considering an argument for a vegetarian conclusion:

This vegetarian argument draws further support from the fact that the intuitions embedded in the conventional consciousness are about species. After all, there are a variety of extreme cases (newly born infants, severely retarded individuals, people who are near death) in which many of the subtler features of human beings are not present but in which the conventional consciousness accords to the people in question far more rights than those normally accorded to animals. This makes it far more difficult to believe that there are some characteristics (a) possessed by all human beings, (b) not possessed by all animals, and (c) which justify the moral distinctions drawn by the conventional consciousness.[19]

How is one to respond to this argument? The reply which Brody suggests is as follows:

There is a religious response to this vegetarian argument which runs as follows: when God created the world, he intended that man should use certain other species for food, clothing, etc. God did not, of course, give man complete freedom to do what he wants with these creatures. They are not, for example, to be treated cruelly. But, because that was God's intention, man can, and should use these creatures to provide him with food, clothing, etc.[20]

Brody's over-all view, in short, is this. Other things being equal, the possession of a functioning brain endows something with a right to life. Moreover, other things being equal, a non-human animal with a brain whose functioning is superior to that of the brain of some human will have a right to life that is at least as serious as that of the human. But other things are *not* equal, since God has given humans

[18] Ibid., pp. 155-6.

[19] Baruch A. Brody, 'Morality and Religion Reconsidered', pp. 592-603 in *Readings in the Philosophy of Religion: The Analytic Approach*, edited by Baruch A. Brody, 1974. See p. 602.

[20] Ibid.

permission to kill other animals, and if God gives one permission to do something, that action is not morally wrong.

Brody is here adopting the position known as theological voluntarism—the view that God can choose any moral standards he pleases. Thus, although Brody holds that, as a matter of fact, God has not given us permission to torture animals, Brody would say that if God *had* given us permission to do that, then it would not be wrong. It is only by adopting this outlook that Brody is able to hold that the possession of a functioning brain by a human makes it wrong to kill it, but the possession of a functioning, and possibly superior, brain by a non-human animal does not make it wrong to kill it. Thus Brody is able to reject abortion without embracing vegetarianism. But the price is high indeed, and it is not surprising that Brody thought it best not to discuss these issues in his book on abortion.

A much more forthright and clear-headed advocate of the view that it is capacities that make something a person is Eike-Henner Kluge. After characterizing a rational being as one capable of perception, thought, self-awareness, and the use of language, Kluge says:

A person is an entity that is a rational being; that is to say, it is an entity that has the present capabilities of symbolic awareness in the manner characteristic of rational beings as defined above. A person is an entity—any entity, irrespective of the precise nature of its constitution—that is either presently aware in a manner characteristic of rational beings, or can become thus aware without any change in the constitutive nature of its composition.[21]

Before examining this view, and the support that Kluge offers for it, we need to get clear about what is involved in the notion of a capacity. Two contrasts are important. First, that between immediately exercisable capacities, and blocked or suppressed capacities. Second, that between capacities and potentialities.

To attribute an immediately exercisable capacity to something is to make a statement about how the thing would be behaving, or what properties it would have, if it were now to be in certain circumstances, or in a certain condition. Where

---

[21] Eike-Henner W. Kluge, *The Practice of Death*, 1975, p. 91.

the thing is a person, the conditions in question will usually involve reference to some desire or choice. Thus, to say that Mary is now capable of running a five-minute mile is to say that if Mary were now to try to run a five-minute mile, were appropriately dressed, were on a track where there is not too much wind, and so on, then she would succeed in running a mile in five minutes. This is what I mean by an immediately exercisable capacity.

Suppose, however, that Mary is drunk. In one sense, she is no longer capable of running a five-minute mile. Yet one might still attribute that capacity to her. In such a case, one might speak of blocked capacities—the idea being that all of the 'positive' factors required for the immediately exercisable capacity are present, but there are also negative factors that prevent the exercise of the capacity.

It is very important not to confuse the concept of a capacity—whether in the narrow sense that covers only immediately exercisable capacities, or in the broader sense that also includes blocked capacities—with the concept of a potentiality. To attribute a certain potentiality to an entity is to say at least that there is a change it could undergo, involving more than the mere elimination of factors blocking the exercise of a capacity, that would result in its having the property it now potentially has. It may also be to say that there are now factors within the entity itself that will, if not interfered with, cause it to undergo the relevant change. (This, and other distinctions with respect to potentialities, will be explored more fully in the next chapter, which is concerned with the question of the moral relevance of potentialities.)

How is the term 'capacity' to be construed when it is claimed that it is an individual's capacities that determine whether it is a person? It is clear that it must be used in the broad sense. An individual who has been knocked unconscious has very few immediately exercisable capacities. If it is capacities that make something a person, and if a temporarily unconscious, normal adult human being is to count as a person, then 'capacities' must cover both immediately exercisable capacities and blocked capacities.

What reasons can be offered for holding that capacities by

themselves determine whether something is a person? Kluge is one of the few authors who have addressed themselves to this question. He offers two considerations in support of this claim. The first is found in the following passage:

> . . . over and above the notion of pure potentiality and potentiality properly speaking, there is the notion of potentiality that we ascribe to a sleeping cat when we say that potentially it is awake. In other words, there is the notion of a potentiality where the realization of that potentiality does not involve a constitutive change in the relevant and defining aspects of the being in question: There is no essential, specific difference between a cat when asleep and a cat when awake.
>
> It is this third notion of potentiality, and not the other two, that provides a clear reason for saying that a potential person has the same moral status as an actual person. For, in this sense of the term, a potential person has all the essential constitutional characteristics of a person. What it lacks is merely the final actualization. Since it has the essential constitutive characteristics of an actual person, it will also thereby have those rights and privileges that accrue to an actual person by virtue of that constitution. The claim that it has the same moral status as an actual person is now seen to be well-founded.[22]

This argument turns upon an important assumption that has not been explicitly stated: *a 'fully actualized' person has the rights he does by virtue of his constitution.* For if a fully actualized person has some rights not simply by virtue of his constitution, but by virtue of his having been in relevant psychological states—for example, having enjoyed conscious experiences, or having had certain desires—the fact that some things that are not fully actualized persons have the same constitution, and thus, presumably, the same capacities as fully actualized persons, will not entail that the former have any of the rights possessed by the latter.

The assumption that fully actualized persons have the rights they do by virtue of their constitution is thus a crucial assumption, and one for which Kluge offers no support. Moreover, given the connection between a thing's capacities and its constitution, anyone who questions whether capacities by themselves are morally significant will also question whether a thing's constitution is, in itself, morally significant. As a result, Kluge's first argument in no way advances the issue.

[22] Ibid., p. 17.

The only other support that Kluge offers for the view that capacities are morally relevant occurs in the following passage: 'Personhood will depend solely on rational awareness. Nor need this awareness be actually present: the mere potential for it, as a constitutive potential, will suffice. In this way an individual, whether awake, asleep, or in a coma, will count as a person just as long as his constitutive nature is such as to permit rational awareness.'[23] The suggestion here is that one advantage of the view that it is an entity's capacities that determine whether it is a person is that the sleeping individual is not deprived of his personhood on such an account. This is certainly desirable, but alternative accounts also accomplish this, and without being exposed to the difficulties the present view encounters.

Let us now turn to the case against this view. In the first place, advocates of the claim that it is capacities that determine whether an entity is a person generally offer no reasons for rejecting the alternative view—advanced by many who defend a conservative position on abortion—that it can be seriously wrong to kill something because of its potentialities, and not merely because of its capacities. In the passage quoted above, Kluge assumes that something has the rights it does by virtue of its constitution. But why should this assumption be preferred to the anti-abortionist one that an organism has rights by virtue of its genetic constitution, or, more precisely, by virtue of the genetically determined psychological capabilities it will later develop? An argument is needed in support of the contention that it is capacities, rather than potentialities, that are morally relevant. As Kluge offers none, his position is open to the charge of arbitrariness as a result.

The claim that it is an entity's capacities that determine whether it is a person involves two contentions. First, that something cannot be a person unless it possesses certain capacities. And second, that the possession of certain capacities is sufficient to make something a person. The second objection concerns the first of these claims. Consider an adult human being that has suffered brain damage that makes it

[23] Ibid., p. 91.

impossible for the organism to enjoy any consciousness at all, let alone rational awareness. Such damage might be of two very different sorts. On the one hand, the damage might involve the complete destruction of those structures that are the positive, constitutional basis of consciousness and rational awareness. On the other hand, the damage might leave those structures intact, but damage other parts of the brain so that the structures in question are isolated, with the result that it is impossible for the capacities for consciousness, and for rational awareness, to be exercised as long as the damage goes unrepaired. In the latter case, one might wish to say that the capacity for consciousness and rational awareness is still present, albeit blocked. So let us confine our attention to a case in which the relevant structures have been destroyed, and where one can say that there is no longer any capacity for consciousness, let alone for rational awareness. If a capacity for rational awareness were a necessary condition for something's being a person, one would be forced to say, in such a case, that there was no longer any person associated with the organism, and thus that, if one were to kill the organism, or allow it to die, one would not be guilty of having destroyed a person.

I think that this conclusion can be shown to be unacceptable. The crucial point is that it might very well be possible to repair such damage, and that the result of doing so might be an organism that not only was capable of rational awareness, but that had the memories, beliefs, attitudes, personality traits, and so on, characteristic of the person who previously existed. Would the resulting individual be identical with the individual who existed prior to the damage, or merely be a replica? The view that he would be a replica does not seem plausible. A person who revives from a coma is not a replica of the person who existed previously. Yet a coma may very well involve brain damage that temporarily destroys the constitutional basis for rational awareness. Why should one distinguish between cases where the damage can be repaired by the organism itself, and cases where it cannot?

Once it is granted that the resulting person is identical with the person who existed previously, the argument can be put as follows. If something can be a person only if it possesses a capacity for rational awareness, then it follows that in destroying an organism that has suffered the sort of damage described above, one cannot be destroying any person. But if the damage is repairable, and if the result would be the revival of the person who previously existed, then the destruction of the organism, by making impossible any such revival, thereby destroys the person in question. Hence it cannot be the case that there is a person only where there is a capacity for rational awareness.

The third objection is directed against the claim that the possession of certain capacities is sufficient to make something a person. Suppose that some day it is possible to construct adult human beings in the laboratory, building them up cell by cell. Assume further that an individual's mental states are either identical with, or at least dependent upon, its brain states, so that one can, by properly programming an individual's brain, determine what beliefs, desires, and personality traits the resulting individual will have. Finally, let us assume that the construction is carried out at a very low temperature, so that the individual is completely unconscious throughout. The question is: Would it be wrong to destroy such an adult human being, at a time before it had enjoyed any conscious experiences at all?

Opinions differ. Some believe, often quite firmly, that it would not be at all wrong to destroy such an organism. Others believe, often equally firmly, that it would be wrong, and seriously so. Most people, perhaps, find the question a puzzling one, and have no strong intuitions on the matter. As it stands, then, the question may seem unhelpful. I believe, however, that it is possible to develop this case further in a way that will provide one with a reason for holding that it is not wrong to destroy such an organism.

What one needs to do is to bring the deprogramming/reprogramming strategy to bear upon the case. Suppose, then, that our frozen Frankenstein has originally been constructed on the model of Billy Graham. That is to say, its brain circuitry is such that when it is unfrozen, the result will be a person whose beliefs, attitudes, capacities, and personality traits are those of Billy Graham. Before the organism is thawed out, however, our scientist undergoes a conversion, and becomes unhappy with the model chosen. So he proceeds to reprogramme the brain, using Bertrand Russell as a model. He then raises the organism's temperature, and the result is a person with the beliefs, attitudes, capacities, and personality traits that characterized Bertrand Russell.

Has the scientist done something morally wrong? I suggest that most people would feel that he has not. But how can one make sense of such intuitions, given that it would be seriously wrong to carry out such reprogramming on a normal adult human being? The answer must be that in the case of the frozen organism, the deprogramming/reprogramming operation cannot involve the destruction of one person, and the creation of another. This, in turn, can be the case only if *either* one has the same person before and after reprogramming, *or* one does not have any person before reprogramming. In view of the absence of both psychological continuity and causal continuity, the first possibility must be rejected. Hence the only way to make sense of the intuitions concerning the act of deprogramming and reprogramming is by adopting the view that the reason the action is not wrong is that there is no person there to be destroyed. Prior to the advent of consciousness there is at most a potential person.

Another objection to the view that the possession of certain capacities suffices to make something a person turns upon what may be called the moral symmetry principle. What this principle states, very roughly, is this. Suppose that C is some type of collection of causally related states of affairs existing at different times. C might be an enduring individual, or it might be merely a sequence of events. Suppose that E is some type of state of affairs to which collections of type C sometimes give rise. Assume further that collections of type C would not be morally significant were it not for the fact that they can give rise to states of type E. Then the moral symmetry principle asserts that, other things being equal, there is no moral difference between, on the one hand, interfering with a causally interrelated collection of states of affairs of type C, so that it never gives rise to a state of type E, and, on the other, intentionally refraining from producing states of affairs so interrelated that they constitute a collection of type C.

This principle is not uncontroversial. In the present section, however, it will be best simply to state the argument that is based upon it. The moral symmetry principle will then be discussed at length in chapter 6, where a more precise statement of the principle will be offered, and objections to it considered.

The argument runs as follows. Let C be some type of physical structure that, if appropriately stimulated, will give rise to rational awareness. Assume further that physical structures of type C would not be morally significant were it not the case that they can give rise to rational awareness. Structures of type C thus possess, in the world as it is, the capacity for rational awareness. In a world in which there were different psychophysical laws, however, structures of type C might not possess the capacity for rational awareness, and so, other things being equal, structures of type C would not be morally significant.

The question is whether it is wrong to destroy a structure of type C at some time before it has given rise to rational awareness. Applying the moral symmetry principle to this situation leads to the conclusion that, other things being equal, there is no moral difference between intentionally destroying a physical structure of type C at some time before it has given rise to rational awareness, and intentionally refraining from performing some actions that would bring into existence a physical structure of type C. Therefore it is intrinsically wrong to destroy something possessing an unexercised capacity for rational awareness only if it is equally wrong intentionally to refrain from producing something with the capacity for rational awareness. But intentionally refraining from conception—which need involve nothing more than abstinence from intercourse—is surely not seriously wrong in itself.[24] Or if it is, at least not as seriously wrong as killing a person. Hence the destruction of an entity with a capacity for rational awareness that has never been exercised cannot be as seriously wrong as the destruction of a

---

[24] Most people would hold, I think, that there is nothing intrinsically wrong with intentionally refraining from reproducing. The issue is, however, rather more problematic than most people take it to be. Arguments bearing upon this question will be discussed in chapter 7.

person. Thèrefore it cannot be the capacity for rational awareness that makes something a person. And since precisely the same argument can be advanced with respect to any capacity, it follows that the possession of certain capacities cannot by itself suffice to make something a person.

5.5 Death and the Concept of a Person

In the final section of this chapter, I want to consider an alternative approach to the question what makes something a person. We have seen that this is a very difficult issue. Some writers have suggested that it might be better to approach it less directly. Perhaps one should begin by focusing upon the concept of death, and by trying to get clear about the conditions under which a person has ceased to be. The conclusions thus arrived at can then be used to attack the problem of the beginning of personal existence, thereby generating, in an oblique fashion, an account of what it is that makes something a person.

It is not at all easy to see why this approach should be thought fruitful. If one is puzzled about the properties something must have to be a person, surely one will be equally puzzled, and in precisely the same ways, about when a person has come into being, and about when a person has ceased to be? How can these issues be other than different sides of the same coin? Still, the fact is that some philosophers are employing this general approach, and are claiming to establish quite important conclusions by means of it.

A representative statement of this general line of argument can be found in chapters 6 and 7 of Baruch Brody's *Abortion and the Sanctity of Human Life*. Brody's formulation of the argument involves two technical philosophical notions: that of an individual's *essential properties*, and that of a *natural kind*. The first of these notions he explains as follows: 'We shall say that an object o_1 has a property P_1 essentially just in case o_1 has P_1 and would go out of existence if it lost it: just in case the loss of it would involve a substantial change.'[25]

Given this notion of an essential property, the notion of a

[25] Op. cit., p. 137.

natural kind is explained by Brody as follows: 'We shall say
that any property had essentially by some object and accidentally by none (whether actual or potential) determines
what is called a natural kind and that the set of objects
having that property is a natural kind.'[26]

It may be helpful to illustrate these notions. Suppose that
a cat with white hair has its hair dyed black. Then the cat
that has black hair today is identical with the cat that had
white hair yesterday. Having white hair is thus only an acci-
dental property of the cat, not an essential one. Consequently
the class of things with white hair cannot constitute a natural
kind. Compare this with the case where a tree is chopped up
for firewood. Brody wants to say that once this has been
done, there is nothing that is identical with the tree that
previously existed. If something is to be identical with a tree,
it must also be a tree. So it would seem that being a tree is an
essential property of any object that has it. The set of trees
is therefore a natural kind.

This is all much more problematic than Brody realizes.
Consider the tree that has been chopped up. Given that the
resulting pile of wood is not a tree, one certainly cannot say
that it is the same tree as one that previously existed. But
there are other ways of referring to the tree. One can, for
example, simply refer to it as a collection of matter. But
when this is done, it is the same collection of matter that at
one time is a tree, and a bit later a pile of wood. That collection of matter, then, can lose the property of being a tree
without ceasing to be. So given Brody's account, being a tree
cannot be an essential property of that collection of matter,
even at the time when it is in fact a tree. It follows from this
that being a tree is not an essential property of trees, and
therefore that the set of trees does not constitute a natural
kind. And in general, both essential properties, and natural
kinds, turn out to be much scarcer on Brody's account than
he imagines to be the case.

Having introduced the notions of an essential property and
of a natural kind, Brody advances two claims about natural
kinds which are needed for his argument:

[26] Ibid., p. 98.

1. Only the possession of properties had essentially by every member of a natural kind is necessary (essential) for membership in that natural kind.

2. The possession of all properties had essentially by every member of a natural kind is sufficient for membership in that natural kind.[27]

As Brody points out, these claims would not be true if they were extended from natural kinds to classes in general. He thinks, however, that they are correct as they stand. Though I believe that he is mistaken on this matter, let us accept these claims for the sake of discussion. His basic line of argument can then be summarized as follows:

(1) Let us agree to use the expression 'human being' so that it applies to all and only individuals that both belong to the biological species *Homo sapiens* and have a right to life.

(2) Something ceases to be a human being when its brain is no longer functioning, or at least, when it is no longer capable of functioning.

(3) Therefore, in view of the definition of an essential property, the property of having a (human) brain that is capable of functioning is an essential property of any human being.

(4) Every individual possessing a (human) brain that is capable of functioning also possesses every property that is an essential property of every human being.

(5) The class of human beings is a natural kind.

(6) Any individual that has a (human) brain capable of functioning, since it therefore possesses all of the properties that are had essentially by all human beings, must, in virtue of claim 2 above, be a human being.

(7) Therefore any individual possessing a (human) brain capable of functioning has a right to life.[28]

The conclusion is certainly significant. If correct, it follows that my contention, in the previous section, that capacities alone are not sufficient to make something a person, must be

---

[27] Ibid., p. 98.
[28] The premisses in this argument occur at steps (1), (2), (4), and (5). For the first premiss, see p. 3. For the second and third, pp. 107-8. For the final premiss, see pp. 100-2.

mistaken. For if a human organism has the capacity for thought, it certainly has a brain that is capable of functioning, and hence, in view of the conclusion of Brody's argument, must have a right to life.

But Brody's argument is in fact defective in a number of ways, and irreparably so. In the first place, given Brody's characterization of what it is to be a natural kind, it is not true, contrary to what is claimed at step 5, that the class of human beings constitutes a natural kind. For this to be true, it would have to be impossible for there to be something that was a human being at one time, and something different at a later time. Brody himself mentions an objection to this claim that seems quite decisive:

> The following objection might be raised: it is true that, in the normal course of events, when a human being is no longer a human being, it also no longer exists. But perhaps there are ways in which human beings could stop being human beings but still continue to exist. Consider the case of Gregor in Kafka's *Metamorphosis*. Has not he survived his amazing transformation although he is no longer a human being? And given that this is so, it follows that being human is not an essential property of human beings.[29]

Brody's response to this objection is as follows:

> It is very difficult to know what to say about this objection because it is very difficult to know what to say about the case of Gregor. Despite its literary strength, it is not clear that Kafka has succeeded in presenting us with a coherent picture of Gregor in an insect's body. But assume that he has. The objector seems to be impressed with the continuities through this change when he assures us that it is still Gregor and with the discontinuities when he assures us that it is no longer a human being. The justification for this asymmetrical treatment is unclear. To the extent that one thinks it is still Gregor, should not one also think that it is a human being (even if in the body of a bug), and to the extent that one thinks it is not a human being, should not one think that it is not Gregor (even if it does have many of his thoughts, feelings, and emotions)?[30]

This reply is certainly very weak. One of the possibilities that Brody suggests—that Gregor has survived the transformation, and survived as a human being, albeit with the body of a bug—is simply incompatible with his own use of the expression

---

[29] Ibid., pp. 100–1. [30] Ibid., p. 101.

'human being', which he explicitly sets out in the introduction of his book: 'The final point is terminological. When, in this book, I use the phrase "human being", I mean "a member of the species homo sapiens who has a right to life similar to the right to life had by you, me, and so on".'[31] If Gregor has the body of a bug, he is certainly no longer a member of the species *Homo sapiens*.

It should perhaps be remarked, however, that there could be somewhat different transformations where it would make sense to hold that Gregor was still a human being. For the resulting organism, rather than being a bug through and through, might consist of a body that was mainly that of a bug, but which contained a human brain. The case we are imagining here, however, is one in which the whole body of the resulting organism, including the brain, is non-human.

The result is that the only alternative open to Brody is to claim that Gregor cannot possibly have survived such a transformation. I think it is possible, however, to describe the transformation in such a way that this alternative is not acceptable. The crucial points would be, first, that psychological states and capacities remain unchanged throughout the transformation, and second, that the transformation of Gregor's brain from a human to a non-human one should exhibit causal continuity, together with a preservation of what might be called, in a broad sense, all the 'information' encoded within the brain. Given such causal continuity and psychological constancy throughout the transformation, it would not seem plausible to maintain that Gregor cannot have survived.

A second defect in Brody's argument occurs at step 4, where it is claimed that any individual possessing a (human) brain capable of functioning also possesses every property that is an essential property of every human being. The natural question to ask is: Capable of functioning *in what sorts of ways*? Brody notices this problem, and responds as follows:

There are, after all, progressive stages in the physical development and functioning of the brain. For example, the fetal brain (and nervous

[31] Ibid., p. 3.

system) does not develop sufficiently to support spontaneous motion until some time in the third month after conception. There is, of course, no doubt that that stage of development is sufficient for the fetus to be human. No one would be likely to maintain that a spontaneously moving human being has died, and similarly, a spontaneously moving fetus would seem to have become human.[32]

A rather brisk treatment of a serious issue. And quite unsatisfactory. Recall the case mentioned in section 4.2, where the upper parts of the brain of a normal adult human being are so severely damaged, and irreparably so, that the neurological basis of consciousness, memory, personality, thinking, and all of the higher mental functions, is completely destroyed, but where the brain stem is left intact, so that basic bodily functions such as respiration and circulation continue to be maintained. It was contended that the killing of such a human organism would not violate anyone's right to life. Now consider a slightly different case, where the damage is less severe. Again, the neurological basis of all of the higher mental functions is completely destroyed, but the basis of a very rudimentary consciousness and of some spontaneous movement remains. We have, let us suppose, a human organism whose mental life is comparable to that of an earthworm. I cannot see that this changes the situation. Surely we still want to say that the person who once existed has ceased to be, and thus that to kill the human organism that remains is not to violate anyone's right to life. If so, not all members of the species *Homo sapiens* that are capable of spontaneous movement have a right to life, and hence, not all are humans in Brody's sense, since that entails the possession of a right to life.

This defect in Brody's argument could be remedied by introducing reference to *specific* functions. This change would not affect the logical structure of the argument, but it would certainly affect the conclusion. One could no longer conclude, as Brody wants to, that any individual with a (human) brain capable of any functioning at all is a person. One would have to say instead that any individual with a (human) brain capable of functions F_1, F_2, etc., is a person.

[32] Ibid., p. 110.

This in turn would undermine Brody's contention that twelve-week-old human foetuses have a right to life, since they do not have brains capable of functioning in the relevant ways.

Moreover, once one introduces reference to specific functions, one is confronted with the very difficult question of which functions are the morally relevant ones. Brody tries to avoid this question by relying upon a simple-minded account of the death of a person that ignores ways in which a person might be destroyed through brain damage that falls short of complete brain death. Had he considered such possibilities, he would have been confronted with the whole range of alternatives discussed in section 5.3. Nor would the decision as to which is correct have been any less puzzling: nothing is gained by focusing upon the question of when a person ceases to be, rather than upon the question of what it is that makes something a person. Indeed, as the discussions by Brody and others illustrate, there is a serious danger that something will be lost, since it is very easy to confine one's attention to the sorts of cases one tends to encounter. This is certainly understandable, since the issues raised by such cases are pressing ones, and it is very important to have a satisfactory legal and moral view of them. But if one is interested in the much broader question of what it is to be a person, it will not do to confine one's attention to cases that tend to arise. There are crucial issues that only emerge when one considers a range of possible cases.

Another defect in Brody's argument also occurs at step 4, and it is a serious one indeed. It turns upon another point about death—one that was made in connection with the earlier reprogramming example. The point is that there are ways in which human persons can be destroyed without *any* destruction of the *general* capacities of any human organism. It is certainly conceivable that mental states are either identical with brain states, or causally dependent upon them. And if either were the case, then all of an individual's memories, beliefs, desires, attitudes, and personality traits could be destroyed by altering his brain states. This could be done, moreover, without destroying the basic structure of the brain, and hence without destroying any of the general capacities—such as the capacity for self-consciousness, or for rational thought—possessed by the human in question. Such an act of deprogramming would destroy a person, even though it would not impair the general functional capacities of the brain involved. For personal identity presupposes a relation of causal dependence between mental states existing at different times. When the relevant causal chain is broken, as it is when an individual's brain is altered in the manner described, the basis of personal identity is destroyed, and it is impossible for any future person to be identical with the person who previously existed.

One property, therefore, that a human person can lose only on pain of ceasing to be is that of standing in a certain causal relation to earlier mental occurrences. This, then, must be an essential property of human persons, and Brody has offered no reason at all for thinking that any individual possessing a (human) brain that is capable of functioning will possess this property. Indeed, the case of the deprogrammed individual is a counter-example. At the time of deprogramming one has an individual possessing a (human) brain that is capable of functioning, but there is no causal connection, of the appropriate sort, between present mental events and past ones.

Brody's argument is, in short, unsound in a variety of ways. The source of these defects is Brody's refusal to grapple with some of the central issues discussed above. He has no real answer to the crucial question of the properties that make something a person. Nor does he address the issue of whether certain capacities by themselves suffice to make something a person, or whether some exercise of those capacities is also necessary.

It would certainly be possible to deal with these issues in the context of a discussion of the conditions under which a person has ceased to be. This would require, however, a much more subtle consideration of the death of persons than is offered by Brody. And once one undertakes a more subtle treatment, it immediately becomes clear that this alternative approach to the question of what it is that makes something a person does not in any way facilitate a resolution of the difficult issues.

6

Potential Persons

The preceding two chapters dealt with issues which bear upon two very common objections to abortion: first, the objection that abortion is wrong because it involves the killing of an innocent human being; and second, the objection that abortion is wrong because it involves the destruction of a person. The first objection is, I argued, mistaken: membership in a particular biological species is not in itself morally significant. The second objection is yet to be answered, though the groundwork has been laid by the attempt to determine what properties make something a person.

This chapter, and the next, are concerned with two other philosophically important objections to abortion. The first, which will be examined in the present chapter, involves the claim that the destruction of potential persons is intrinsically wrong. The second, which will be discussed in chapter 7, turns upon the contention that abortion is wrong because it prevents the actualization of a possible person. In popular thinking, at least, these two objections are often confused with one another. We shall see, however, that they are quite distinct, and raise very different issues.

6.1 Potential Persons, Latent Persons, and Possible Persons

In order to understand and evaluate these two objections to abortion, we need to get very clear about the underlying notions. First, the concept of a potential person. How can the phrase 'potential person' be interpreted so that it will be true that biologically normal human foetuses are potential persons? This question is much more difficult to answer than it appears initially. Suppose, for example, that one says that an entity is a potential person if and only if it will, in the normal course of affairs, develop into a person. Since it would seem to be true, on this analysis, that normal human foetuses are potential persons, what is wrong with this account? The answer is that, on this analysis, whether a particular entity is a potential person depends upon what the normal course of affairs is in the situation in question. Consider, for example, a society in which there is a disease that leads to the death of 95 per cent of human foetuses. The statistically normal course of affairs in such a society would be one in which biologically normal human foetuses did not develop into persons. So normal human foetuses would not be potential persons in such a world.

The natural response to this problem is to revise the analysis as follows: an entity is a potential person if and only if it will, if not interfered with, develop into a person. This revision has the merit of eliminating the dependence of an entity's status as a potential person upon what happens to be statistically normal. However it does run afoul of another problem, since it does not seem to be true, on this analysis, that normal human foetuses are potential persons. The reason is that it is not enough that a foetus not be interfered with. It must also be supplied with nutrients and other things, if it is to survive and develop into a person.

It might be claimed that to cut off a foetus's life-support system is to 'interfere' with it, though this, however, would seem to me to be a misuse of that term. In any case, the basic point can be made without challenging this move. For consider a biologically normal human foetus that has had to be removed from the womb due to the death of the mother. To fail to hook it up to a life-support system cannot, under any reasonable use of language, be characterized as interfering with the foetus. The upshot is that either no normal human foetuses are potential persons on the revised account, or else there are at least some that are not, and this is objectionable, since whether an entity is a potential person should depend only upon its properties, not upon its relations to other things.

The basic difficulty involved in finding a satisfactory characterization of the notion of a potential person will become clearer if we consider the concepts of an active potentiality, a latent potentiality, and a passive potentiality. To understand these concepts, we need to introduce a distinction between positive causal factors and negative ones. A book is in a gravitational field. Is the fact that it is in a gravitational field sufficient to ensure that the book is being accelerated? Clearly not. The book may be sitting on a desk. But the gravitational field is the only 'positive' thing that is needed. The book need not have any further properties. It need not stand in any other relation to anything. What is required is only the *absence* of factors that would interfere with, or counteract, the influence of the gravitational field.

An entity may be said to have an active potentiality for acquiring some property P if there are within it all of the positive causal factors needed to bring it about that it will acquire property P, and there are no other factors present within it that will block the action of the positive ones. It has a latent potentiality if all of the positive factors are present within it, but there is some feature of it that will block the action of those factors. Finally, it has a passive potentiality for acquiring property P if other things could act upon it in such a way as to bring it about that it acquires property P.

One would like to characterize a potential person as an entity that has an active potentiality for becoming a person, and a latent person as an entity that has a latent potentiality for becoming a person. But given that normal human foetuses will develop into persons only if treated in certain ways, to define 'potential person' and 'latent person' in this way would have the consequence that human foetuses would not even be latent persons, let alone potential ones.

Is the notion of a potential person to be characterized, then, in terms of the concept of a passive potentiality? This alternative would not seem to be a happy one, since the notion of a passive potentiality covers too many possibilities. Milk powder has a passive potentiality to become milk: one need merely add water. But by the same token, water has a passive potentiality for becoming milk: one need merely add milk powder. Passive potentialities include cases ranging from, at the one end, 'almost active' potentialities, where almost all of the positive factors are present in the entity, and very little has to be added, through to cases, at the other end, of almost totally passive potentialities, where nearly all of the relevant factors have to be added, and where there is little more than a bare receptivity to change imposed from without. To characterize potential persons as entities that have a passive potentiality for becoming persons would have the consequence that random collections of matter that could, with sufficient knowledge and technological advances, be transformed into human organisms, would have to be classified as potential persons.

What one needs to do, apparently, is to pick out a certain range of passive potentialities, toward the active potentiality end of the spectrum, and define the concept of a potential person in terms of that. This range could conceivably be characterized in some precise way, but I cannot see how such a precise specification could be arrived at other than by an arbitrary decision. The alternative is a vague characterization of the range:

> X is a *potential person* if and only if X has all, or almost all, of the properties of a positive sort that together would be causally sufficient to bring it about that X gives rise to a person, and there are no factors present within X that would block the causal process in question.

Similarly, a latent person can be characterized as follows:

> X is a *latent person* if and only if X has all, or almost all, of the properties of a positive sort that together would be causally sufficient to bring it about that X gives rise to a person, together with one or more properties that will block a causal process of the sort in question.

A question that naturally arises is this. If the notions of a potential person and a latent person necessarily involve either vague boundaries, or precise but arbitrary ones, doesn't this raise doubts with regard to the contention that these notions are morally important? This is a serious issue. However it will be best to leave the discussion of it until section 6.3, where the general question of the moral relevance of potentialities will be considered.

Finally, there is the notion of a possible person. This can be dealt with very briefly. To make what might be referred to as a statement about a possible person is just to say that there is some sort of event that might have occurred, or some sort of action that someone might have performed, or refrained from performing, that *would* have resulted in the existence of a person who does not exist as things actually are. So understood, statements about possible persons may be true without there being, anywhere in the world, any positive factors that are causally sufficient, or even almost sufficient, to bring about the existence of a person. The 'existence' of possible persons, so to speak, does not entail the existence of either potential persons or latent persons.

6.2 Potentialities and the Conservative Position on Abortion

Defenders of the conservative position on abortion hold that abortion is seriously wrong in itself, no matter how soon after conception it is performed. In this section I shall argue that when this position is thought through in a critical fashion, it appears to be the case that it stands or falls with the answer to be given to the question of the moral status of potential persons.

The reasons become clear if one considers attempts to defend a conservative view of abortion that do not make any appeal to potentialities. One such line of thought points to the gradual and continuous development of an organism as it changes from a zygote into an adult human being. An advocate of this approach contends that it is arbitrary for a defender of a liberal or moderate position on abortion to draw a line at some point in this continuous process, and to say that abortion is permissible before, but not after, that particular point.

This defence of the anti-abortionist view is unsound. All that follows from the assumption that the development of a human organism is a gradual and continuous process is that if there is some doubt as to precisely what properties make something a person, then it will presumably be impossible to find some point in the development of a human organism such that one is justified in holding that the destruction of a human organism is morally permissible at any stage prior to that point, but morally wrong at any stage thereafter.

It is true that some anti-abortionists have tried to argue that if one cannot justify drawing a line between successive stages in this way, the same moral status must be ascribed to a human organism at every stage of development. That this argument is fallacious can be seen by comparing it with the following argument. Consider a series of objects, starting with a very heavy one, followed by one that is a hundredth of a gram lighter, followed by another that is another hundredth of a gram lighter, and so on down to an object that is very light indeed. It is impossible to find two successive objects, one of which is heavy, and the other not. So we must conclude that all of the objects are heavy. The point is simply that the absence of significant differences between successive members of some series, or between successive stages in some process, provides no reason at all for concluding that there are no significant differences between non-successive stages or members.[1]

As a consequence, even if a pro-abortionist cannot find successive stages such that the destruction of a human organism is morally permissible at the one, but morally wrong at the other, he *may* nevertheless be justified in picking out non-successive stages, and holding that killing is morally permissible at or before the one, and morally wrong at or after the other. Furthermore, if it turns out that the only morally relevant feature of a foetus is whether or not it is a person, then it seems very likely indeed that pro-abortionists *will* be justified in holding that there are non-successive stages with these properties. The reason is this. First, as was argued in the previous chapter, it seems plausible to hold that whatever doubts there may be as to precisely what properties make something a person, an entity cannot be a person unless it has developed to the point where it is capable of at least some sort of mental life. Second, our knowledge of the relation between states of the brain and states of the mind would seem to make it most unlikely that a human organism is capable of enjoying any mental life at all before it has acquired a central nervous system. The fact that the development of a human organism is a gradual and continuous process thus

[1] For a very careful and incisive discussion of arguments such as the above, see Donald Van De Veer's article, 'Justifying "Wholesale Slaughter"', in the *Canadian Journal of Philosophy*, Vol. 5, No. 2, 1975, pp. 245–58.

provides no reason for holding that a human being is a person at every stage of its development.

It might be objected, however, to the second part of this response, that the capacities in question may not have a physical basis. Perhaps they are capacities of an immaterial entity, and one that is present from conception onward. Unless there are reasons for viewing this hypothesis as implausible, one will not be justified in holding that it is unlikely that the capacities are present prior to the development of the central nervous system.

What support might be offered for the claim that there is some non-physical entity—the soul—that is present from conception, and in which the relevant capacities reside? Given that there does not seem to be any evidence of the exercise of such capacities prior to the relevant development of the brain, it is hard to see how one could offer empirical support for the hypothesis. However, there are at least two other sorts of appeals that are possible. The one is that the hypothesis in question is a divinely revealed truth. The other is that it can be supported by philosophical argument.

As regards the former, I believe that there are excellent reasons for holding that it is not a divinely revealed truth that humans have, at every point in their development, immaterial souls that possess the morally relevant capacities. A satisfactory defence of this claim would require, however, a rather lengthy digression into the field of philosophy of religion—a digression that I do not believe is justified in the present context.

What about the second suggestion? Can the thesis that humans have souls, from conception onward, be defended by philosophical argument? This issue will be taken up in section 11.4, where I shall argue that such an approach is not satisfactory.

Let us now consider some other ways in which one might attempt to defend an anti-abortionist position without appealing to potentialities. A second possibility is to argue that membership in a particular biological species can be morally significant in itself, and decisively so, and that the reason abortion is seriously wrong is that it is intrinsically wrong to kill any member of the species *Homo sapiens*. This view was examined, and rejected, in chapter 4.

A third way of attempting to defend a conservative position is to maintain that a human organism is an intrinsically valuable object at every stage of its development, and is so *independently of the fact that it will develop into a person.* This is not, it must be said, a line of argument that anti-abortionists typically advance, and a little reflection makes it clear why it is not. For what could there be about a human organism—once its potentialities are set aside—that would make it intrinsically valuable? One suggestion might be complexity of structure. But given that there are many animals whose structure is more complex than that of a human zygote, and whose destruction is not considered seriously wrong, it seems clear that this explanation will not do. As it is hard to think of plausible alternatives, this approach does not seem promising.

The situation, then, seems to be as follows. The conservative believes that abortion is seriously wrong—comparable, in fact, to the killing of a normal adult human being. On the other hand, though he may believe that it is wrong to kill kittens for no good reason, he does not view the wrongness as at all comparable to that of destroying even a human zygote. The problem that confronts him is how this view can be justified. What morally significant difference is there between a human zygote and a kitten that supports the contention that the killing of the former is seriously wrong in a way that the killing of the latter is not? The popular anti-abortionist appeal to the fact that human zygotes belong to the species *Homo sapiens,* and kittens do not, is unacceptable. Nor can he plausibly hold that human zygotes are persons, while kittens are not. Nor does it seem to be the case, if one focuses only upon the non-potential properties of human zygotes and kittens, and not upon the properties they may later acquire, that there is any property, possessed by human zygotes, but not by kittens, that provides a reason for viewing the former as intrinsically much more valuable than the latter. It would seem, then, that a conservative position on abortion cannot possibly be correct unless the property of being a potential person is in itself a morally significant property, and seriously so.

There are different claims that a conservative on abortion

might advance that would entail that being a potential person is a morally significant property. The most natural, presumably, would be:

(1) Potential persons have a right to continued existence.

In section 5.2 I argued, however, that the concept of a right is such that not just any entity can have rights, and also, that there are different conditions a thing must satisfy to be a *possible* possessor of various rights. In the case of the right to continued existence, I argued that unless there is some time at which a thing possesses the concept of a continuing self or mental substance, it cannot be the sort of thing that can have that right.

If this is correct, then the claim that potential persons have a right to continued existence cannot be a sound basic moral principle, since it is certainly possible for there to be potential persons that do not possess, at any time, the concept of a continuing self. But it is also clear that it cannot even be a sound derived moral principle: human zygotes are potential persons, but they do not, it would seem, possess the concept of a continuing self.

One way of avoiding this difficulty is by abandoning claim (1) in favour of:

(2) Potential persons are intrinsically valuable objects.

This claim also leads to difficulties. The fact that a certain type of object is intrinsically valuable certainly constitutes a reason for not destroying such objects. But it is also a reason for bringing such things into existence. So if the conservative on abortion appeals to (2), he is confronted with the problem of showing why abortion is seriously wrong, while merely refraining from reproduction is not. Unless, of course, he is prepared to argue that people are under a *very* serious prima-facie obligation to propagate.

It seems best to avoid such difficulties by advancing a more modest claim:

(3) The destruction of potential persons is intrinsically wrong, and seriously so.

It is claim (3), after all, that the conservative on abortion

needs if he is to defend his position. The point of advancing
either claim (1) or claim (2) is to advance claim (3), and to
offer some explanation of why the destruction of potential
persons is intrinsically wrong. The explanations in question,
however, involve the anti-abortionist in additional difficulties
of a very serious sort. It seems best to avoid these unnecessary difficulties by confining oneself to the most modest
claim that can provide the basis for a defence of the conservative position on abortion, namely, claim (3).

What I have attempted to show, then, is that a necessary
condition for the conservative's position being defensible is
that claim (3) be correct. Is this also sufficient? If the destruction of potential persons is intrinsically wrong, and seriously
so, does it follow that the conservative view is correct?

In some earlier discussions I assumed that this was so.
However, R. M. Hare has shown that this is a mistake.[2] The
essential point is simply this. In the first place, there is no
incompatibility between the contention that the destruction
of potential persons is intrinsically wrong and the claim that
there is a basic obligation to actualize possible persons.
Indeed, if there is an obligation to actualize possible persons,
it follows that it is wrong to destroy potential persons. And
then, in view of the fact that whatever is entailed by a basic
moral principle must itself be a basic moral principle, it
follows that if it is intrinsically wrong to refrain from actualizing possible persons, it must also be intrinsically wrong to
destroy potential persons. Second, it might also be the case
that the *only* reason it is intrinsically wrong to destroy potential persons is that one is thereby failing to actualize a possible person. If the latter were the case, an extreme conservative
view on abortion would not be correct, for the following
reason. Compare the action of having an abortion, and then
having another child, with the action of refraining from
having an abortion, and not having another child. The conservative on abortion holds that the former action is seriously
wrong, but that the latter is either not wrong at all, or at least
not as seriously so as the former. This view could not be

---

defended by appealing to the wrongness of destroying potential persons if it were wrong to destroy potential persons only
because one is thereby failing to actualize possible ones. For
both the woman who aborts, but then has another child, and
the woman who does not abort, but who does not have a
second child, actualize one possible person and refrain from
actualizing another. Their actions would therefore have to be
viewed as being morally on a par, on the hypothesis in
question.

The relationship between the conservative position on
abortion and the question of the moral status of potential
persons may, therefore, be summed up as follows. There
appears to be little hope of defending a conservative view
unless it can be shown that the destruction of potential
persons is intrinsically wrong, and seriously so. This is not,
however, sufficient. One would also have to show either that
refraining from actualizing possible persons is not intrinsically
wrong, or that, it if is, the wrongness of destroying potential
persons cannot be adequately explained in terms of it, so that
destroying potential persons is more seriously wrong than
merely refraining from actualizing possible persons.

6.3 The Morality of Destroying Potential Persons

Is it intrinsically wrong to destroy potential persons? In this
section I shall set out a number of arguments in support of
the view that it is not. Some of the arguments are, I believe,
unsatisfactory, for reasons which I shall indicate. The remain-
ing arguments seem to me correct. Objections to them will be
considered in subsequent sections.

Argument 1: Identity Conditions and Potential Persons

This first argument is an attempt to apply a line of argument
used above, in connection with persons, to the case of potential persons. The argument involves two contentions. First,
that if it were possible to programme a given set of beliefs,
attitudes, and personality traits into a developing potential
person, subsequent reprogramming would not be wrong
provided that it was done while the organism was still merely

a potential person. Second, that such reprogramming would necessarily alter the identity of the potential person, since it might well result in the actualization of a completely different possible person. But if the identity of the potential person has been altered, then one potential person has been destroyed, and another created. Now in the case of persons, we certainly do not think it is morally permissible to destroy one person, provided that another is thereby produced. How then can one account for the fact that it does not seem wrong to destroy one potential person, provided that we produce another? Isn't the explanation simply that it is not wrong to destroy potential persons?

This argument does not seem entirely satisfactory. It does, I believe, have force when it is directed against the claim that potential persons have a right to life. Rights attach to individuals, and one is not justified in violating one individual's right to continued existence in order to produce some other individual with a comparable right. But if it is being asserted only that the destruction of potential persons is wrong, and not that they have a right to continued existence, the argument is not successful. For it may be that the reason it is wrong to destroy potential persons is that they are intrinsically valuable entities. If that were so, one would have a perfectly good explanation of why it was not wrong to destroy one potential person, provided one produced another. Reflection on the identity conditions for potential persons does not seem to show that the destruction of potential persons is not intrinsically wrong.

Argument 2: Persons Versus Potential Persons

The second argument is one set out by Mary Anne Warren in her very well-known article on the morality of abortion:

Suppose that our space explorer falls into the hands of an alien culture, whose scientists decide to create a few hundred thousand or more human beings, by breaking his body into its component cells, and using these to create fully developed human beings, with, of course, his genetic code. We may imagine that each of these newly created men will have all of the original man's abilities, skills, knowledge, and so on, and also have an individual self-concept, in short that each of them will be a bona fide (though hardly unique) person. Imagine that the whole project will take only seconds, and that its chances of success are extremely high, and that our explorer knows all of this, and also knows that these people will be treated fairly. I maintain that in such a situation he would have every right to escape if he could, and thus to deprive all of these potential people of their potential lives; for his right to life outweighs all of theirs together, in spite of the fact that they are all genetically human, all innocent, and all have a very high probability of becoming people very soon, if only he refrains from acting.[3]

In a more recent article she refers to this line of argument, and indicates that she no longer wants to rest much weight upon it:

Unfortunately, arguments of this sort, which appeal to our intuitions regarding unusual or bizarre situations, are never conclusive. Proponents of the potentiality principle may well have intuitions different from my own, and even if they do not the case is still not closed, since our intuitions about such cases, while they may serve to clarify (the consequences of) our existing moral convictions, cannot establish what our moral convictions *ought* to be. The potentiality principle, like any specific moral claim, must ultimately be defended or refuted on the basis of some overall conception of the nature of morality.[4]

Though I certainly agree with Warren's insistence on the need to defend moral claims by reference to a general theory of morality, rather than by appealing to moral intuitions, I feel that the argument is being set aside too quickly, and for the wrong reason. For I think that many people who would hold that it is wrong to destroy potential persons would also share her feelings about the 'bizarre' case in question. If this is right, the case would seem to point to an inconsistency in the attitudes of at least many conservatives on abortion with respect to the moral status of potential persons, and hence would provide such people with an excellent reason for reconsidering their position.

The real problem with the argument is that it does not in fact do this. For I think that a conservative who shared Warren's intuitions about this case would argue that the morally relevant construal of the expression 'potential person'

[3] Mary Anne Warren, 'On the Moral and Legal Status of Abortion', *Monist*. Volume 57, Number 1, 1973, pp. 43–61. See pp. 59–60.

[4] Mary Anne Warren, 'Do Potential People Have Moral Rights?', *Canadian Journal of Philosophy*, Vol. 7, No. 2, 1977, pp. 275–89. See p. 278.

is such that, while human foetuses are potential persons,
human cells are not. If this is right, there is no inconsistency
in the attitudes in question.

This response does not show there is nothing of value in
the argument. It shows only that there is an assumption that
is crucial to the argument, but which Warren does not make
explicit, and hence does not argue for, namely, that there is
no morally significant interpretation of 'potential' according
to which human foetuses, but not human cells, are potential
persons.

Argument 3: The Unrestricted Potentiality Principle

The structure of this third argument is as follows. The potentiality principle that the conservative on abortion requires is
really a restricted version of a more general principle. Moreover, the restricted principle is acceptable only if the unrestricted principle is also acceptable. The general principle,
however, has consequences which are clearly unacceptable.

What is the most modest principle that the anti-abortionist
can employ in defending his position? I suggest that it is the
following:

The Biologically Restricted Potentiality Principle

The destruction of a biologically unified potential person
is intrinsically wrong, and seriously so, where X is a biologically unified potential person if and only if X is a biological organism and X has all, or almost all of the properties
of a positive sort that together would be causally sufficient
to bring it about that X develops into a person, and there
are no factors present within X that would block the
causal process in question.

There is a weaker principle which might be proposed, namely:

It is intrinsically wrong, and seriously so, to kill any biological organism that is a potential person.

This more modest principle would not, however, be adequate.
The reason is that just as it is possible to destroy a person
without killing any organism, so it is also possible to destroy

a potential person without killing any organism. If the conservative on abortion were to rely on the second, more modest principle, he would have no way of ruling out, as morally wrong, two-step abortions in which a chemical that destroys all potentiality for developing into a person is first injected into the brain of the foetus, and then the organism, now no longer a potential person, is destroyed. The principle employed must rule out all destruction of biologically unified potential persons, not merely the killing of such organisms.

The next step in the argument involves the contention that if the biologically restricted potentiality principle is acceptable, so is the following:

The Unrestricted Potentiality Principle
The destruction of a potential person is intrinsically wrong, and seriously so, where X is a potential person if and only if X is an entity, or system of entities, that has all, or almost all of the properties of a positive sort that together would be causally sufficient to bring it about that X gives rise to a person, and where there are no factors present within X that would block the causal process in question.

In this unrestricted form, the potentiality principle applies not only to biological individuals, but also to non-biological individuals, and to systems of entities that are causally interrelated in the appropriate way.

What reason is there for holding that the biologically restricted potentiality principle cannot be acceptable unless the unrestricted principle is also acceptable? The basic thought is simply that if it is wrong to destroy biologically unified potential persons, what reason can there be other than that it is wrong to destroy a certain sort of potentiality? The fact that the potentiality is realized in one way, namely, biologically, rather than in some other, surely cannot be morally relevant.

This view can be reinforced, I think, by reflecting upon some possibilities concerning persons. The persons with whom we are at present acquainted tend to be biological—gods, angels, and devils notwithstanding. However, there is reason to believe that it is possible in principle to construct a complex electronic computer whose sensory, linguistic, and intellectual capacities would be comparable to those of a normal adult human being, and which would at least behave as if it enjoyed sensations, thoughts, feelings, desires, and so on. On some philosophical theories of the mind—such as logical behaviourism and central state materialism—an electronic device with these characteristics would have to be classified as a person. On other theories—such as dualism, and emergent materialism—it would be an open question whether it really enjoyed mental states and hence whether it was a person. For while a dualist, for example, might think that it would be very unlikely that such a device would have a mind, the idea of there being an immaterial mental substance connected in certain ways with a complex electronic computer is in itself logically no more problematic than the idea of such a substance's being associated with certain biological entities. On any theory, then, it is at least logically possible that there should be electronic persons.

If electronic persons are possible, then so are potential electronic persons. That is, there could be an electronic device that, although it did not possess those properties that make something a person, was so programmed that it would alter its own circuitry in such a way that it would come to have those (possibly emergent) properties that make something a person.

The fact that something was an electronic person rather than a biological one would not be morally significant. What matters is that something is a subject of non-momentary interests, or that it possesses self-consciousness, etc., and not whether these properties are biologically or electronically based. And surely it is equally true that if something has the potential of developing into a person, it does not matter whether it will develop into a biological person or an electronic one.

As a consequence, it is unreasonable to accept the biologically restricted potentiality principle without also accepting a corresponding principle dealing with electronic persons. Moreover, it will not do simply to add a principle covering the latter, since the same argument can be repeated for other types of potential persons. As regards computers, for example, whatever can be done electronically can be done mechanically, albeit much more slowly. So if electronic persons are logically possible, so are mechanical ones, and the potentiality principle will have to be extended to cover potential mechanical persons.

Still, might it not be possible to stop short of the unrestricted potentiality principle, by confining the principle to individuals, and refusing to apply it to systems of entities? I think that this can be shown to be unjustified. The first point to note is that there is nothing incoherent in the notion of a person with spatially separated parts. It is, as Strawson argues in Chapter 3 of *Individuals*, only a contingent fact that a given person's experiences are dependent upon states of a single biological organism.[5] Imagine, for example, that you find yourself involuntarily participating in an experiment conducted by an innovative scientist, which involves cutting your head in half along the plane between the two hemispheres of the brain, and then keeping the parts alive. The experiment, unfortunately, is not completely successful, as you have the feeling that you are now only half—or perhaps it is twice—the person you were before.[6] Undaunted, the scientist constructs a radio linkage between the two halves of the brain, and the result is most gratifying. You now experience bodily sensations associated with both halves of your head. You are able to control muscles on either side. You enjoy a unified field of consciousness which once again involves input from sense organs on both sides of your head —although your visual experience may well be of the split-screen variety, if half your head happens to be in New York, and the other half in London.

Perhaps it is not especially likely that such an experiment would in fact have this result. All that matters here, however, is that such an outcome is at least conceivable. If it is, it establishes two important conclusions. First, it is not logically

[5] P. F. Strawson, *Individuals*, 1959, pp. 90-2.

[6] For an account of what happens when the connections between the two hemispheres of the brain are severed, together with a discussion of the possible philosophical implications, see Thomas Nagel's article, 'Brain Bisection and the Unity of Consciousness', pp. 111-25 in *The Philosophy of Mind*, edited by Jonathan Glover, 1976.

necessary that a person's body be a spatially connected whole. Nor is it necessary that all of its parts be of the same general type—such as, all biological, or all electronic. It is logically possible for a person's body to be a whole that is unified causally, rather than spatially, and for its parts to be of different general types.

Given that this is true of persons, what reason could there be for denying that the same can be true of potential persons? If it is wrong to destroy potential persons of a biologically unified sort or of an electronically unified sort, must it not be equally wrong to destroy potential persons that involve either different types of parts, or parts that are spatially separated, but causally connected, or both? It would seem, then, that it is unreasonable to accept the biologically restricted potentiality principle without also accepting the unrestricted potentiality principle.

The argument now proceeds as follows. In the future, it will be possible to construct a machine that will bring together a human sperm cell and an ovum, and then sustain the life of the resulting organism until it becomes capable of independent existence. Suppose that a sperm cell and an unfertilized ovum have been placed in such a machine, and it has been started up. The total system has the potential of giving rise to a person. Indeed, it has a totally active potentiality in this respect, in contrast to that possessed by a human zygote. The zygote requires external assistance—the provision of nutrients and warmth, and the disposal of waste—whereas the system requires nothing beyond the absence of interference. Consider, now, the possibility of doing something to the mechanical part of this system so that the spermatozoon and ovum are never brought together: a conveyor belt carrying the sperm cell to the ovum is cut, so that they languish and die. Is such an action seriously wrong, in the way that killing a normal adult human being is wrong? I suggest that very few people indeed would accept this view. Yet if one applies the unrestricted potentiality principle to the situation, it implies that such an action is intrinsically wrong, and seriously so. The unrestricted potentiality principle thus has consequences that are inconsistent with almost everyone's moral views. Those who are not willing to revise those views must therefore reject the unrestricted potentiality principle. And thus, in view of the argument offered above, to the effect that acceptance of the biologically restricted potentiality principle is reasonable only if acceptance of the unrestricted potentiality principle is also reasonable, it follows that such people must also reject the view that it is intrinsically wrong, and seriously so, to destroy a biological organism possessing the potentiality of developing into a person.

Argument 4: 'Almost Active' Potentialities

A human zygote does not possess the active potentiality for giving rise to a person. This fact made it necessary to adopt, in section 6.1, the somewhat vague characterization of a potential person as an entity having all, *or almost all*, of the properties that are causally sufficient . . . etc. It also makes it possible to extend the previous argument from systems of entities possessing the active potentiality for giving rise to a person to systems almost possessing it.

Consider, then, a system consisting of a woman together with a collection of spermatozoa which could be used to bring about fertilization. This system of living things does not possess the active potentiality for giving rise to a person. But it would seem to be at least as close to having that potentiality as a human zygote *on its own*, and almost as close as a system involving a human zygote inside a woman. And while it is perhaps conceivable that there should be some great moral divide between things with a certain active potentiality, and things that almost have it, it is surely very implausible to hold that there is any sharp difference between two things that almost have a certain potentiality, by virtue of the fact that the one is slightly closer to having it than the other. Any difference should be at most one of degree.

The conclusion is this. *If* it is seriously wrong to destroy a human zygote inside a woman, and is so because one is thereby destroying an 'almost active' potentiality for giving rise to a person, then it must be almost as seriously wrong to destroy the 'almost active' potentiality associated either with an isolated human zygote, or with a system consisting of a normal woman and a collection of spermatozoa. The potentiality

associated with the latter could, however, be destroyed by
means of spermicide. The question, then, is whether the
anti-abortionist is prepared to maintain that the destruction
of sperm, given the presence of willing and able women, is
seriously wrong. If not, it would seem that he cannot be
justified in holding that it is seriously wrong to destroy the
'almost active' potentiality inherent in biologically unified
potential persons.

Argument 5: The Moral Symmetry Principle

A fifth argument in support of the claim that the destruction
of potential persons is not intrinsically wrong turns upon
what I have referred to as the moral symmetry principle. A
rough formulation of this principle was given in section 5.4,
in connection with the question of the moral relevance of
capacities. In this chapter we shall need to take a much closer
look at the principle, and examine objections to it.

Precisely how should the principle be formulated? Perhaps
the best way to approach this question is by considering how
moral principles in general should be expressed. It turns out
that there are some important options with respect to the
fundamental notions to be employed. Often, the concept
of a *prima-facie duty* is taken as the basic ethical notion,
so that moral principles are viewed as stating prima-facie
duties.

This approach has the drawback, however, that the notion
of a prima-facie duty does not, in itself, discriminate between
obligations arising from basic moral principles, and those
arising from derived moral principles. This distinction might
be introduced by means of counter-factual statements as
follows: prima-facie duties that would exist in all possible
worlds correspond to basic moral principles; those of a sort
that would not exist if the world were different in certain
ways correspond to derived moral principles.

This approach is, however, rather roundabout. There are,
moreover, reasons for wanting to avoid the use of counter-
factuals, and references to 'possible worlds', in offering
analyses of concepts. An alternative approach, which does
this, takes the notion of a *wrong-making characteristic* as

basic. One can then explain, in a direct fashion, and without counter-factuals or references to 'possible worlds', both the notion of a prima-facie duty and the distinction between basic and derived moral principles.

The concept of a wrong-making characteristic is not, however, adequate by itself; this approach needs to be augmented in at least two ways. The first is reflected in the fact that most philosophers who have spoken of wrong-making characteristics have also used the notion of *right-making characteristics*. Now it might seem, at first, that this is simply a historical accident, and that from a logical point of view, only the notion of wrong-making characteristics is necessary. However we shall see, in section 6.5, that the attempt to get by with only the one notion involves a conceptually confused view of the characteristics of an action.

The second point is this. Some actions are more seriously wrong than others. The notion of a wrong-making characteristic does not, by itself, provide a way of expressing such facts. One needs a slightly more complicated notion, namely, that of a function relating characteristics of actions to some measure of their intrinsic wrongness.

This functional notion is necessary for another reason. It may be that all the actions open to one possess at least one wrong-making characteristic. Perhaps the only way that one can avoid killing someone is by breaking a promise. One needs to be able to compare the wrongness of killing someone with the wrongness of breaking a promise. One way of doing this is by using some method based upon a measure of the extent to which an action is rendered intrinsically wrong by various characteristics.

It is important to notice that this conceptual approach does not preclude the possibility of absolute moral rules—of rules that should never be broken, whatever the consequences. For the function assigning, to characteristics of actions, some measure of the extent to which actions are wrong by virtue of the possession of those characteristics, can certainly assign infinite weight to one or more characteristics. So there is no problem about capturing the notion of an absolute moral rule within this conceptual framework.

Given this conceptual framework, it is possible to offer a

more precise statement of the moral symmetry principle than
that employed in section 5.4.

Basic Moral Symmetry Principle

Let C be any type of causal process where there is some
type of occurrence, E, such that processes of type C would
possess no intrinsic moral significance were it not for the
fact that they result in occurrences of type E.

Then:

The characteristic of being an act of intervening in a
process of type C that prevents the occurrence of an outcome of type E makes an action intrinsically wrong to
precisely the same degree as does the characteristic of
being an act of ensuring that a causal process of type C,
which it was in one's power to initiate, does not get
initiated.

Is this principle sound? Some philosophers have argued
that it is not, and in section 6.5 I shall take a careful look at
those arguments. In the present section the discussion will be
confined to a preliminary defence of the principle.

Let us begin by asking why some people think that the
principle is unsound. One main reason is that they believe
that there is an important moral distinction between 'what
we owe people in the form of aid and what we owe them in
the way of noninterference,'[7] and that it is more serious to
neglect the latter, 'negative duties', than it is to neglect the
former, 'positive' ones.

For support, this view can appeal to people's intuitions
concerning cases such as the following. Even if it is wrong not
to send food to starving people in other parts of the world, is
it not even more wrong to kill someone? And doesn't this
imply, then, that one's obligation to refrain from killing someone is more serious than one's obligation to save lives?

The moral symmetry principle appears to be incompatible
with this conclusion. For let C be some causal process going

[7] Philippa Foot. 'The Problem of Abortion and the Doctrine of the Double
Effect', *The Oxford Review*, Number 5, 1967, pp. 5–15. See the discussion on
pp. 11 ff.

on within someone's body that is necessary to sustain the individual's life. The process might involve, for example, circulation of the blood. If one disrupts such a process, one will have killed someone. In contrast, if an individual's heart has just stopped beating, and one refrains from starting it up, and therefore from initiating the type of process in question, one has not killed anyone. One has simply failed to save someone. According to the moral symmetry principle, however, interference with the process is morally on a par with refraining from initiating such a process. The principle appears to assert, then, that the characteristic of being an act of killing a person is no more serious a wrong-making characteristic than that of being an act of failing to save someone. Therefore, if the above view is sound, the moral symmetry principle must be rejected.

This attempt to show that the moral symmetry principle is inconsistent with common moral intuitions involves, I believe, a failure to distinguish two very different sorts of moral claims. On the one hand, there are claims about wrong-making characteristics; on the other, claims about the extent to which actions possessing certain characteristics are *generally wrong, all things considered*. It is only claims of the first sort, not claims of the second sort, that are entailed by the moral symmetry principle. Thus, while it entails that being a case of killing, and being a case of failing to save, are equally weighty wrong-making characteristics, it does not imply that acts of killing are, in general, and all things considered, no more seriously wrong than acts of failing to save someone.

The crucial question, then, is which of these two types of claims can be supported by the intuitions that are being appealed to when it is claimed that killing is morally worse than merely failing to save. What I want to maintain is that they support only judgements of the second sort; they do not support any claim about the relative weights of wrong-making characteristics.

The reason is this. When one is asked to compare acts of killing and acts of failing to save, one naturally considers typical cases. Such cases will tend to differ in other respects that are morally significant, with the result that in comparing typical acts of killing with typical acts of failing to save, one is being moved by differences other than that between killing and letting die. Thus, for example, the *motivation* likely to be associated with the two types of actions is different. If someone performs an action he knows will kill someone else, this will usually be grounds for concluding that he wanted to kill that person. In contrast, failing to help someone may indicate only apathy, laziness, selfishness, or an amoral outlook: the fact that a person knowingly allows another to die will not normally be grounds for concluding that he desired that person's death. Someone who knowingly kills another is thus likely to be more seriously defective from a moral point of view than someone who fails to save another's life.

Another typical difference is this. Action usually involves more effort than inaction. It does not generally require any effort on my part to refrain from killing someone, but saving someone's life may often require a large expenditure of energy. One must therefore ask how large a sacrifice a person is morally required to make in order to save the life of another. If the sacrifice of time and energy, or the potential risk involved, is quite large, it may be that one is not morally obliged to save the life of another, in that situation. Superficial consideration of such cases might lead one to introduce the distinction between positive and negative duties, but again it should be clear that to do so is probably to advance an incorrect explanation of one's moral intuitions. The point, it would seem, is not that one has a greater duty to refrain from killing others than to perform actions that will save them, other things being equal. It is rather that positive actions may often involve significant cost or risk—factors that are certainly relevant to any decision about what to do. If the potential cost, or risk, is very high, this may outweigh one's prima-facie obligation to save someone else.

A third morally relevant difference between typical acts of killing, and of failing to save, is that an act is not a killing unless it results in someone's death, whereas one may fail to save someone who is then rescued by someone else. Again, if our moral responses are not to lead us astray, we must confine our attention to cases in which the failure to save someone inevitably results in that person's death.

The argument, then, is that typical cases of killing and

failing to save differ in a number of morally significant respects, among which the most important are the agent's motivation, the cost and risk involved, and the probability that death will result. If one wants to appeal to moral intuitions in order to evaluate the moral symmetry principle, one must be careful to confine one's attention to pairs of cases that do not differ in these, or other significant respects. And I am suggesting that when people feel that the principle is unacceptable, it is because they are considering pairs of cases that do differ in other morally significant respects.

Let us consider two examples where such differences are absent. First, compare the following: (1) Jones is about to shoot Smith, when he sees that Smith will be killed by a bomb unless he warns him. Jones's reaction is: 'How fortunate —that will save me the trouble of killing him myself.' So Jones allows Smith to be killed by the bomb, even though he could easily have warned him. (2) Jones wants Smith dead, and shoots him. In the former case, Jones has merely refrained from saving Smith's life. In the latter, he has killed Smith. Yet most people presented with such a case do not seem to feel that the two actions differ with respect to the degree of moral wrongness.

A second, slightly less direct example, is this. A diabolical machine contains two innocent children, John and Mary. An observer has sufficient information about the construction of the machine to know that no matter what he does, one of the children will perish, and one will emerge unharmed. He also knows that if he pushes a certain button, it will alter the situation so that the child that would have died will survive, while the child that would have survived will now be destroyed. He has no way of knowing, however, whether it is John, or Mary, who will survive if he pushes the button.

How does pushing the button compare with doing nothing? If he pushes the button, he initiates a causal chain that leads to the destruction of one of the children. He will have killed one of the children, though he does not know which one. On the other hand, if he does not push the button, he does not initiate any causal chain, and so he has not killed anyone. He has merely refrained from saving one of the children. But even though this is so, does one really want to say that the action of intentionally refraining from pushing the button is morally preferable to the action of pushing it, in spite of the fact that precisely one innocent child perishes in either case? The best action, it seems to me, might be to flip a coin to decide which action to perform, thus giving each person an equal chance of surviving. But if that is not possible, it seems to me a matter of indifference whether one pushes the button or not. And again, most people with whom I have discussed this example apparently share these intuitions.

These two examples seem to provide considerable support for the view that the moral symmetry principle is, first impressions notwithstanding, quite in accordance with our ordinary moral intuitions, and that it only seems counter-intuitive if one fails to get clear precisely what the principle asserts. However there are some questions that need to be raised about these two appeals to intuitions. This is especially so in the case of the diabolical machine. These issues will be discussed in section 6.5.

There is a way in which one can reduce the initial appearance of counter-intuitiveness that the moral symmetry principle has for many people. That is by explicitly building into the statement of the principle reference to other morally relevant factors that may be present in typical cases, and which may make a difference in the wrongness of the two actions. Thus, one might specify that the motivation should be the same in the two cases, that the action should involve no risk, and minimal expenditure of energy, that the actions should have no further consequences, and that the actions should be intentional.

The advantage of this type of formulation, which I have adopted elsewhere, is that it explicitly draws attention to factors that must be kept constant in evaluating the principle. But there are also disadvantages. The resulting principle is necessarily more complex, and the fundamental claim being advanced is to some extent concealed. On the whole, then, the present approach seems best. The moral symmetry principle itself is set out in its most basic form, that is, as a claim that two sorts of characteristics of actions are wrong-making to precisely the same degree. One can then go on to emphasize that, in evaluating this principle, it is necessary—

just as it is in evaluating any principle about wrong-making characteristics—to take into account other characteristics that particular actions may have, and that may enter into one's over-all evaluation of the action.

Given this more precise formulation of the moral symmetry principle, and preliminary defence of it, let us turn to the statement of the fifth argument against the view that the destruction of potential persons is intrinsically wrong. Suppose that at some time in the future a chemical is discovered that, when injected into the brain of a kitten, causes it to develop into a cat possessing a brain of the sort possessed by normal adult human beings. Such cats will be able to think, to use language, to make decisions, to envisage a future for themselves, and so on—since they will have all of the psychological capacities possessed by adult humans. If one maintains that it is seriously wrong to kill adult members of the species *Homo sapiens*, one must also, in view of the discussion in chapter 4, hold that it would be seriously wrong to kill cats that have undergone such a process of development.

Second, imagine that one has two kittens, one of which has been injected with the special chemical, but which has not yet developed those properties that, in themselves, make something a person, and the other of which has not been injected with the chemical. Compare now the actions of injecting the former with a 'neutralizing' substance that will interfere with the transformation process and prevent the kitten from developing those properties that would make it a person, and the action of intentionally refraining from injecting the second kitten with the special chemical. It is possible that both actions are prima facie seriously wrong. The basic moral symmetry principle has no implications with respect to that issue. But it does entail that the former action is no more seriously wrong than the latter.

Third, compare a kitten that has been injected with the special chemical, and then had it neutralized, with a kitten that has never been injected with the chemical. It seems clear that it is no more seriously wrong to kill the former than the latter. For although their bodies have undergone different processes in the past, there is no reason why the two kittens need differ in any way with respect to either their present properties or their potentialities.

Fourth, again, consider two kittens, one of which has been injected with the special chemical, but which has not yet developed those properties that would make it a person, and the other of which has not been injected with the chemical. It follows from the previous two steps in the argument that the combined action of injecting the first kitten with the neutralizing substance and then killing it is prima facie no more seriously wrong than the combined action of intentionally refraining from injecting the second kitten with the special chemical and then killing it.

Fifth, one way of neutralizing the action of the special chemical is simply to kill the kitten. And since there is surely no reason to hold that it is more seriously wrong to neutralize the chemical and kill the kitten in a single step than in two successive steps, it follows that it is prima facie no more seriously wrong to kill a kitten that has been injected with the special chemical, but that has not yet developed into a person, than intentionally to refrain from injecting the special chemical into another kitten and then to kill it.

Next, compare a member of *Homo sapiens* that has not developed far enough to have those properties that make something a person, but that will later come to have them, with a kitten that has been injected with the special chemical, but that has not yet developed into a person. It is clear that it cannot be prima facie any more seriously wrong to kill the human organism than to kill the kitten. The potentialities are the same in both cases. Neither is yet a person. The only difference is that in the case of a human foetus the potentialities have been present from the beginning of the organism's development, while in the case of the kitten they have been present only from the time it was injected with the special chemical. This difference in the time at which the potentialities were acquired is surely not morally relevant.

It follows from the previous two steps in the argument that it is prima facie no more seriously wrong to kill a human organism that is a potential person, but not a person, than it is intentionally to refrain from injecting a kitten with the special chemical, and to kill it instead.

According to the potentiality principle, however, the destruction of potential persons is intrinsically wrong, and seriously so. If this were true, it would follow from the conclusion of the argument just stated that an action of intentionally refraining from injecting a kitten with the special chemical, and killing it instead, would be intrinsically wrong, and seriously so. Now most people would certainly want to reject this latter conclusion. Whether they are right in doing so, however, raises some difficult issues, as we shall see in chapter 7. But if the claim is defensible, it will follow, by virtue of the argument just stated, that the destruction of potential persons is not seriously wrong.

Why have I stated the argument in terms of kittens and chemicals with wondrous properties? After all, one could replace the references to kittens and special chemicals by references to unfertilized human egg cells and spermatozoa, and the argument offered would be unaffected. My reason for the more fanciful formulation is that it serves to establish a stronger conclusion, due to the fact that kittens possess consciousness, together with some other rudimentary mental states, while human egg cells do not. Because of this, the argument shows that the destruction of potential persons possessing consciousness (and a rudimentary mental life) is not seriously wrong. This stronger conclusion is not needed in connection with the conservative view of abortion, but it is relevant to some moderate positions, as we shall see in chapter 8.

For the moment, however, it may be helpful to put things in terms of spermatozoa and ova. The thrust of the argument, then, is that the destruction of a human organism that is a potential person, but not a person, is prima facie no more seriously wrong than intentionally refraining from fertilizing a human egg cell, and destroying it instead. Since intentionally refraining from procreation is surely not seriously wrong, neither is the destruction of potential persons.

But is it really clear that intentionally refraining from procreation is not intrinsically wrong, even seriously so? May there not be a serious prima-facie obligation to produce additional people, contrary to the intuitions of most people? In which case the present argument does not show that the conservative position on abortion is mistaken. It shows only that most conservatives, since they do not hold that intentionally refraining from procreation is *just as wrong* as destroying a potential person, accept an untenable combination of views. They must either abandon the view that the destruction of potential persons is seriously wrong, or else adopt the view that intentionally refraining from procreation is just as seriously wrong. But the present argument does not show that it is the former, rather than the latter, that should be done.

This critical point is well taken. The question of whether there is an obligation to produce additional persons, and perhaps even a very serious one, is both important and difficult, and it will not do to rest one's answer to it simply upon an appeal to common intuitions. I shall take a very careful look at this issue in the next chapter, where I shall attempt to show that refraining from producing additional people is not a serious wrong-making characteristic of actions. If my argument there is satisfactory, that conclusion, together with the present argument, will establish that the destruction of potential persons is not seriously wrong.

Argument 6: Moral Comparability Principles

Two variations on the preceding argument deserve to be at least briefly mentioned. They are suggested by the reflection that someone not quite convinced, for example, that failing to save is, in itself, just as seriously wrong as killing, may very well accept one of the following, weaker claims:

(1) Failing to save someone is, in itself, almost as seriously wrong as killing.

(2) Killing and failing to save are comparable in the technical sense of there being some number n such that failing to save n people is, in itself, more seriously wrong than killing one person.

These claims can be generalized into principles similar to, but more modest than, the basic moral symmetry principle. In the case of the second we have:

The Moral Comparability Principle

Let C be any type of causal process where there is some type of occurrence, E, such that processes of type C would possess no intrinsic moral significance were it not for the fact that they result in occurrences of type E.

Then:

There is some number n such that the characteristic of being an act of ensuring that n causal processes of type C, which it was within one's power to initiate, do not get initiated, makes an action intrinsically wrong to at least as great a degree as does the characteristic of being an act of intervening in a process of type C, thereby preventing the occurrence of an event of type E.

Given the moral comparability principle, one way of proceeding is simply to parallel the preceding argument. This will lead to the conclusion that there is some number n such that intentionally refraining from bringing into existence n persons is in itself at least as seriously wrong as destroying a potential person. Then, if it is granted that it is not seriously wrong intentionally to refrain from creating n persons, it follows that the destruction of a potential person is not seriously wrong.

Many would grant the additional assumption required here, on the ground that one is under no obligation at all to bring additional persons into existence. It is worth noting, however, that there is a variant of the argument that avoids this assumption, albeit at the cost of weakening the conclusion. Consider the moral status of destroying a potential person that, if allowed to become a person, will lead an unhappy life. The moral comparability principle implies that there is some number n such that the destruction of such a potential person is, in itself, no more seriously wrong than intentionally refraining from bringing into existence n people who will lead unhappy lives. If it is not seriously wrong to refrain from bringing into existence n people who will lead unhappy lives, it follows that it is not seriously wrong to destroy a potential person that will lead an unhappy life.

In the modified form, this sixth argument does not show that the destruction of potential persons is not intrinsically wrong. However, it still tells against the view of abortion that the overwhelming majority of conservatives advance, since they reject the claim that abortion is morally permissible where the resulting person will lead an unhappy life.

I have outlined six arguments in support of the view that the characteristic of being an act of destroying a potential person is not a wrong-making characteristic. The first two arguments appear unsound, for the reasons indicated. The other four arguments are, in my opinion, correct, and I shall attempt to defend this view by considering, in the next two sections, objections and counter-arguments that have been advanced in the philosophical literature.

6.4 Objections and Counter-arguments

There are two ways of responding to an argument. The one is to construct a counter-argument that leads to a denial of the claim in question. To the extent that one has reason to believe that the counter-argument is itself sound, one has reason to believe that something must be wrong with the original argument, even though one may not be able to say exactly where the problem lies. The other way of responding to argument involves showing precisely how the argument is unsound: a certain premiss is unacceptable, or a certain step in the reasoning is invalid.

In the present case there has been a striking lack of counter-arguments. There have been significant attempts to show that there is a prima-facie obligation to actualize *possible* persons, whether potential or not. There have also been attempts to show that potentialities are relevant in at least some contexts. But I know of no argument that both supports the claim that the destruction of potential persons is intrinsically wrong, and is compatible with the view that there is no prima-facie obligation to actualize possible persons. Most proponents of the view that the destruction of potential persons is intrinsically wrong exhibit no inclination to offer any support for this contention, in spite of the fact that arguments against it are well known.

Counter-arguments supporting the claim that there is a prima-facie obligation to actualize possible persons will be taken up in chapter 7. The discussion in the present section will be concerned mainly with some objections to two of the arguments advanced in the previous section, namely, the arguments based upon the unrestricted potentiality principle and upon the moral symmetry principle.

First, the argument based upon the unrestricted potentiality principle. Although advanced in 1973, there has been little discussion of it. The only person who, to my knowledge, has attempted to refute it, is Philip Devine. His response is as follows.[8] If one holds *only* that it is *intrinsically wrong* to kill organisms that are potential persons, then one should also hold that it is intrinsically wrong to destroy a potentiality for giving rise to a person, regardless of whether that potentiality is associated with a biologically unified individual, or with some system of causally interrelated entities. On the other hand, if one holds that *the reason* it is intrinsically wrong to destroy organisms that are potential persons is that such potential persons have *a right to life*, then there is no reason to hold that it is wrong to destroy such potentialities when they are not associated with biologically unified individuals, since only the latter can have a right to *life*. And since this *is* the reason why it is intrinsically wrong to destroy organisms that are potential persons, it follows that the argument based upon the unrestricted potentiality principle is unsound.

This objection is unsatisfactory for two reasons. In the first place, the claim that potential persons can have a right to life is extremely problematic, in view of the discussion of rights in section 5.2. And secondly, even if one grants, for the sake of discussion, that some potential persons can have a right to life, what reason is there for restricting this to organisms? The only ground that Devine offers is this: 'Only organisms can have a right to life. But the same point can be reached if we speak not in terms of a right to life but of a

---

[8] Philip Devine, 'Tooley on Infanticide', Eastern Division Meetings of the American Philosophical Association, 1973, pp. 7 ff. Devine also mentions the present argument, albeit more briefly, in his more recent work, *The Ethics of Homicide*, 1978, p. 75.

moral rule against certain kinds of killing, for only an organism can be killed.'[9]

In setting out the generalized potentiality argument in the previous section I have, however, already ruled out this move. Recall the relevant points. First, the notion of non-biological persons is not incoherent. There could be mechanical systems that, though they did not grow or reproduce, possessed minds that were capable of self-consciousness, of rational thought, of having enduring interests, and so on. Second, although one could not strictly speak of such beings as having a right to *life*, one could attribute a right to *continued existence* to them—which is what one really wants to attribute to human persons, in any case, given that there are ways of destroying a human person without killing an organism. Third, one would want to attribute a right to continued existence to them, given that whether an entity is unified mechanically rather than biologically cannot be morally significant. Fourth, there is nothing incoherent in the notion of a person whose physical basis does not consist of a single spatio-temporal object. And finally, if it is not morally relevant in the case of persons whether the causal unification is biological or mechanical or electronic, or whether the physical basis consists of a single physical object or a collection of appropriately interrelated objects, what reason can there be for holding either of these things to be relevant in the case of potential persons? Devine has none to offer, and surely, there is none.

Let us now turn to objections to the argument based upon the moral symmetry principle. The most important objections are directed against that principle itself. These will be considered in the next section. Here I shall consider objections that claim that even if the moral symmetry principle is accepted, the conclusion does not follow.

First, an objection advanced by Larry Davis.[10] The gist of Davis's objection is that the moral symmetry principle, as I stated it, can only be applied to a causal process of type C provided that the outcome of type E is the only part of the

---

[9] Ibid., p. 8. Compare *The Ethics of Homicide*, p. 75.
[10] Lawrence H. Davis, 'Could Fetuses and Infants Have a Right to Life?', pp. 8–10.

process that has *intrinsic* moral significance. So if the moral symmetry principle is to be applied to the process involved in a human organism's developing into a person, one must assume that the fact that the organism is a potential person does not have intrinsic moral significance. But to make this assumption is to beg the question at issue between the conservative and his critics, since the very basis of the conservative's position is that it is *intrinsically* wrong to destroy potential persons.

This objection rests upon a misunderstanding of the moral symmetry principle. The misunderstanding becomes clear if one considers the formulation advanced in the previous section. The relevant clause is the requirement that 'processes of type C would possess no intrinsic moral significance were it not for the fact that they result in occurrences of type E'. The crucial point to note is that this clause does not entail that no part of a process of type C is intrinsically significant, other than the outcome of type E. It asserts only that if processes of type C *were not* thus causally related to outcomes of type E, such processes would have no intrinsic moral significance. Application of the moral symmetry principle does not require, then, the assumption that it is not intrinsically wrong to destroy potential persons. All that is needed is the assumption that if the laws of nature were different, so that normal human zygotes remained in a stable state, and did not develop into persons, there would be nothing intrinsically significant about such organisms.

I am myself partly responsible for Davis's misconstrual of the moral symmetry principle, since my earlier formulations were not as precise as they should have been. The best way of stating the principle is that adopted in the previous section. By formulating it as a statement about the relative seriousness of wrong-making characteristics that are related in certain ways, the thrust of the principle is made clear, namely, it imposes certain constraints upon the basic moral principles that one can accept. It is therefore a thesis about relations between properties that have intrinsic moral significance.

As a result, Davis is mistaken in thinking that the argument based upon the moral symmetry principle tacitly assumes that there is nothing intrinsically wrong with the destruction of potential persons. The basic structure of the argument, on the contrary, is simply this. Assume that the destruction of potential persons is intrinsically wrong, and seriously so. In view of the moral symmetry principle, it follows that refraining from conception is also intrinsically wrong, and seriously so. But this conclusion is unacceptable. So we must reject the claim that the destruction of potential persons is intrinsically wrong, and seriously so.

A second criticism of the argument based upon the moral symmetry principle has been advanced by Edward Langerak.[11] He contends that the argument involves fallacious reasoning at step two—the step at which it is inferred from the moral symmetry principle, that if one has a kitten that has been injected with the special chemical, but which has not yet developed those properties that make something a person, and another kitten that has not yet been injected with that chemical, it is prima facie no more seriously wrong to inject the former with a neutralizing substance than to refrain from injecting the latter with the special chemical.

Why does Langerak think that the inference in question is mistaken? The reason he offers is that it involves, he thinks, a confusion between potential entities and possible entities, where this distinction is just a generalization of that between potential persons and possible persons, set out in section 6.1. This distinction is itself perfectly acceptable. But Langerak is mistaken in thinking that one can accept the moral symmetry principle *and* maintain that there is an important moral distinction between, on the one hand, destroying a potential entity of a given sort, and, on the other, intentionally refraining from actualizing a possible entity of that sort. For the moral symmetry principle has been explicitly formulated so as to be applicable to pairs of actions, one of which involves a potential entity, and the other only a possible entity. Whenever there is a causal process leading to some outcome of type E, there is a potential entity of that type. To interfere with such a process is to destroy a potential entity of type E.

---

[11] Edward Langerak, 'Correspondence', *Philosophy & Public Affairs*, Volume 2, Number 4, 1973, pp. 410–16.

On the other hand, to refrain from initiating a process of that type is merely to refrain from actualizing a possible entity of type E. The wrong-making characteristics of actions that the moral symmetry principle asserts are equally weighty necessarily differ in this respect: one involves potential entities, and the other only possible entities.

It would seem, then, that what Langerak should be questioning is not the logic of the argument, which appears perfectly sound, but the moral symmetry principle itself. One might either reject it completely, for reasons to be considered in the next section, or one might try to advance a restricted version of it that could not be used in the present argument.

What might such a restricted version look like? It would have to say, presumably, that the characteristics of destroying a potential entity of type E, and of failing to actualize a possible entity of that type, are morally equivalent unless there is a morally relevant difference between potential and possible entities of type E. And this, I suggest, would make the principle circular and useless. In order to apply the principle, one would have to know whether there is a morally relevant difference between potential entities and possible entities of the given type. But one of the ways in which there may be a moral difference is that it may be wrong to prevent the actualization of one but not of the other. So it would seem that one could not know whether the restricted version of the moral symmetry principle was applicable in a given case unless one first knew whether preventing the actualization of potential entities of the relevant type was morally on a par with preventing the actualization of possible entities of that type, which is precisely the sort of question the moral symmetry principle is supposed to answer. I think, then, that there is no hope for a restricted version of the principle: if it is not right as it stands, it must be more or less completely rejected—aside from the possibility of weakened principles of the comparability sort.

A third criticism of the argument based upon the moral symmetry principle has been advanced by Larry Thomas:

> That Tooley begs the question by resting his argument . . . upon the moral symmetry principle is obvious. For this principle is exactly parallel to the time prior to human conception and the time afterwards.

And the symmetry principle tells us that if it is not wrong to prevent conception, then it is not wrong to stop the process of human development after conception. But the very issue which the symmetry principle is intended to settle is whether or not it is morally wrong to stop human development after conception (and prior to the attainment of self-consciousness). Thus, in the absence of independent arguments for the soundness of the symmetry principle, we cannot use this principle to establish that the potentiality for self-consciousness is not a morally relevant consideration.[12]

Does the argument, in appealing to the moral symmetry principle, beg the question? The claim that it does is rather puzzling. In the first place, it does not follow from the moral symmetry principle alone that the characteristic of being an act of destroying a potential person is not a wrong-making characteristic. One needs the additional premiss that the characteristic of being an act of refraining from actualizing a possible person is not wrong-making. Thomas, in his discussion, ignores the fact that this additional assumption is necessary. Perhaps he feels that it is too uncontroversial to deserve notice. We shall see in chapter 7, however, that this is not the case.

Second, the implications of the moral symmetry principle are not restricted to issues connected with the question of the intrinsic wrongness of destroying potential persons. The principle is an extremely general one. It applies to any type of causal process that has some outcome such that the process would have no intrinsic significance were it not for that outcome. This generality ensures that the argument cannot be a case of begging the question.

Thomas, in fact, shifts his ground, toward the end of the passage quoted, from claiming that the argument begs the question, to pointing out that the moral symmetry principle requires independent support if it is to be used to establish any conclusions about the moral relevance of potentialities. This I should certainly agree with. However it is not true, as Thomas in effect suggests, that I simply take the principle for granted. Both here, and in the discussion to which Thomas refers, I have emphasized the fact that the principle may

[12] Larry L. Thomas, 'Human Potentiality: Its Moral Relevance', *The Personalist*, Volume 59, 1978, pp. 266–72. See p. 268.

seem, at first glance, to have implications that some people think counter-intuitive. And I have tried to provide support for the principle by arguing that if one gets clear as to precisely what it asserts, and then focuses upon pairs of actions that do not differ with respect to other morally relevant factors, it becomes apparent that the principle does not in fact conflict with our ordinary moral intuitions. If this is right, it is surely a fairly impressive fact, given the generality of the principle. Whether it is right will be explored carefully in the next section.

At the beginning of this section I mentioned that, aside from arguments directed at showing that there is a prima-facie obligation to actualize possible persons, virtually no arguments have been advanced to support the claim that the destruction of potential persons is intrinsically wrong. The only argument I have encountered, in fact, is this. Consider a normal adult human being that is in a coma due to brain damage. Unless the term 'capacity' is used loosely, we cannot speak of such an individual as having capacities for self-consciousness, for rational thought, etc. It has only the potentiality of re-acquiring those capacities. Nevertheless, one certainly does not think that it is morally permissible to kill such an individual. If it is possible for the individual to recover, it is just as wrong to kill him as it is to kill a normal adult human being who is not in a coma. So potentialities *do* have moral weight. And if they count in this context, if their presence serves to make it seriously wrong to destroy something, why should they not count equally in the case of potential persons?[13]

The first point to be made about this argument is that any conclusion it supports cannot be restricted to active, or 'almost active' potentialities. Consider a case where a previously normal adult human being is in a coma due to brain damage that it cannot itself repair, but which could be repaired by others. In such a case there is certainly no capacity

---

[13] This line of argument is suggested, for example, by Larry Thomas' discussion on pp. 268 ff., op. cit. However Thomas would not accept the last step in this argument, since he says that the conservative position is 'mistaken in its contention that having the potential for self-consciousness is sufficient for something having a right to life.' (p. 269.)

for self-consciousness, or for rational thought, etc. But there is also no active potentiality for these things. Nor need it be the case that there is an 'almost active' potentiality. Provided that the physical bases of the individual's memories, beliefs, and personality traits remain, the physical bases of self-consciousness, rational thought, and other higher mental functions can be completely obliterated, and the person still survive. What is crucial, as I emphasized in section 5.5, is that those parts of the brain that are the physical bases of the states upon which personal identity depends have not been destroyed. So nothing even remotely like an active potentiality for rational thought, or for self-consciousness, etc., need be present in something for the destruction of that thing to be the destruction of a person.

The above argument for the moral relevance of potentialities cannot, moreover, be salvaged by defining the expression 'potential person' so it applies to entities with potentialities that are virtually at the passive end of the active/passive scale. This would include far too much, as becomes clear if one considers the possibility of cloning. For however complex the cloning of humans may be, it is clear that much more would be needed to repair massive brain damage of the sort envisaged here. The upshot is that if one mistakenly assumes that it is potentialities that count, one will be unable both to defend the view that persons can survive certain sorts of extreme brain damage, and maintain, at the same time, that the destruction of living human cells is not seriously wrong.

The second point is that potentialities for self-consciousness, rational thought, etc., are not sufficient, contrary to what the argument claims, to make it wrong to destroy an organism that is in a coma. For the injury may have deprogrammed the organism's brain, with the result that while *it* will shortly revive, and enjoy self-consciousness, etc., it will not have any of the memories, beliefs, attitudes, personality traits, and so on, of the person previously associated with that human organism. An organism may continue to possess certain general potentialities after the associated person has been destroyed. In addition to general potentialities, there must be states of certain sorts standing in appropriate causal relations to corresponding earlier states—the types of states being those upon which personal identity depends. Accordingly, it is simply not true that general potentialities suffice to make it wrong to destroy a human organism in a coma, even though the organism was once a person. And if general potentialities are not sufficient in this case, the present argument has failed to provide one with any grounds for thinking that general potentialities suffice to make it wrong to destroy organisms that are not yet persons.

6.5 Causing and Allowing to Happen: The Moral Symmetry Principle

In section 6.3 I claimed that the moral symmetry principle, properly understood, is supported by our ordinary moral intuitions, and I offered a preliminary defence of that contention. It may be best to begin the present section by confronting some doubts that might be thought to bear upon the two examples to which I appealed above. First, consider the following discussion from an article by Judith Jarvis Thomson:

> Morally speaking it may matter a great deal how a death comes about, whether from natural causes, or at the hands of another, for example. Does it matter whether a man was killed or only let die? A great many people think it does: they think that killing is worse than letting die. And they draw conclusions from this for abortion, euthanasia, and the distribution of scarce medical resources. Others think it doesn't, and they think this shown by what we see when we construct a pair of cases which are so far as possible in all other respects alike, except that in the one case the agent kills, in the other he only lets die. So, for example, imagine that
>
> (1) Alfred hates his wife and wants her dead. He puts cleaning fluid in her coffee, thereby killing her,
>
> and that
>
> (2) Bert hates his wife and wants her dead. She puts cleaning fluid in her coffee (being muddled, thinking it's cream). Bert happens to have the antidote to cleaning fluid, but he does not give it to her; he lets her die.
>
> Alfred kills his wife out of a desire for her death; Bert lets his wife die out of a desire for her death. But what Bert does is surely every bit as bad as what Alfred does. So killing isn't worse than letting die.
> But I am now inclined to think that this argument is a bad one.[14]

[14] Judith Jarvis Thomson, 'Killing, Letting Die, and the "Trolley Problem"', *Monist*, Volume 59, Number 2, 1975, pp. 204–17. See p. 204.

If this is right, then my attempt to lend intuitive support to the moral symmetry principle by appealing to the very similar case of Jones and Smith must also be unacceptable. We need to consider, then, precisely why Thomson thinks the Alfred/Bert argument is a bad one:

Compare the following argument for the thesis that cutting off a man's head is no worse than punching a man in the nose. 'Alfrieda knows that if she cuts off Alfred's head he will die, and, wanting him to die, cuts it off; Bertha knows that if she punches Bert in the nose he will die—Bert is in peculiar physical condition—and, wanting him to die, punches him in the nose. But what Bertha does is surely every bit as bad as what Alfrieda does. So cutting off a man's head isn't worse than punching a man in the nose.'[15]

The point, then, is that there must be something wrong with the Alfred/Bert argument since it is possible to construct a parallel argument—the Alfrieda/Bertha argument—that has an obviously unacceptable conclusion. But if the conclusion of the latter argument is to be clearly unacceptable, it must be interpreted in a certain way, namely, as asserting something like: cutting off a man's head is not *in general* any worse than punching a man in the nose. For if the conclusion were instead interpreted as asserting that the cutting off of a man's head is not *in itself* any more wrong than punching a man in the nose, the conclusion would be perfectly acceptable. Consequently, the above criticism does not apply to the Jones/Smith argument, since the conclusion of that argument is that two characteristics are, as wrong-making characteristics, equally weighty, and not that actions possessing those characteristics are, in general, equally wrong.

Let us now turn to the case of John, Mary, and the diabolical machine, and consider an objection suggested by Richard Trammell's comment on that argument:

Failure to meet a negative duty makes the realization of some good impossible which would have been realized if one had not acted at all. But in evaluating whether or not an action prevents the realization of a 'good', one must consider the over-all results of the action. In the case given by Tooley, whether one does or does not push the button, one person lives and one person dies. Therefore regardless of which action

[15] Ibid., p. 204.

one chooses, there is no over-all good to be realized and no negative nor positive duty involved.[16]

Trammell's position here is unusual in at least two respects. The first is that, while, on the one hand, he wishes to defend the view, generally associated with anti-consequentialist positions, that negative duties are more serious than the corresponding positive ones, he seems, on the other hand, to accept the consequentialist contention that where two actions do not differ with respect to their over-all consequences, they are morally on a par.

The second unusual feature, and the more important one, is that while Trammell maintains that the obligation to refrain from killing is more serious than the obligation to save someone, he wants to deny that there is anything wrong with killing one person if that is the only way to save someone else. Virtually everyone else who holds that killing is intrinsically more wrong than letting die also holds that killing John in order to save Mary is intrinsically more wrong than refraining from killing John and letting Mary die. Indeed, they will normally appeal to the former claim in support of the latter.

Is there any way of lending plausibility to Trammell's rather unusual view? The best attempt that I know, and one which cleanses Trammell's position of its apparent consequentialist elements, runs as follows. What should be done is determined by the right-making and wrong-making characteristics of the actions open to one. An action may be obligatory because it has a right-making characteristic and no wrong-making characteristics, or because its right-making characteristics outweigh its wrong-making characteristics. Similarly, an action may be wrong because it possesses a wrong-making characteristic and no right-making characteristics, or because its wrong-making characteristics outweigh its right-making characteristics. Now consider the sorts of actions we are interested in here. An action is prima facie wrong if it is an act of killing, or an act of refraining from saving. It is prima facie obligatory if it is an act of saving

---

[16] Richard L. Trammell, 'Saving Life and Taking Life', *Journal of Philosophy*, Volume 72, Number 5, 1975, pp. 131-7. See p. 137.

someone's life, or an act of refraining from killing someone. Suppose then that these characteristics are assigned the following weights—positive weights indicating right-making characteristics, and negative weights wrong-making characteristics:

Saving someone's life	+2
Refraining from killing someone	+1
Refraining from saving someone's life	−1
Killing someone	−2

This assignment of weights implies that an act of killing someone is prima facie more wrong than an act of refraining from saving. But it also implies that an act of killing someone in order to save someone else is prima facie no more wrong than an act of both refraining from killing and refraining from saving someone. Each act possesses one right-making characteristic and one wrong-making characteristic, and the sum is the same in each case, namely zero.

Are we to conclude, then, that Trammell's position is merely an uncommon one, and that there is no reason for preferring the more widely accepted view? I think not. I believe that the common view is to be preferred, on the ground that the way in which I have attempted to make sense of Trammell's position involves a confusion. The basic point is this. It can be a characteristic of an act that it is not an act of killing, or not an act of saving someone's life. But it is *not*, in the same way, a characteristic of an act that it is one of *refraining* from killing, or one of refraining from saving someone's life. An act can be an act of refraining from doing something only if doing that thing is among the alternatives open to the agent; it is a characteristic not of the act itself, but of the act taken together with the set of alternatives to which it belongs. So, for example, if Mary is alone on the beach, nothing she does can be described as an act of refraining from saving someone's life. What is needed, then, is an account of right-making and wrong-making characteristics, and of the way in which obligations are determined by such characteristics, that does not confuse characteristics of individual actions with characteristics of actions taken together with the available set of alternatives. The following seems the simplest and most natural approach:

(1) Right-making and wrong-making characteristics are always characteristics of the individual act itself, not characteristics of the act together with the set of alternatives.

(2) Weights are associated with each right-making and wrong-making characteristic, with the possibility that some characteristics may be assigned 'infinite' weight relative to others.

(3) The extent to which an individual action is, in itself, prima facie obligatory is determined by summing the weights associated with its right-making and wrong-making characteristics.

(4) Whether an action is wrong, relative to a certain set of alternative actions, is determined by considering the difference between its prima-facie obligatoriness and the prima-facie obligatoriness of the best action belonging to the set.

Consider a simple illustration, which involves only one right-making characteristic, and one wrong-making characteristic, weighted as follows:

Saving the life of one person	+1
Killing someone	−3

Let A_1 be some action that neither kills anyone, nor saves anyone's life, and let A_2 be an action that kills someone, but saves four other people. The prima-facie obligatoriness of A_1, considered in itself, will then get assigned the measure zero. It is thus an action that, other things being equal, there is no objection to performing. But suppose that A_2 is an action that is available to the agent. The prima-facie obligatoriness of A_2 will be plus one. If A_1 and A_2 are the only actions available, A_2 will thus be the best action available, and A_1 will be assigned a wrongness measure of minus one—the difference between its prima-facie obligatoriness and that of the best action in the set of alternatives. A_1, though morally neutral considered in itself, is morally wrong given the available alternatives. And this seems to be precisely the right way of viewing the situation. Considered in itself, there is nothing wrong with A_1. Most of the actions we perform are actions that neither kill nor save. An action such as A_1

becomes wrong only when the set of actions available to one contains some morally superior action.

It should now be clear why it is that virtually everyone who holds that killing is worse than letting die also holds that it is prima facie wrong to kill in order to save, and also why they are inclined to argue from the former to the latter. Suppose that John has only two available actions, one of which kills someone, and the other of which does not. If we assign the weight $-x$ to the wrong-making characteristic of killing, this will also represent the over-all wrongness of his choosing to kill someone, given the two choices open to him. Suppose now that Mary also has only two available actions, one of which saves someone, and the other of which does not. If we assign the weight $+y$ to the right-making characteristic of being an act which saves someone, then if she performs the act that does not save the person, she will be performing an act whose prima-facie obligatoriness is zero, but whose over-all wrongness, given the alternatives, is $-y$.

If, now, one is to maintain that John, in killing someone, did something more seriously wrong than Mary, in refraining from saving someone, one has to choose x and y so that x is greater than y. But consider then the case of a person who has to choose one of the following actions:

A_1:   Killing one person, thereby saving another.

A_2:   Doing nothing.

The prima-facie obligatoriness of A_1 will be equal to $-x + y$. That of A_2 will be zero. So if x is larger than y, as it must be if one is to hold that killing is more seriously wrong than refraining from saving, the number assigned to A_1 will be negative, and hence less than that assigned to A_2. If one's choice is restricted to A_1 and A_2, then, it is wrong to do A_1 rather than A_2.

The upshot is that the following inference, which Trammell in effect rejects, but which is very widely accepted, is a perfectly reasonable one:

Killing is intrinsically worse than letting die.

Therefore:

It is intrinsically wrong to kill one person in order to save another.

Trammell's rejection of this inference reflects, I have argued, a confusion between the characteristics of an action and the characteristics of an action together with the set of alternatives available to the agent.

The relevance of this to the case of John, Mary, and the diabolical machine is simply that the argument implicitly involves the above inference. The logic of the argument, though not made explicit above, is really this. Assume that killing is intrinsically more wrong than letting die. Then it follows that it is intrinsically wrong to kill one person to save another. But the diabolical machine case shows that the latter is not so. Hence we must reject the assumption that killing is intrinsically more wrong than merely letting die. Trammell attempted to undermine this argument by rejecting the key inference. However we have just seen that the inference is a perfectly reasonable one.

As a consequence, neither the argument from the case of Smith and Jones, nor the argument from the case of John, Mary, and the diabolical machine, seems exposed to any logical objections. There is thus a substantial prima-facie case for the claim that the moral symmetry principle is in agreement with the ordinary moral intuitions of most people.

Let us now consider some objections to the principle itself. I shall begin by considering two objections that rest upon misunderstandings. The first is contained in an article by Leonard Carrier, who says that my appeal to the moral symmetry principle serves to underline my 'consequentialist approach to moral values', and that the counter-examples which he advances to the principle 'can thus be interpreted as a criticism of the doctrine that consequences are the sole arbiters of right and wrong.'[17]

The moral symmetry principle is not, however, a consequentialist principle. True, most consequentialists would, I think, find it appealing. Indeed, it would seem to follow from act-consequentialism. However it is also perfectly

---

[17] Leonard S. Carrier, 'Abortion and the Right to Life', *Social Theory and Practice*, Volume 3, Number 4, 1975, pp. 381–401. See p. 400.

compatible with a thoroughgoing deontological position. The central ethical concept involved in stating the principle is, after all, a quantitative version of the familiar deontological notion of a wrong-making characteristic, and the principle contains no reference at all to the goodness or badness of states of affairs. As a result, the moral symmetry principle is perfectly consistent with the claim that the rightness or wrongness of actions cannot be reduced to the goodness or badness of resulting states of affairs. The moral symmetry principle says only that if causing something to happen is intrinsically wrong, so is allowing it to happen, and to the same degree. The principle is studiously neutral with respect to what account, if any, is to be given of right-making and wrong-making characteristics.

A second possible misunderstanding of the moral symmetry principle is illustrated by a criticism advanced by Philip Devine. He proposes a counter-example based upon the following two actions:

Action M: An individual refrains from giving information to the enemy even though he knows that the enemy will torture a child as long as he refuses to divulge the information.

Action N: An individual tortures a child in order to induce the enemy to give him information.

Devine contends that it is 'surely monstrous'[18] to view these two actions as morally equivalent. I think that the issue here is rather more problematic than he suggests. However let us grant that Devine is right about this. Do we then have a counter-example to the moral symmetry principle? Clearly not. The principle states, very roughly, that intentionally refraining from bringing about some state of affairs is as wrong as interfering with a causal process that otherwise will lead to such a state. It does not assert that intentionally refraining from *preventing someone else* from doing something is as wrong as doing it oneself. So the moral symmetry principle does not assert that actions M and N are morally equivalent.

[18] Phillip Devine, 'Tooley on Infanticide', p. 10.

Mightn't one argue, however, that although the moral symmetry principle does not entail that actions such as M and N are morally equivalent, one can formulate a generalized moral symmetry principle that does have this implication, and that ought to be accepted by anyone who embraces the original principle? Certainly, one can formulate such a principle. The difficulty is in justifying the claim that anyone who accepts the original principle ought to accept the generalization of it. For suppose that one has a principle that entails that intentionally refraining from preventing someone else from doing something, and doing it oneself, are morally equivalent actions. It can then be shown that such a principle has a consequence that most people would reject.

The consequence in question arises as follows. Assume that intentionally refraining from preventing someone else from doing something, and doing it oneself, are morally equivalent actions. It would seem to be true, in general, that if Q and R are morally equivalent actions, then so are the actions of intentionally refraining from Q and intentionally refraining from R. Applying this general principle to the present hypothesis leads to the conclusion that intentionally refraining from intentionally refraining from preventing someone else from doing something is morally equivalent to intentionally refraining from doing it oneself. The former, however, is surely morally equivalent to preventing someone else from doing something. So we are forced, if we accept the original assumption, to conclude that preventing someone else from doing something is morally equivalent to intentionally refraining from doing it oneself.

This conclusion, however, is grossly counterintuitive. When one prevents someone else from doing something, one is *interfering* with that person's freedom of action. One is not doing this when one intentionally refrains from doing something oneself. There is, then, a difference between the two actions which most people would view as morally significant.

Thus there is a prima-facie case against any extension of the moral symmetry principle that results in a principle entailing that intentionally refraining from preventing someone else from doing something is morally equivalent to doing it oneself. I do not wish to assert that this prima-facie case cannot be overcome. The point is simply that, on the one hand, it must be overcome before one can justifiably claim that anyone who accepts the original moral symmetry principle ought to accept the generalization of it, and that, on the other, any argument that was successful in overthrowing this objection to extending the principle would ipso facto give one a reason for rejecting Devine's contention that it is 'monstrous' to view actions M and N as morally equivalent.

Having noted these misinterpretations of the moral symmetry principle, let us turn to objections to the principle itself. The natural place to begin is by considering a possible counter-example:

Charles is a great transplant surgeon. One of his patients needs a new heart, but is of a relatively rare blood-type. By chance, Charles learns of a healthy specimen with that very blood-type. Charles can take the healthy specimen's heart, killing him, and install it in his patient, saving him. Or he can refrain from taking the healthy specimen's heart, letting his patient die.[19]

Most people seem to feel that in this situation Charles must not kill the healthy person in order to save his patient. And doesn't this show that the moral symmetry principle conflicts with our ordinary moral intuitions?

I do not believe that it does. My reason will emerge if we consider the following two examples, which Thomson juxtaposes:

David is a great transplant surgeon. Five of his patients need new parts —one needs a heart, the others need, respectively, liver, stomach, spleen, and spinal cord—but all are of the same, relatively rare, blood-type. By chance, David learns of a healthy specimen with that very blood-type. David can take the healthy specimen's parts, killing him, and install them in his patients, saving them. Or he can refrain from taking the healthy specimen's parts, letting his patients die.

Edward is the driver of a trolley, whose brakes have just failed. On the track ahead of him are five people; the banks are so steep that they will not be able to get off the track in time. The track has a spur leading off to the right, and Edward can turn the trolley onto it. Unfortunately

<hr/>

[19] Judith Jarvis Thomson, 'Killing, Letting Die, and the Trolley Problem', p. 205. A number of writers have appealed to this sort of case. See, for example, Daniel Dinello's proposed counter-example to Jonathan Bennett's claim that the distinction between killing and letting die is not morally significant in itself, in 'Killing and Letting Die', *Analysis*, Volume 31, 1971, pp. 85–6.

there is one person on the right-hand track. Edward can turn the
trolley, killing the one; or he can refrain from turning the trolley, killing the five.[20]

Thomson suggests that it would be morally permissible for
Edward to turn the trolley, but not for David to cut up his
healthy specimen. If we assume, for the sake of discussion,
that this is the right view of the matter, how are we to
explain the difference? In both cases it is a choice between
killing one and allowing five to die. Why should killing be
justified in one case, and not in the other? The only answer is
that there must be some morally significant feature present in
one case, but not in the other. What might that be? Thomson's answer is that in the trolley case the lone individual has
no more claim not to be run over by the trolley than each of
the other five individuals, whereas in the medical case the
healthy person has more of a claim to his organs—simply
because they are his—than the other five individuals.

This seems to be a plausible view of the matter. This line
of thought can be reinforced, moreover, by comparing the
cases of Charles and David with the following related case,
suggested by Jeff McMahan. Mark is a great transplant
surgeon, in a situation very similar to that of David. Five of
his patients, all of the same, relatively rare, blood-type,
require various bodily parts if they are to survive. Mark
knows of a healthy person of the right blood-type, but that
individual is not interested in supplying the needed organs.
By chance, however, that person is involved in an accident,
and the situation is such that he will not survive unless Mark
calls for an ambulance immediately. So Mark can refrain
from rendering aid, allowing the person to die, and then use
his organs to save the lives of his five patients. Or he can save
the person's life, thereby allowing his five patients to perish.
I think that most people who would hold that David ought
not to kill someone in order to get parts for his five patients
would also hold that Mark ought not to allow someone to die
in order to get organs for his five patients. If so, the relevant
judgements here cannot be explained in terms of a distinction

[20] Op. cit., p. 206.

between killing and letting die. The crucial factor must be that the organs belong to the one person.

The upshot is that the case of Charles is not a counter-example to the moral symmetry principle. For the choice is not merely one between killing and letting die; it is also one between allowing a person to keep things to which he has a claim, and giving them to someone else who does not have a comparable claim to them. The presence of this other, morally relevant feature prevents the case from being a counter-example to the moral symmetry principle.

This outcome should not come as a surprise. I have tried to show that there are examples, such as the case of John, Mary, and the diabolical machine, that provide intuitive support for the principle. If other examples appear to conflict with the principle, there must be something amiss somewhere. For the situation is not comparable to that with a generalization, where there can be both instances and counter-instances. The issue is whether a certain distinction is morally significant, and it cannot be significant in some cases and not in others. Therefore, if one is confronted with two examples, each involving a choice between causing something, and allowing the same sort of thing to happen, and it seems that the actions are morally equivalent in one case and not in the other, one knows that there must be some morally significant feature that is present in one case and not in the other. The question, then, is which examples involve the obscuring factor. Is it the examples that I have offered in support of the principle? Or is it the proposed counter-examples? I believe that one is justified in thinking that it is the proposed counter-examples that are likely to involve some additional, obscuring factor. For in the first place, this is clearly so in the case of many proposed counter-examples, such as the case of Charles. And secondly, the examples offered in support of the principle have been deliberately constructed in such a way as to minimize the possibility that there is some other morally relevant factor that is cancelling out the contribution of the purportedly significant difference between causing and allowing to happen.

The most extended critique of the moral symmetry principle is found in two articles by Richard Trammell. In the one, he advances objections to the principle itself. In the other, he outlines reasons why the distinction between causing and allowing to happen must be viewed as morally significant. First, then, his objections to the moral symmetry principle. Trammell begins by pointing out that the formulation of the moral symmetry principle that he is considering can be seen as asserting that causing and allowing to happen are morally equivalent *provided that* three conditions are satisfied: (1) the motivation is identical in the two cases; (2) the expenditure of energy is minimal; (3) both action and inaction are intentional. To these, Trammell adds a fourth restriction, which he suggests is implicit in my discussion: (4) the causal process in question has no potential value. Trammell points out that these qualifications upon the general claim about the relation between causing and allowing to happen are of two very different types: 'Type I qualifications specify that the action and inaction which we compare must be equal in regard to some variable, without any further restriction on that variable. Type II qualifications specify that the action and inaction must be equal in regard to some variable with a *further restriction on the range of that variable*.'[21] Trammell then observes that while restriction (1) is a Type I qualification, restrictions (2), (3), and (4) are all Type II qualifications.

The importance of this is that while Type I restrictions seem perfectly in order, Type II restrictions may well be dubious. The more that are introduced, the less application the principle has. And, what is even more serious, the more grounds there are for suspecting that the restrictions have been introduced in order to avoid, in an *ad hoc* way, embarrassing consequences.

I believe that Trammell is right about this, and that Type II restrictions are suspect. But when the moral symmetry principle is properly formulated, it does not incorporate such restrictions. As I pointed out in section 6.3, what is essentially involved is a claim about the equivalence of two wrong-making characteristics. And when reference to wrong-making

---

[21] Richard Louis Trammell, 'Tooley's Moral Symmetry Principle', *Philosophy & Public Affairs*, Volume 5, Number 3, 1976, pp. 305–13. See p. 306.

characteristics is made explicit, there is no need to refer to other morally significant variables of actions, and hence no need for restrictions either of Type I or of Type II.

So far, then, all is well. But Trammell believes that the moral symmetry principle, even in its fully restricted version, conflicts with our ordinary moral intuitions, and that the removal of restrictions (2), (3), and (4) intensifies this conflict. I shall attempt to show that Trammell is mistaken.

First, an objection that Trammell believes tells against even the fully restricted version of the principle. He asks us to consider the following case:

(1) Jones sees that Smith will be killed unless he warns him. But Jones is apathetic. So Smith is killed by the bomb even though Jones could have warned him. (2) Jones is practising shooting his gun. Smith accidentally walks in the path and Jones sees Smith; but Jones's reaction is apathy. Jones pulls the trigger and Smith is killed.

This is a slightly modified version of the Jones/Smith example to which I appealed in support of the moral symmetry principle. Here, however, the action and inaction involve apathy rather than hatred. Trammell suggests that my choice of an example in which Jones's motivation is extreme hatred of Smith makes it more difficult for one to be sensitive to other important differences—differences which he feels emerge when we consider the modified case where it is apathy that is involved: 'Now even though Jones's apathy in Case 1 is clearly wrong, surely it is more wrong in Case 2.'[22]

What I want to suggest is that Trammell's own intuitions about this case may reflect a failure to distinguish, in the present context, between two very different judgements: (1) a judgement as to the relative wrongness of the actions in question; (2) a judgement as to the moral undesirability of the character traits that are likely to underlie the actions in question. Now it is clear, in our world, that a person who doesn't care whether he kills people or not thereby has a more undesirable character trait than a person who doesn't care whether he saves people or not. If the latter person is driving a car, he may not bother to stop if someone carelessly steps into the street, whereas the former may drive up on the footpath and run people down. And in general, there are vastly many more opportunities for people to cause destruction than for them to allow destruction that they could have prevented. But this is a fact about our world, and one can imagine a rather different world in which this was not so—a world, for example, in which it was very difficult indeed for one person to kill another, but in which there were constant opportunities for people to save one another from natural disasters. In such a world, I suggest, our ranking of the two traits of character would be different: apathy about saving people would be viewed as a more serious defect than apathy about killing. And in such a world there would, accordingly, be little temptation to share Trammell's intuitions about the modified Jones/Smith case.

This response to Trammell's first objection receives additional support from the diabolical-machine example. In that example, no restriction was placed upon the underlying motives, other than that they be the same in both cases. Compare, then, the case of a person who apathetically pushes the button, killing John, but saving Mary, with the case of one who apathetically refrains from pushing the button, thereby refraining both from killing John and from saving Mary. Very few people, I believe, would hold that one of these actions was morally worse than the other. Now we have seen, of course, that the bearing of this example upon the moral symmetry principle is slightly less direct than might at first appear. However I have also argued that Trammell's attempt, in his article, 'Saving Life and Taking Life', to resist the claim that this example supports the principle, rests upon a failure to distinguish between the characteristics an action has in itself and the 'characteristics' it has when viewed as belonging to a set of alternatives. If I am right about this, then the case of the diabolical machine also serves to show that the prima-facie obligation to avoid an action in which one apathetically kills someone is no greater than the prima-facie obligation to avoid an action with the so-called characteristic of being an action of apathetically allowing someone to die.

Let us now consider the three sorts of objections that Trammell believes the moral symmetry principle is exposed to when the three Type II restrictions are dropped. First, Trammell maintains that the moral symmetry principle is exposed to counter-examples once the restriction to actions that involve minimal risk or effort is removed:

Proponents of the distinction between negative and positive duties assert that in a wide range of circumstances we are morally obligated to undergo a greater sacrifice to avoid killing another person than to save that person. For a concrete illustration, consider the following:

(1) Jones sees that Smith, a stranger, will die unless he (Jones) acts to save him. It will cost Jones most of his life-savings, $5,000, to save Smith. Jones has no ill-feelings toward Smith, but decides not to make the sacrifice necessary to save him. (2) Jones sees that if he continues in his present course of action, he will directly kill Smith. It will cost Jones most of his life-savings to change his plans and thus avoid killing Smith. Jones has no ill-feelings toward Smith, but decides not to make the sacrifice necessary to avoid killing Smith.

Now even if one believes that Jones has some obligation to try to save Smith, surely he has an even greater obligation to avoid killing Smith.[23]

I believe it can be shown that this is not a plausible moral view. There is, however, something unsatisfactory about the illustration suggested by Trammell. It is unclear why the burden of sacrificing $5,000 in order to save Smith has to be borne entirely by Jones, and I think that this may cloud the intuitions of some people. So let us consider a slightly different example from which this unclear feature has been removed:

Jones has used his life-savings of $5,000 to purchase a railway car, which is now careering down the tracks. The tracks branch, one branch leading to a gorge where Jones's train will be completely destroyed, and the other leading to a siding where the car will come to a stop, but only after killing Smith, who has fallen, unconscious, on the tracks. Jones has no way of removing Smith from the tracks in time, or of stopping the car. (1) The position of the switch is such that the railway car will turn on to the siding, killing Smith, but coming to a stop. Jones can

[23] Ibid., p. 309.

switch it to the other branch, thus saving Smith, but totally destroying his $5,000 railway car. Jones decides to do nothing. (2) The position of the switch is such that if Jones does nothing, his car will career into the gorge and be totally destroyed. He decides to flip the switch, saving his car but killing Smith.

Confronted with this example, most people seem to have difficulty detecting the moral difference which Trammell claims exists between Jones's actions in the two cases. Moreover, the claim that there is no difference can, I think, be strongly supported as follows. It seems very plausible that there are some sacrifices that are so great that it is morally . preferable for mankind not to make those sacrifices in order to save a single person. Let M be the smallest sacrifice of which this is the case. Then, if Trammell were right, the following two statements would seem to be true:

(1) Not making sacrifice M is morally preferable to saving a single individual;
(2) Not killing a single individual is either morally preferable to, or else at least as good as, not making sacrifice M.

It then follows from (1) and (2) that:

(3) Not killing an individual is morally preferable to saving an individual.

Trammell's moral views, then, would seem to commit him to the view that in the famous trolley case where there is an individual lying on each track, it is morally preferable to allow the trolley to run over the individual on the track along which the trolley is going to move, rather than to switch the trolley to the other track, thus killing the other individual. But the idea that there is a moral difference here is surely, at least upon critical reflection, quite implausible.

The second objection that Trammell believes arises once the restrictions are removed from the moral symmetry principle concerns actions and inactions that involve negligence:

It would seem that we have a greater obligation to know the consequences of our actions, so as to avoid nonintentional killing, than to know the consequences of what we do not do, so as to avoid nonintentional failure to save. The following modification of Tooley's example illustrates this distinction:

(1) Jones is daydreaming and thus fails to see that Smith is about to be killed by a bomb. So Smith is killed by the bomb, and Jones has unintentionally failed to save him. (2) Jones is daydreaming as he practises shooting his gun. He fails to notice Smith walking into the path of his bullet. So Jones unintentionally kills Smith.

This example provides intuitive support for the claim that, other things being equal, it is more seriously wrong to act unintentionally in such a way as to kill than to fail unintentionally to act in such a way as to save.[24]

The defect in this objection is that it does not take into account the *change* that a given action (or inaction) may make in the *probability* of the occurrence of an event of a certain sort. Mary knows that there is some non-zero probability that the steering on her car will fail as she is driving along a street packed with pedestrians, and that her car will run up on to the footpath, killing and injuring several people. Nevertheless, she drives her car along the street, the steering does fail, and someone is killed. If Mary's action is wrong at all, it is at least not wrong to the extent that it would be if she had instead fired a gun at a group of people, thereby killing one. Why is this so? The answer, surely, is that driving a car along a busy street increases only slightly the likelihood that someone will be killed, whereas firing a gun at a group of people substantially increases that likelihood.

Once this factor is taken into account, it is clear that Trammell's example provides no support for the claim that the distinction between action and inaction is morally significant in itself. The probability that someone will die is increased much more, in normal circumstances, if Jones daydreams while practising shooting his gun, than if Jones simply day-dreams. The difference in probability is certainly morally relevant, and that it is also sufficient to explain the difference in one's moral feelings in the two cases becomes clear, I suggest, if one considers the following case:

Jones is a witness to a scene in which terrorists plant a bomb, and has been left by a friend to stand guard and

[24] Ibid., p. 310.

warn passersby against entering the sabotaged building while the friend goes off to summon the bomb-squad. Jones falls to daydreaming, thus unintentionally allowing someone to wander to his doom inside the building.[25]

Would we not view Jones as just as blameworthy in such a case as in the one where he day-dreams while practising shooting his gun?

Trammell's final objection to the moral symmetry principle is that it has unacceptable consequences when applied to causal processes that will, if not interfered with, give rise to something valuable. He illustrates his point by means of the following examples: 'In the midst of a severe famine, farmer A decides not to plant corn but to plant a flower garden. Farmer B decides to plant corn, but one week before harvest of the corn would have been possible, he decides to destroy the corn and plant a flower garden.' Trammell says: 'Now corn is something which has value. Farmer B, by his neglect of the imminent realization of the value connected with fruition of the grain, commits a more serious wrong than farmer A, who decides not to plant corn at all.'[26]

Once again, Trammell is appealing to moral intuitions that have not been subjected to critical reflection. It is certainly true that Trammell's claim about the relative wrongness of the actions of farmer A and farmer B seems plausible. Imagine, for example, that given five more minutes' growth, farmer B's crop would be ready for harvesting. Isn't it clear that, if he destroys it, he does something more wrong than farmer A? But one needs to ask what the *ground* of this judgement is, and when this is done, it becomes clear that there is no reason to attribute the difference to the fact that farmer B is destroying something with potential value, whereas farmer A is not. In the first place, in planting corn, farmer B may have influenced others not to plant it, so that the consequences of his planting corn, and then destroying it, may very well be worse than if he had never planted it at all. Second, the sacrifices farmer A and farmer B must make in order to save people from starvation are not the same. Farmer A, by planting corn, would be committing himself to all the work involved in looking after it, and would have to live without a flower garden for three months. Farmer B has already done most of the work, and needs to deprive himself of a flower garden for only a very short period of time. Third, given that crops may fail for a variety of reasons, the probability that farmer B's crop will issue in something valuable is greater than the probability that farmer A will produce something valuable if he plants a crop. These last two points show that the fact, in the case of farmer B, of the 'imminent realization' of something of value, is morally relevant, but not for the reason that Trammell suggests. Its relevance is, first, that the sacrifice that farmer B now needs to make in order to save people is less than what farmer A would have to make, and second, that the probability that farmer B's crop will come to fruition is greater than the probability of a similar outcome from farmer A's planting. Consequently, there is no need to reject the moral symmetry principle in order to explain why farmer B's action is more seriously wrong than farmer A's.

Trammell's objections to the moral symmetry principle all appear, then, to be unsound. Let us now turn to his second article, 'Saving Life and Taking Life', in which he attempts to provide positive grounds for thinking the distinction between causing and allowing to happen is morally significant. He begins by offering the following 'paradigm case' in support of the view that there is a greater obligation to refrain from killing someone than to save someone:

If someone threatened to steal $1,000 from a person if he did not take a gun and shoot a stranger between the eyes, it would be very wrong for him to kill the stranger to save his $1,000. But if someone asked from that person $1,000 to save a stranger, it would seem that his obligation to grant this request would not be as great as his obligation to refuse the first demand—even if he had good reason for believing that without his $1,000 the stranger would certainly die.[27]

This example does not, however, support Trammell's view, since there is a difference between the action and the inaction that may very well be morally significant. The former involves killing in order to prevent someone from

[27] Op. cit., p. 131.

stealing $1,000 from one; the latter involves letting someone die rather than contributing $1,000 to save him. So the example is defective in the same way as Devine's example.

The lack of parallelism could be repaired by considering whether there is any moral difference between killing someone to prevent someone else from robbing one of $1,000 and letting someone die in order to prevent that. Alternatively, one could remove the 'threat to steal' element, and consider something like the railway car example discussed above. In either case, it seems to me that any intuitive feeling that there is a difference thereby vanishes.

Let us now consider the account Trammell offers of the underlying factors that, he believes, make the distinctions between acting and allowing to happen a morally significant one. The first of the three factors that he mentions is a matter of the extent to which a duty can be discharged:

A number of factors underlie the distinction between negative and positive duties, one of which is the dischargeability of a duty. It is an empirical fact that in most cases it is possible for a person not to inflict serious physical injury on any other person. It is also an empirical fact that in no case is it possible for a person to aid everyone who needs help. The positive duty to love one's neighbor or help those in need sets a maximum ethic which would never let us rest except to gather strength to resume the battle. But it is a rare case when we must really exert ourselves to keep from killing a person.[28]

Trammell's empirical claims point to a certain innocence, as Carolyn Morillo notes in her article, 'Doing, Refraining, and the Strenuousness of Morality'. For it no longer appears to be true that it requires very little effort to avoid killing people. Massive consumption in advanced societies gives rise to widespread pollution, which seriously affects the health, and shortens the lives, of vast numbers of people. As a result, 'minimum morality may become very strenuous indeed': 'We are being asked to refrain from those activities which pose a serious threat to life. And all that this requires is that we alter radically our whole consumption oriented way of life, closing off vast ranges of activity we have come to take for granted.'[29]

[28] Ibid., p. 133.
[29] Carolyn R. Morillo, 'Doing, Refraining, and the Strenuousness of Morality, *American Philosophical Quarterly*, Volume 14, Number 1, 1977, pp. 29-39. See p. 39.

The basic point, however, concerns the form of Trammell's argument—specifically, the fact that it turns upon empirical claims. In our world, saving everyone possible would require tremendous effort, whereas refraining from killing does not. Trammell employs this empirical claim to arrive at a conclusion about the relative seriousness of certain obligations: the duty to save is less serious than the duty to refrain from killing.

But the world could be different. It is easy to imagine a world in which people rarely needed to be saved, but where virtually every action would kill someone. In that world, refraining from killing would require tremendous effort, while saving everyone possible would not. Parity of reasoning would force one to conclude that in that world, the duty to refrain from killing would be less serious than the duty to save.

If Trammell's argument were sound, then, we would be forced to conclude that the relative seriousness of the duty to save and of the duty to refrain from killing vary from one world to another. This conclusion is, I suggest, unacceptable. The duties in question are grounded simply upon the facts that being an act of killing a person is a wrong-making characteristic, and being an act of saving a person is a right-making characteristic. And by definition, such characteristics do not vary, in seriousness or otherwise, from one world to another.

What is one to do if, like Trammell, one is concerned that morality not be too strenuous? Trammell believes that in the world as it is, a morality that imposes intolerable burdens can be avoided by holding, for example, that the principle that one should save lives imposes a less serious obligation than the principle that one should refrain from killing. He fails to notice that in a different world, one would have to hold that it was the former principle, rather than the latter, which imposed the more serious obligation, if one were not to be faced with an intolerable burden. And the problem is that one cannot have it both ways, since the principles in question are *basic* moral principles, and so cannot vary depending upon the nature of the world.

There is, however, a coherent alternative. *If* one wants to ensure that morality never imposes intolerable burdens, one need merely maintain that there is another basic moral principle that, in all worlds, places limits upon the sacrifices an individual is morally required to make for others—be it to save them, or to avoid killing them, or whatever. In this way one can avoid having an ethical point of view that would, in some worlds, 'never let us rest except to gather strength to resume the battle', and one can do this without embracing the incoherent idea of basic ethical principles that vary from one world to another.[30]

The second factor that Trammell believes underlies the distinction between acting and refraining, and makes it a morally significant one, is what he refers to as 'optionality':

Some actions either destroy a good or make it impossible for anyone else to realize a certain good; whereas other actions do not destroy and perhaps leave open to others the option of realizing the good in question. Suppose that the continuation of *x*'s life is good. Then obviously if someone kills *x*, not only does the killer fail to contribute toward the realization of this good; he also closes everyone else's option to do so. But if a Levite or priest merely passes by on the other side of *x*, then at least the option is left open for some Good Samaritan to come along and provide *x* the aid he needs to live.[31]

The problem with this is that if one is to show that there is a moral difference between causing and allowing to happen, one must be careful to ensure that other relevant factors do not vary from one situation to the other. One obviously relevant factor is the probability that a certain sort of outcome, such as someone's death, will result from action, or from inaction, as the case may be. Trammell fails, here, to keep that factor constant.

In order to keep it constant, cases of killing must be compared, not with cases of failing to save, where it is possible

---

[30] Bruce Russell, in his article, 'On the Relative Strictness of Negative and Positive Duties', *American Philosophical Quarterly*, Volume 14, Number 2, 1977, pp. 87–97, criticizes Trammell along rather similar lines. Russell contends that the proper conclusion to draw from the facts that Trammell cites is 'not that people are not morally required to expend as much effort or incur as much risk to help the needy as to avoid injuring anyone. It is rather that the amount of effort can be distributed with a certain amount of leeway when it comes to aiding the needy, given that to try to aid everyone would lead one beyond the bounds of moral obligations.' (p. 94.)

[31] 'Saving Life and Taking Life', p. 135.

the person may be saved by someone else, but with cases of allowing to die, where 'allowing to die' is so construed that one cannot be said to have allowed someone to die unless they do die as a result of one's inactivity. Alternatively, if one wants to focus upon cases of failing to save, the appropriate comparison is not with actions that are certain to result in someone's death, but with actions whose probability of leading to death is the same as when one fails to save someone. When this is done, there is no difference in 'optionality' between corresponding cases of bringing about and of allowing to happen.[32]

A third factor that Trammell believes makes negative duties more serious than positive ones is what he refers to as 'responsibility':

A fire is started by Miller. Both Miller and Thompson, who also happens on the scene, witness a woman on the third floor crying for help. According to the responsibility factor, if everything else is equal, Miller is more obligated to try to save the woman than Thompson, because Miller is responsible for the woman being in the situation of needing to be saved, whereas Thompson is not. In general, if x kills y, then x is responsible for y's death. But if x fails to save y, then x may or may not be responsible for y being in the situation in which y needs to be saved. The more directly involved x is for y's needing to be saved, the more responsible x is for helping to rescue y.[33]

What does Trammell mean by 'responsibility'? In particular, is it a matter of moral responsibility for a state of affairs, or simply a matter of being part of the causal chain that brought the state about? Bruce Russell, in his discussion of Trammell, thinks that it is the latter, and he then points out that if a person accidentally and non-negligently thrusts someone into a dangerous situation, that person, being only causally, and not morally responsible, is not under a greater obligation to save the person than is anyone else.[34]

---

[32] Compare Russell's discussion, op. cit., pp. 91-2, and Morillo's discussion, op. cit., p. 35. Morillo also sets out, in section I of her paper, a method of describing acts that is very helpful in the present context. The framework she recommends involves a distinction between the 'decision perspective' and the 'results perspective', and it also involves an explicit specification of the likelihood that an implemented decision will lead to a given, ethically significant consequence. (pp. 30-2.)

[33] Trammell, ibid., pp. 135-6.   [34] Russell, op. cit., p. 92.

Russell's interpretation may be right. A footnote to the passage quoted above, however, inclines me to think that Trammell is referring to moral responsibility, although the footnote also suggests that Trammell has not really made up his mind on this matter. In any case, let us consider the significance of this third factor if it is taken to be moral responsibility.

In order to do so, we need to get clear about the argument Trammell is advancing. There are two arguments that might be extracted from the passage quoted above. The first is this. If John kills Mary, John is responsible for Mary's death. If John merely allows Mary to die, John may very well not be responsible for Mary's being in a situation where she needs to be saved. So killing always involves responsibility, by definition, while letting die does not. But, as the case of Miller and Thompson shows, responsibility adds to the seriousness of the relevant obligation. Therefore the obligation not to kill is in itself more serious than the obligation to save.

This argument is invalid. From the fact that John may allow Mary to die without being responsible for her being in a situation in which she needs to be saved, it does not follow that letting die need not involve any responsibility factor. If John lets Mary die he is responsible for her death—that is, for precisely what he would be responsible for if he killed her. So killing and letting die do not differ with respect to any responsibility factor.

One way in which Trammell might try to resist this response is to opt for the non-moral construal of 'responsibility'. Then there is a difference between killing and letting die. But then he is exposed to Russell's objection, mentioned above.

This explains, perhaps, why Trammell fails to get completely clear about how he is interpreting the term 'responsibility'. If it is to be a morally relevant factor, it must be interpreted in the moral sense. But if the preceding argument is to be acceptable, it must be interpreted in the non-moral, causal sense.

There is a second reconstruction of Trammell's argument, suggested by Russell. According to it, the argument involves two premisses:

(1) The duty to bring aid on the part of those who are

responsible for some injury or danger is greater than the
duty to bring aid on the part of those who are not responsible for the injury or danger;
(2) The duty to bring aid on the part of those who are
responsible for some injury or danger is of exactly the
same strength as the duty not to injure or endanger in the
first place.

From this it follows immediately that the duty not to injure
or endanger is greater than the duty to bring aid on the part
of those who are not responsible for the injury or danger.[35]

Russell's response to this argument is that, contrary to
Trammell's view, it is plausible that the duty to bring aid on
the part of those who are responsible for some injury or
danger is stronger than the duty not to injure or endanger in
the first place, and thus premiss (2) is false.[36]

It may not be clear that Russell is right in maintaining that
the problem lies with premiss (2). What is clear, however, is
that it is *not* reasonable to accept both premisses. This can be
seen as follows. First, *if* one holds that John has a stronger
obligation to save Mary if he is morally responsible for her
being in danger than if he is not, it would seem that one
should *also* hold that if John places Mary in a situation where
her life is threatened, and she escapes, through no help of his,
then John has a greater obligation not to kill her than not to
kill someone else. For it can be argued, with equal plausibility
in either case, that John has wronged Mary, and thus owes
her more than someone he has not wronged. Second, how
does John's obligation to save someone he has put in danger
compare with his obligation not to kill someone whom he has
put in danger, but who has escaped? Suppose John has tied
both Mary and Jim to the main trolley line, and that Mary
has been removed, but placed on a siding. John is now confronted with the choice of leaving the trolley on the main
line, where it will kill Jim, or switching it onto the siding,
where it will kill Mary. In one case he refrains from killing
Mary, but allows Jim to die. In the other he saves Jim, but
kills Mary. Confronted with this example, most people feel
that there is no moral difference between switching and not

<hr>

[35] Ibid., p. 92.   [36] Ibid., p. 93.

switching the trolley. If these intuitions are right, the obligation not to kill someone whose life one has previously endangered is no stronger than the obligation to save someone whose life one has placed in jeopardy. And this, together with the claim that the obligation not to kill someone whose life one has previously put in jeopardy, but who escaped without one's assistance, is stronger than the general obligation to refrain from killing—a claim that cannot plausibly be rejected without also rejecting premiss (1) of Trammell's argument—entails that the obligation to save someone whom one has placed in danger is stronger than the general obligation not to kill. In short, one cannot reasonably accept both premiss (1) and premiss (2) in the second reconstruction of Trammell's argument. The upshot is that none of the three reasons that Trammell advances in support of the view that negative duties are more serious than the corresponding positive ones is acceptable.

Trammell attempted to refute the moral symmetry principle by offering detailed objections to it. An alternative way of attacking that principle would involve attempting to establish some general moral theory that is incompatible with it. Among the more important moral theories that have this property is the one defended by Alan Donagan in his recent book, *The Theory of Morality*. It may be useful to conclude this survey of possible objections to the moral symmetry principle by examining the position defended by Donagan.

The relevant parts of Donagan's discussion are as follows. First, he sets out what he takes to be the fundamental principle of morality. In its preferred formulation, this states: '*It is impermissible not to respect every human being, oneself or any other, as a rational creature.*'[37] Then he goes on to develop, in some detail, a system of morality based upon that fundamental principle. In setting out that system, Donagan makes use of the distinction between perfect and imperfect duties—between actions that are never permissible, and actions that are morally required provided that the action is not, in the individual case, also an action that is never permissible. It is in terms of this distinction that

[37] Alan Donagan, *The Theory of Morality*, 1977, p. 66.

Donagan construes what he calls the 'Pauline principle', i.e. the claim that it is never permissible to do evil that good may come of it. On Donagan's interpretation this is just the analytically true assertion that it is never permissible to violate a perfect duty in order to satisfy what would otherwise be an imperfect duty.

Donagan also advances a number of substantive claims about perfect and imperfect duties however, and it is these that are of interest here. First, Donagan holds that there are perfect duties. His view here contrasts sharply with that of many present-day moral philosophers, who would contend that for any type of action that is prima facie impermissible it is possible to conceive of a situation in which the consequences of not performing an action of that sort would be so horrendous that the action would be, not merely permissible, but obligatory.

Second, there is Donagan's allocation of duties to the perfect/imperfect categories. The duty not to kill people who satisfy certain conditions (innocent people who are not, even unwittingly, a threat to one?) is a perfect duty. In contrast, the duty to save people satisfying precisely the same conditions is only an imperfect duty. Donagan derives the latter duty from what he calls the principle of beneficence—a principle that, for him, specifies our imperfect, non-institutional duties to others: 'It is impermissible not to promote the well-being of others by actions in themselves permissible, inasmuch as one can do so without proportionate inconvenience.'[38] If the system of morality set out by Donagan is correct, then, it is impermissible to kill someone in order to save others, and the moral symmetry principle must be rejected.

Finally, there is Donagan's defence of the moral outlook in question. Donagan attempts to find a ground for the fundamental principle in man's rational nature—more specifically, in the Kantian idea that rational nature exists as an end in itself. Donagan maintains that once this idea is granted, the fundamental principle follows unproblematically. The problem is thus one of establishing the ground.[39]

[38] Ibid., p. 85   [39] Ibid., pp. 229 ff.

Perhaps the place to begin an examination of the system of morality set out and advocated by Donagan is with the fundamental principle. As noted above, Donagan's preferred formulation of it is: 'It is impermissible not to respect every human being, oneself or any other, as a rational creature.' The first point to be made is that if the argument in chapter 4 is sound, this cannot be a basic moral principle; no basic moral principle can contain expressions referring to particular biological species. One needs, then, to shift to some such principle as: 'It is impermissible not to respect every creature that is either actually rational, or else potentially rational.'

Second, and this is the important point in the present context, Donagan's formulation of his fundamental principle is very misleading. This can be seen as follows. In view of the principle of beneficence, one does have a prima-facie duty to save others from threats to their lives or well-being. Donagan holds that the principle of beneficence follows from his fundamental principle. So his interpretation of the latter must be such that, for example, to allow someone to die when one could have saved that person with little sacrifice and without acting immorally is to fail to respect that individual as a rational creature. One can thus fail to respect someone not merely by doing certain things to him, but also by failing to do certain things for him. If these things were on a par, there would be no ground for complaint about Donagan's formulation of his fundamental principle. But Donagan holds that they are not on a par: the duty not to kill an 'innocent' person is a perfect duty; the duty to save an 'innocent' person an imperfect one. This crucial asymmetry, however, is completely concealed by Donagan's preferred formulation of his fundamental principle.

My reason for emphasizing the misleading quality of Donagan's preferred formulation is twofold. First, the fundamental principle, so formulated, appears considerably more plausible than it otherwise would. Second, it also lends an air of unmerited reasonableness to some of Donagan's most central claims and arguments, as we shall see shortly.

Why should one accept the fundamental principle proposed by Donagan? The structure of the justification he offers is outlined in the following passage:

The ground of the fundamental principle of morality (*oberstes prak-tischen Prinzip*), according to Kant, is that rational nature exists as an end in itself (*die vernünftige Natur existiert als Zweck an sich selbst*). From this ground it obviously follows that no rational being should ever be used merely as a means; always, even when he is being used as a means, he must at the same time be treated as an end. And that may also be expressed as: every rational creature is to be respected as such; which, in turn, in its application to human beings, yields the fundamental principle of common morality—every human being is to be respected as being a rational creature.

The argument from ground to principle is plain. The problem is whether the ground can be established.[40]

Donagan is inviting the reader to embrace the argument, and to ponder the obscure question of whether the ground can be established. This invitation should be declined; the argument itself is plainly invalid. The premiss is that rational nature exists as an end in itself. This is hardly a transparent saying. However there are passages in Kant which perhaps make what he is saying sufficiently clear: 'Suppose, however, there was something *whose existence* had *in itself* an absolute value, something which as *an end in itself* could be a ground of determinate laws; then in it, and in it alone, would there be the ground of a possible categorical imperative—that is, of a practical law.'[41] It seems, then, that an end in itself is some-thing that has value in itself, and not merely relative to other possible ends that one might have. Now if something does have value in itself, there is a sense in which it follows that one should not, in one's treatment of it, view it merely as a means to some end. One should take into account the fact that it is intrinsically valuable. But it does not follow from this that one should never use it only as a means in the sense that Donagan has in mind. This is clear if one considers a concrete case. A bomb is in a room containing a dozen people. Mary, who is not in the room, can remove it, but only by placing it in the vicinity of John. If Mary removes the bomb, it does not mean that she does not view John as an individual who is valuable in himself. It may merely be that she views the people in the room as having the same status,

---

[40] Ibid., p. 229.
[41] Immanuel Kant, *Groundwork of the Metaphysic of Morals*, p. 428, from the translation by H. J. Paton, *The Moral Law*, 1956, p. 95.

and decides that it would be better to maximize the number of rational creatures whose lives are preserved.

In short, what Donagan labels a 'plain' argument involves a sliding from (1) rational nature is an end in itself, through (2) no rational being should be used only as a means—where this is construed as asserting that the fact that an individual is rational should always be taken into account—and onto (3) no rational being should be used only as a means—where this is construed as ruling out killing, but not failing to save, in certain corresponding situations. The move from (1) to (2) is fine; that from (2) to (3) is simply invalid. Donagan's fundamental principle, involving as it does a crucial asymmetry, cannot be derived from the Kantian premiss.

There are, of course, other ways in which one might construe the expression 'end in itself'. Donagan, unfortunately, does not say what he has in mind. But one possibility that deserves to be mentioned has been suggested to me by Stanley Benn: something is an end in itself if certain occurrences involving it provide one with a reason for acting one way rather than another. Given this interpretation, a thing's being intrinsically valuable is just one way in which it might be an end in itself.

A shift to this more general interpretation does not, however, save Donagan's argument. The fact that a certain action of Mary's will kill John is a reason for her not acting in that way. But the fact that she can by acting in that way save a number of people is equally a reason for so acting. To construe 'end in itself' in terms of reasons for acting does not entail any asymmetry of the sort implicitly present in Donagan's fundamental principle.

The problem, in short, is that the ground offered by Donagan does not appear to involve any asymmetry with respect to acting and refraining from acting, while his fundamental principle does. As a consequence, Donagan's argument in support of his fundamental principle cannot be valid. But because Donagan's formulation of his fundamental principle does not make the asymmetry explicit, it is possible to overlook this problem. If the asymmetry were made explicit, I think that it is very unlikely that Donagan would be tempted to view his argument as unproblematic.

Another crucial claim, and supporting argument, occurs in Donagan's response to Jonathan Bennett's much-discussed article, 'Whatever the Consequences',[42] in which Bennett criticizes moral systems containing prohibitions that admit of absolutely no exceptions. In reply to Bennett, Donagan advances the following claim: 'For any member of the class of deontological systems in which the sole fundamental principle ordains respect for beings of a certain kind—and I do not think that Bennett would maintain that members of that class are as such irrational—demonstrably must contain both a counterpart of the Pauline principle and unconditional prohibitions of certain kinds of action.'[43]

This is a rather surprising contention. Why should there be any connection at all between a moral system's having as its sole fundamental principle one that enjoins respect for beings of a given sort, and either unconditional prohibitions, or any counterpart of the Pauline principle? Donagan's answer is contained in the following argument:

Let *S* be a deductive moral system, having as its single first principle that all *K*s are to be respected as *K*s. Grant that there are goods proper to *K*s which they rationally pursue, and evils proper to them which they rationally avoid. *S* must, in that case, contain precepts enjoining the promotion of those goods and the avoidance and relief of those evils. However, since those precepts derive from the first principle—that respect may not be withheld from any *K*—they must also embody the restriction that it is impermissible, whether in promoting those goods or in avoiding or relieving those evils, to withhold respect from *K*s as *K*s; or, in other words, to violate any of the prohibitory precepts in which various kinds of withholding such respect are specified. Such a restriction is plainly a counterpart of the Pauline principle: it ordains that evil (the withholding of respect from *K*s as *K*s) must not be done that good may come of it.[44]

This argument is unsatisfactory. In the first place, it begins with an implicit assumption that seems clearly unjustified. For Donagan, in advancing this argument, is claiming to show that '. . . any member of the class of deontological systems in which the sole fundamental principle ordains respect for beings of a certain kind . . . demonstrably must contain both

[42] Jonathan Bennett, 'Whatever the Consequences' *Analysis*, Volume 26, 1965, pp. 83–102.
[43] Op. cit., p. 157.   [44] Ibid., p. 157.

a counterpart of the Pauline principle and unconditional prohibitions of certain kinds of action'. In supporting this claim, he asks us to consider 'a deductive moral system, having as its single first principle that all *K*s are to be respected as *K*s'. However there are alternative ways of formulating a deontological system containing a single fundamental principle that ordains respect for things of a certain sort. Thus, rather than employing a universally quantified principle stating that all *K*s are to be respected as *K*s—as Donagan wrongly assumes one must—one can base the system upon the principle that there is only one wrong-making characteristic of actions, namely, failure to respect *K*s as *K*s.

Secondly, no acceptable moral system can incorporate the principle that all *K*s are to be respected as *K*s. The reason is that allowing a number of innocent *K*s to be destroyed is certainly to fail to respect those *K*s as *K*s. So if one were to adopt the principle that respect may not be withheld from *any K*—a principle that Donagan contends is in no way irrational—one would have to hold that it is impermissible to allow a number of innocent *K*s to be destroyed. But the situation may be one in which one can prevent innocent *K*s from being destroyed only by destroying some other *K*. Whatever one does, there will be one or more *K*s that one has failed to respect as *K*s. To adopt Donagan's method of formulating the deontological system in question means that one is driven to the unacceptable conclusion that one can, without having done anything wrong, find oneself in situations where whatever one does is morally wrong.

Moreover, this problem cannot be resolved by *adding* something to the system—such as the Pauline principle. The fact that there are situations in which every action is impermissible, in view of the principle that all *K*s are to be respected as *K*s, is unaffected by any supplementation of that principle by one or more other principles. The only way to remove the difficulty is by abandoning that principle in favour of some alternative.

One possibility is to adopt the wrong-making characteristics formulation. This is, I believe, by far the most plausible approach, given the problem of actions with terrible consequences. Alternatively, one can introduce some distinction between different ways in which one may fail to respect some *K*s as *K*s—such as that between cases of causing and cases of allowing to happen. Then, given that distinction, one might do as Donagan does, and adopt the view, first, that one should never *do* anything that involves a failure to respect any *K* as a *K*, and second, that to the extent that is compatible with that, one should never allow anything to happen that involves a failure to respect *K*s as *K*s. But equally, one could adopt the view that one's primary obligation is to prevent occurrences that, if allowed, would involve a failure to respect some *K*s as *K*s, and then, to the extent that it is compatible with that primary obligation, that one should never do anything involving a failure to respect *K*s as *K*s.

In conclusion, then, Donagan is mistaken, first of all, in thinking that a deontological system containing as its sole principle one enjoining respect for *K*s as *K*s will contain a counterpart of the Pauline principle that one should never do evil that good may come of it. It might equally well contain a reverse Pauline principle, asserting that one should never refrain from doing evil when good will result. Or, more plausibly, it might contain neither.

And second, Donagan is also mistaken in thinking that such a deontological system would unconditionally prohibit actions that involve failure to respect any *K* as a *K*. For given situations that actually occur, such an unconditional prohibition would have the absurd consequence that one could, through no moral fault, find oneself confronted with situations in which whatever one did was morally wrong.

Finally, let us consider whether the system of morality that Donagan proposes agrees with the moral intuitions of most people. The crucial question is whether people in general believe that certain moral rules should take the form of unconditional prohibitions. Do they believe, for example, that one should never kill an innocent person no matter how many lives will be saved?

One would have expected Donagan to grapple with this problem in chapter 6 of his book, which deals with 'Consequentialism'. Unfortunately, he tends to skirt the issue, and focuses his discussion on much more problematic questions, such as whether one should kill someone if someone else threatens to kill a number of people unless one does so. One case that he does discuss, albeit briefly, is that in which a number of people are trapped underground, and will drown unless they blast themselves out, but know that if they do so, they will kill some picnickers. Donagan says that many 'would intuitively condemn the blowing up of the innocent picnickers as murder'.[45] I think this is doubtful, even where the number of picnickers is only slightly less than the number trapped. I also think that many who might initially be inclined to condemn the action would not do so upon reflection, if they were to consider the points raised above in defence of the moral symmetry principle. The main point, however, is that Donagan is committed to a much stronger claim than that the duty not to kill is more serious than the duty to save: he is saying that the former is infinitely more serious than the latter. This means that what he should be considering is the intuitions people have when they are asked about cases in which the number of innocent, trapped people becomes larger and larger relative to the number of picnickers.

Donagan does, in the end, confront this sort of case:

> Whenever a defender of traditional morality protests that there are moral rules which, whatever the consequences, must not be broken, such as the rule prohibiting murder—the killing of the materially innocent—a natural reaction is to confront him with imaginary horror upon imaginary horror, and to inquire whether it would not be permissible, nay right, to commit murder if these horrors would be the consequences of his not committing it.[46]

Donagan's response is that the sort of consequentialist escape clause suggested by such reflection is both 'crude and unnecessary':

> For, in laying down that its precepts are to be observed no matter what the consequences, traditional morality does not imply that they are to be observed, let us say, if the consequences should be the death of everybody on earth. It has been constructed at every point with careful attention to the nature both of human action and of the world in which it takes place. The worst efforts of 'situation ethics' to invent situations in which the consequences of abiding by traditional morality would be some world calamity have resulted in nothing but absurd fantasies. In short, the nature of traditional morality is such that observing it cannot, except by unpredictable accidents, have calamitous consequences.[47]

[45] Ibid., p. 179.   [46] Ibid., p. 206.   [47] Ibid., p. 206.

Readers who are hesitant about associating themselves with 'the worst efforts of "situation ethics"' may be satisfied by this reply. However it is clear that Donagan's response here is not really satisfactory, since it is simply false that it is only by *unpredictable accidents* that the observation of 'traditional morality' could have calamitous consequences. There is no difficulty in constructing a doomsday case in which Mary *knows* that the world will be destroyed unless she murders John. To reply by labelling such cases 'absurd fantasies' is to abandon argument in favour of abuse. To the extent that the intuitions that are shared by Donagan and the overwhelming majority of people on these matters are correct, such logically possible fantasies provide grounds for believing that no adequate system of morality can be a deductive system involving exceptionless prohibitions of the sort advocated by Donagan. Consequentialist considerations show, then, that Donagan's proposed moral outlook is intuitively unacceptable.

To sum up. Donagan sets out a system of morality which, if correct, shows that the moral symmetry principle must be rejected. Donagan defends that system of morality by contending, first of all, that the fundamental principle of that system can be derived from the view that rational nature exists as an end in itself. However we have seen that, in view of the asymmetry involved in his fundamental principle, no such entailment exists. Second, Donagan attempts to show that any system having as its sole fundamental principle respect for beings of a certain sort must involve unconditional prohibitions, together with some counterpart of the Pauline principle. We have seen that this claim is also false.

Donagan has not, therefore, provided any sound reason for accepting the moral system that he proposes, and there are, on the other hand, good reasons for rejecting it. In particular, in asserting that certain actions are never to be done under any circumstances, he is putting forward a view that is incompatible with the moral intuitions of the overwhelming majority of people.

In this section I have tried to examine the most important objections to the moral symmetry principle. I have argued that when the principle is correctly formulated—namely, as a thesis about related right-making and wrong-making characteristics—it does not conflict with the reflective intuitions of most people, and that, in general, the objections that have been directed against it are unsound.

7

Possible Persons

In section 6.3 a number of arguments were advanced in support of the view that it is not wrong, or at least not seriously so, to destroy potential persons. In the case of the argument based upon the moral symmetry principle I pointed out, however, that the argument shows that the destruction of potential persons is not wrong (or not seriously so) only on the assumption that it is not wrong (or not seriously so) to refrain from producing additional persons. The same is true of some of the other arguments, such as that involving the generalized potentiality principle. The present chapter will be devoted to an examination of this crucial, underlying assumption.

Is there a prima-facie obligation to produce additional persons? Or, alternatively, to produce additional persons with certain characteristics, such as persons who will be happy, or who are capable of leading satisfying lives? If there is such a prima-facie obligation, how serious is it? Or, if it turns out that there is no such *obligation*, might it not none the less be a good thing in itself to produce additional people, or at least additional people who will lead satisfying lives? Might the world not be intrinsically *better* for having more people, or more people with certain properties?

The discussion has two main aspects. On the one hand, a number of interesting and important philosophical arguments have recently been advanced in support of affirmative answers to one or more of the above questions. Some of these arguments raise difficult issues indeed. However I shall attempt to show that none of the arguments provides one with a good reason for holding either that there is a prima-facie obligation, or that it is in itself a good thing, to produce additional persons, or additional persons with certain properties.

Second, a number of philosophers have attempted to formulate some appealing, general ethical thesis that will have the consequence that, considered in itself, there is no moral reason to produce additional persons, even if they would lead especially satisfying lives. Some such theses seem initially very plausible. But on reflection, it turns out that they have quite unpalatable consequences. I shall attempt to show, however, that there is a plausible general thesis that is free of unacceptable consequences, and which implies that, considered in itself, there is no moral reason to produce additional persons, regardless of how satisfactory their lives will be.

7.1 Hare's Golden Rule Argument

Perhaps the place to begin is with an interesting and much discussed article by Hare, entitled 'Abortion and the Golden Rule',[1] in which he attempts to show that there is a prima-facie obligation to produce additional people. Hare's primary appeal is to 'a type of argument which, in one guise or another, has been the formal basis of almost all theories of moral reasoning that have contributed much that is worth while to our understanding of it'.[2] The argument can be stated in different ways. Rather than his own preferred, universal prescriptivist formulation, Hare sets out a version based upon an extension of the Golden Rule:

I shall use that form of the argument which rests on the Golden Rule that we should do to others as we wish them to do to us. It is a logical extension of this form of argument to say that we should do to others what *we are glad was* done to us. Two (surely readily admissible) changes are involved here. The first is a mere difference in the two tenses which cannot be morally relevant. Instead of saying that we should do to others as we wish them (in the future) to do to us, we say that we should do to others as we wish that they had done to us (in the past). The second is a change from the hypothetical to the actual: instead of saying that we should do to others as we wish that they had done to us, we say that we should do to others as we are glad that they did do to us. I cannot see that this could make any difference to the spirit of the injunction, and logical grounds could in any case be given, based on the universal prescriptivist thesis, for extending the Golden Rule in this way.[3]

[1] R. M. Hare, 'Abortion and the Golden Rule', *Philosophy & Public Affairs*, Volume 4, Number 3, 1975, pp. 201-22.
[2] Ibid., p. 207. [3] Ibid., p. 208.

Given this extension of the Golden Rule, Hare argues that it follows immediately that there is a prima facie obligation to produce additional people:

> . . . when I am glad that I was born (the basis, it will be remembered, of the argument that the Golden Rule therefore places upon me an obligation not to stop others being born), I do not confine this gladness to gladness that they did not abort me. I am glad, also, that my parents copulated in the first place, without contraception. So from my gladness, in conjunction with the extended Golden Rule, I derive not only a duty not to abort, but also a duty not to abstain from procreation.[4]

Is this argument sound? If it is, it would seem to necessitate quite a radical revision of the ethical outlooks of most people. The reason is this. First, although the Golden Rule does not explicitly talk about *the extent* to which a given action is obligatory, it would seem to entail statements that do. John may want others both to refrain from robbing him, and to save his life when he is in danger. But he may also prefer being robbed to being allowed to die. The latter preference, together with the Golden Rule, would seem to support the view that the duty to save someone is more serious than the duty not to rob. And in general, the Golden Rule would seem to entail that we should do A rather than B to others if we would prefer others to do A rather than B to us. Secondly, most people would, I think, say that they would prefer being killed at age thirty, say, to never having been conceived. It is possible this attitude is somehow confused. For it is sometimes felt that there is something odd about preferences over alternatives, one of which is that the individual in question *never* existed. One source of the feeling of oddness is that there seems to be an intimate conceptual connection between preferences and choices, and an individual can never be confronted with a choice among alternatives, one of which involves his never having existed. But if there is an objection to talk about preferring being murdered at age thirty to never having been conceived, it will also tell against Hare's argument. So we can assume, without prejudice to Hare, that sense can be made of the preference in question. It then follows, in view of the Golden Rule's implications about

[4] Ibid., p. 212.

the relative wrongness of different actions, that it is prima facie more wrong to refrain from actualizing a possible person than to murder an actual person.

This conclusion not merely conflicts with the moral intuitions of most people, but does so very strongly. Indeed, I suspect that most people would agree with the moral outlook expressed by Mary Anne Warren in the following passage:

Imagine that you are approached by alien scientists, who propose to create billions of replicas of you, that is billions of new people with your genetic code, by separating the cells of your body and using each to clone a new individual. Being moral, the aliens first ask your permission for this operation, assuring you that all these new people will be given the chance to lead reasonably happy lives on some distant planet where they will not contribute to the earth's overpopulation problems. My intuition is that you would have absolutely no moral obligation to agree to such a proposal at the cost of your own life; and indeed I think that you would not be obligated to agree even if they were to promise eventually to reconstitute you as good as new. Hence I think that any right to life which a potential person as such might have is at least billions of times as weak as that of an actual person.[5]

What then, if anything, is wrong with Hare's argument? The fundamental flaw, I believe, is as follows. The crucial quantifier in the original, unextended Golden Rule, ranges over actual persons. That is to say, the 'others' whom the Golden Rule asserts one should treat in certain ways are actual individuals, existing at some time or other. If one extends the Golden Rule *merely* by removing tense restrictions, and by shifting from reference to what we would like others to do to us, to reference to what we are glad they did to us, one does not alter the range of the quantifier: the others will still be persons who are actual at some time or other. But when the extension is of this sort, the resulting principle has *no* implications with respect to abortion, or with respect to the production of additional persons.

[5] Mary Anne Warren, 'Do Potential People Have Moral Rights?', *Canadian Journal of Philosophy*, Volume 7, Number 2, 1977, pp. 275–89. See p. 278. Warren first advanced this intuitive argument in her article, 'On the Moral and Legal Status of Abortion', *Monist*, Volume 57, Number 1, 1973, pp. 43–61. See pp. 59–60.

This contention may initially strike one as dubious. For after all, one of the things that Mary's parents did is to produce her, and she is glad that they did. So why doesn't it follow that she ought to produce other persons? The reason is that the action that led, ultimately, to Mary's existence, was not something that her parents did *to* Mary. It was something they did to parts of the physical world. A pleasant rearrangement of biological entities resulted in an organism that subsequently gave rise to the person, Mary. Similarly, any activity of Mary that gives rise to other people will not be something she does *to* those people.

A natural response is that one can simply extend the Golden Rule in a slightly different way. Rather than saying, as Hare does, that we should do *to* others what we are glad was done to us, we can say that we should perform those actions that stand in some relation R to other persons such that we are glad that there were actions of that sort that stand in relation R to us. Thus extended, the principle certainly will imply there is a prima-facie obligation to produce additional persons.

This extension, however, is logically of a very different sort from the other. Suppose that one performs an action that, judged by the original unextended Golden Rule, is morally wrong. Then there will be some actual individual, existing at some time or other, whom one has harmed, or failed to benefit. This means that the obligation that one has failed to meet can be viewed as an obligation *to* that individual. The same will be true in the case of the first extension of the Golden Rule. But it will not be true of the second one. If one refrains from producing an additional person, one acts contrary to the second extension of the Golden Rule, but there will not be, in that case, any actual individual, existing at any time, whom one has either harmed or failed to benefit, or to whom one had an obligation that one failed to meet.[6]

Does this mean that the extended Golden Rule is really incoherent? The answer is that it does not. There would seem,

---

[6] This point is put very clearly and forcefully by T. G. Roupas in his article, 'The Value of Life', *Philosophy & Public Affairs*, Volume 7, Number 2, 1978, pp. 154–83. See pp. 162–3.

for example, to be nothing unintelligible about the notion of obligations that are not obligations *to* any individuals. Indeed, in what follows we shall see that there are good reasons for acknowledging at least some obligations of precisely this sort.

My point, then, is not that the extended Golden Rule is conceptually muddled. It is simply that the move from the original Golden Rule to the second extension of it involves more than the two changes mentioned by Hare, viz. the change of tenses, and the shift from a reference to how we would like others to act to a reference to how we are glad they did act. The 'generalization' of the Golden Rule involves a move from a principle that gives rise to obligations that can always be viewed as obligations to individuals, and the breaking of which normally involve an infliction of harm upon, or a failure to benefit, the individual in question, to a principle that gives rise to obligations that need not have either of these characteristics.

These differences do not show that the second extension of the Golden Rule is incorrect. However, the fact that there are these differences, together with the fact that the revised Golden Rule has consequences that conflict strongly with the ordinary moral intuitions of most people does, I believe, show that additional support must be forthcoming, before one can be justified in holding that the revised version of the Golden Rule is an acceptable moral principle.

7.2 Roupas's Objective Value Argument

Another line of argument bearing upon the morality of producing additional persons has been advanced by T. G. Roupas. His argument, in contrast to Hare's, is not intended to show that there is a prima-facie obligation to produce additional persons. It is concerned instead with questions of value. Thus, one of the conclusions that Roupas wishes to establish is that the world is a better place, other things being equal, if it contains additional people who are glad that they exist.

Roupas's argument involves connecting the objective values of different complete states of affairs with the subjective preferences of individuals. The connection is via a

notion of objective preference, which is explained in the
following passage:

Let S_1 and S_2 be complete states of affairs, and let A_1, A_2, A_3, . . .
be all the individuals, actual or hypothetical, in either S_1 or S_2. Suppose
that a given actual person x is trying to decide which of S_1 and S_2 is
objectively preferable. In making this decision x suppresses his knowledge of which, if any, of the individuals A_1, A_2, A_3, . . . he himself in
fact happens to be. For each A_i in turn, x considers which of S_1 and
S_2 he subjectively prefers on the assumption that he is the individual
A_i. . . . Finally, in the light of the conditional preferences obtained by
this means, x asks himself which of S_1 and S_2 he prefers on the supposition that there is an equal likelihood of his being any of the individuals A_1, A_2, A_3, . . .[7]

The objective preferences of individuals, thus defined,
need not coincide. One reason is that the procedure described
for determining objective preferences involves decision under
conditions of uncertainty, and people differ about what
principles are appropriate in such circumstances. Another is
that the subjective preferences of individuals differ. But
Roupas argues that there will be important cases in which the
objective preferences of all individuals—or at least, all rational
individuals—will coincide. And he holds that when all rational
individuals would objectively prefer S_1 to S_2, that is a sufficient reason for concluding that the objective value of S_1 is
greater than that of S_2.

One such case is this. Let S_1 be a state of affairs that
differs from S_2 only in that it contains one or more additional individuals—beyond those that exist in S_2—who are
glad, throughout their lives, that they exist. Now, provided
that one grants that any rational individual will, as a matter
of fact, prefer a life in which he is glad he is alive to complete
non-existence, it follows that any rational individual will
objectively prefer S_1 to S_2. The reason is this. Every
individual who exists in S_2 also exists in S_1 and, by hypothesis, is just as glad that he exists when in S_1 as when in
S_2. On the other hand, there are one or more individuals
who exist in S_1, and who are glad that they exist, and who do
not exist in S_2. Therefore any person who prefers a happy

---

[7] Roupas, op. cit., pp. 171-2.

existence to non-existence, if he is asked which world he would prefer to see actualized, without knowing which individual, actual or possible, he will be, will choose S_1, since he cannot be worse off in S_1 than in S_2, and he may be better off, since he may happen to be an individual who exists in S_1 but not in S_2. Hence if S_1 differs from S_2 only in containing additional people who are glad they exist, S_1 is objectively better than S_2.

One way of responding to this argument is to challenge the assumption that a rational individual will prefer a world in which he exists, and is glad that he exists, to a world in which he does not exist at all. Roupas points out that this assumption has been questioned by philosophers such as Thomas Nagel and Bernard Williams.[8] He contends, however, that it would be 'very odd indeed' if it were rational to prefer a longer life to a shorter life for oneself, but not to prefer some life to none at all, and he offers the following account of the mistake upon which the view in question rests:

The mistake lies . . . in the assumption that where a person is *here and now* contemplating two complete states of affairs S_1 and S_2, it is not rational for him to prefer S_1 to S_2 unless he fares better in S_1 than he fares in S_2. That this assumption is at best questionable appears as soon as we compare it with another assumption about rational preference: that as long as more net good befalls a person in S_1 than befalls him in S_2 (whether he shows up in both S_1 and S_2 or not), it is rational for him to prefer S_1 to S_2. This alternative assumption is no less plausible than the one being challenged, yet it contradicts that one in its implications for the case at hand.[9]

The issue strikes me as rather more problematic than Roupas is prepared to allow. The reason was mentioned earlier: it is tempting to hold that there is a fairly tight conceptual connection between preferences and the choices one would make in the corresponding situations. So there is a prima-facie difficulty in making sense of talk about preferences among alternatives some of which involve worlds in which one never existed. One could never be confronted with such a choice. The question, then, is whether there is a plausible analysis of the concept of preferring that does allow one to talk about such preferences.

8 Ibid., pp. 166-7.   9 Ibid., p. 167.

I am inclined to think that there is. Consequently, I do not think that the defect in Roupas's argument lies in his assumption that people who have not been corrupted by certain philosophical arguments will, if rational, prefer some life to none at all. If there is an error, it seems rather to lie in the method of constructing objective value rankings out of subjective preferences.

That something is wrong with Roupas's method is strongly suggested by some of its consequences. First, compare the following two worlds. A contains 100 people, each of whom enjoys 100 units of happiness. B contains the same 100 people, each enjoying 120 units of happiness, together with an additional 100 people, each of whom enjoys only 1 unit of happiness. The reason that the first group is happier in world B than in world A is that in World B all the unpleasant tasks are carried out by the addditional 100 people, which is why they lead lives that are just barely worth living. How does world A compare with world B? Everyone who exists in world A also exists in world B, and is better off there. And those who exist only in world B lead lives that are (just barely) worth living. So every individual who is actual either in world A or world B should prefer his state in world B. Roupas's approach then implies that world B is objectively better than world A—that is to say, a world can be improved by adding some minimally happy serfs who will increase the happiness of other members of society.

Second, Roupas's approach appears to lead to what Derek Parfit has referred to as the Repugnant Conclusion—where this is the view that for any world containing a finite number of people leading extremely satisfying lives, there is a better world that contains a larger number of people, but each of whom leads a life that is just barely worth living.[10] The argument that shows this is Parfit's Mere Addition Argument, and may be stated as follows. Let A be a world containing 100 people, each enjoying 100 units of happiness. Let A+ be a world that differs from A only in the addition of some extra happy people. These additional people do not affect the 100

[10] Derek Parfit discusses his Mere Addition Argument in his paper, 'On Doing the Best for our Children', pp. 100–15 of *Ethics and Population*, edited by Michael Bayles, 1976. See especially Parfit's discussion in footnotes 11 and 34.

people who exist both in A and in A+. In short, A+ contains the 100 people who exist in world A, enjoying precisely the same level of happiness—100 units—together with, let us say, 100 additional people, each enjoying 10 units of happiness. Finally, let world B contain the same 200 people as are in world A+, but where each person enjoys 60 units of happiness. How do these three worlds compare, given Roupas's method of determining objective value? First, consider worlds A and A+. Everyone who exists in A also exists in A+, and is precisely as well off. On the other hand, there are people who exist in world A+, but not in world A. All of them enjoy, in world A+, lives that are worth living. As a result, Roupas's approach implies that world A+ is objectively better than world A. Second, compare worlds A+ and B. Roupas's method by itself does not imply that world B is better than world A+. To have any implications as to the relative value of these two worlds the method must be supplemented by some account of the principles a rational person will follow in making decisions under conditions of uncertainty. But it turns out that every plausible account of those principles leads to the same result in the present case. Suppose that one should choose in such a way as to avoid disastrous outcomes. Then one should choose world B rather than world A+. Suppose, on the other hand, that the rational procedure is to choose the world where one's expected level of happiness is greatest. Again, this will be world B, where the average level of happiness is 60, rather than world A+, where it is 55. The upshot is that if one accepts Roupas's method of constructing objective value rankings out of subjective preferences, it is difficult to avoid the conclusion that world B is better than world A+. And this, together with the previous consequence that world A+ is better than world A, forces one to conclude that world B is better than world A. Roupas's approach implies, therefore, that it is a good thing to double the population, even if the average level of happiness must be cut by 40 per cent.

This argument can, of course, be repeated. Such iteration will generate a sequence of worlds containing more and more people at successively lower levels of happiness. Roupas's approach thus forces him to accept Parfit's Repugnant

Conclusion, and to hold that a world containing a massive number of barely happy people is better than a world that contains a smaller number of people leading extremely satisfying lives.

Nor does the repugnancy end there. Consider the following three worlds, each of which contains only people who are minimally happy at every point in their lives. C contains 100 people who will live to age 70. C+ contains the same 100 people, with the same life expectancy, together with an additional 100 people who will live only to age 30. World D contains the same 200 people as world C+, but now with a life expectancy of 55. Application of the same argument as above shows that Roupas's approach commits him to the conclusion that world D, which contains more people living substantially shorter lives, is better than world C. Iterating this argument, and combining its conclusion with the previous one, leads to the result that a world containing a massive number of people living extremely short, minimally happy lives, is a better world than one containing a smaller number of people living long and very happy lives.

These objections would appear very damaging. There is, however, a serious question concerning the criticism that Roupas's approach leads to the Repugnant Conclusion. It arises from the fact that the Mere Addition Argument can be put in a more general way than it was above, so that it does not appeal to principles peculiar to Roupas's approach. The question then becomes how anyone can avoid being forced to accept the Repugnant Conclusion. Unless it can be shown that the more general version of the argument is somehow faulty, it cannot be fair to criticize Roupas on the ground that his approach runs foul of the Mere Addition Argument.

This problem will be tackled in section 7.4, when I discuss Parfit's Mere Addition Argument itself. There I shall attempt to show, first, that the argument can be answered, and thus that one can avoid being driven to the Repugnant Conclusion, but second, that the argument, in the more specific form set out above, is still a telling objection to Roupas's position.

Why does Roupas's approach generate the above consequences? The relevant feature is that, in comparing two complete states of affairs, S_1 and S_2, one is to assume an equal likelihood of one's being any of the individuals who is actual in *at least one* of those states of affairs. This is not the only way of proceeding. One might instead compare S_1 with S_2 by assuming that if S_1 were actual, there would be an equal likelihood of one's being any of the individuals who is actual in S_1, while if S_2 were the case, there would be an equal likelihood of one's being any of the individuals who is actual in S_2. The latter method of making comparisons would lead to quite different results.

Roupas attempts to counter this sort of objection. He refers to Hare's critical study of Rawls's book, *A Theory of Justice*, in which Hare rejects Rawls's construal of the original position on the ground that 'in Rawls' system the interests of possible people are simply not going to be taken account of'.[11] Roupas contends that the proper way of setting up the original position depends upon whether one is concerned with justice or with value. Given that no one is being treated unjustly when a hypothetical person is denied existence, the original position is properly restricted to actual individuals if one's concern is with justice. But the situation is quite otherwise when one is concerned with value:

Hare's criticism of Rawls is therefore misconceived inasmuch as justice and not value was Rawls' concern. On the other hand if (objective) value is the concern, then purely hypothetical individuals must be given equal consideration with actual individuals . . . This is because of the logical form of value judgements: such judgements predicate value of complete states of affairs, within which actual and hypothetical individuals show up in exactly the same way.[12]

The argument advanced by Roupas in this passage is unsound. It is true that in evaluating a given possible world it makes no difference whether the individuals who are actual *in* that world are in fact actual, or merely hypothetical. But it does not, of course, follow from this that in evaluating a given possible world one should take into account, not merely the individuals who are actual *in* that world, but also those who are actual only in other worlds, and hence

[11] R. M. Hare, 'Rawls' Theory of Justice—I and II', *Philosophical Quarterly*, Volume 23, 1973, pp. 144–55 and 241–52. See p. 245.
[12] Roupas, op. cit., p. 177.

hypothetical *in* the world in question. So Roupas has offered us no reason for thinking that in evaluating a given world one should consider individuals, be they actual or hypothetical, who are not actual in the world in question.

The outcome is this. On the one hand, the positive argument that Roupas offers in support of his approach has turned out to be unsound. On the other, his approach has some consequences that are quite implausible. It would seem, then, that one is justified in setting aside Roupas's attempt to show that, other things being equal, the world is a better place if it contains additional people who are glad they exist.

7.3 Obligations to Produce Additional Persons: Two Attempted Disavowals

I have considered, and offered grounds for rejecting, two attempts to show that there is a prima-facie moral reason, of an intrinsic sort, for adding happy people to the world. In this section I shall examine two attempts to show that there cannot be any prima-facie obligation, of an intrinsic sort, to produce additional persons, regardless of how satisfactory their lives would be.

7.31 Obligations to Individuals

One attempt to argue that there cannot be any prima-facie obligation, of an intrinsic sort, to produce additional persons, even ones who will lead very satisfactory lives, turns upon the claim that all obligations are obligations *to* (actual) individuals. This point granted, the conclusion follows swiftly. Consider an action that would produce additional people. The only individuals to whom this action necessarily makes a difference are the people produced by it. So given the assumption that all obligations are obligations to individuals, there can be a prima-facie, intrinsic obligation to perform the action only if there is a prima-facie obligation to the individuals who will be produced. But if the action is not performed, those individuals will not exist, so there certainly will not be any obligation to them that the action be performed. A decision not to produce additional people, then, cannot in itself be contrary to any prima-facie obligation that one has. Therefore, unless there can be obligations that can be honoured, but not breached, there cannot be any prima-facie, intrinsic obligation to produce additional persons.[13]

What is one to say about the crucial assumption that all obligations are obligations *to* individuals? A number of philosophers appear to accept this principle. Thus Jan Narveson, in his article 'Future People and Us', says: 'The idea, namely, is that there are people, in this case future ones, *to whom* we owe something or other. And indeed, it is plausible to generalize this and hold that duties must always be duties *to* someone or other: if no person is affected by an action, then that action (or inaction) cannot be a violation or fulfillment of a duty.'[14] In a similar vein, Thomas Schwartz, in an article arguing that we have no obligations to distant future generations, advances the following claim about our obligations to adopt some social policy P: 'I don't see how we can be *morally required* to adopt P unless we owe it to *someone* to adopt P—unless our *not* adopting P would, in some broad sense, *wrong* someone.'[15]

The view that all obligations are obligations *to* individuals is, however, exposed to a very strong objection. Suppose that John knows that, as a consequence of a genetic defect, any child he has will be condemned to a rather brief life full of excruciating pain. The claim that it would be prima facie seriously wrong for John to have a child in such circumstances would be widely accepted indeed. Yet on the view in question, if John does refrain from having a child, we will not be able to say that he acted in accordance with an important obligation, since there will never be any (actual) individual to whom the obligation in question was owed. In short, if there is a prima-facie obligation not to produce individuals whose lives will be worth not living, then not all obligations can be

---

[13] Compare Jan Narveson's discussion on pp. 43-4 of his article, 'Future People and Us', in *Obligations to Future Generations*, edited by R. I. Sikora and Brian Barry, 1978, pp. 38-60.

[14] Ibid., p. 43.

[15] Thomas Schwartz, 'Obligations to Posterity' pp. 3-13 in Sikora and Barry, op. cit. See pp. 11-12.

obligations to individuals.[16] The first attempt to establish that there cannot be any prima-facie, intrinsic obligation to produce additional persons must be set aside as unsatisfactory.

7.32 Wronging or Harming Individuals

A second attempt to justify the claim that there can be no prima-facie, intrinsic obligations to produce additional people, regardless of what sort of lives they would lead, appeals to one of the following two principles:

An action is, in itself, prima facie wrong only if performance of that action would necessarily make it the case that there would be someone for whom the action is *worse* than the non-performance of the action would have been.

An action is, in itself, prima facie wrong only if performance of that action would necessarily make it the case that there would be someone who would be *wronged* by the action.[17]

These principles seem quite plausible, and there are a number of philosophers who accept at least one of them. A version of the second principle, for example, is explicitly affirmed by Schwartz in the passage quoted above, and I believe that it is also implicitly embraced by Narveson in his article, 'Future People and Us'. On the other hand, the first principle appears to lie at the heart of Mary Anne Warren's argument in her article, 'Do Potential People Have Moral Rights?'[18]

If either principle is correct, the desired conclusion once again follows quickly. Suppose that Mary can produce a person who will enjoy a satisfactory life. If Mary does this, then it may be possible to say that her action has made it the case that there is someone who is better off than would be the case had she not performed the action. But on the other hand, if Mary chooses not to produce the person, it will not, in general, be true that there is some (actual) individual for whom things are *worse* as a result. Nor will it be the case in general that there is someone who is *wronged* by her decision not to produce a person who would lead a very satisfactory

---

[16] Jefferson McMahan, 'Problems of Population Theory', *Ethics*, Volume 92, Number 1, pp. 96–127. See p. 102.

[17] Compare McMahan, op. cit., pp. 101 and 102 respectively.

[18] Op. cit., pp. 285–6.

life. Therefore it follows, by virtue of either of the two principles, that there cannot be any prima-facie, intrinsic obligation to produce additional people.

This attempt to repudiate obligations to produce additional people is superior to the first attempt, since one can allow for the possibility of a prima-facie obligation to refrain from producing miserable people. For if one deliberately produces an individual whose life is so bad that it is worth not living, it seems plausible to hold both that one has wronged that individual, and that the action is one that is worse for him—though, as noted above, some philosophers have argued that the latter sort of claim involves conceptual confusion.

The second approach is, however, exposed to other important objections. A succinct statement of one that has been advanced by a number of writers is offered by Jonathan Glover:

Another reason has to do with the continuance of the human race. Suppose we could take a drug which would render us infertile, but make us so happy that we would not mind being childless. Would it be wrong for everyone now alive to take it, ensuring that we would be the last generation? Would it have mattered if the human race had become sterile thousands of years ago? Some people are indifferent to either of these possibilities, and I have no argument to convince them. But other people, including me, think that to end the human race would be about the worst thing it would be possible to do. This is because of a belief in the intrinsic value of there existing in the future at least some people with worth-while lives.[19]

Glover is right, I believe, in thinking that most people not only would like to see the human race continue, but would view its disappearance as an undesirable outcome. It is another question, however, what account is to be given of this widely shared feeling. Glover suggests that it reflects a belief that there is *intrinsic* value in the future existence of at least some people with worthwhile lives, but he does not appear to offer any support for this interpretation. Many desires that people have, after all, can only be satisfied if there are future generations. Many people would like to see man's understanding of reality continue to advance. Many would like to see a society

---

[19] Jonathan Glover, *Causing Deaths and Saving Lives*, 1977.

in which goods are more equitably distributed, and in which justice is achieved. Many would like to see people learning to interact in ways rather more rational than is the case now. The mere fact that people have such desires, and that some of their activities are directed toward such ends, itself gives one a reason for ascribing value to the continued existence of mankind.[20] In the absence of further argument, then, it would seem that one can explain the feelings that people have about the continued existence of the human race without attributing to them the belief that the continued existence of the human race possesses *intrinsic* value.

If this response can be sustained, as seems plausible, then the prospects for this second attempt at repudiating obligations to produce additional persons might seem very bright. For the underlying principles do have wide appeal, and if the extreme case where one allows the human race to come to an end does not pose an unanswerable objection, then one might think that other objections should occasion little difficulty. In the next section we shall see, however, that this is emphatically not the case.

7.33 Parfit and the Identity Problem

The crucial objection to the second attempt to show that there cannot be any prima-facie, intrinsic obligation to produce additional people has been formulated by Derek Parfit. The objection can be put in two slightly different ways, one of which is concerned with the actions of individuals, and the other with a choice between two social policies. Let us begin by considering the version of the argument in which one is to compare the actions of two women:

The first is one month pregnant, and is told by her doctor that, unless she takes a simple treatment, the child she is carrying will develop a certain handicap. We suppose again that life with this handicap would probably be worth living, but less so than a normal life. It would obviously be wrong for the mother not to take the treatment, for this will handicap her child. . . .

[20] Compare Jonathan Bennett's approach to this issue in his paper, 'On Maximizing Happiness', pp. 61–73 in Sikora and Barry, op. cit. See especially the discussion on pp. 66–9.

We next suppose that there is a second woman, who is about to stop taking contraceptive pills so that she can have another child. She is told that she has a temporary condition such that any child she conceives now will have just the same handicap; but that if she waits three months she will then conceive a normal child. It seems clear that it would be wrong for this second woman, by not waiting, to deliberately have a handicapped rather than a normal child. And it seems (at least to me) clear that this would be just *as* wrong as it would be for the first woman to deliberately handicap her child.[21]

Why does this pose a problem for the two theses appealed to in section 7.32, to the effect that for an action to be in itself prima facie wrong, either it must make it the case that there is someone for whom it is worse, or it must wrong someone? The reason is that in the case of the second woman there is, it would seem, no actual individual for whom the action is worse, or who has been wronged, as a result of the woman's refusal to wait three months. The child that results will, by hypothesis, live a happy life, albeit not as happy as that of a normal child. But the woman's decision is certainly not worse for that child, since if the woman had waited three months, *it* would never have existed at all. Similarly, it is difficult to see how it can be plausibly claimed that the woman has wronged her child, given that the child will enjoy its life, and that she has done the best that she could for *that* child.

Is there any response to this argument? One possibility is to grant that what the second woman does is wrong, but then to argue that it can be explained in a way compatible with the theses being considered. The idea would be to explain the wrongness of what the second woman does in terms of *side effects*. Producing a defective child will normally have an adverse effect upon other members of society. Why may not this provide an adequate account of our feeling that what the second woman does is wrong?

One problem with this response is that it does not explain Parfit's intuition—which would, I believe, be shared by many —that what the second woman does is not merely wrong, but

---

[21] Derek Parfit, 'Rights, Interests, and Possible People' in *Moral Problems in Medicine*, edited by Samuel Gorovitz *et al.*, 1976, pp. 369-75. See pp. 373-4. The same argument is also set out by Parfit in his article, 'On Doing the Best for Our Children', pp. 100-2.

just as wrong as what the first woman does. Second, and more importantly, the argument can be formulated in a way that rules out the appeal to side effects:

Suppose we have a choice between two social policies. These will alter the standard of living—or, more broadly, the quality of life. The effects of one policy would, in the short term, be slightly better, but, in the long term, be much worse. Since there clearly could be such a difference between two policies, we need not specify details. It is enough to assume that, on the 'Short Term Policy,' the quality of life would be slightly higher for (say) the next three generations, but be lower for the fourth generation, and be *much* lower for several later generations.

We can next note a second fact about the difference between the policies. The particular members of the fourth and later generations, on the Short Term Policy, would not have been born at all if instead we had pursued the Long Term Policy. Given the effects of the policies on the details of people's lives, different marriages would increasingly be made. More simply, even in the same marriages, the children would increasingly be conceived at different times. As we argued, this would be enough to make them different children.[22]

The argument is the same as in the case of the second woman. On the one hand, everyone who will exist regardless of whether one adopts the Short Term Policy or the Long Term one will be better off under the former. On the other, those who will exist only if the Short Term Policy is adopted will certainly not be any worse off if that policy is adopted, since they will enjoy at least minimally satisfactory lives, and the alternative for them, in view of Parfit's point about identity, is not existing at all. So if the Short Term Policy is adopted, there will be no one who is worse off. And given this, it is hard to see how it can plausibly be argued that adoption of the Short Term Policy will have the result that someone is wronged. On either of the theses we are considering, then, one would seem to be forced to conclude that it is not morally wrong to adopt the Short Term Policy.

The difference between this case, and the case of the women, is that one cannot appeal to adverse side effects on other people, since *no one* who will exist given the Short Term Policy is worse off than they would otherwise be. The upshot is that there are only two choices. Either one must hold that there is nothing morally objectionable about

---

[22] Parfit, 'On Doing the Best for Our Children', pp. 101–2.

choosing the Short Term Policy, or one must abandon the two theses appealed to in section 7.32 in support of the claim that there cannot be a prima-facie, intrinsic obligation to produce additional persons.

Is it possible to take the bold line, and to hold that there is nothing morally wrong with opting for the Short Term Policy, so that this and the next few generations enjoy affluence, while later generations are condemned to lives that are worth living, but only barely so? Some philosophers have certainly accepted this view. Among the most forthright is Thomas Schwartz:

> You've heard it said that we own certain things to posterity, remote as well as near. These things include an adequate supply of natural resources, a clean environment, a healthy and varied gene pool, a rich cultural heritage and a limit on population size.
> I disagree: Whatever we may owe ourselves or our near posterity, *we've no obligation extending indefinitely or even terribly far into the future to provide any widespread, continuing benefits to our descendants*. The contrary claim rests on an identifiable fallacy.[23]

Schwartz's defence of this view is twofold. First, as we have seen, he appeals to the general theses that all obligations are obligations to actual individuals, and that an action cannot be wrong unless there is someone who is wronged by it. Second, he suggests that the reason people intuitively feel that we have obligations with respect to remote generations is that they fail to notice that different people will exist under different social policies.

If the second claim were correct, it would be quite decisive. But is it? The evidence seems to be against it. Most people— though admittedly not all—do not seem to abandon the view that we have obligations concerning remote generations when they are confronted with the identity point. So Schwartz's contention that the view rests upon 'an identifiable fallacy' does not seem to be generally true.

If this is right, Schwartz must fall back upon the first line of defence, and appeal to the fact that the view that there are obligations to remote generations conflicts with certain very general ethical theses. The question, however, is how this conflict should be resolved. Should one abandon the view

---

[23] Schwartz, op. cit., p. 3.

that there are obligations to remote generations or should one abandon the general theses? Schwartz favours the former. Most philosophers, in contrast, feel that it is the general theses that should be abandoned. One would like to be able to bring some deeper argument to bear upon this issue. But in the absence of such an argument, I think that one should back the more widely shared, reflective intuition. The second attempt to establish that there cannot be any prima-facie, intrinsic obligation to produce additional persons must be jettisoned in the face of Parfit's argument.

7.4 The Repudiation of Obligations to Produce Additional Persons: A Third Attempt

With the failure of the above two attempts to establish that there cannot be any prima-facie obligation to produce additional persons, the prospects of finding any plausible general thesis that entails this conclusion may not seem especially bright. In this section, however, I shall attempt to formulate such a thesis. My starting point will be another important, but troubling argument, set out by Derek Parfit. The attempt to determine what is wrong with this argument will lead to the view I wish to advance. I shall then go on to argue that the general thesis in question enables one to deal, in a very plausible way, with certain arguments that have recently been advanced in support of the contention that there is a prima-facie obligation to produce additional happy people.

7.41 Parfit's Mere Addition Argument

One of the objections directed against Roupas's argument in section 7.2 was that his method for determining objective value leads to the Repugnant Conclusion, that is, to the view that for any world containing a finite number of people leading extremely satisfactory lives, there is a better world, containing a larger number of people, each of whom leads a life that is just barely worth living. I pointed out that there was a problem with this criticism, however, in that the argument used against Roupas can be put in a more general way such that, while it still leads to the Repugnant Conclusion, it does not appeal to principles that are specific to Roupas's method. This raises the question of whether the Mere Addition Argument can fairly be employed against Roupas. The time has come to address this issue.

The general version of Parfit's Mere Addition Argument may be put as follows.[24] As before, let A be a world containing 100 people, each enjoying 100 units of happiness. Let A+ be a world that differs from A only in the addition of some extra happy people. These additional people do not affect in any way the 100 people who exist both in A and A+. In short, A+ contains the 100 people who exist in world A, enjoying precisely the same level of happiness—100 units—together with, let us say, 100 additional people, each enjoying 10 units of happiness. Finally, let world B contain the same 200 people as are in the world A+, but where each person enjoys 60 units of happiness. How do these three worlds compare in value? First, consider worlds A and A+. Parfit suggests that it is plausible to hold that A+ is *not worse* than A, since the only difference between those two worlds is that A+ contains some additional people who all lead lives worth living, and who do not in any way reduce the happiness of those who exist both in A and in A+.

Can this view be resisted? There appear to be two main reasons that have been advanced for challenging the claim that A+ is not worse than A.[25] These are, first, that the average level of happiness is lower in A+ than in A, and second, that there is an unequal distribution of happiness in A+, but not in A. Parfit's response to the first objection is that while a lower average is often a bad thing, it is not at all easy to see why a lower average should be thought objectionable if no one is worse off, 'if it involves no loss of any kind, but mere addition'.[26]

What about the inequality point? Does it provide grounds for holding that A+ is worse than A? The response here seems to be that while inequality is undesirable, other things being

---

[24] Parfit, in advancing his Mere Addition Argument, is not attempting to show that the Repugnant Conclusion is reasonable. What he is doing is drawing attention to an apparent inconsistency in the moral intuitions of most people.

[25] McMahan, op. cit., pp. 122-3.

[26] Derek Parfit, 'Overpopulation' (1973 Draft), p. 4.

equal, when one is comparing A+ with A other things are not equal. For the alternative to the inequality in the distribution of happiness that exists in A+ is for the group that is worse off in that world not to exist at all. And given that the worse off group benefits from the inequality, while the better off group does not suffer from it, how can the inequality be taken as a ground for holding that world A+ is worse than world A?[27]

The next step in the argument involves comparing B with A+. Parfit thinks that it is plausible to hold that B is better than A+, and, as McMahan points out, considerable support can be offered for this view:

> For example, B has both a larger total and a higher average. The appeal to the average in this case, moreover, seems appropriate, since the same number of people are, on average, better off in B, which is also superior both in terms of the maximin rule and on grounds of equality. Again, the appeal to equality here seems more appropriate than in the preceding case, since in this case the avoidance of inequality does not involve the nonexistence of the worse-off group.[28]

If it is granted both that B is better than A+, and that A+ is not worse than A, it would seem to follow that B is better than A. The argument can then be repeated indefinitely, generating a sequence of better and better worlds, containing more and more people at ever lower levels of happiness, until one arrives at a world containing a massive number of people leading lives that are just barely worth living. The later world is, according to the Mere Addition Argument, better than the original world, which contained a smaller number of very happy people.

Before we go on to consider what might be wrong with this argument, some observations on the argument itself are in order. In the first place, it is not claimed, at step one in the argument, that A+ is *better* than A. The contention is merely that A+ is no worse than A. This is emphasized by both Parfit and McMahan,[29] and their reasons for doing so appear to be that they think that the claim that A+ is better than A would not be especially plausible.

The second point concerns a possible criticism of the

---

[27] This response is from McMahan, op. cit., p. 123.
[28] Ibid., p. 123.　　　　　　　[29] Ibid., p. 122.

formulation of the Mere Addition Argument offered above. The criticism, which is due to Ronald Dworkin,[30] is that the inference from the claims that A+ is not worse than A, and that B is better than A+, to the conclusion that B is better than A, assumes that it follows from the fact that A+ is *not worse* than A that A+ is *at least as good* as A. But this latter assumption is not justified. There are two very different situations in which it is true to say that A+ is not worse than A, The first is where A+ is at least as good as A. The other is where A+ and A are for some reason incapable of being compared. If it is the latter that one has in the case of A+ and A, one cannot conclude, from the fact that B is better than A+, that B is better than A. Worlds A and B may also be incapable of being compared.

There are two responses to this objection. The first is to modify step one, so that the conclusion being drawn is that A+ is at least as good as A, and not merely that A+ is not worse than A. With this modification, the argument will go through as before.

The second possibility is this. Rather than inferring, from the claims that A+ is not worse than A, and B is better than A+, that B is better than A, one can draw the more modest conclusion that B is not worse than A. The grand conclusion will then be that the world that contains a massive number of people with lives barely worth living is at least not worse than a world containing a small number of people enjoying extremely satisfying lives.

Which modification should one adopt? The second may seem very appealing initially. For on the one hand, one is shifting to a more modest claim at the first step of the argument, and on the other, since the grand conclusion is little more appealing than the original Repugnant Conclusion, the argument would seem to retain its full force.[31]

A problem lurks, however. Consider the argumentation offered at step one. *How* does it lend support to the claim that A+ is not worse than A? In particular, does it do so by lending support to the claim that A+ and A are incapable of being compared? The answer is perhaps not entirely clear,

---

[30] Ibid., p. 123.   [31] Compare McMahan, op. cit., p. 123.

but my own inclination is to say that the considerations advanced provide *no* support for the claim that A+ and A are incapable of being compared, and thus that they support the claim that A+ is not worse than A *only if* they support, just as strongly, the claim that A+ is at least as good as A. If this is so, the second modification of the argument cannot be superior to the first modification.

But if this were right, the whole argument would appear problematic, since it is not clear that the first response to Dworkin's point is satisfactory. The problem is this. Consider another world, A+*, which is as follows. Everyone who exists in world A also exists in world A+*, and enjoys precisely the same level of happiness. In addition, A+* also contains the 100 additional people found in world A+, but in A+* they enjoy only five units of happiness each, rather than the 10 units they enjoy in A+. Now the arguments that were used to support the conclusion that A+ is at least as good as A can equally well be used to support the claim that A+* is at least as good as A. But A+ is surely better than A+*, since it differs from the latter only in that the worst off people in A+* are somewhat better off in A+. It then follows that world A+ must be better than world A, and not merely as good.[32] But, as was pointed out above, Parfit and McMahan appear to believe that it is important that the Mere Addition Argument not claim that A+ is better than A. If they are right about this, it would seem that the first way of modifying the argument is not satisfactory. The only hope is to opt for the second modification, and to attempt to show that the considerations appealed to at step one *do* support the conclusion that worlds A+ and A are incapable of being compared, and that that is the reason why A+ is not worse than A.

It is unclear to me whether the latter view can be made plausible. I shall not, however, pursue this issue, since the central problem with the Mere Addition Argument appears to lie elsewhere. What does need to be noticed, though, is that the problem just considered does not affect the version of the Mere Addition Argument used against Roupas in the previous

---

[32] Ibid., p. 123.

section. For the specialized version of the argument employed there involved showing that it follows from Roupas's principles not merely that A+ is not worse than A, nor even than A+ is at least as good as A, but that A+ is better than A. This feature enables that version of the argument to escape the present difficulty.

7.42 A Response to the Mere Addition Argument

What, if anything, is wrong with Parfit's Mere Addition Argument? I think it may help if we consider a scaled down, but fleshed out, version of the problem. Susan is committed to having at least one child, and is physically capable of having at most two. If she does nothing special, she can have two children of average capabilities. If she takes a certain drug, her first child will be superior in all respects, but if she then proceeds to have a second child, it will be significantly defective, though it will still enjoy a life worth living. Assume, finally, that the difference between the superior child and an average child is less than that between the defective child and an average child, so that if Susan has both the superior child and the defective child they will be, on average, less well off than an average child.

Susan is interested, then, in choosing among the following three actions:

A: She has a superior child, and no others.
A+:   She has a superior child, and then a defective one.
B: She has two average children.

Can it be argued that A+ is no worse than A? It would seem that it could. Susan takes the drug and gives birth to a superior child. Should she have a second child? If she does, it will be defective. But it will enjoy life, and its existence, we may assume for the sake of argument, will not adversely affect anyone else. So if Susan decides to have another child, thus performing action A+, she will merely be adding another happy person to the world. So it would seem that action A+ cannot be worse than action A.

That this judgement is not acceptable can, I suggest, be seen as follows. First, consider the case of Cynthia. If Cynthia has only one child, she can afford to provide it with an education known to produce individuals who are superior in all respects. If she has two children, she will not be able to provide both of them with such an education. She will have to choose between providing only one with the vastly superior education, while sending the other to a rather unsatisfactory school, and sending both children to a good, but not outstanding, school. Cynthia, then, is confronted with choices very similar to Susan's:

C: Cynthia can raise a superior child, and no other.
C+:   Cynthia can raise a superior child, and then an inferior one.
D: Cynthia can raise two average children.

Can it be claimed that C+ is no worse than C? Such a claim is exposed to an immediate objection. If Cynthia chooses to perform C+, the inferior child that she thereby raises can complain, and surely correctly, that it has been treated unfairly. For that very same child would have existed if Cynthia had chosen action D rather than C+, and by choosing C+, Cynthia has deprived that child in order to benefit the other child. Since each child has a right to a good education, C+ is open to a moral objection. Action C, in contrast, is not. There is, in that case, no individual whose right is violated.

The case of Susan differs from the case of Cynthia in that if Susan chooses action A+, the defective person who results will not be able to claim that he is worse off than he might otherwise have been, or that his rights are not satisfied to the extent they would have been if Susan had acted otherwise. But if Parfit is right about the case of the other two women, Mary and Jane—and I am now convinced, very strongly, that he is—then this difference between the cases of Susan and Cynthia does not matter. The fact that the two children produced by action A+ are not identical with those produced by action B, while the same two children are involved in action C+ and in action D, cannot be a morally relevant factor. The upshot is that one cannot hold that C+ is worse than C without also holding that A+ is worse than A. But C+ is worse than C. Therefore A+ is worse than A.

If this is right, the flaw in the Mere Addition Argument lies in the first step. It would be nice, however, if one could explain why the first step may seem quite appealing initially. The source of the apparent plausibility emerges, I think, if one considers the following case. The population of the earth cannot be further increased without disastrous consequences. It is possible, however, to produce people who will live on Mars. If we do this, they will enjoy lives worth living, but not as satisfactory as those enjoyed by people living on earth, due to the harshness of the Martian environment. We wish to decide, then, between the following two actions:

A: Maintaining the earth's population, but not producing any additional people.

A+: Maintaining the earth's population, while also producing some additional people who will lead slightly less satisfactory lives on Mars.

How are we to rank these two actions? The answer, I suggest, depends upon whether there is a third alternative available to us, of the following form:

B: Maintaining the earth's population, while producing additional people, at some cost to our own standard of living, who will enjoy more satisfactory lives than people living on Mars would.

When an action of type B is available, we may speak of its being possible to redistribute happiness more equitably, though such 'redistribution' may, just as in the case of Susan, in contrast to that of Cynthia, involve distribution over different individuals than those who would exist under the less satisfactory distribution.

Consider, then, the two cases. First, that in which an alternative of type B is available, so that redistribution is possible. In that case, one must hold that A+ is worse than A, just as in the case of the corresponding judgements in the cases of Susan and Cynthia. Second, the case in which no alternative of type B is available, so that redistribution is impossible. Here, I think, it might be claimed that A+ is not worse than A, since in choosing A+ one is not bringing into existence individuals who have less of what they deserve than would be the case with other individuals one might have produced.

If this is right, then there may be cases in which the mere addition of happy people does not make the world a worse place. What I am suggesting is that the first step in the Mere Addition Argument derives its plausibility mainly from such cases. But such cases cannot in fact lend support to the argument as a whole, since they presuppose that redistribution is impossible, and thus that the sort of alternative that is needed at the second stage of the Mere Addition Argument cannot possibly be available.

If this diagnosis is correct, it is possible to reject the general version of the Mere Addition Argument, and along with it, the Repugnant Conclusion, while employing a more specialized version of the argument as an objection against Roupas's method of determining objective value. For Roupas's principles lead to the conclusion that A+ is better than A, *regardless* of whether redistribution is possible.

7.43 A Third Attempt

In this section I wish to sketch a third attempt to set out very general ethical principles that imply that the fact that an action will produce additional persons, or additional persons with certain properties—such as that of leading very satisfying lives—cannot be a right-making characteristic. The view I shall be advancing arises very naturally out of the above discussions of Parfit's two arguments, and I believe that it is a very important feature of the present view that it is able to handle those arguments in an intuitively plausible way.

Additional support for the view will be offered in the three sections which follow. In sections 7.44 and 7.45 I shall consider two arguments that have been advanced in support of the claim that there can be obligations to produce additional persons, and I shall attempt to show that the view being recommended here provides a plausible account of what is wrong with those arguments. Then, in section 7.46, I shall consider some important objections to my general approach.

One way of developing my view, which may be helpful, is by an analogy with moral principles relevant to promising. Suppose, first of all, that I make a promise which I do not keep. Have I done something prima facie wrong? Not necessarily, since there may have been circumstances that made it impossible for me to keep my promise. This suggests something like the following principle:

P_1: If it is possible for one to keep a promise, then it is prima facie wrong not to do so.

Suppose, however, that I make a promise, foreseeing that it will be impossible for me to keep it. My failure to keep the promise cannot be judged prima facie wrong by virtue of principle P_1. Yet surely I have done something wrong. What one needs, apparently, is another principle:

P_2: It is prima facie wrong to make a promise one knows one will not be able to keep.

Given these two principles, one would also like to have a principle dealing with the relative seriousness of these two wrong-making characteristics of actions. John makes a promise which he decides not to keep. Mary makes a comparable promise which she foresees she will be unable to keep. How do these actions compare? I do not see how one can argue the issue. My inclination, though, is to view the actions as wrong to the same degree, and thus to accept the following principle:

P_3: Making a promise one knows one will be unable to keep, and failing to keep a comparable promise, when it is possible for one to do so, are prima facie wrong to precisely the same degree.

What I now want to do is, first, to suggest three very general principles that are analogous to the above principles:

Q_1: If it is possible not to violate an obligation concerning some individual, then it is prima facie wrong to do so.

Q_2: It is prima facie wrong to bring it about that there is an individual concerning whom there is an obligation that cannot be satisfied.

Q_3: Violating an obligation of some type R, which one has regarding some individual, when it is possible not to do so, and bringing it about that there is an individual with respect to whom there is an obligation of type R which cannot be satisfied, are prima facie wrong to precisely the same degree.

Second, I want to advance the following general thesis about the conditions under which an action is prima facie wrong:

> S: An action is prima facie wrong if and only if it involves a failure to fulfil an obligation regarding some individual, when it was possible to do so, or it makes it the case that there is some individual with respect to whom there will be an obligation that cannot be fulfilled.

If principle S is correct, it follows that there is no prima-facie obligation to produce additional persons. For refraining from producing additional persons does not in itself either violate an obligation with respect to any individual, or make it the case that there is an individual with respect to whom there are obligations that cannot be met.

Let us now consider how principle S fares when confronted with some of the troublesome cases considered above. First, is S compatible with the claim that there is a prima-facie obligation not to produce a miserable person? Clearly it is. One might, for example, advance the following claim:

The Right to a Worthwhile Life Principle

> T_1: Every individual has a right to life that is worth living.[33]

This principle is certainly compatible with S, and, together with it, entails that it is prima facie wrong to bring into existence a miserable person.

Second, Parfit's case of the two women. There are a number of alternatives here. I would suggest appealing to some very general principle, such as:

> T_2: Every person has a right to an equal chance of enjoying those natural resources, both environmental and genetic, that a person living in his society might enjoy, and that make it possible for one to lead a satisfying life.

[33] It is natural to say that some lives are worth living, others are worth not living, and still others are neutral. In view of this, a more accurate, albeit slightly awkward formulation of T_1 would be: 'Every individual has a right to a life that is not worth not living.'

Given such a principle, it follows from ‘S that what the first woman does is wrong, since she deprives a particular person of the chance of being normal. But it also follows from S that what the second woman does is wrong, since she brings it about that there is an individual who has no chance of being normal. Moreover, Q_3 implies that what the two woman do is equally wrong, in agreement with Parfit's judgement about this case.

Third, the related case of the two social policies. It follows from S, together with T_2, that it is prima facie wrong to adopt the Short Term Policy. For given that the Long Term Policy is an available alternative, people living in the future could enjoy a standard of living much closer to what we enjoy than they will if we adopt the Short Term Policy. Principle T_2 implies that they have as much right to enjoy such a standard of living as we do. Therefore, if we choose the Short Term Policy, we do something wrong, since we bring it about that there will be people whose chance of enjoying such a standard of living is not equal to our own.

Finally, Parfit's Mere Addition Argument. In section 7.42 it was noted that the second step in the argument is ruled out if redistribution is not possible. So let us assume that redistribution is possible, and ask how A+ compares with A. There will then be a standard of living which additional people might enjoy, and which is enjoyed by the 100 people who exist both in A and in A+, but which the 100 additional people have no chance of enjoying. It therefore follows from S together with T_2 that it would be wrong to bring about A+ rather than A.

7.44 Anglin and the Extra Person Obligation

To further test the plausibility of the view just advanced, let us consider how it fares when confronted with two recent attempts to establish that there are prima-facie obligations to produce additional persons. The first is found in William Anglin's article, 'The Repugnant Conclusion'.[34] Anglin's

[34] William Anglin, 'The Repugnant Conclusion', *Canadian Journal of Philosophy*, Volume 7, Number 4, 1977, pp. 745-54.

over-all strategy in his article is, first, to discuss the reasons
why the Repugnant Conclusion might be thought repugnant.
Second, to argue that if there is an 'Extra Person Obligation'
—understood as an obligation to add another happy person,
even at some small cost to those already around—then the
Repugnant Conclusion is not repugnant. And third, to show
that there is in fact an Extra Person Obligation.

It is the latter that is of interest here. Anglin's statement of
his argument may be summarized as follows:

> (1) Suppose a woman has a choice between having a child
> that will be neither happy nor unhappy, and undergoing
> an operation that will involve a small amount of discom-
> fort, but that will enable her to have a very happy child.
> Then there is a prima-facie obligation for her to do the
> latter.
> (2) There is no moral difference between producing a
> person who will be neither happy nor unhappy, and not
> producing anyone at all.
> (3) It follows from (1) and (2) that given a choice between
> not producing anyone at all, and producing a very happy
> person, at some small cost to oneself, there is a prima-
> facie obligation to do the latter.

Peter Singer, in a critical discussion of Anglin's argument,[35] maintains that while premiss (1) is acceptable,
premiss (2) is not. Singer's diagnosis seems very plausible,
and, with a slight qualification, is supported by the approach
adopted above. First, as regards premiss (1), S together with
T_2 implies that in a world where people are generally at least
somewhat happy, it is prima facie wrong to produce a person
who will be neither happy nor unhappy. One will then need a
further principle to the effect that the prima-facie wrongness
of such an action is more serious than the prima-facie wrongness of inflicting a small amount of discomfort upon oneself,
but such a principle is hardly problematic. Second, given that
one is dealing with a world in which most people are at least
minimally happy, S together with T_2 does entail, contrary to

---

[35] Peter Singer, 'Anglin on the Obligation to Create Extra People', *Canadian
Journal of Philosophy*, Volume 8, Number 3, 1978, pp. 583-5.

premiss (2), that there is a moral difference between producing a person who will be neither happy nor unhappy, and not producing anyone at all. In the former case, but not in the latter, one is producing a person who will not have an equal chance of happiness, and so one is doing something that is prima facie wrong according to S together with T_2.

As noted above, this account diverges slightly from Singer's. For it implies that premiss (1) is acceptable, and premiss (2) unacceptable, only if one is considering a world where most people are at least minimally happy. But I think that it can be seen that this divergence is plausible. Consider a world in which everyone is neither happy nor unhappy. Would one still think premiss (2) is mistaken, and that there is a moral difference between producing a person who will be neither happy nor unhappy, and producing no one at all? I suggest that one would not. If this is right, it provides an additional reason for adopting the approach that I am advocating.

7.45 Sikora's Argument

The second argument for the view that there is a prima-facie obligation to produce additional happy people is found in an interesting article by Richard I. Sikora. A slightly modified version of his argument runs as follows. It starts out from two moral claims that appear to be such as would be generally accepted:

(1) Provided that p is sufficiently small, it is not in itself morally wrong to perform an action that will lead, with probability p, to the existence of a thoroughly wretched person, and, with probability $(1 - p)$, to the existence of a happy person.
(2) To bring into existence a thoroughly wretched person is wrong in itself.

But if it is wrong to bring about a certain result, it is also wrong, albeit not to the same degree, to do something that will lead, with non-zero probability p, to the same result, and with probability $(1 - p)$ to some outcome that has no moral significance. So it follows from (2) that:

(3) For non-zero probability p, it is wrong in itself to perform an action that will lead, with probability p, to the existence of a thoroughly wretched person, and, with probability (1 − p), to an outcome that has no moral significance.

Then, if one compares (1) with (3), it is apparent that the bringing into existence of a happy person cannot be an event that has no moral significance. Hence, either there is a prima-facie obligation to bring happy people into existence, or the existence of happy people is at least something that is valuable in itself.[36]

The intuitive appeal of Sikora's argument is clear. If it is wrong in itself to create a wretched person, but not to risk doing so when there is a sufficiently good chance of producing a happy person, must it not be the case that the production of a happy person is a positive consideration that outweighs the risk of bringing someone wretched into existence? And how is this to be explained except on the assumption that the creation of happy people is prima facie obligatory, or, at least, good in itself?

I shall attempt to show that Sikora's argument involves, however, a subtle confusion which, once noticed, drains the argument of its apparent plausibility. To appreciate the confusion, compare the cases of the following three women, all of whom are interested in having five children. Amy is pregnant for the first time, and if nothing is done, she will give birth to a normal child, but will be unable to have any more children. On the other hand, if an operation is performed, this will result in her giving birth to a defective child, but will also enable her to produce four more children, all of whom will be normal. Amy decides to have the operation. Becky is not pregnant. If she becomes pregnant immediately, she will give birth to a normal child, but will be unable to have any more children. If she waits three months, her first child will be defective, but the next four will be normal.

---

[36] R. I. Sikora, 'Utilitarianism: the Classical Principle and the Average Principle', *Canadian Journal of Philosophy*, Volume 5, Number 3, 1975, pp. 409-19. The argument is found on pp. 414-15. Sikora also sets out this argument on pp. 136-7 of his article, 'Is It Wrong to Prevent the Existence of Future Generations?', in Sikora and Barry, op. cit., pp. 112-66.

Becky decides to wait three months. Finally, the case of Cathy. She is told that if she has five children, all of them will be normal at birth, but that she should expect that one of them will catch a disease that will make it defective. Cathy has five children, and one of them does contract the disease.

Let us begin by considering the case of Amy. First, what should one say about her action if one adopts the view being advanced by Sikora? According to that view, either there is a prima-facie obligation to produce happy people, or the production of happy people is at least something whose goodness can counterbalance our prima-facie obligation not to produce unhappy people. This means that Amy's decision to make a normal child defective in order to produce four additional normal children may turn out to be morally right, given Sikora's approach. Whether it is or not will depend upon the relative weight that he assigns to the two conflicting factors: making a normal child defective, and producing normal, happy children. Perhaps he would hold that four additional normal children is not enough. But in any case, there will be some number, n, such that Sikora is committed to holding that it is morally right to make a normal child defective in order to produce n additional normal children— a conclusion which, I suggest, few people would find plausible, either initially or upon reflection.

Amy's action gets assigned a very different moral status when judged by the view advanced in section 7.43. According to that view, her action possesses a wrong-making characteristic, but no counterbalancing right-making characteristic. For in making a normal person defective, she violates that person's right to an equal chance of enjoying those things that make for a satisfying life. It is true that she is also producing four normal people—and hence, presumably, four individuals whose rights can be satisfied. But this cannot be a right-making characteristic. For if it were, it would be prima facie wrong to refrain from bringing it about that there is someone whose rights can be satisfied, and this is incompatible with principle S—which says that there are only two ways in which an action can be prima facie wrong: by violating someone's right, or by bringing it about that there is someone with a right that cannot be satisfied.

The next question is whether one can hold that what Amy does is wrong without also holding that it is prima facie wrong to reproduce if there is a chance of producing a defective child. To see that one can, let us go on to consider the cases of Becky and Cathy. The case of Becky differs from the case of Amy only in that Becky, rather than making a normal child defective, merely decides to have a defective child rather than a normal one. If Parfit is right about the Identity Problem issue, what Becky does is precisely as wrong as what Amy does. Believing that he is right on this matter, I have set out principles that entail this conclusion. Principle Q_2, together with T_2, implies that it is prima facie wrong to produce a defective child when one could instead produce a normal child, and principle Q_3 implies that this is just as wrong as making a normal child defective. The actions of Becky and Amy are morally on a par.

Can one avoid drawing the same conclusion about Cathy? The answer is that one can. Both Becky and Amy did something knowing that the result would be the existence of a person who would have *no chance* of being normal. Cathy does not do this. She produces five normal children, knowing that one of them will become defective. But this is compatible not only with its being the case that all of her children have an equal chance of being normal, but with all of her children having as good a chance of being normal as one can have in the environment in question. The actions of Amy and Becky both violate T_2, the principle of the right to an equal opportunity; the action of Cathy does not. Her action, therefore, is not morally comparable to theirs.

It should now be possible to indicate, very briefly, the subtle confusion on which Sikora's argument trades. It is a confusion between:

(1a) Provided that p is sufficiently small, it is not in itself morally wrong to perform an action that will lead, with probability p, to the existence of a person who is certain to be thoroughly wretched, and, with probability $(1 - p)$, to the existence of some other person who is certain to be happy,

and

(1b) Provided that p is sufficiently small, it is not in itself morally wrong to perform an action that will lead to the existence of a person who will be, with probability p, thoroughly wretched, and, with probability $(1 - p)$, happy.

Given (1a), Sikora's argument does show that the bringing into existence of a happy person cannot be an event that has no moral significance. But (1a) is unacceptable, for reasons just discussed. On the other hand, while (1b) is acceptable, it does not enable one to derive the conclusion that the production of additional happy people has positive moral significance. The conclusion to which Sikora's argument does lead, when (1) is interpreted as (1b), is the very different, and quite acceptable conclusion, that either there is a prima-facie obligation to make existing people happy, or, at least, it is a good thing to do so.

7.46 McMahan's Objections

Can there be prima-facie obligations to produce additional people? In grappling with this issue, I have had to consider some very perplexing questions that arise in the area of ethics known as population theory. The answers I have proposed have been formulated in terms of a particular conceptual framework: that of rights. One could, if one wanted, advance the same account without using that framework. None the less, I suspect that it is a significant feature of the account being proposed that the simplest, and most natural formulation of it, is in terms of rights.

Other philosophers have also felt that many of the very difficult ethical questions that arise within population theory are at least less intractable when tackled within a rights framework, rather than, as is much more commonly the case, within a broadly utilitarian framework. This view has, however, been challenged, and in this section I want to consider some of the objections that have been directed against a rights approach. I shall attempt to show that, though some of these raise serious difficulties for many approaches of this general sort, they do not tell against the view advanced here.

The question of a rights approach is carefully discussed by Jeff McMahan in the article mentioned above. McMahan points out that such an approach has distinct advantages. However he also thinks that there are important difficulties, and that in the end such an approach is not satisfactory.

McMahan mentions five difficulties. First, there is what he refers to as a formal objection. It arises in connection with the obligation not to produce miserable people. The question is how this obligation is to be described if we adopt the framework of rights: '. . . it would seem that we must say either that in preventing these people from existing we would be honoring rights without bearers, or that the rights which these people have can exist only when they are violated—in other words, that these people possess rights which can be violated but not honored.'[37]

McMahan views this as an interesting problem, but he seems to think that a satisfactory answer is possible. In part because, as he points out: 'There are numerous cases in which our behavior is controlled by a regard for rights which people might, but do not have—for example, when one avoids entering into certain relations with a person because one would be unable to honor the rights which the person would then acquire against one.'[38]

Let us turn, then, to the four substantive objections mentioned by McMahan. We shall see that all of them turn upon a certain feature of the particular rights approach that McMahan considers. The feature in question is the claim that people have a right to a certain minimum level of welfare. Now this claim is not part of the approach I am suggesting. It is replaced, in a sense, by T_2—the principle of the right to an equal opportunity. We need to consider, however, whether this change really enables one to escape the difficulties in question.

The first of these four objections is that 'the specification of the acceptable minimum level of welfare must be to some extent both arbitrary and socially relative'.[39] The problem of the arbitrariness involved in choosing the acceptable minimum is clearly avoided when one shifts to the equal opportunity

---

[37] McMahan, op. cit., p. 125.   [38] Ibid., p. 125.
[39] Ibid., p. 126.

principle. But what about the point that what people have a right to will depend upon the society they are in? This point still applies. But is it objectionable? It is true that the right to an equal chance of enjoying those things that are available in one's society and that make it possible to lead a satisfying life will give rise to quite different derivative rights in very wealthy societies and in very poor ones, *provided that re-distribution is not possible.* Without this proviso, the conclusion would be unacceptable. With it, it is hard to see that it is in any way implausible.

The second objection concerns Parfit's Mere Addition Argument for the Repugnant Conclusion. If one appeals to a right to a minimum level of welfare, then that will prevent one from arriving at the Repugnant Conclusion, but one will still be able to arrive at a conclusion that is far from appetizing. For one will be able to show that given a society with a finite number of people who lead very satisfying lives, there will be a better society that contains a larger number of people all of whom enjoy the minimally acceptable level of welfare.

The reason the problem reappears if one appeals to a right to a minimum level of welfare is that such an appeal does not show that there is *in general* anything wrong with the reasoning in the Mere Addition Argument: the argument only becomes objectionable beyond a certain point. In contrast, the approach being recommended here implies that the Mere Addition Argument is unacceptable at the very first step. The present approach, therefore, does not fall prey to the modified version of the argument.

The third objection concerns the Identity Problem: 'If there is a choice between two policies, one of which requires minor sacrifices now in order to maintain a high quality of life in the future, while the other provides minor benefits now at the cost of lowering the future quality of life to just above the stated minimum, no one will be worse off, and no one's rights will be violated, if we choose the latter.'[40] The present approach is also immune to this objection. The Short Term Policy is wrong because it makes it the case that there

---

[40] Ibid., p. 124.

are people who have less of a chance of enjoying those things that make it possible to lead a satisfying life than society could provide, while others have more.

This brings us to McMahan's final objection, to the effect that an approach which appeals to rights entails the conclusion that it is wrong to conceive a child whose life, while below the minimum, would nevertheless be worth living—a conclusion which seems counter-intuitive: '. . . it is arguable that conceiving a person with a life below the minimum but above zero would not constitute a violation of his rights at all. For, if the person is later glad that he was conceived, this might be regarded as tantamount to his retroactively waiving his right. If it is reasonable to assume that this tacit waiving will occur, then it is to that extent reasonable to assume that no violation of rights occurs when the person is conceived.'[41] Once again, this objection, as it stands, does not apply to my approach, since I do not wish to claim that one has any non-derivative right to a minimum level of welfare beyond that which renders life barely worth living. But it would seem that the objection is easily reformulated, so that it does apply. Thus, might it not be argued that on the view that I am recommending it follows that it is wrong to produce people whose level of happiness will be lower than that of those who already exist, and that this consequence is counter-intuitive?

Thus restated, the appeal of this final objection is precisely that of the first step in the Mere Addition Argument, and my response is the same. There are two cases that need to be distinguished: that where redistribution is possible, and that where it is not. First, the case where redistribution is not possible. There is not, on the present approach, any objection to producing additional people no matter how low their level of happiness, *provided that* one is doing the best that one can, and that their lives are not ones that are worth not living. Second, the case where redistribution is possible. We produce, let us say, a group of minimally happy serfs. Their existence benefits those of us who would have existed anyway, and they are glad they were conceived, since the only real alternative for them would be non-existence: we would not have produced them if we had to give them an equal share of the world's resources. The present approach implies that it would be prima facie wrong to add such a group of minimally happy serfs to the world. But this, I suggest, is in no way counter-intuitive.

My response, in brief, is this. Any appeal the reformulated objection may have derives from a failure to distinguish between the case where redistribution is possible and the case where it is not. Once this distinction is made, it can be seen that the present approach leads to plausible answers in both cases.

7.5 Summing Up

In this chapter I have examined some attempts to establish that there can be prima-facie obligations to produce additional persons, or additional persons with certain properties, such as that of enjoying very satisfying lives. I have tried to show that such attempts either involve unsound argumentation, or lead to intuitively unacceptable consequences.

I have also considered some attempts to support the claim that there cannot be any prima-facie obligation to produce additional persons, however satisfactory their lives may be. The two most common lines of argument were seen to be untenable. I then went on to propose a third approach that seems more promising.

At the heart of the third approach is the idea that while an action may be prima facie wrong either because it violates an obligation one has with respect to some individual, or because it brings it about that there is an individual with respect to whom one has an obligation that cannot be satisfied, it cannot be prima facie wrong because it involves a failure to bring it about that there is an individual with respect to whom one has obligations that could be satisfied. From this it follows that while there may be a prima-facie obligation *not* to produce additional persons under certain circumstances, there cannot be a prima-facie obligation to produce additional persons.

My defence of this approach was twofold. On the one hand, I attempted to show that when this fundamental idea is conjoined with two more specific principles—to the effect that every individual has a right to a life worth living, and a right to an equal chance of having those things that make possible a satisfying life—one is able to develop plausible answers to some arguments that are otherwise very puzzling indeed. On the other hand, I attempted to show that the present approach is not exposed to the objections that appear to tell against some other attempts to appeal to the framework of rights in order to deal with problems in the area of population theory.

8
Moderate Positions on Abortion

The liberal view is that abortion should always be permitted, on the ground that, first, abortion is never wrong in itself, at any stage in the development of a human foetus, and that second, the practice of abortion need not involve any undesirable consequences. The anti-abortionist, in contrast, maintains that abortion is wrong in itself, and seriously so, being comparable to the killing of a normal adult human being, and therefore that it is almost never permissible. This chapter will consider some alternatives to these two extreme positions.

8.1 A Classification of Moderate Views on Abortion

There are three main types of considerations that might lead one to adopt a moderate position on abortion. In the first place, one might agree with the liberal that abortion is never wrong in itself, but hold that there should be some legal restrictions upon its availability on the ground that complete acceptance of the practice would have undesirable consequences.

Second, one might agree with the liberal with respect to abortions performed sufficiently early, but dissent with respect to later abortions. One might hold, for example, that there is good reason to believe that human organisms become persons at some point before birth, and thus that late abortions should practically never be permitted. Or, more agnostically, one might simply maintain that the morality of abortion becomes increasingly problematic as the human organism develops, either because of crucial empirical information that bears upon the morality of destroying a foetus, and that we do not presently have—such as knowledge about the type of mental life a human foetus enjoys at different points in its development—or perhaps because the morally relevant concept of a person is not yet sufficiently clear for its applicability to be determined with confidence in all cases. Given this view, it would seem reasonable to place no restrictions upon early abortions, but to require that increasingly stringent conditions be met as the foetus becomes more mature, and the uncertainty about its status as a person becomes increasingly greater.

Finally, one might adopt a moderate position because of disagreement with both liberals and conservatives about the relevant wrong-making characteristics involved, or about the weight to be assigned to them. There are a number of important possibilities here. One might agree with the conservative that abortion is prima facie seriously wrong, but hold that there are a number of circumstances in which abortion is morally permissible, all things considered. Alternatively, one might agree with the liberal view that human foetuses are not persons, but think that there are other, albeit less weighty factors, that also need to be taken into account. Or thirdly, one might hold that both the liberal and the conservative are mistaken in assuming that sharp lines are to be drawn in this area, on the ground that the properties that bear upon the permissibility of killing an individual are ones that admit of degrees.

The discussion in this chapter will be confined, on the whole, to positions based upon considerations of the third sort. The reason is that in order to evaluate moderate positions of the first and second sorts, one needs to determine, on the one hand, whether the acceptance of certain practices that are not in themselves immoral might have undesirable consequences, and, on the other, at what point a human being becomes a person. These are issues that arise, more forcefully, in connection with the question of the morality of infanticide, which will be discussed in part III. The evaluation of moderate positions based upon the first two types of considerations is best left until then.

8.2 A Moderate View of Abortion: Initial Difficulties

Moderate positions on abortion are quite widely accepted, as many people feel that although abortion should not be available on demand, it should be permitted under certain circumstances. The conditions under which it is held to be permissible are quite varied. Often one of the conditions is temporal: abortion is permissible before a certain point, but not after, except under special circumstances. Such a line has been drawn in different ways. Abortion is permissible before the foetus has become capable of independent existence, but not after. Or before quickening, but not after.

Another type of condition relates to the child that will result from the pregnancy. Abortion is often thought to be morally acceptable if it is known that the child will be grossly defective, either physically or mentally.

Other conditions concern the circumstances that led to conception. If it was the result of rape, or of incestuous intercourse, it is often held that abortion is permissible.

Still others turn upon the effect that bearing the child will have upon the woman. Many people believe that if having the child will seriously affect the woman's physical or psychological health, that is an adequate reason for allowing the woman to have an abortion.

Finally, many people feel that socio-economic considerations are relevant, so that if the parents are poor, or already have several children, etc., that is a reason for allowing an abortion.

In spite of the widespread appeal of such views, they are rejected by most philosophers. Let us briefly consider why this is so, beginning with the view that abortion is permissible up to a certain point, but not thereafter. The main problem here is not with the general idea of a dividing line, but with the properties typically employed in drawing that line. Consider, as an illustration, viability. The possession of this property does not seem to be either a necessary or a sufficient condition of its being seriously wrong to destroy something. Thus, on the one hand, if a normal adult human being comes to require, through injury or disease, a complex life-support system in order to survive, it does not follow that that person no longer has a right to life. And on the other, it is not thought to be seriously wrong to kill most living things, for trivial reasons, although they are certainly capable of independent existence. It is apparently a mistake, then, to assign to the capacity for independent existence the sort of moral significance that moderates on abortion often do. The same is true of other ways in which a line is typically drawn.

What the moderate should be doing, it would seem, is asking at what point in its development a human organism becomes a person. To answer this question, he must first decide what it is that makes something a person. As we saw in chapter 5, a variety of more or less plausible answers have been proposed—such as the capacity for rational thought, the presence of self-consciousness, the ability to view oneself as a continuing entity, and so on. The relevant point here, how-ever, is simply that the lines that moderates have traditionally drawn, at various points in the development of a human foetus, do not involve *any* of these properties, nor is there any reason for thinking that they involve properties that are even correlated with any plausible person-making characteristics.

Second, what rationale can be given for the view that while abortion is in general wrong, at least after a certain point in the development of the foetus, it is permissible under some of the circumstances mentioned above? It may seem at first that this question should not occasion any difficulties for the moderate. Can he not simply reply that, while the destruction of a human foetus is prima facie wrong, there may be counterbalancing, right-making characteristics, which make abortion morally permissible, all things considered, in certain circumstances? The problem, however, is that he needs to provide an account of the wrongness of destroying human foetuses that will allow the other factors he cites to serve as overriding considerations. It will not do, for example, for the moderate to take the view that the killing of human foetuses, or of human foetuses past a certain point of development, is wrong for the same reason that it is wrong to kill normal adult human beings. For the factors that he regards as making abortion permissible would not, in general, be regarded as factors which make it permissible to destroy a person. We do not believe that the fact that someone is defective, physically or mentally, makes it permissible to kill that person. Nor do we think that it is permissible for parents to kill some of their children to protect their own well-being, either physical or psychological, let alone for socio-economic reasons.

Some of the factors cited by moderates as making abortion permissible may reasonably be regarded as overriding, even if it is just as wrong to destroy a human foetus as to kill an adult human. Many conservatives, for example, would agree that abortion is not wrong if there is a serious threat to the woman's life. And, as emerged in the earlier discussion of Judith Jarvis Thomson's defence of abortion, the fact that conception results from rape may well make abortion permissible, on the ground that the woman is no more responsible than other people for the foetus's standing in need of a life-support system. Most factors cited by the moderate, however, are not such as one would normally take as grounds that make it permissible to kill someone, or to allow them to die. If the moderate's position here is to be defensible, then, he needs some account of the wrongness of destroying human foetuses that makes it prima facie wrong, but far less seriously so than the killing of normal adult human beings.

To sum up. The moderate holds that abortion is in general wrong, but that there are circumstances that render it permissible. The circumstances in question are of two types: temporal and non-temporal. Each gives rise to difficulties. If the defender of a moderate view wants to hold that abortion is permissible before a certain point in the development of the foetus, but generally not thereafter, he must specify some morally relevant property that the foetus acquires at that point. And if he wants to maintain that abortion is prima facie wrong, at least past a certain point, but not wrong all things considered if certain conditions are satisfied, then he needs to offer an account of the prima-facie wrongness of abortion that allows the factors he cites to function as overriding considerations. Given the sorts of considerations that the moderate typically advances, however, it will not do for him simply to take over the grounds that conservatives offer in support of the claim that abortion is prima facie wrong. For those grounds would make abortion so seriously wrong that its wrongness could not be counterbalanced by most of the factors that the moderate takes to be relevant. The defender of a moderate view needs, then, a quite different account of the prima-facie wrongness of abortion.

8.3 Can the Difficulties Be Surmounted?

Advocates of a moderate position on abortion have rarely grappled with either of these problems. It would seem, however, that there are two main approaches that might be tried. First, one could hold that there is some characteristic of individuals, other than that which makes something a person, that also makes the destruction of something intrinsically wrong, though not to the degree that being a person does. If there is a period of time, before humans become persons, during which they possess that property, the way will be open for a defence of a moderate view. How moderate, of course, will depend upon how serious the wrong-making characteristic is. If it makes the destruction of an individual quite seriously wrong, the resulting position will, on most points, coincide with the conservative view. On the other hand, if the wrong-making characteristic is a rather trivial one, the resulting view will diverge only slightly from a liberal perspective. The strength of the wrong-making characteristic will therefore be crucial.

In outline, this is fine. The problem comes when one asks what the wrong-making characteristic is. Most answers with any initial plausibility have, in effect, already been ruled out by earlier discussions. It is sometimes suggested, for example, that the achievement of a certain level of physiological development—such as the possession of a rudimentary central nervous system—is a characteristic that makes it wrong to destroy an individual. It is surely clear, however, in view of arguments of the sort advanced in chapter 4, that no property that is described in physical, rather than psychological terms, can plausibly be viewed as entering into a wrong-making characteristic.

Alternatively, it might be proposed that the possession of a certain potentiality is sufficient to make the destruction of an individual intrinsically wrong. This suggestion, however, is exposed to some of the same objections as the view, considered in chapter 6, that it is intrinsically wrong to destroy potential persons. In view of the moral symmetry principle, for example, it cannot be wrong to destroy non-persons possessing some potentiality unless it is also wrong, and equally so, to refrain from producing individuals with that potentiality. This can then be combined with the general view advanced in chapter 7 to provide a defence of the claim that there cannot be any potentiality possessed by human foetuses, such that it is intrinsically wrong to destroy anything possessing that potentiality.

Another possibility is that it is intrinsically wrong to destroy something that possesses certain general, unexercised capacities. The moral symmetry principle entails, however, that it is intrinsically wrong to destroy non-persons possessing some general capacity only if it is also intrinsically wrong, and equally so, to refrain from producing individuals with that capacity. The general view advanced in the preceding chapter implies, however, that there is no type of individual that it is intrinsically wrong to refrain from producing.

A final alternative, which deserves very serious consideration, is the view that it is intrinsically wrong to destroy any individual that possesses consciousness—or at least, consciousness together with desires. The suggestion that consciousness, together with desires, suffices to make something a person, was dismissed rather quickly in chapter 5. The reason was, in part, a matter of widely shared intuitions. If it were true that consciousness, together with desires, is sufficient to make something a person, most of us would have to revise, in a very radical way indeed, our views on the permissibility of killing animals belonging to other species—even animals very far down the evolutionary scale. Such killing would have to be viewed not merely as intrinsically wrong, but as very seriously so.

The main reason, however, for thinking that consciousness together with desires cannot suffice to make something a person is brought out by the reprogramming example. To reprogramme a normal adult human is to destroy a person. Yet there remains a human organism that enjoys not only consciousness plus desires, but all of the higher mental states enjoyed by human persons. It is very hard to see how this can be explained unless one holds that one of the essential features of a person is a certain sort of unification of mental life over time. But if this is right, consciousness together with desires cannot suffice to make something a person.

But even if consciousness, together with desires, does not make something a person, may it not be the case that it is still intrinsically wrong to destroy such beings, albeit not as seriously so as it is to destroy persons? Indeed, is this not our ordinary moral view? Would not most people, for example, regard a person who killed mice simply because he enjoyed doing so as morally defective in some way?

Perhaps the first point to be made about this line of thought is that, to the extent that it rests upon an appeal to people's ordinary moral views, it leads to a position on the morality of abortion that is virtually indistinguishable from a liberal one. For even if people do think that it is wrong to destroy sentient beings for no reason at all, it is clear that they do not view it as seriously wrong. Otherwise they could not take the fact that they enjoy the taste of steaks as adequate justification for killing cattle.

Second, there is the following argument. Let A be some organism that has enjoyed consciousness, together with momentary desires, and that could do so in the future. Assume, further, that A is not the sort of organism that can enjoy a mental life that is unified over time. Let B be an organism that is qualitatively indistinguishable from A, but which has just been constructed, and hence which has never enjoyed any experiences or momentary desires. Is there any moral difference between the following two actions:

A is completely destroyed, but B is allowed to go into a physical state of type P, which gives rise to a conscious state of type E;

B is completely destroyed, but A is allowed to go into a physical state of type P, which gives rise to a conscious state of type E?

In both cases, the world will contain a conscious state of type E. Does it matter whether it is A or B that enjoys that state? It is important, here, not to lose sight of the fact that A and B are incapable of enjoying a mental life that is unified over time in any way. For I want to suggest that if one is tempted to say that it is better if A enjoys the conscious state, it is because one is imagining some psychological connection between A's earlier experiences and the present experience of type E. But this possibility is, by hypothesis, ruled out. The only connection between experiences enjoyed by A at different times is that they are causally dependent upon states of a single organism, and it is very hard to see why this relation should be morally significant.

Let us assume, then, that this causal relation is not morally significant. It follows that:

(1) It is in itself no more seriously wrong to destroy an organism of type M that has previously enjoyed states of consciousness than it is to destroy one that has not—where an organism is of type M only if it is incapable of enjoying a mental life that is unified over time in any way.

This can be combined with the following premiss, which is entailed by the moral symmetry principle:

(2) It is in itself no more wrong to destroy an organism of type M that has never enjoyed any conscious states than it is to refrain from creating such an organism.

The result will be:

(3) It is in itself no more wrong to destroy an organism of type M that has previously enjoyed states of consciousness than it is to refrain from creating an organism of that type.

Is there a prima-facie obligation to produce organisms that will have experiences, but whose mental life will never be unified over time in any way? If there is, how serious an obligation is it? I am inclined to think that no such obligation exists. In the first place, the moral intuitions of most people provide no reason for suspecting that there is an obligation to create organisms of type M. Second, it would be surprising, surely, if there were a prima-facie obligation to create organisms of type M, but no obligation, at least equally strong, to produce additional people. In view of the conclusion of chapter 7, then, it seems very unlikely that there is any obligation, even a very weak one, to produce organisms that will have experiences, but never enjoy a temporally unified consciousness. Finally, the basic thesis developed in chapter 7 can be applied directly. If an action cannot be wrong unless it either violates an obligation with respect to some individual, or makes it the case that there is an individual with respect to whom there are obligations that cannot be met, then it follows that it cannot be intrinsically wrong to refrain from producing an individual of type M.

If this is correct, it follows, in view of (3) above, that it cannot be intrinsically wrong to destroy an organism that has enjoyed states of consciousness, but which does not enjoy a mental life that is temporally unified. A moderate position on abortion cannot be defended, therefore, by appealing to the proposition that it is intrinsically wrong to destroy something which, though not a person, does possess consciousness together with desires.[1]

Where does this leave the first attempt to defend a moderate position on the morality of abortion? I believe that it shows that such an approach is unlikely to succeed. The question was whether there is some property, possessed by human organisms before they become persons, that makes their destruction intrinsically wrong, though not as seriously so as it would be if they were persons. My approach to this question has been to survey what seem to be the most plausible candidates—namely, the achievement of a certain level of physiological development, the possession of some potentiality, the possession of some unexercised capacity, and the possession of consciousness, possibly together with momentary desires. I have tried to show that none of these properties serves to make the destruction of something intrinsically wrong. In the absence of other suggestions as to what the morally relevant property might be, I believe that we are justified in setting aside this first attempt to defend a moderate position on the morality of abortion.

A second way of attempting to make sense of a moderate position on abortion is as follows. The liberal on abortion thinks that the morality of killing is to be understood in terms of some property, which a thing either has or doesn't have, and which makes something a person. If something has that property, it is seriously wrong to destroy it. If it lacks that property, it can be destroyed for any reason. But there

[1] Compare Wayne Sumner's attempt to defend a moderate position on abortion in his recent book, *Abortion and Moral Theory*, 1981, especially pp. 128-46 and pp. 195 ff.

are alternative views that need to be considered. One possibility is that personhood depends upon the presence of a group of properties, and that the presence of only some of the members of that group is sufficient to make it intrinsically wrong to kill something, albeit not to the degree that it is intrinsically wrong to destroy persons.[2] A second possibility is that the property (or properties) that makes something a person may admit of degrees, and be morally significant in whatever degree it is present. Perhaps it is similar, in this respect, to the property of causing pain. It is wrong to cause pain, but the degree of wrongness is not always the same. It depends upon the amount of pain produced.

If either of these alternative models of the morality of killing is correct, it follows that it is not possible to place all individuals in one of two classes: those it is seriously wrong to kill, and those that can be destroyed for any reason. What one will have is a spectrum, ranging from things that may be destroyed at will, through things that may only be destroyed given some significant counterbalancing consideration, up to things that are persons, and hence which may be killed only for the most serious reasons.

Views of this general sort have been espoused by a number of philosophers. Wayne Sumner, for example, has advocated a 'developmental' view according to which one 'must allow for the gradual acquisition by the fetus of the status of a moral person and the accompanying right to protection of life'.[3] Similarly, Edward Langerak has suggested that 'the closer a potential person develops to being an actual person, the higher we rank his right to life'.[4]

The most careful exposition of this general point of view, however, is found in Norman Gillespie's interesting article, 'Abortion and Human Rights'.[5] Gillespie attempts to show, first, that the most plausible basis for a moderate position on abortion lies in the view that there is some comparative

---

[2] This possibility was suggested by Jefferson McMahan.

[3] L. W. Sumner, 'Toward a Credible View of Abortion', *Canadian Journal of Philosophy*, Volume 4, Number 1, 1974, pp. 163–81. See p. 180.

[4] Edward Langerak, 'Correspondence', *Philosophy & Public Affairs*, Volume 2, Number 4, 1973, pp. 410–16. See p. 416.

[5] Norman C. Gillespie, 'Abortion and Human Rights', *Ethics*, Volume 87, Number 3, 1977, pp. 237–43.

property such that the wrongness of destroying something is dependent upon the extent to which it possesses that property; and second, that there is nothing incoherent in the notion that the wrongness of destroying something is a function of the extent to which it possesses some comparative property. If that view is wrong, it is wrong for substantive moral reasons, not as a matter of logic.

I believe that Gillespie makes out a reasonably plausible case for the first contention, and that he is undoubtedly right about the second. He does not, however, offer any suggestions as to what the comparative property might be. As a result, he has shown only that a defence of this sort cannot be precluded.

What might the comparative property be? Some writers have suggested that it is degree of physiological development, but in view of the discussion above, it is clear that that cannot be right: no characteristic that is described in purely physical terms can, as such, enter into the characterization of a wrong-making property.

Another possibility involves a thing's potentialities. Generally speaking, of course, the potentialities of a human organism do not undergo significant change during the period of foetal development. However *the likelihood* that the individual's potentiality for developing into a person will be realized does change, and I think that some philosophers have felt that this is a morally relevant factor.

This possibility has, however, in effect been ruled out by the line of argument developed in chapters 6 and 7 in support of the claim that it is not intrinsically wrong to destroy something that will, if not interfered with, necessarily develop into a person. For if it is not intrinsically wrong to destroy something that is otherwise certain to become a person, it is surely not intrinsically wrong to destroy something that will, with probability p, develop into a person.

While a human's potentialities remain more or less constant during its development before birth, this is not true of its capacities. They undergo great alteration throughout that period. So it might be suggested that it is the extent to which a human organism has acquired various capacities possessed by persons that determines how wrong it is to destroy it. In view of the earlier discussion, of course, it cannot be the mere possession of a certain capacity, to some degree or other, that is morally relevant: the capacity must be one that the organism either has exercised, or is exercising.

What might the relevant capacity be? The most common suggestion, I think, is that the wrongness of destroying something depends upon the *level of consciousness* that the individual has become capable of enjoying. The popularity of this view may be due in part, however, to the vagueness of the expression, 'level of consciousness'. On one interpretation, the suggestion seems to be that it is the variety and structural complexity within an organism's momentary field of consciousness that determines how wrong it is to destroy it. So construed, there are two points that need to be made. First, even if this line of thought could be made plausible, it would support a view of abortion that differed significantly from the liberal view only if it also entailed a very radical revision of common moral views about the treatment of animals. For the experiences enjoyed by a human foetus do not, for reasons which will emerge in section 11.4, compare very favourably with those enjoyed by mature animals belonging to many species, with respect to either variety or structural complexity. Therefore level of consciousness, so construed, makes abortion wrong only if it makes the killing of many animals even more wrong.

Second, recall the argument advanced above against the view that it is intrinsically wrong to destroy something that enjoys consciousness, possibly together with momentary desires. That argument can be modified to bear upon the present suggestion. Let A be an organism that has enjoyed, and that is capable of enjoying, consciousness of level n— where level of consciousness is a function of the variety and/or structural complexity of one's field of consciousness at a given moment. Let B be an organism that is qualitatively indistinguishable from A, but which has just been constructed, and hence which has never enjoyed consciousness of level n. Is there any intrinsic moral difference between the following two actions:

A is completely destroyed, but B is allowed to go into a physical state that will give rise to consciousness of level n;

B is completely destroyed, but A is allowed to go into a physical state that will give rise to consciousness of level n?

In both cases, the world will contain a momentary state of consciousness of level n. Does it matter whether that state is associated with A or with B? It seems to me that if A and B are organisms whose experiences cannot be psychologically unified over time, it makes no difference at all whether the conscious state of level n is associated with A or with B. If so:

It is no more seriously wrong in itself to destroy an organism that has previously enjoyed consciousness of level n than it is to destroy an organism of the same type that has not yet enjoyed consciousness of level n, provided the organisms are not of a type whose states of consciousness are psychologically unified over time.

The moral symmetry principle, however, entails that:

It is no more seriously wrong in itself to destroy an organism that is capable of enjoying consciousness of level n, but has not yet done so, than it is to refrain from creating such an organism.

And from these, it follows that:

It is no more seriously wrong in itself to destroy an organism that has previously enjoyed consciousness of level n (but whose conscious states are not unified over time), than it is to refrain from creating an organism capable of enjoying consciousness of level n.

The reasons for thinking that there is no prima-facie obligation to create beings that will enjoy simple consciousness, possibly together with momentary desires, can then be appealed to in support of the claim that there is no prima-facie obligation to create organisms that will enjoy consciousness of level n. Accordingly, it cannot, apparently, be intrinsically wrong to destroy organisms that have previously enjoyed consciousness of level n.

The upshot is that if the expression, 'level of consciousness', is construed in terms of the variety and structural complexity of momentary states of consciousness, it does not seem to be the case that the wrongness of destroying something is a function of its level of consciousness. But other interpretations are possible, and there are two in particular that deserve examination. According to one, an organism's level of consciousness is a matter of the cognitive capacities that it exercises. According to the other, it is a matter of the extent and/or the ways in which consciousness is unified over time.

The former position may be quite appealing if one starts out from the view that it is rationality that makes something a person, and then pursues, in a vigorous fashion, the issue of precisely what is involved in rationality. For the capacity for rational thought seems, upon reflection, to involve a number of distinct capacities, and it may not be easy to draw a plausible line between those that are essential and those that are not. So it may be natural to conclude both that there are different cognitive capacities that are relevant to the issue of whether it is wrong to destroy a given organism, and that the wrongness depends upon how many of those capacities are present in the individual, or perhaps, upon the extent to which each is fully developed.

If, on the other hand, one does not think that it is rationality that makes something a person, the claim that it is intrinsically wrong to destroy anything that is rational to some degree or other is likely to have little appeal. In section 5.3, however, I attempted to show, first, that rationality is not in itself sufficient to make something a person, and second, that something need not be rational to be a person, unless rationality is construed in a weak sense that involves nothing more than the capacity for having thoughts, or for making temporal judgements. If these claims are correct, it would seem that we can also reject the view that the wrongness of destroying something is a function of the extent to which it exercises rational thought.

What of the other alternative mentioned above, viz. that the destruction of something is intrinsically wrong to the extent that the individual enjoys consciousness that is unified over time? As it stands, this view does not seem adequate. For as was argued in section 5.3 in the discussion of whether self-consciousness suffices to make something a person, there are reasons for thinking that it cannot be intrinsically wrong to destroy something unless it has preferences. But this claim might simply be granted, at least for sake of discussion, and this final suggestion modified to read:

> The destruction of an individual with preferences is intrinsically wrong to the extent that the individual's consciousness is unified over time.

In section 5.3 I attempted to defend the view that it is being a subject of non-momentary interests that makes something a person. We saw, however, that it is not at all easy to decide *precisely* what conditions must be satisfied in order for desires and preferences existing at different times to be unified into a single, non-momentary interest. One explanation of this difficulty is that unification is really a matter of degree, so that any attempt to draw a sharp line will necessarily involve an element of arbitrariness.

The notion that unification of consciousness over time, and its moral significance, are a matter of degree, is an idea that I now find rather appealing. The appeal is related to enduring doubts that I have about the moral status of non-human animals. Consider a very mundane occurrence. Two cats, Sheep and Woofer, are playing. Sheep sees Woofer coming, and hides behind a corner. Sheep can no longer see Woofer, but he crouches down, and when she appears, he springs. What is one to say about the mental life of Sheep as he crouches, prepared to pounce?

Many people, I believe, find it very tempting to attribute to non-human animals, in such situations, mental representations of future events that they are eagerly anticipating. A number of philosophers, on the other hand, contend that this is a mistake—or, at least, that any such mental representations are not *thoughts*.[6] The reasons offered usually involve the claim that there is a necessary connection between thought and language, so that no individual incapable of using language can possibly enjoy thoughts. The issues raised are somewhat

---

[6] See, for example, Donald Davidson, 'Thought and Talk', in *Mind and Language*, edited by S. Guttenplan, 1975, and S. P. Stich, 'Do Animals Have Beliefs?' *Australasian Journal of Philosophy*, Volume 57, Number 1, 1979, pp. 15-28.

complex, and it will not be possible to pursue them here.[7] It is my opinion, however, that the arguments are unsound. I also am inclined to believe that it is reasonable to attribute to animals in such situations thought episodes of *roughly* the sort one is naturally inclined to attribute to them, though this latter opinion is quite a tentative one.

The crucial issue here, however, is this. Suppose that it does turn out that some non-human animals have thoughts and desires about the future. Does that make them persons? The answer, I suggest, is unclear. The reason is that there may still be significant differences between the ways in which their mental lives are unified over time, and the way in which the mental life of a normal adult human being is unified over time.

Normal adult human beings can think of their lives as extending indefinitely into the future. They can also recall past events extending back over many years. Perhaps cats, for example, have a much more limited view. Perhaps they are capable only of envisaging a future that extends a few minutes beyond the present, and of recalling—in the sense of 'recall' that involves thought episodes—the more or less immediate past. Would such differences be morally significant? There is some reason for thinking they would be. Any limitation upon one's capacity to envisage a future for oneself will entail restrictions upon the projects one can choose to undertake. Similarly, if one's capacity for recall is limited to the immediate past, one will be unable, after a short period of time, to view past undertakings as things that one has done oneself. The sense that one has of oneself as a continuing entity will be very different from that possessed by normal adult human beings. And it seems to me that these differences may very well be relevant when it is a matter of the extent to which desires existing at different times are to be viewed as belonging to a single non-momentary interest.

My present views on this matter are tentative in the extreme. Nevertheless I am inclined to think both that the property that makes something a person is one that admits of

---

[7] For a careful discussion of some of the central issues, see John Bishop 'More Thought on Thought and Talk', *Mind*, Volume 89, Number 353, 1980, pp. 1-16.

degrees, and that the destruction of something is intrinsically wrong to the extent that it possesses the property in question.

Even if this view turns out to be right, however, it does not follow that the correct position on the morality of abortion is a moderate one. There is still the crucial question of the extent to which, as a matter of fact, human foetuses possess the morally relevant property. This issue will be taken up in part III, when we turn to consider the question of the point at which humans become persons. Another issue that bears upon the tenability of some moderate positions on abortion will also be taken up in part III, namely, the question whether the practice of abortion has seriously undesirable consequences. Only then shall we be in a position to arrive at a final conclusion concerning the tenability of a moderate view.

9

A Brief Summary

We have covered most of the issues that I believe are crucial to the question of the morality of abortion. Those that remain will be dealt with in the discussion of infanticide in part III. We shall then be in a position to decide what view should be taken on the morality of abortion. At this point, however, I think it will be useful to summarize briefly the conclusions that I have tried to establish, and the questions that remain.

The main theses that I have advanced, and argued for, are as follows:

(1) One cannot, in general, decide the issue of the permissibility of abortion without tackling the question of the moral status of the foetus. There may be cases in which a woman's rights have sufficient weight to render abortion morally permissible even if a human foetus has a serious right to life. This is the case, presumably, if the woman's life is threatened, and may also be the case when the pregnancy results from rape. But it does not appear to be so in most cases.

(2) The fact that a foetus developing inside a human female belongs to the biological species, *Homo sapiens*, is not *in itself* morally significant. For in so far as properties are described in purely physical terms, they cannot enter into right-making and wrong-making characteristics.

(3) The non-potential property that makes an individual a person—that is, that makes the destruction of something intrinsically wrong, and seriously so, and that does so independently of the individual's value, is the property of being an enduring subject of non-momentary interests. It is not the possession of, or the exercise of, any of the following: the capacity for rational thought; the capacity for free action; the capacity for self-consciousness.

(4) The destruction of potential persons is not intrinsically wrong.

(5) It is not intrinsically wrong to refrain from producing additional persons, or additional persons who will have certain properties.

(6) There does not appear to be any property, unrelated to the property that makes something a person, that makes the destruction of something intrinsically wrong, and that does so independently of the entity's value.

(7) It may be the case that the property that makes something a person is one that admits of degrees, and that the wrongness of destroying something is a matter of the degree to which it possesses the property in question.

The main issues that have yet to be dealt with are the following:

(1) At what point in the development of a human organism does it become a person?

(2) If the property that makes something a person admits of degree, and is morally significant to whatever degree it is present, at what point in the development of a human organism does it first become wrong—even if only minimally so—to destroy it?

(3) Is acceptance of the practice of abortion necessarily accompanied by undesirable consequences, even if abortion is not intrinsically wrong?

If the conclusions stated above are correct, the anti-abortionist position is *virtually* ruled out. For there are three main lines of argument that an anti-abortionist can offer in support of his claim that abortion is intrinsically wrong, and seriously so. First, he may argue that abortion is seriously wrong because it involves the killing of innocent human beings. Second, he may argue that abortion is seriously wrong because it involves the destruction of potential persons. Third, he may contend that abortion is seriously wrong because it involves the destruction of persons. None of these arguments appears to be tenable. The first two fail because they appeal to unacceptable moral principles. The fact that an organism belongs to a particular biological species—*Homo sapiens*—does not in itself make it wrong to destroy it. Neither does the fact that it is a potential person. The third argument, on the other hand, is mistaken for factual reasons. For whatever may be true of a human organism at later points in its development, it seems most unlikely indeed that a fertilized human egg cell is a person, given that it has no central nervous system, and hence, presumably, neither enjoys nor is capable of enjoying any mental life whatever.

In part III, however, I shall consider an argument that conservatives on abortion sometimes offer in support of the apparently very implausible claim that human zygotes are persons. I shall also consider an argument that maintains that abortion is wrong, not because it destroys persons, but because it harms them. I believe that both arguments are unsound. If so, we shall be left with a choice between an extreme liberal position, and one of the moderate positions set out in the previous chapter. The decision among these alternatives will turn upon the answers to the three questions listed above.

PART III
INFANTICIDE

10

Present-day Attitudes, and the Historical and Anthropological Background

10.1 Present-day Attitudes: Is There a Need for a New Perspective?

First, with respect to moral innocence, we can take babes in arms as paradigms. Here I should argue that no reasons can be given for why it is wrong to kill babies; neither are any reasons needed. If anything can be taken as a brute datum for moral philosophy, surely the principle 'Do not kill innocent babies' is a very good candidate—much more plausible for an ethical primitive than, say, 'promote your self-interest' or 'maximize the general utility' (other candidates that have been offered for ethical primitives). The person who cannot just *see* that there is something evil about killing babies could not, I suspect, be made to see anything else about morality and thus could not understand any reasons that one might attempt to give. And any 'ethical' theory which entailed that there is nothing wrong at all with killing babies would surely deserve to be rejected on the basis of this counterexample alone. Miss G. E. M. Anscombe puts the point in the following way:

If someone really thinks, *in advance*, that it is open to question whether such an action as procuring the judicial execution of the innocent should be quite excluded from consideration—I do not want to argue with him; he shows a corrupt mind.

Jeffrie G. Murphy[1]

Recently at least two philosophers have published defenses of abortion that allow as how infanticide is also at worst imprudent. Query: Will their essays create anything comparable to the public outrage generated by the now infamous work of Jensen and Herrnstein? Not bloody likely. Why not, for their assault on the conscience and intellect of civilized people is surely no less brutal and blundering? Well, without discounting numerable other salient differences, part of the answer is that Jensen and Herrnstein are social scientists, and, for good reasons and bad alike, we listen when social scientists, even those of minor

---

[1] Jeffrie G. Murphy, 'The Killing of the Innocent', *Monist*, Volume 57, Number 4, 1973, pp. 527–50. See pp. 536–7.

distinction, speak out on matters touching upon public policy. Their counterparts in philosophy are not invited onto the stage. . . . Why is this? Just look at a typical philosophical performance: Abortion, an issue inspiring no unanimity among any random class of persons (as is evidenced by the turbulent condition of laws on the matter), provides the occasion for a blithe dismissal of a prohibition endorsed by a mono-lithic consensus and enforced by every present Western legal system. Once again a philosopher has thrown the baby out with the bath water (and the very premeditation of the performance only deepens the onlooker's despair); and once again, having walked upon the stage, the philosopher turns his back to his audience (and then walks off, for he has no responsibilities for what follows). And then, when the crowd remains unmoved except to laughter and derision, the philosopher deems it benighted. But the explanation of the crowd's response is not what the philosopher says, but *that* he says it. At least since Socrates philosophers have been regarded with hostile suspicion or amused contempt because, at least since Socrates, they have regarded others with hostile suspicion or amused contempt. They are not listened to because they do not listen. That may be an instance of a psychological law, but here the point is also that philosophers are not listened to because what they say is not worth listening to, and is not because they do not listen (to anyone but themselves), and so they are in no position to speak (to anyone but themselves).

Roger Wertheimer[2]

The preceding quotations illustrate, albeit somewhat dramatically, some recurrent weaknesses in present-day discussions of abortion. I shall begin by considering these defects, for I believe that an awareness of them makes it much easier to appreciate why the question of the morality of infanticide stands in urgent need of re-examination.

Many philosophers believe that infanticide is intrinsically wrong, and seriously so—for the same reason, and to the same degree, as the killing of an adult human being. Some offer arguments in support of this view, as we shall see in the next chapter. Most, however, are content to appeal to the fact that virtually everyone feels that infanticide is seriously wrong. Thus Roger Wertheimer, in the passage just quoted, refers to 'a prohibition endorsed by a monolithic consensus and enforced by every present Western legal system'.

I believe that such an appeal is unsatisfactory, for a number of reasons. In the first place, there is a serious

---

question whether philosophers who make such an appeal are right about the facts. Is it true that most people think that infanticide is morally on a par with killing an adult? I believe that it is true that the vast majority of people feel that the killing of a *normal* infant is morally wrong, and it may also be true that they believe that it is seriously wrong. But the situation seems very different in the case of infants that are not normal, where at least a very substantial minority—and possibly a majority—believe that infanticide ought to be permitted. In a recent Australian Gallup Poll, for example, 55 per cent of those interviewed thought that the law should allow life to be painlessly terminated in the case of babies who are either 'mentally abnormal' or 'physically seriously deformed'.[3] This certainly shows that there is no consensus on infanticide in general. But it also suggests that there is probably no consensus on infanticide even in the case of normal infants. For what moral views are to be ascribed to those who think that infanticide should be permitted when the infant suffers from certain defects? Do such people believe that the killing of a normal infant is morally on a par with the killing of a normal adult? If they do, why do they not think that the law should also permit the painless termination of life in the case of an adult who is 'mentally abnormal' or 'physically seriously deformed'? Perhaps the people in question are simply inconsistent on this matter. But before that conclusion is embraced, there is a more charitable view that deserves to be considered. Namely, that most people who accept infanticide in the case of defective infants do so because they do not assign normal human infants precisely the same moral status as normal human adults. In the absence of much more careful and detailed surveys, I would suggest that this is the most plausible interpretation of the facts. And if it is correct, then at least a substantial minority, and possibly even a majority, accept a moderate position on the morality of infanticide, according to which infanticide is not to be treated as a crime in the case of infants suffering from certain defects, and, even in the case of normal infants, is not wrong to the same degree as the

[3] As reported in *The Advertiser*, Adelaide, Australia, 2 Oct. 1978, p. 10.

killing of a normal adult human being. Consequently, the contention there is a 'monolithic consensus' on infanticide appears simply false.

Second, if one is going to appeal to moral intuitions to resolve ethical issues, it is crucial that such an appeal should be as *reflective* as possible. What this involves was discussed in section 1.5, where two factors were stressed. First, there is the extent to which the moral feelings in question are shared by others. And here it is very important not to confine oneself to one's own social group, or one's own society, however enlightened they may seem to be. One should investigate the extent to which other societies, both now and at other times, have the same moral intuitions.

The second factor concerns certain sorts of explanations of shared moral feelings. Religions, for example, have traditionally offered people package deals—part of the package being a set of moral principles. As a result, moral agreement may, in many cases, reflect religious agreement. The consensus, until quite recently, on various principles of sexual morality, is a case in point.[4]

As long as there is good reason for believing that the religion in question is correct, the fact that it is responsible for the sharing of certain moral views raises no problem. But if there are grounds for doubting or rejecting the religion, these will also be grounds for discounting any moral consensus that it has produced, unless that consensus derives from considerations that are independent of its religious claims.

Very few people who appeal to moral intuitions in defence of the view that infanticide is seriously wrong even touch upon either of these issues, and I know of no account that seriously grapples with both factors. How does the argument fare when this is done? This issue will be considered in the next section.

There is a third, very serious objection to any attempt to support the claim that infanticide is seriously wrong by appealing to moral intuitions. It arises out of a point that was made in section 1.5, to the effect that an appeal to moral intuitions can have very little plausibility unless the appeal is

---

[4] See, for example, Wayland Young's *Eros Denied* (1964).

restricted to principles that are either (1) basic moral principles themselves, or (2) principles that can be derived from other principles that are both basic and in accordance with moral intuitions.

The plausibility of this contention is perhaps clearest when the point is expressed in terms of the concepts of right-making and wrong-making characteristics. Assume, for the sake of discussion, that there is a faculty of moral intuition. Is it at all plausible to suppose that it would provide us with intuitive knowledge of the fact that certain natural characteristics are associated with right-making and wrong-making characteristics, without also providing us with knowledge of what the right-making and wrong-making characteristics in question are? This would make such a faculty mysterious indeed. So it seems reasonable to hold that if there is a faculty of moral intuition, it will provide us with knowledge of the relevant right-making and wrong-making characteristics.

How does this bear upon attempts to support the view that infanticide is in itself seriously wrong by appealing to moral intuitions? The answer is that it turns out to be very difficult to specify a *basic* moral principle that people will generally view as intuitively correct, and from which it follows, without any additional problematic assumptions, that infanticide is wrong. The difficulty can be illustrated by Murphy's discussion, quoted at the beginning of this section. Murphy suggests that the principle, 'Do not kill innocent babies', can plausibly be viewed as an 'ethical primitive'. But a little reflection shows that in fact it is not reasonable to view·it as a basic moral principle. For Murphy is not using the term 'baby' in the broad sense in which it covers new-borns of any species: he has in mind the narrower, and more common meaning of the term, according to which it applies only to new-born members of a particular biological species—*Homo sapiens*. The principle to which Murphy is appealing, then, cannot be a basic moral principle, in view of the considerations advanced in section 4.2. Purely biological concepts cannot enter into right-making or wrong-making characteristics. Hence the principle advanced by Murphy is not one that can be supported by appeal to moral intuitions.

There are, of course, other principles that one might

appeal to in this context, such as 'It is wrong to destroy potential persons', or 'It is wrong to destroy persons.' But it seems to be the case that all such principles suffer from at least one of three defects. Either, like Murphy's principle, they are not basic moral principles, and hence not appropriate candidates for principles grounded directly on moral intuitions; or, like the principle that it is wrong to destroy potential persons, they are not such as most people find intuitively plausible; or, like the principle that it is wrong to kill persons, they cannot be applied to human babies without invoking some additional premiss whose acceptability is far from clear. If this is correct, there is no hope of defending the view that infanticide is wrong by a simple, direct appeal to moral intuitions.

In the light of these three considerations, the widespread and casual way in which philosophers appeal to moral intuitions in support of the contention that infanticide is intrinsically wrong is a puzzling phenomenon. The considerations that have been offered here are not esoteric, and they seem quite decisive.

It seems, then, that one is justified in concluding that if it is to be shown that infanticide is wrong, this will have to be done by means of an *argument*, and one, moreover, that involves both moral principles, and non-moral, factual claims. The next chapter will be devoted to an examination of such arguments.

One other point, illustrated by the introductory quotations, also deserves comment—namely, the rather emotional quality of many discussions of infanticide. In response, it might be suggested that such emotion is not necessarily inappropriate. After all, how would one react to a suggestion, say, that murder and torture are really fine things? The comparison, however, is not apt. The reason emerged in the final consideration just advanced against any appeal to intuitions in this context, namely, that an individual who questions whether infanticide is morally wrong need not, and probably does not, disagree with *most* people about any *basic* moral principles, such as the principle that it is wrong to destroy persons. Nor, as we shall see shortly, need it be the case that such a person is rejecting any straightforward and obviously correct non-moral claim. The issue of the morality of infanticide is a serious one, and it deserves to be approached in a much more open-minded and dispassionate fashion than is usually the case.

10.2 The Historical and Anthropological Background

To what extent has infanticide been practised in other societies? What were their attitudes toward it? If the attitudes and practices of other societies were substantially different from what is prevalent in our own society, how are such differences best explained? These are the questions to be considered in the present section.

Historically, the situation is as follows. In technologically less advanced societies, infanticide was widely accepted, up into the present century. It was very common to destroy infants that were deformed or diseased or illegitimate or regarded as ill omens. But the practice was not restricted to such cases. In many societies, custom determined how many children a family should have, and infanticide was enjoined as a means of achieving the desired family size. In such societies the practice of infanticide was extremely prevalent.[5]

This was the case, for example, in most of the South Sea Islands. It was very common in Melanesia, and even more so in Polynesia. It was almost universally practised in Australia among the Aborigines, where a woman might be punished for rearing too many children. The practice was not as general in New Zealand, but it was still quite frequent, and not regarded as seriously wrong. It was rejected by some tribes in North and South America, but very common in others. It was practised less in Africa than in the South Sea Islands, but in some cultures, such as the Swahili, infanticide was very common, and not seriously disapproved of.[6]

Infanticide was also widely accepted in more highly developed cultures. It was a common practice among the ancient Arabs, who sometimes regarded it as not merely permissible, but a duty. Female infanticide was common in

---

[5] E. A. Westermarck, *The Origin and Development of Moral Ideas* (1906–8). See chapter 17, pp. 394–6.

[6] Ibid., chapter 17, pp. 396–405.

the poorer districts of China, and although prohibited by both Buddhism and Taoism, was not regarded as wrong by most people. In India, infanticide was accepted during the Vedic age, and the practice was common, over a long period of time, in various Hindu castes.[7]

Infanticide was also accepted and practised by the two most advanced cultures of ancient Europe, Greece and Rome. In Greece, exposure of weak and deformed infants was an ancient custom and, in at least one state, Sparta, was required by law. Exposure of healthy infants was not generally approved of, but it was practised very widely, and not regarded as a serious offence.

This attitude toward infanticide was shared by the greatest of the Greek Philosophers, Plato and Aristotle. Aristotle, in the ideal legislation proposed in his *Politics*, holds that deformed infants should not be allowed to live.[8] Plato, in the *Republic*, goes further, and advocates the destruction not only of defective children, but of those who are the product of inferior parents, or of individuals past the ideal child-bearing ages.[9]

The status of infanticide in Rome was very similar. The exposure of healthy infants was probably less common; however this apparently reflects, not a difference in moral outlook, but the need for a population sufficient to maintain a large army. So while the killing of healthy infants was disapproved of, it was not viewed as an especially serious crime. And the destruction of weak or deformed infants was not merely accepted, but required by custom, and possibly even by law.[10]

The upshot is that there is a very remarkable gulf between the historical facts about the practice of infanticide, and what most people in present-day Western society take those facts to be. The situation is succinctly summed up by Laila

[7] Ibid., chapter 17, pp. 407–8, and chapter 18, page 485.
[8] Aristotle, *Politics*, book 7, chapter 16.
[9] Plato, *Republic*, book 5, 460.
[10] Westermarck, op. cit., chapter 17, pp. 408–11. Compare William L. Langer's account of Greek and Roman attitudes and practices on pages 354–5 of his article, 'Infanticide: A Historical Survey', *History of Childhood Quarterly*, Volume 1, Number 3, 1974, pp. 353–65.

Williamson, at the beginning of her recent article, 'Infanticide: An Anthropological Analysis':

Infanticide is a practice present-day westerners regard as a cruel and inhuman custom, resorted to by only a few desperate and primitive people living in harsh environments. We tend to think of it as an exceptional practice, to be found only among such peoples as the Eskimos and Australian Aborigines, who are far removed in both culture and geographical distance from us and our civilized ancestors. The truth is quite different. Infanticide has been practised on every continent and by people on every level of cultural complexity, from hunters and gatherers to high civilizations, including our own ancestors. Rather than being an exception, then, it has been the rule.[11]

How are we to account for the differences between societies that practised infanticide, and those, such as our own, that emphatically reject it? What I want to maintain is that no satisfactory understanding of those differences is possible unless they are seen as involving a difference in moral outlook. Some writers, in contrast, seem to believe that the difference is merely with regard to the prevalence of infanticide in other societies. As a result, they think that the difference can be explained by reference to factors such as the difficult conditions of life in primitive societies. But the difference between societies is not merely with regard to the frequency with which infanticide is practised. The crux is a difference in how people feel about infanticide. For the anthropological evidence indicates that exposure of infants was apparently carried out without any deep sense of regret, and, particularly in the case of weak and deformed children, was thought of as a perfectly natural way of behaving.[12]

It might be suggested, however, that this difference in feeling, rather than reflecting a difference in the moral principles accepted, is due to parental love being weaker in cultures that practised infanticide. Certainly, this is a possibility. But it is not borne out by the evidence. The testimony of anthropologists is that, in most societies where infanticide was prevalent, once a decision had been made to allow a child

---

[11] Laila Williamson, 'Infanticide: An Anthropological Analysis', pp. 61–75 in *Infanticide and the Value of Life*, edited by Marvin Kohl, 1978. See p. 61. Readers who are interested in examining primary source material will find this article especially helpful.

[12] Westermarck, op. cit., chapter 17, pages 396–7 and 403–4.

to live, the care and concern shown by its parents were by
no means inferior to that typical of present-day Western
society.[13]

There is also much more direct evidence that the differences in practices and feelings reflect a difference in moral
outlook. Thus, on the one hand, it has been observed, in the
case of more primitive cultures, that a different status was
often assigned to infants; they were not regarded as 'fully
human'—or, as I should prefer to say, as persons:

The killing is made easier by cultural belief that a child is not fully
human until accepted as a member of the social group. This acceptance may take place when the child is named, or when it appears
strong enough to survive, or when it shows 'human' characteristics,
such as walking and talking. The time varies from a few days to several
years after birth. The Peruvian Amahuaca, for instance, do not consider children fully human until they are about three years old.[14]

In the case of more highly developed cultures, on the other
hand, one has the evidence provided by direct pronounce-
ments on the morality of infanticide, such as those of Plato
and Aristotle referred to above.

What accounts for this remarkable difference of opinion
on the morality of infanticide? By far the most important
factor was the emergence of Christianity as the dominant
religion in Europe, and its subsequent influence upon law
and morality.[15] Long before the advent of Christianity, of
course, infanticide had been unequivocally rejected by
Judaism. But the Jewish religion has never been a missionary
religion, and as a result, it had little direct effect in shaping
the opinions of people in the ancient world on the morality
of infanticide. The situation was quite otherwise with Christianity, which actively sought political power in order to further
its missionary ends. Nevertheless, in spite of Christianity's
vigorous and unrelenting opposition to infanticide, attitudes and practices changed very slowly. Infanticide was an

---

[13] Ibid., chapter 17, pp. 404-5. Williamson, op. cit., pp. 63-4.

[14] Williamson, op. cit., p. 64. The passage is in the 'ethnographic present'.

[15] John T. Noonan, Jr., 'An Almost Absolute Value in History', pp. 1-59 in
The Morality of Abortion, edited by John T. Noonan, Jr., 1970. See pp. 3-18.
Compare also Glanville Williams, 'The Legal Evaluation of Infanticide', pp. 115-
29 in Kohl, op. cit. See p. 116.

important factor in limiting population growth in Europe until the nineteenth century,[16] despite the fact that it was considered a crime deserving punishment by death, often administered in unusually cruel ways, such as burial alive.

The Christian church appealed to a variety of considerations in support of its contention that infanticide was wrong. One of the grounds it offered, for example, involved the idea that human life is a gift from God, that it is something he has made, that it exists by his providence, and that, as a result, it is an offence against God to destroy human life at any point in its development.[17] The most fundamental ground, however, lay in the idea that there is something that human infants, no less than adult human beings, possess, namely, an immortal rational soul, and that it is this that sets man off from all other animals, and explains why the killing of humans is seriously wrong, while the killing of other animals is not. Thus Lecky, in his *History of European Morals*, comments that:

To the Pagans, even when condemning abortion and infanticide, these crimes appeared comparatively trivial, because the victims seemed very insignificant and their sufferings very slight. The death of an adult man who is struck down in the midst of his enterprise and his hopes, who is united by ties of love or friendship to multitudes around him, and whose departure causes a perturbation and a pang to the society in which he has moved, excites feelings very different from any produced by the painless extinction of a new-born infant, which, having scarcely touched the earth, has known none of its cares and very little of its love. But to the theologian this infant life possessed a fearful significance. The moment, they taught, the foetus in the womb acquired animation, it became an immortal being, destined, even if it died unborn, to be raised again on the last day, responsible for the sin of Adam, and doomed, if it perished without baptism, to be excluded forever from heaven and to be cast, as the Greeks taught, into a painless and joyless limbo, or, as the Latins taught, into the abyss of hell.[18]

The obvious point to be made about the grounds offered by the Christian church for thinking that infanticide is wrong is that they involve specifically religious claims. Now the fact

[16] Thomas McKeown, *The Modern Rise of Population*, 1976, pages 143-61. Also Langer, op. cit., pp. 357-62.

[17] Compare Noonan, op. cit., pp. 10-11.

[18] W. E. H. Lecky, *History of European Morals*, 3rd edition, 1910, volume 2, pp. 22-3. Compare Westermarck, op. cit., chapter 17, p. 411.

that the church's arguments against infanticide rest upon theological premisses need not distress the orthodox Roman Catholic, since he may very well believe that one can, for example, offer a *purely philosophical proof* of the claim that man possesses an immortal soul.[19] The liberal Roman Catholic, in contrast, is in a rather less comfortable position, since he may have grave doubts about the latter claim. As a result, the fact that the church's arguments against infanticide involve theological assumptions is not one that he can welcome, especially when it is a matter of attempting to justify legislation which is to apply even to those who do not accept the theological claims in question. The liberal, accordingly, usually attempts to play down the religious content of the arguments. John T. Noonan, Jr.'s approach may be taken as typical: 'The Christian position as it originated did not depend on a *narrow* theological or philosophical concept. It had no relation to theories of infant baptism. It appealed to no *special* theory of instantaneous ensoulment. It took the world's view on ensoulment as that view changed from Aristotle to Zacchia.'[20] But while Noonan is prepared to claim that the Christian position did not rest upon any 'narrow' theological assumptions, he is sufficiently familiar with the primary source material to realize that it cannot be denied that the arguments did involve theological premisses: 'There was, indeed, theological influence affecting the theory of ensoulment finally adopted, and, of course, ensoulment itself was a theological concept, so that the position was always explained in theological terms.'[21] Readers who are familiar with liberal Protestant theology, and especially with the 'demythologization' of the Gospel message will realize, of course, that this passage does not concede as much as it might appear to at first sight. When a theological liberal remarks that a certain position was always 'explained' in theological terms, one can be reasonably confident that he

[19] The claim that the existence of an immortal soul in man can be demonstrated is advanced in most standard Roman Catholic textbooks in the field of philosophical psychology. See, for example, Joseph F. Donceel, *Philosophical Psychology*, 1955, chapters 14 and 18.
[20] Noonan, op. cit., p. 51. The emphases are mine, not Noonan's.
[21] Ibid.

will go on to say that the theological concepts are mere trappings, and that the essential message or argument can be restated without loss in language that involves no theological concepts at all. Accordingly, it is not surprising when Noonan immediately proceeds to say:

> But the theological notion of ensoulment could easily be translated into humanistic language by substituting 'human' for 'rational soul'; the problem of knowing when a man is a man is common to theology and humanism.
>
> If one steps outside the specific categories used by the theologians, the answer they gave can be analyzed as a refusal to discriminate among human beings on the basis of their varying potentialities. Once conceived, the being was recognized as a man because he had man's potential. The criterion for humanity, thus, was simple and all-embracing: if you are conceived by human parents, you are human.[22]

Noonan has managed to compress a remarkable amount of confusion and imprecision into a short passage. The central question raised by his discussion, however, is whether the arguments in question can be demythologized without distorting their essential character. I believe that they cannot, and in the next chapter I shall support this claim by showing, in the case of the central argument, that once one grants the main theological premises, there is an argument that does what the demythologized alternatives suggested by Noonan do not do, namely, provide one with an excellent reason for holding that abortion and infanticide are seriously wrong, where the reason does not depend upon any moral principles that a non-religious person would wish to deny.

This issue is not, however, relevant in the present context. The points that are important here are these. First, the arguments that Christianity actually employed to support its contention that infanticide is wrong involved theological assumptions. As a consequence, those who do not accept those theological assumptions cannot justifiably appeal to the resulting change in moral intuitions about infanticide as grounds for believing that infanticide is wrong.

Second, the situation would not be significantly different if, contrary to fact, the church had appealed to non-theological

[22] Ibid.

arguments. The reason is that, for the vast majority of people, religious beliefs are a matter of faith, rather than evidence and argumentation. The mere fact that the church taught that infanticide was seriously wrong, for whatever reason, was what brought it about that people in general came to share this view of the matter.

The basic conclusion, then, is this. Even if one waives the general philosophical objections to any attempt to settle the question of the morality of infanticide by appealing to intuitions, there are particular, empirically-based objections that make such an appeal methodologically unsound in this case. First, the moral intuitions of people in most societies regarding infanticide have differed significantly from those which are common in present-day Western society. Second, when one examines the way in which the present consensus has come about, it is apparent that one has no grounds for assuming that the change in moral feelings about infanticide represents moral progress unless one is prepared to hold—as most philosophers who appeal to moral intuitions in this area are not—that the underlying theological assumptions are reasonable ones.

11

Objections to Infanticide

11.1 Introductory Remarks

As noted earlier, present-day attitudes toward infanticide vary greatly, depending upon whether the infant is normal, or suffers from some serious defect. The discussion here will be confined to the case of infanticide involving normal human infants.

In the preceding chapter, I indicated why the question of the morality of infanticide cannot be settled by an appeal to moral intuitions. An argument is required. Moreover, any argument must, if it is to be satisfactory, do more than merely provide grounds for thinking that infanticide is wrong; it must also explain why it is wrong. This will involve specifying the wrong-making characteristic that is possessed by acts of infanticide. This means that arguments need to be formulated in terms of basic moral principles, not in terms of derived ones.

In this chapter I shall consider the most important attempts to defend the view that infanticide, at least when it involves normal infants, is seriously wrong. Some of the arguments can be dealt with rather quickly, since they turn upon principles that have already been considered, and rejected above. Other arguments will require much more extended examination, and these I shall leave to the last.

11.2 Arguments Examined in the Discussion of Abortion

Argument 1: The Appeal to Species Membership

The reason which many people would offer for holding that infanticide is wrong is that it involves killing an innocent member of the biological species, *Homo sapiens*. This view is unsatisfactory in the case of infanticide for the same reasons that it is unsatisfactory in the case of abortion—reasons which were set out in chapter 4. Thus, in the first place, it does not seem to be the case that the killing of innocent human beings, considered in itself, is always wrong. Second, even if this principle were true, it would not provide us with an ultimately satisfactory account, since principles involving reference to membership in a particular biological species cannot be basic moral principles.

Argument 2: An Obligation to Produce Additional Persons

A second possible account of the wrongness of infanticide appeals to the claim that there is a prima-facie obligation to produce additional persons. On some views, this obligation is a very weak one. If this were so, infanticide would be wrong in itself, but there would be many circumstances in which it would be permissible, all things considered. On other views, the obligation may be a very strong one indeed. This seems to be so, for example, given Hare's view of the matter—as was argued in section 7.1. It does not necessarily follow, however, if the obligation is a strong one, that there will be very few cases in which infanticide is justifiable. It may turn out that infanticide is quite often permissible. The reason why this is so is set out very clearly by Hare.[1] The basic point is that if there is a prima-facie obligation to produce additional persons, this will sometimes be a reason *for* infanticide, and not merely a reason against. John and Mary may be capable, for example, of raising only one more child. Suppose that Mary gives birth to a baby suffering from serious defects. If they destroy it, they have, at that point, prevented the production of an additional person. But on the other hand, destroying it will make it possible for them to produce an additional person at a slightly later time, and if there is a sufficiently high chance that their next child will be healthier, the best course of action, all things considered, may be to destroy their present baby and have

---

[1] R. M. Hare, 'Survival of the Weakest', pp. 364-9 in *Moral Problems in Medicine*, edited by Samuel Gorovitz *et al*. See also pp. 211-13 of Hare's 'Abortion and the Golden Rule'.

another. In contrast, if one thought that infanticide was wrong because it involved the killing of a human being, or the destruction of a person, there would not be any sufficient counterbalancing considerations in the situation and it would therefore be seriously wrong, all things considered, for John and Mary to destroy one baby in order to have another.

The approach to the morality of infanticide that underlies this second argument is an interesting one, and deserves to be taken very seriously.[2] For as was emphasized in chapter 7, the issue of whether there is an obligation to produce additional persons is a very difficult one. Nevertheless, I believe that one is justified in concluding, for reasons set out in that chapter, that there is no prima-facie obligation, either weak or strong, to produce additional persons, and therefore that this second argument should be set aside.

Argument 3: An Obligation Not to Destroy Potential Persons

A third objection to infanticide turns upon the contention that there is a prima-facie obligation to refrain from destroying potential persons. This claim was examined at some length in chapter 6, where I argued that there are excellent reasons for holding that there is nothing intrinsically wrong with destroying potential persons.

This completes the discussion of arguments that have already been examined in connection with abortion. The next two sections will be concerned with arguments which, though relevant to abortion as well, have not yet been considered.

11.3 Infanticide as Wronging Persons

Many people would maintain that infanticide wrongs persons, on the ground that human infants are persons, and infanticide wrongs them by destroying them. In the present section, however, I want to consider a very different line of argument, which maintains that infanticide wrongs persons even if

[2] Jonathan Glover, in his admirably dispassionate discussion of infanticide in chapter 12 of his book, *Causing Death and Saving Lives*, 1977, adopts such an approach, though he also stresses other considerations.

human infants do not possess those properties that make something a person.

The basic idea involved in the present argument will become clear if we consider for a moment the general approach to the morality of killing followed in chapter 5. The discussion centred upon the question of the (non-potential) properties that, independently of a thing's value, make it seriously wrong to destroy something. Part of the rationale for approaching things in that way was provided by the reprogramming example, which was taken as showing that one could destroy persons without killing any organism. But this way of formulating the issue involves an unstated, and by no means uncontroversial assumption, namely, that to kill a normal adult human being is to *destroy* a person. Many people, both religious and non-religious, believe that a person's existence does not end with the destruction of his body, and so would view the above way of formulating the issue as not entirely satisfactory.

The difficulty, however, is that it does not seem possible to offer a 'religiously-neutral' account of the morality of killing. For it would seem that, on any plausible view of morality, whether people survive death, and what their prospects are if they do, may have a bearing upon *how* wrong it is to kill someone. Suppose, for example, that death, rather than being the end of a person's existence, is merely a matter of being transferred to another world where one enjoys a life very similar to what one presently enjoys. Murder would still be wrong, since it would, among other things, sever a person's relations with others to whom he was deeply attached. Yet it is surely plausible to say that it would not be as wrong as it would be if death represented the end of a person's existence.

How is one to deal with this problem? To consider even a representative sample of views on the afterlife would have necessitated a much lengthier discussion. I decided, therefore, to confine the discussion to a consideration of what view of the morality of killing would be plausible if it were the case that death was the end. Partly because this represents, to some extent, an intermediate view: death could be much better, but it could also be much worse. And partly because it seems to me that there is not, unfortunately, any good reason for believing that we shall survive the destruction of our bodies.

Be that as it may, the point of interest here is how a rather different view can have a crucial bearing upon the morality of abortion and infanticide. The view in question involves the proposition, not only that human persons survive death, but that all humans, regardless of their degree of development, have an immaterial and immortal soul. The relevance of this stronger claim is brought out by the following line of argument:

(1) There is, in every living human organism, an immaterial soul that will survive the destruction of the body. Moreover, every human soul is such that either it possesses the capacity for self-consciousness (or rationality, etc.), or it is such as will *inevitably* come to possess and exercise that capacity.

(2) Let it be granted that it is the possession and exercise of a capacity for self-consciousness (or rationality, etc.) that makes something a person. What account, then, is to be given of the wrongness of killing persons? The account cannot be based upon the claim that it is wrong to destroy persons. For though that is certainly the case, killing a normal adult human being does not involve this, if premiss (1) is true. The wrongness of killing, on this view, is rather a matter of cutting short a person's earthly existence, and transferring him, involuntarily, to another realm of existence.

(3) Let it also be granted, for the sake of argument, that human foetuses, and even human infants, are not persons. It will still be just as wrong to kill them as to kill humans that are persons, and it will be wrong for *precisely the same sort of reason.* For just as, given (1), killing a human person deprives someone of the opportunity of enjoying a more extended earthly existence, so, given (1), killing a human nonperson makes it the case that there *will be* a person later on who will have been deprived of the opportunity of enjoying any earthly existence at all.

This is an interesting argument, for a number of reasons. In the first place, though the argument has a definite religious flavour, with its appeal to the view that humans have immortal souls, it does not involve any ethical principles that non-religious people would be likely to reject. For the only ethical assumption is that an action is prima facie wrong if it results in someone's being deprived of something they would otherwise have, the wrongness of the action depending upon the seriousness of the deprivation.

Second, the argument may illuminate the appeal to potentialities. In considering the appeal to potentialities in chapter 6, the view examined, and argued against, was that the destruction of potential persons is intrinsically wrong, where a potential person is something that will give rise to a person, if not interfered with. The present argument suggests quite a different way of viewing the appeal to potentialities, and one that involves a different notion of a potential person. A potential person, on this view, is not something that will become a person *if not interfered with*; it is something that will become a person willy-nilly. And the reason, therefore, that it is wrong to destroy a human foetus is not that one is destroying a potential person, but that one is thereby depriving the person who will later come into being of the opportunity of enjoying life in this realm of existence.

This argument may also explain why some people are inclined to draw such a sharp distinction between passive and active potentialities, and hence why they view abortion as morally very different from intentionally refraining from conception. If an active potentiality is nothing more than something that will develop into a certain sort of thing if not interfered with, it is very puzzling why interference with an active potentiality should be thought of as morally different from non-actualization of a passive potentiality, in a case where only minimal assistance is needed to convert the passive potentiality into an active one. But if a potential person is something that will necessarily develop into a person, regardless of what is done, the distinction makes perfectly good sense. If one refrains from actualizing a passive potentiality, there will never be anyone who will be harmed as a result, whereas if one destroys something with an active potentiality, there will be.

Similarly, this argument may explain why some people accept the potentiality principle, but wish to reject any extension of it to *generalized* (active) potentialities. If a human embryo is only, or at most, something that will develop into a person if not interfered with, it is difficult to see how it can be wrong to destroy it for that reason, unless it is also wrong to disrupt a system of objects so interrelated that the system will, if not interfered with, give rise to a person. The distinction between active potentialities that reside in systems and those that inhere in individuals appears arbitrary and without moral significance. On the other hand, if a human embryo involves something that will necessarily give rise to a person, then the distinction between this potentiality, and the weaker sort associated with systems of objects, is clearly a morally significant one.

Finally, this argument suggests that it may not be possible to 'demythologize' certain arguments against abortion in the way that John Noonan Jr. and others are wont to suppose. For what is at the heart of the argument we are now considering is the notion of an unstoppable potentiality. And unless there is, in human organisms, some immaterial something that will survive the destruction of the body, there will not be any unstoppable potentiality in a human organism, and so one will not be able to say that abortion and infanticide are wrong because they bring it about that a given potentiality gets diverted, with the consequence that some future person is deprived of an opportunity he would otherwise enjoy. The proposition that man has an immortal soul, then, may very well be absolutely essential to certain traditional anti-abortion arguments, rather than, as Noonan and others tend to assume, mere theological trappings that can be discarded without loss.

Let us now turn to an evaluation of the argument. At first sight, the argument may appear to stand or fall with the crucial factual assumption that humans have immortal souls. For as I stressed in setting out the argument, it seems not to involve any distinctively religious, *ethical* claims. The basic principle to which it appeals is that it is prima facie wrong to act in ways that impair the interests of actual persons—either ones existing now or ones that will exist at some future time.

And this is a principle that would be accepted by most people, religious or not. So it would seem that if the argument is to be criticized, one must take issue with the claim that humans have immortal souls.

This conclusion is, however, mistaken. There is another factual assumption that is necessary if the argument is to go through, namely, that when human organisms are destroyed, via abortion or infanticide, the life that the immortal human souls will thenceforth come to enjoy is *inferior to what they would enjoy on this earth.* For if it is not inferior, their interests are not being impaired by being thus transferred to another realm of existence. They are not suffering any loss, even though they are by definition being deprived of the opportunity of life on *this* earth: it is simply a matter of offering one benefit rather than another.

Now it might be thought that this rejoinder is exposed to the objection that it also implies that there is nothing wrong with killing normal adult human beings. But it is clear that this does not follow. An adult human will have formed various attachments to people and places. As a result, even if he continues to exist, after death, in a realm no less attractive than this one, he still has grounds for complaint about having been murdered: he has been forcefully separated from family and friends, from places and things that are part of his life, from most of the projects he has been engaged in. Consequently, even if it is granted for the sake of discussion that humans have immortal souls, the argument involves a fallacious inference in moving to the conclusion that abortion and infanticide are morally comparable to the killing of humans who are persons.

Does the argument even provide any prima-facie reason against abortion and infanticide? It seems to me that it does not, unless the crucial auxiliary assumption, to the effect that the life to be enjoyed by the appropriate human souls is inferior to what they would enjoy here, can be defended. Within traditional Christianity, of course, this assumption was taken for granted. For, in the first place, to abort a foetus, or to kill an infant, was believed to deprive a person of the opportunity of working out his own eternal destiny. And second, as Lecky pointed out in the passage quoted earlier, it was the Christian view, for a long time, that foetuses and infants that died without baptism would, by virtue of Adam's sin, either 'be cast, as the Greeks taught, into a painless and joyless limbo, or, as the Latins taught, into the abyss of hell.'[3] From a traditional Christian perspective, then, abortion and infanticide might well impair a person's interests in two ways, by robbing him of the opportunity of achieving salvation and, with it, eternal happiness, and by plunging him immediately into a realm of existence that would be less satisfactory than what he probably would have enjoyed on this earth.

If, however, one sets aside this traditional Christian perspective, is there any reason to believe that the killing of a human being, before it has acquired those properties that make it a person, has the result that a particular immortal soul enjoys a less satisfactory life than it otherwise would have? I do not believe that there is. If life on earth were glorious for most people, and this seemed to be a rather lucky accident, there might be reason for believing that people who missed out on earth were likely to be less well off. But since life on earth is not really like that, there does not seem to be any reason—revelation aside—for supposing that, if humans have immortal souls, they will be worse off if they do not have a chance of living on this earth.

To sum up, we have seen that it is possible for abortion and infanticide to wrong actual persons without destroying them, and for this to be the case even if human foetuses and infants are only potential persons. But is there any reason for thinking that abortion and infanticide are in fact wrong in this way? In this section I have examined an argument in support of the claim that this is the case. The ethical principle on which the argument rests seems perfectly acceptable. On the other hand, the argument involves two theological, or quasi-theological assumptions of a factual sort: the one, that humans have immortal souls; the other, that a person is worse off starting life in the next world rather than in this one. I believe that the first claim is dubious, though I have not argued that here. I shall be considering it briefly in the next

---

[3] Lecky, *History of European Morals*, pp. 22-3.

section. The ground that has been offered here for rejecting the argument is that there is no reason at all to accept the second factual assumption.

11.4 Infanticide as Destroying Persons: Preliminary Considerations

11.41 Introductory Remarks

The most important objection to infanticide, in my opinion, claims that infanticide is intrinsically wrong, and seriously so, because it involves the destruction of a person. If this view is correct, there would seem to be a serious question with respect to at least late-term abortions. The reason is this. Birth is certainly a dramatic event. The human infant ceases being dependent upon the mother's life support system, and presumably begins to enjoy, for the first time, more complex visual experiences. But in the light of the earlier discussion of what it is that makes something a person, it does not seem plausible to view any of these changes, striking though they may be, as ones in which a human being acquires some person-making characteristic. If infanticide involves the destruction of a person, it seems very likely, then, that this will also be true of some late-term abortions.

Does infanticide involve the destruction of persons? The problem with this question, as it stands, is that the term 'infant' covers far too much ground. It is sometimes so construed, for example, that it applies to any child under the age of seven. But even if it is employed in a more restricted sense according to which it applies only to pre-toddlers, it is clear that human infants, so understood, vary radically with respect to mental life and psychological capabilities. These differences may turn out not to be morally significant, but it cannot be sound to predicate one's discussion on the assumption that they are not.

The question I propose to consider, then, is whether new-born human infants, or neonates, that have been carried to term, and that are neurophysiologically normal, are persons. The terms 'new-born' and 'neonate' are admittedly imprecise.

What I shall mean, in the present discussion, is an infant within a week or so of birth.[4]

How can one decide whether normal, full-term, new-born humans are persons? First, it is necessary to determine, as I attempted to do in chapter 5, what properties something must have in order to be a person. Then it would seem that, second, an empirical investigation is called for, to find out whether new-born humans do in fact possess the morally relevant properties. There is, however, an alternative approach that, if successful, shows that there is no need for a detailed empirical study of human development. This alternative approach to the problem involves an attempt to establish, by means of certain metaphysical considerations, that every human being, at every point in its development, is a person. This line of argument will be examined in the next section. I shall then go on, in section 11.5, to consider the detailed scientific evidence bearing upon the question of whether human infants are persons.

11.42 A Metaphysical Approach

The argument to be examined in this section involves an attempt to demonstrate that a rational soul is present in human beings from conception onward. At the heart of the argument are a number of philosophical claims that were advanced, and defended, by the well-known Roman Catholic philosopher, St. Thomas Aquinas. The conclusion of the argument, on the other hand, was explicitly rejected by Aquinas.

Given that Aquinas accepted the crucial philosophical assumptions, why did he reject the conclusion? The explanation that is usually offered by those present-day Thomists who accept the argument is that Aquinas was labouring under some biological misinformation, to the effect that the

---

[4] This usage is slightly more restrictive than what is common. *The Penguin Medical Dictionary*, edited by Peter Wingate, 1972, gives: 'neonatal. Of new-born babies, conventionally limited to the first four weeks of life.' *Black's Medical Dictionary*, 31st edition, edited by W. A. R. Thomson, 1976, states: 'Neonatal mortality is the mortality of infants under one month of age.' For broader construals, see *The Compact Edition of the Oxford English Dictionary*, Volume I, 1971, p. 1426.

development taking place from conception onward is not a continuous one. It is then contended that if he had had the biological knowledge that we now possess, he would have accepted the conclusion in question. Thus Germain Grisez, for example, says that '. . . others have argued plausibly on Aquinas' philosophical principles that if he had known what we know about human physiology, including what we know about the specific and individual definiteness of the zygote, he would not have held the Aristotelian theory of delayed animation.'[5]

This view of the matter is, however, by no means uncontroversial. It has been strongly disputed, for example, by the Roman Catholic philosopher, Joseph Donceel. In his well-known article, 'Immediate Animation and Delayed Hominization', Donceel argues, first, that Aquinas held that 'a substantial form can exist only in matter capable of receiving it';[6] second, that in the case of humans this means that 'the human soul can exist only in a highly organized body';[7] and, therefore, third, that a rational soul cannot be present in a human until the brain is 'fully developed'.[8]

Which view of the matter is correct? The issue is, I believe, a rather murky one, and I shall not pursue it here. My basic impression, however, is that the rejoinders to Donceel—from scholastic writers such as Grisez—are, in general, philosophically weak.

Let us now turn to the argument itself. I shall begin by offering an informal sketch that will bring out the basic steps. The argument starts out from the everyday observation that adult human beings, at least, possess the capacity for rational thought, and for acquiring knowledge. If one reflects, philosophically, upon this, one is led to ask what must be the case if adult humans are to have these capacities. In response, a philosophical argument is offered that is intended to show that no purely physical being could possibly have these

---

[5] Germain C. Grisez, *Abortion: The Myths, the Realities, and the Arguments*, Washington, 1969, p. 283. A similar view is expressed by Norman St. John-Stevas in his book, *The Right to Life*, New York, 1964, p. 32.

[6] Joseph F. Donceel, S. J., 'Immediate Animation and Delayed Hominization', *Theological Studies*, Volume 31, 1970, pp. 76-105. See p. 79.

[7] Ibid., p. 79.   [8] Ibid., p. 83.

capacities. Adult humans must possess, then, something immaterial—which we may refer to as a rational soul—in order for them to be capable of rational thought, and of acquiring knowledge.

The next stage of the argument involves further reflection upon the nature of human beings. Consider the ways in which humans differ from inanimate things. One way is with respect to the possession of rationality. But there are other ways that are also both obvious and striking. Humans are, for example, living things, and they possess consciousness. These differences between humans and inanimate things also stand in need of explanation. What account can be given? The explanation that is suggested by proponents of the present argument is that the rational soul that is present at least in adult human beings is responsible not only for rationality and cognition, but also for consciousness and for life processes. The ground that is offered in support of this view is that there is a certain unity evident in the interrelationships among biological processes, consciousness, and rationality. This unity is most naturally explained on the hypothesis that all of these aspects of human beings are dependent upon a single entity, rather than upon three different entities. The immaterial soul, which explains a human's capacity for rationality and cognition, must therefore also be the basis of human consciousness and of human biological processes.

The third stage in the argument involves considering human biological development. The central points here are that human development, from conception onward, both exhibits a certain sort of continuity, and is directed by the organism itself, rather than being controlled from without. These features indicate that throughout the process one has a living thing of the same sort, rather than a succession of different types of living things. It is then contended that philosophical reflection upon the nature of change forces one to postulate, in such a case, a single entity, or 'substantial form', that is present throughout, and that explains the continuity of the process of development, and its control from within.

This conclusion, together with the earlier conclusion that in the case of adult human beings it is the rational soul that is responsible for biological processes and consciousness as well as for rationality and cognition, implies that the entity that is responsible for the biological development of a human being from conception onward must be that entity which, in the case of adult humans, is the rational soul.

The final stage in the argument is concerned with the question of whether the entity that at a later time is the rational soul need always have involved the *capacity* for rationality and cognition. Perhaps only the corresponding *potentialities* were present initially. The force of this objection becomes clear if one considers present-day views concerning the relation between mind and body which claim that the capacity for rational thought, for example, depends upon the presence of certain complex structures in the brain. If such views were correct, one would be forced to conclude that the capacity for rationality is definitely not present in humans in early stages of development. It is at this point, then, that it becomes clear why the claim that the entity that explains the capacity for rationality is necessarily *immaterial* plays a crucial role in the argument. If it could be something physical, it might very well possess that capacity at later stages, while lacking it at earlier ones. In contrast, if the basis of rationality must be an immaterial soul, then it may be possible somehow to argue that the entity in question cannot possess the capacity for rational thought at one time without possessing it at all times—owing, perhaps, to some inherent limitations upon the sorts of changes that immaterial entities can undergo.

The grand conclusion, then, is that from the moment when one first has a living human being, one also has something possessing the capacities for consciousness, rationality, and cognition. Given appropriate claims about the properties that make something a person, it will then follow immediately that human beings are persons from conception onward.

Such is the basic argument. Expressed in a more precise and explicit form, it might be put as follows:

(1) Mature humans possess, at least derivatively, a capacity for knowledge and rational thought.
(2) Only something immaterial can be a non-derivative possessor of a capacity for knowledge and rational thought.

(3) An entity can possess a capacity only if it, or something involved in it, possesses that capacity non-derivatively.

(4) Therefore, there is present in mature human beings an immaterial something—which we may call a rational soul —that possesses, in a non-derivative way, a capacity for knowledge and rational thought.

(5) In mature human beings there is a single entity that is responsible for, and controls, not only intellectual activities, but also sense experience and life processes.

(6) It is a biological fact that there are structures present in a human organism, from the zygote stage onwards, that ensure that the organism's development will proceed in a continuous fashion, without radical breaks, and that the organism will develop into a being with characteristics that make it a being of a certain type.

(7) In view of (6), it is extremely reasonable to conclude that there is a single entity that is responsible for, and controls, the development of an individual human organism at every point throughout its existence.

(8) It follows from (5) and (7) that that thing which is responsible for, and controls, intellectual activity in the case of a mature human being is identical with that thing which is responsible for, and controls, the biological development of the human individual at every earlier point, from conception onwards.

(9) If an entity is immaterial at one time, it is immaterial at every other time at which it exists.

(10) It is impossible for there to be an immaterial entity, X, such that X exists at times t_1 and t_2, and possesses a capacity for knowledge and rational thought at time t_2, but not at the earlier time t_1.

(11) It follows from (8), (9), and (10) that there is, in every human organism that will attain maturity, an entity that is responsible for, and controls, the biological development of that organism from conception onwards, and that possesses, at every point throughout that process, a capacity for knowledge and rational thought.

(12) It is extremely improbable that human organisms that happen not to reach maturity differ from human organisms

that will reach maturity with respect to the property mentioned in (11).

(13) Therefore it is very likely that all human beings involve an entity that, at every point throughout the development of the human being, possesses a capacity for knowledge and rational thought.

(14) It is the possession of a capacity for knowledge and rational thought that makes something a person.

(15) Hence all human beings, from conception onwards, are persons.

How satisfactory is this argument? Is the reasoning acceptable? And are the premisses plausible? In formulating the argument, I have tried to make the reasoning relatively tight, even if not impeccable. On the other hand, I believe that there are serious problems with some of the premisses. Many are quite implausible, and some extremely so.

There does not seem to be any reason, for example, to accept the premiss introduced at step (1), viz., that all mature humans possess a capacity for knowledge and rational thought. For some mature humans have brain defects that appear to make them incapable of rational thought. This means that (1) needs to be replaced by something like:

(1*) Mature human beings that are neurologically normal possess, at least derivatively, a capacity for knowledge and rational thought.

This change, however, will carry through to the conclusion of the argument, which in turn will have to be revised to read:

(15*) All human beings that are neurologically normal are, from conception onwards, persons.

Another premiss that is far from plausible is that introduced at step (2), to the effect that only something immaterial can be a non-derivative possessor of a capacity for knowledge and rational thought. This is a very strong assumption indeed. For it is not merely being asserted that a materialist view of the mind is unsatisfactory. Nor is it being claimed merely that states of cognition and/or of rational thinking involve immaterial aspects. It is being claimed that the basic subject of the capacity for knowledge and rational thought is an immaterial *entity*. The reason this is crucial is that while many philosophers would insist that thought-episodes are events that involve, or perhaps consist entirely of, non-physical properties, most philosophers who take this view also hold that the existence of a brain with a certain structure is causally necessary if a human person is to enjoy any mental states at all, let alone do any reasoning. If this view is right, it would seem that the capacity for reasoning must either be viewed as a property of the brain itself—with thoughts and other mental states being viewed as emergent states of the brain—or as a property of a composite entity, consisting of the brain together with an immaterial mind, and not as a property of any non-physical entity alone.

What reason is there for holding that the capacity for cognition and rational thought is, at bottom, a property of an immaterial entity alone, rather than a property of the brain, or a property of the brain together with the mind? The following passage will provide a rough idea of the type of argument traditionally offered for this view:

The forms of sensible things have a more perfect mode of existence in the intellect than in sensible things, for in the intellect they are simpler and extend to more things; thus, through the one intelligible form of man, the intellect knows all men. Now, a form existing perfectly in matter makes a thing to be actually such—to be fire or to be colored, for example; and if the form does not have that effect, then the form is in that thing imperfectly, as the form of heat in the air carrying it, and the power of the first agent in its instrument. So, if the intellect were composed of matter and form, the forms of the things known would make the intellect to be actually of the same nature as that which is known. And the consequence of this is the error of Empedocles, who said that 'the soul knows fire by fire, and earth by earth'; and so with other things. But this is clearly incongruous. Therefore, the intelligent substance is not composed of matter and form.[9]

The underlying structure of this argument seems to be this:

(i) An individual cannot have knowledge of a certain sort

[9] St. Thomas Aquinas, *Summa Contra Gentiles*, book 2, chapter 50, paragraph 5. The quotation is from James F. Anderson's translation, 1955, p. 150.

of thing unless the appropriate universal is present in his mind.[10]

(ii) When a universal is present in anything material, that thing, or some part of it, necessarily has the property in question.

(iii) It is not true that whenever the mind has knowledge of things of type P, the mind, or some part of it, has property P.

(iv) Therefore the mind cannot be anything material.

A detailed account of the error involved in this argument would take us very far afield indeed. For while the fundamental mistake falls within epistemology, it has its ultimate source, I believe, within ontology—specifically, within the theory of universals. It will not be possible here to offer more than a summary account of Aquinas's error, and its source.

The fundamental error in the argument lies in the unsound model of knowledge that is invoked at step (i)—that is, in the view that knowledge of things of some type P involves the presence in the knowing mind of the appropriate universal, P. This model has been more or less entirely abandoned in present-day theory of knowledge. It is true, of course, that if what one knows is that one is presently in a mental state of type P, then the relevant universal, P, will be present in one's mind. It may even be the case that the universal is not merely present in one's mind, but present in the relevant cognitive state, since some philosophers hold that, for example, to be in pain, and to know that one is in pain, is not to be in two distinct states. Finally, it may be true, as advocates of the Representative Theory claim, that all knowledge of non-necessary truths ultimately rests upon knowledge of one's own present mental states. But even if all this were granted, the result would be nothing like the view that Aquinas is advancing. For the advocate of the Representative Theory wants to maintain that one can have knowledge of things other than one's own present mental states, and that when

---

[10] Compare book 2, chapter 49, paragraph 4 of the *Summa Contra Gentiles*, where Aquinas asserts: 'But the intellect understands things by those forms of theirs which it has in its possession.' Also, his *Summa Theologica*, part 1, question 75, article 5, where Aquinas says: 'Now a thing is known in so far as its form is in the knower.'

one does, it is not the case that the relevant properties are present in one's mind. What is present in the cognitive state is the corresponding *concept*. When John knows that there is something green in the next room, it is not the property (or universal) greenness that is present in his mind, but the concept of that property. And when Mary knows that John is in pain, or that he believes that there is something green in the next room, it cannot be the case that the corresponding properties are present in Mary's mind, for *these* properties are properties of minds, which means that if they were literally present in Mary's mind, she would be in pain, and she would believe that there was something green in the next room. What is present in her mind is the concept of being in pain, and the concept of believing that there is something green in the next room.

The root of Aquinas's mistaken epistemology is, I want to suggest, the fact that he was not a realist with regard to universals. This claim may strike some as mildly preposterous, since it is a truism in certain circles that Aquinas was a 'moderate realist'. But truisms have a habit of turning out false, and this seems to be a case in point. Thus Francis P. Clarke, in his article 'St. Thomas on "Universals"', begins by remarking:

In many handbooks of the history of philosophy one finds as a summary of the 'problem of universals' that the 'correct' answer is found in the three-fold statement:

Universals are *ante rem* in the mind of God;

Universals are *in re* in that the essence represented in the mind is in each particular;

Universals are *post rem* in the (human) intellect.

As far as St. Thomas is concerned, I shall show that the first two are not true, and that the third can be accepted only with qualifications.[11]

In a similar vein, the position that F. C. Copleston attributes to Aquinas is that '. . . universals as such exist in the mind and not extramentally . . .'[12] If these authors are right, Aquinas was not really a realist. What, then, was his position? This is not an easy question. David Armstrong in his recent

[11] Francis P. Clarke, 'St. Thomas on "Universals"', *Journal of Philosophy*, Volume 59, 1962, pp. 720-5. See p. 720.
[12] F. C. Copleston, *Aquinas*, 1955, p. 175.

two-volume work on universals has suggested that Aquinas's view *may* have been a combination of Particularism with Concept Nominalism, that is, of the view that the properties and relations of particulars are themselves (first-order) particulars, with the reductive doctrine that for particulars to have the same property, or to have the same relation, is for them to fall under the same concept.[13]

The important point here, however, is simply that once one gets over the confusion between universals and concepts, and recognizes that it is concepts, not universals, that are present in the mind in cognitive states, the ground is cut from under the argument set out above for the immateriality of the mind: premiss (i) is not acceptable.

This fundamental error in Aquinas's epistemology and metaphysics also infects a number of other arguments that he offers in support of the contention that the intellect cannot be material. One of his central arguments, for example, appeals to the claim that '. . . no body can receive the substantial form of another body, unless by corruption it lose its own form'.[14] Another proceeds: 'Therefore, it is only as individuated that a form is received into a body. If, then, the intellect were a body, the intelligible forms of things would not be received into it except as individuated. But the intellect understands things by those forms of theirs which it has in its possession. So, if it were a body, it would not be cognizant of universals but only of particulars. But this is patently false. Therefore, no intellect is a body.'[15] Both these arguments collapse once it is realized that it is concepts, not universals, that are present in the mind when it has knowledge.

Let us return now to the anti-abortion argument. Another premiss that deserves serious scrutiny is that introduced at step (5), to the effect that there is, in mature human beings, a single entity that controls, not only intellectual activities, but also life processes and sensory experiences. Whether this

[13] David M. Armstrong, *Nominalism and Realism—Universals and Scientific Realism*—Volume I, 1978, p. 87.

[14] *Summa Contra Gentiles*, book 2, chapter 49, paragraph 3. Compare the argument in his *Summa Theologica*, part 1, question 75, article 2.

[15] *Summa Contra Gentiles*, book 2, chapter 49, paragraph 4. Compare the argument in the *Summa Theologica*, part 1, question 75, article 5.

premiss is defensible depends upon how the expression 'single entity' is construed. Consider some non-human animal, such as a cat. Is there a single entity responsible for both its life processes and sensory experiences? In one sense, yes. For it is by virtue of its brain that the cat is alive and has sense experiences. But in another sense, the answer is no, since life processes and sensory experiences depend upon different parts of the brain, and it is possible for there to be brain damage that results in permanent unconsciousness, but not in the cessation of life processes.

The upshot is that if 'single entity' is construed narrowly, it seems simply false that there is a single entity in humans that controls intellectual activities, sensory experiences, and life processes. For whatever may be true of intellectual activities, it is surely true that perception and life processes depend upon different parts of the brain, and that there can be damage that destroys the basis of sensory experience while allowing life processes to be maintained.

Suppose, then, for the sake of the argument, that 'single entity' is generously construed, so that something with parts that are capable of independent existence and functioning counts as a single entity if its parts normally function in a way that involves mutual interaction. The problem with this defence of the premiss introduced at (5) is that it either makes the premiss introduced at step (9) unacceptable, or it makes the inference at step (11) invalid.

The reason is this. The premiss introduced at step (9) asserts that something that is immaterial at one time is immaterial at every other time at which it exists. When 'single entity' is construed broadly, a question arises as to precisely what this premiss asserts. For there would not seem to be anything impossible in the notion of something that is partly material, partly immaterial. The entity whose existence is supposed to have been established by step (8), then, might turn out to consist of the human brain together with an immaterial something with which it interacts. As a result, if the premiss introduced at (9) is intended to refer only to *completely* immaterial things, the inference from (8), (9), and (10) to the conclusion stated at (11) will be fallacious. On the other hand, if what is being asserted at (9) is that if something is at least partially immaterial at one time, it is at least partially immaterial at every other time at which it exists, there is no reason to accept it. For in the first place, there is nothing incoherent in the notion of an emergent property. A physical system, when it goes into a certain state, may causally give rise to properties quite distinct from those that existed previously. When a switch is thrown completing an electric circuit, a magnetic field is established. Why may it not be the case that, as a number of philosophers believe, the relation between the mind and the brain is similar? When the central nervous system has developed to a certain degree, it gives rise to consciousness and other mental states. If one holds that the new properties are non-physical ones, the case does differ from that of the magnetic field and the electric circuit, but there does not seem to be any reason why there cannot be non-physical emergent properties that are causally based upon purely physical properties. The premiss introduced at step (9), if interpreted so as to preclude this possibility, is therefore unacceptable.

The final premiss on which I wish to comment is that introduced at step (10), viz. the claim that it is not possible for an immaterial entity that lacks a capacity for knowledge and rational thought to come to have such a capacity. This premiss is essential to the argument. If it is rejected, all that follows from the other assumptions is that there is, in every human, an immaterial something that initially controls life processes, later makes possible sense experience, and later still makes possible cognition and rational thought. One would not be able to conclude that the capacity for rational thought is present in the immaterial entity from conception onwards. The most that one would be justified in ascribing to it initially would be an active potentiality that would result in its later having a capacity for rational thought.

Is there any reason for believing that the premiss introduced at step (10) is true? I cannot see that there is. Consider purely physical systems. The capacities of such systems can certainly change, and they can change, moreover, not as a result of action from without, but due to internal mechanisms. Thus there is no problem about programming a computer so that it can, by playing games of draughts against itself, and evaluating the outcomes, gradually modify its draughts-playing programme so that it acquires the capacity to beat human opponents that it couldn't initially. If physical systems can be so structured that they can alter their capacities in this way, why cannot the same be so for immaterial entities? And in particular, why could there not be an immaterial entity so structured that, although it does not have a capacity for rational thought, it will necessarily come to have that capacity? Immaterial entities can, after all, be in different states at different times, so why should there not be properties P and Q that satisfy the following three conditions:

(i) if an immaterial entity has property P at time t, it will not have the capacity for rational thought at time t;

(ii) any immaterial entity possessing property P at time t will, by virtue of laws of nature, come to have property Q at a later time t*;

(iii) any immaterial entity that has property Q at time t will also have a capacity for rational thought at time t.

These conditions do not appear to be mutually inconsistent. Hence, in the absence of a further argument, there does not seem to be any reason to accept the claim advanced at step (10).

An argument that might, I think, be appealed to at this point, runs as follows. The human soul is immaterial not merely in the ordinary sense of being incorporeal, or non-physical. It is immaterial in a technical sense, which can be roughly explained as follows. Some changes in the world, such as the death of a plant, are what are known as 'substantial changes', in that they involve a ceasing to be of one type of thing, or substance, that thereby brings about the existence of other types of things. Now the term 'matter', in Thomistic philosophy, is used to refer to what underlies, to what is the common subject of, such substantial change. To say that something is immaterial, in this technical sense, then, is to say that it cannot undergo substantial change. The human soul, therefore, cannot undergo any substantial change; it cannot change from one type of being to another. And what type of thing is the human soul? It is a rational soul. So whatever may be true of immaterial entities in general, it is certainly not possible for a human soul to be rational at one time and not at another, since that would entail that it had undergone substantial change.

This argument is not acceptable. In the first place, the arguments offered in support of the claim that humans have a soul that is immaterial in the technical sense are just the arguments we have already considered, and found wanting, in connection with the premiss introduced at step (2). But second, the argument would still be completely unsatisfactory even if it were granted, for the sake of argument, that the human soul is immaterial. The reason is that the argument needs the assumption that the human soul is a certain type of thing, namely, one whose essence involves the *capacity* for rationality. For if one adopted instead the more modest assumption that a human soul is a type of thing that involves at least the active *potentiality* for rationality, there would not be any substantial change involved if a human soul possessed the capacity for rationality at one time and not at another. To employ the argument just outlined in defence of step (10)—or some variant of (10) restricted to human souls—is therefore to beg one of the central questions at issue here.

The upshot is that the attempt to demonstrate, by means of a rationalistic, metaphysical argument, that all humans possess the capacity for cognition and rational thought, is intellectually unsound, and radically so. Given our present scientific knowledge it would, of course, be most surprising if it were otherwise. The differences in mental capacities, not merely between man and other animals, but between animals belonging to different species, are accompanied by differences in brain structure. It is also known that brain damage of various sorts is accompanied by different types of impairment of mental functioning. Similarly, as the human brain, along with the rest of the body, deteriorates through ageing, there is a decline in one's mental powers. These facts would be curious indeed if it were true that there is, in every human at every point in time, an immaterial substance with the capacity for rational thought. Why should man have a more highly developed brain if St. Thomas were right in maintaining that one does not understand by means of any part of the

body?[16] Or why should brain damage affect mental functioning, given that on the view in question, the capacity for
rational thought is still there, no more impaired after the
brain damage than before? It is sometimes suggested that the
soul is like a pianist with her hands tied: the capacity to play
is there, but the exercise of that capacity is temporarily
blocked. The analogy is fine. But it throws no light at all on
why damage to the brain should prevent an immaterial soul
not merely from *exhibiting*, but even from *exercising* the
capacity for rational thought—a capacity that belongs to it,
and which, it is held, the soul can exercise once it is severed,
by death, from its union with the body. In contrast, all of
these facts concerning the relations between the structure
and states of the brain, and mental functioning, fall neatly
into place once it is recognized that the brain is, at the very
least, causally essential for all mental functioning, including
rational thought.

11.5 Infanticide as Destroying Persons: The Scientific Evidence

11.51 Introductory Remarks

Let us turn, then, to an empirical approach to the question of
the point at which a human becomes a person. Assume, for
the moment, that we do have a satisfactory answer to the
ethical question of the properties that make something a
person. The issue then is how we can determine whether a
human at a certain stage of development possesses the
morally relevant property or properties.

There is, as we saw in section 5.3, considerable disagreement about what it is that makes something a person. All of
the answers that survive even mild scrutiny, however, agree at
least on this: the relevant feature is *psychological* in nature.
Something is a person by virtue of the sort of mental life that
it enjoys, or has enjoyed, or is capable of enjoying. So the
problem is one of arriving at justified conclusions about the
mental states and/or capabilities of others.

---

[16] See, for example, his *Summa Theologica*, question 75, article 2.

There are three types of considerations that are relevant to judgements about the mental states of others: (i) their linguistic behaviour; (ii) their non-linguistic behaviour; (iii) their neurophysiological states. In the case of normal adults, we rely very heavily upon linguistic behaviour in arriving at beliefs about mental states and capacities. In the case of foetuses and infants, our conclusions about the individual's mental life and psychological capacities must rest upon observations of non-linguistic behaviour together with information about the development of the central nervous system and the states that it is in at different times.

What sorts of reasoning are involved in moving from such considerations to conclusions about the psychological states and capabilities of an organism? Given information about the individual's behaviour, the reasoning would seem to be a matter of what has been called an inference to the best explanation. That is to say, one postulates mental states and capacities of those types that seem necessary in order to explain the behaviour exhibited by the organism. Given neurophysiological information, on the other hand, the reasoning must involve an appeal to established correlations between brain states and mental states. One can, for example, study adult human beings, where linguistic behaviour is available, and attempt to determine for any given type of mental state, M, whether there is some type of brain state, B —which may be very complex—such that a human individual is in a mental state of type M when, and only when, the individual's brain is in a state of type B. Such correlations can then be applied to humans before they are capable of using language, and if one has reason to believe that a given individual's brain is in a state of type B, it would seem reasonable to conclude that the individual is enjoying a mental state of type M.

There would not seem to be any difficulty in principle, then, in arriving at justified beliefs about the mental lives and psychological capabilities of human embryos, foetuses, and neonates. In practice, of course, the conclusion may be less firmly based than one would like, because, for example, of an absence of well-established and detailed correlations of brain states with crucial mental states. As a result, there will be, given our present knowledge, a range of development such that it will be genuinely unclear what sort of mental life a human organism falling within that range enjoys, or is capable of enjoying. But there should also be a range of less fully developed human organisms, within which one can draw conclusions about probable mental life and capabilities that are sufficiently well grounded for the purposes at hand—that is, for deciding whether a human at a certain stage of development is a person, and hence such as it would be seriously wrong to destroy.

But how useful will such information be, if one does not know what it is that makes something a person? That depends upon the extent of our ignorance. It could be very helpful even if there is no 'simple' characteristic, P, such that one is now justified in believing that it is P that makes something a person. For it might be possible to find a list of properties that one is justified in believing possesses either or both of the following characteristics: (i) Nothing can be a person unless it has at least one of the properties on the list; (ii) Anything that has all of the properties is a person. Most people, I suggest, would agree that anything that has, and has exercised, all of the following capacities is a person, and that anything that has never had any of them is not a person: the capacity for self-consciousness; the capacity to think; the capacity for rational thought; the capacity to arrive at decisions by deliberation; the capacity to envisage a future for oneself; the capacity to remember a past involving oneself; the capacity for being a subject of non-momentary interests; the capacity to use language. Given such a list, the information provided by a scientific study of human development will enable one to conclude that humans up to a certain point in their development are not persons, since they possess none of the properties on the list, and that humans beyond some other stage are definitely persons, since they possess all of the properties on the list. And such conclusions, though they would leave unresolved the question of the status of humans between those two points, might very well enable one to deal with those moral issues that are most pressing from a practical point of view.

11.52 The Views of Kluge and Blumenfeld

Let us now turn to the basic issue. Given what is known about human development, is it reasonable to think that a neonate is a person? Philosophers have devoted remarkably little attention to this question—partly because the question of the morality of infanticide has been only infrequently discussed, and partly because, when it has, the dominant tendency has been to suppose that infanticide can be ruled out by an appeal to one's intuitions. Some philosophers, however, have maintained that, given plausible moral principles, the relevant empirical evidence does support the view that neonates are persons. Perhaps the place to begin, then, is by examining some attempts to defend this claim.

Of the attempts with which I am familiar, the most vigorous is that of Eike-Henner Kluge in chapters 1 and 4 of his book, *The Practice of Death*.[17] He has also advanced essentially the same position in his more recent article, 'Infanticide as the Murder of Persons'.[18] The later discussion, however, is very unsatisfactory in a number of ways. Crucial claims that are argued for in the book are often simply asserted in the article. Objections that have been advanced against his earlier discussions are simply ignored, and there are serious distortions of the positions of other philosophers.[19] His earlier discussion, therefore, will be the main focus of attention.

Kluge holds that human organisms, probably by about the fourth month, and certainly by the sixth month, are

[17] Eike-Henner W. Kluge, *The Practice of Death*, 1975.

[18] In Marvin Kohl's *Infanticide and the Value of Life*, 1978, pp. 32–45.

[19] As regards the first point, my own critical notice of Kluge's book, published in the *Canadian Journal of Philosophy*, Volume 6, Number 2, June 1976, pp. 339–57, contains quite detailed criticisms of Kluge's claims and argumentation. Kluge neither mentions the article, nor attempts to answer the objections raised.

As regards the second point, Kluge attributes to me two views that I have never held. First, the view that neonates do not have a right to life because they lack 'full social interaction and role', and second, the view that 'the right to freedom from intolerable pain or subnormal human experience takes precedence over the right to life'. (For the former, see pages 36 and footnote 16, and for the latter, page 39 and footnote 23. Kluge cites an article of mine in these footnotes, but offers no page references, even though he does so in other footnotes.)

persons,[20] and *a fortiori*, that human infants are certainly persons. This contention rests upon a moral claim and a factual claim. The former concerns what it is that makes something a person: 'An entity is a person if and only if *either* it now is perceptually aware, reasons and makes judgments, and is self-aware, *or* it is in a state of constitutive potential with respect to these.'[21] Where, for Kluge, an entity is in a state of constitutive potential with respect to some activity if it could come to engage in that activity without undergoing any 'constitutive structural change' in its make-up.[22] The basic suggestion, then, is that something is a person if, and only if, it either presently enjoys a certain sort of mental life, or has the *capacity*—as contrasted with the mere potentiality, be it active or passive—to do so.

This moral claim was examined above in section 5.4. There I argued that the possession of certain capacities is neither a necessary nor a sufficient condition for being a person, so that Kluge's account of what it is that makes something a person must be rejected.

The factual claim on which Kluge's position rests is that humans, probably from about the fourth month, and certainly from the sixth month, possess the 'constitutive potential', or capacity, for perceptual awareness, reasoning and judgement, and self-awareness. Why does Kluge hold that this is so? He offers two types of evidence in support of this claim: first, that provided by electroencephalograms; second, direct anatomical evidence of brain development. With regard to the former, Kluge says:

The nervous system in general and the brain in particular evince electrical activity of varying degrees of intensity, frequency, and complexity. This can be recorded by means of electroencephalographs. The electro-encephalograms (EEGs for short) that result have a characteristic nature which—whether the human being is asleep or awake—can serve to distinguish his nervous activity from that, say, of a cat, a frog, or even a monkey. EEGs, then, reflect a difference in neurological activity of man vis-a-vis other animals.[23]

[20] *The Practice of Death*, p. 98, and 'Infanticide as the Murder of Persons', p. 36.

[21] 'Infanticide as the Murder of Persons', p. 35. Cp. *The Practice of Death*, p. 36.

[22] 'Infanticide as the Murder of Persons', p. 34. Cp. *The Practice of Death*, p. 17.

[23] *The Practice of Death*, p. 93. Cp. 'Infanticide as the Murder of Persons', p. 35.

And as regards brain development, Kluge says: 'Furthermore —on a slightly different tangent—the brain of a human being has certain structures, particularly in those parts of it that are termed the nonlimbic cortex, which are characteristic of the human brain. They are thought to be the physiological basis for symbolic processes and self-awareness.'[24]

How do human foetuses and neonates fare when judged by these standards? What are the EEGs of foetuses and new-borns like? How developed are their brains in those respects thought to underlie rational awareness? In his more recent discussion, Kluge asserts that: '. . . generally speaking, by the end of the fourth month of the gestation period, certainly by the sixth, the constitutive potential for personhood is present. Differently, at that point the brain of the fetus is structurally and functionally sufficiently developed so as to leave no doubt that the above criteria for personhood in the consti-tutive sense, are met.'[25]

However, Kluge does not, in this article, offer any evidence to support this confident claim. At no point in his article does he describe, for example, either the EEGs of foetuses or infants, or the state of development of the relevant parts of the brain. The reader who is interested in the relevant evidence must turn to the chapter on infanticide in *The Practice of Death*, where Kluge does grapple with the scientific facts. But there we find, for example, when he is considering an argument in support of infanticide, that he accepts the following contentions:

(1) '. . . when we examine the EEGs of babies and children, it emerges that they do not evince the amount of electrical activity typical of adult and fully conscious human beings. Nor are the electrical currents of the same wave lengths'[26]

(2) The EEGs of newborn babies 'resemble closely those of a frog.'[27]

(3) The EEGs of small children are not even as complex as those of the great apes.[28]

These facts about EEGs certainly do not support Kluge's

[24] *The Practice of Death*, p. 93.
[25] 'Infanticide as the Murder of Persons', p. 36.
[26] *The Practice of Death*, p. 195.   [27] Ibid., p. 195.
[28] Ibid., p. 195.

contention that newborn infants possess the capacity for rational awareness. On the contrary, they tend to count against it. I say 'tend to', since it is unclear precisely what EEGs are a measure of, and hence difficult to know how much weight should be placed upon such evidence.

What about the much more crucial evidence provided by direct anatomical observations of the brain at different stages of development? Does it support Kluge's thesis? Kluge is prepared to admit that the central nervous systems of foetuses and infants are immature:

Completion of the central nervous system—myelination of the nervous fibers, attainment of the complexity of adult brain waves, and completion of intersystemic connections—is not fully accomplished until approximately five years of age; behavioral characteristics are not fully present and operative until age fourteen. At the fetal stage, certainly, fissure development in the cortex is not at all pronounced.[29]

If so, how can it be claimed that foetuses beyond about four months have the capacity for rational awareness? Kluge's answer is this:

The argument as stated assumes, although it does not say so explicitly, that in order for there to be what we have previously defined as a properly human, personlike potential of rational awareness, the neurological base of that awareness (or its analogue) must be systemically complete and fully developed in all its aspects. That assumption is mistaken. It misses completely the crucial point of the concept of structural completeness which was central to our definition of personhood. It is not that the structure as a whole must be complete, down to the last nerve path and down to the last intercellular connection. What is important is that the structural makeup in its essential human blocks is there, that certain developments in the limbic and nonlimbic cortex are structurally present. It is structural completeness in this sense, not neurological completeness as to mass and axons, that is important. These structures, however, as we have stated before, are present very early on, in the fourth month or so of the gestation period. They may not be interconnected. But that is not essentially a matter of adding new cells and cellular structures. It is a matter of interconnecting, by means of the processes of cells already there, the structures that already exist.[30]

Certainly, the complete development of the brain is not needed for one to be capable of self-consciousness and the

[29] Ibid., p. 196.   [30] Ibid., p. 197.

symbolic processes involved in rational thought and language. But Kluge has evaded the crucial issue: Has the brain of a foetus beyond about the fourth month developed to the point where it presently possesses the capacities for self-consciousness, rational thought, and the use of language? Kluge has been content merely to maintain that the brain of such a foetus is structurally complete, in the sense that all the important parts are there. He happily admits that these parts may not be interconnected. Apparently he thinks that the absence of such interconnections is of no interest. But why isn't it absolutely crucial? A radio with all its parts, but not wired together, does not have the capacity to receive radio waves. If one is interested in *capacities*—as Kluge is—rather than in mere potentialities, then the appropriate notion of structural completeness is not merely that of all the parts being there, but of the parts being connected up in those ways necessary to endow the thing with the relevant capacities.

To sum up, what has gone wrong with Kluge's argument is this. He begins by distinguishing between capacities and mere potentialities, and by arguing that only the former are of moral interest in the present context. He then introduces the notion of constitutional or structural completeness. The reason for introducing this notion is that to the extent that the capacities of a thing are determined by the nature of its parts and their interrelations, it is natural to say that when the structure of a thing is complete it will possess all the capacities things of that sort normally possess. Finally, in the passage just considered, Kluge argues that the brain of a human is structurally complete from about the fourth month of foetal development onward. But in doing this he has shifted to a different sense of structural completeness, namely, one in which it is not necessary for the parts to be connected up in the appropriate ways. Given this sense of structural completeness, there is no reason at all to say that once an object is structurally complete it will possess all the capacities that objects of its kind normally possess. On the contrary, the reasonable supposition is that it will lack most of the capacities it will have once its parts are appropriately interconnected. Kluge's argument in support of the contention that infants and older foetuses are capable of rational awareness is thus fallacious.

Another writer who holds that infanticide is morally wrong, and who approaches the issue in a rather similar way, is Jean Beer Blumenfeld.[31] However her approach diverges from Kluge's in at least two important respects. First, she believes that the point at which a human organism becomes a person is considerably later than the fourth month or so favoured by Kluge, on the ground that 'it is not until "the final fetal months" that the brain attains its characteristically human structure'.[32] In support of the latter contention, Blumenfeld offers a variety of evidence. First, there is the anatomical evidence:

The earliest fissures appear during the fourth month, yet throughout the first half of fetal life the exposed surface of the brain remains quite smooth. In the later months, however, other fissures arise and complete the series. Developing at the same time as this last group are the numerous but shallower sulci. The secondary and tertiary sulci, peculiar to the human brain, are developments of the final fetal months. Previous to their appearance the brain resembles that of an adult monkey.[33]

Second, there is the evidence provided by the study of tissue development in the central nervous system:

The present observations taken together with previous studies indicate that *dendritic spine* development in the human cerebral cortex does not represent a continuous process traceable to early fetal phases of dendritic differentiation. Rather, cortical neuronal spine development occurs in a relatively brief time frame (28 to 32 weeks g.a.) in which the cerebral cortex acquires synaptic organizations that are not evident in the previable fetus of 25 weeks. The development of this new synaptic substrate can be expected to have dramatic effects upon intracortical and cortical input–output neuronal operations. Indeed it is not unreasonable to suspect that the development of axospinodendritic synapses in cerebral cortex between 28 to 33 weeks g.a. is of central importance in the emergence of state-related behaviors in the preterm infant.

---

[31] Jean Beer Blumenfeld, 'Abortion and the Human Brain', *Philosophical Studies*, Volume 32, 1977, pp. 251–68.

[32] Ibid., p. 265.

[33] Leslie Brainerd Arey, *Developmental Anatomy*, 7th edition, 1974, p. 496. Quoted by Blumenfeld, op. cit., p. 265.

Cajal, who originally discovered dendritic spines and immediately recognized their importance, must be allowed the last word on the subject: 'The spines . . . are the last morphological details to appear in the nerve cell. . . . Their appearance indicates functional maturity of the neuron.'[34]

This brings me to the second main point of divergence between Blumenfeld's argument and Kluge's. It might be expected that, having argued that a human foetus, by about the eighth month, possesses a brain with a characteristically human structure, Blumenfeld would go on to claim that such an organism therefore possesses some morally relevant psychological property, such as a capacity for rational thought. If she did argue in this way she would, of course, be open to the objection lodged against Kluge, namely, that the possession of a brain with a characteristically human structure is not sufficient to endow something with a capacity for rational thought: certain very complex interconnections are also essential. However Blumenfeld is apparently aware of this point, since she concedes, quite explicitly, that human infants do not possess the ability to think.[35] None the less, she is not prepared to accept infanticide—apparently because she believes that it can be shown to be impermissible by appeal to 'moral intuitions'.[36] The upshot is that she is driven to maintaining that no satisfactory criterion of what it is that makes something a person can be formulated solely in terms of psychological characteristics.[37] How, then, is an adequate criterion to be stated? Blumenfeld is not completely explicit on this matter, but her view appears to be that any satisfactory criterion will also have to refer to an individual's species, and to the brain structure that is characteristic of members of that species. On this view, an individual will be a person, regardless of the mental life or psychological capacities that it either has enjoyed or is now enjoying, provided that it has a brain that has developed to the point where it possesses a structure that is 'characteristic' of a

---

[34] Dominick P. Purpura, 'Morphogenesis of Visual Cortex in the Preterm Infant', in *Growth and Development of the Brain*, edited by M. A. B. Brazier, (1975), pp. 46–7. Quoted by Blumenfeld, op. cit., pages 265–6.
[35] Op. cit., p. 262.   [36] Ibid., p. 266.   [37] Ibid., p. 262.

species whose members typically possess the capacity for rational thought.

While Blumenfeld's rejection of infanticide rests, therefore, upon facts about the development of humans, it does not involve any claims about the mental life or psychological capacities of human infants. The crux of her argument is a certain moral principle—according to which whether or not a given individual is a person may depend upon the species to which that individual belongs. If a principle of the sort that Blumenfeld proposes were sound, infanticide would be wrong. But I have argued, in section 4.2, that such a principle is not acceptable.

The approaches of Kluge and Blumenfeld appeal to empirical facts. But there is a very significant feature that their approaches share with the metaphysical approach considered earlier, namely, a refusal to treat as relevant judgements about the mental life and capabilities of a human at various stages of development, based upon information about the times at which humans acquire different behavioural capacities. I believe that any approach that treats such information as irrelevant is unsound. I also believe that it is no accident that the approaches we have considered share this short-coming, since, as we shall see, it is very difficult to support the claim that new-born humans are persons by appealing to facts about their psychological development.

11.53 The Scientific Evidence: Human Psychological Development

In this section and the next I shall survey the relevant scientific knowledge concerning the development of human beings. The present section deals with human psychological development as evidenced by changes in behavioural capacities. The next section is concerned with the underlying neurophysiological development.

My account of the scientific evidence will be reasonably detailed. There are at least two reasons for this. In the first place, if the general approach to the question of the morality of abortion that I have defended above is at least along the right lines, then a decision as to when abortion is morally justified depends upon answers to two very different sorts of questions. The first is a philosophical question: What non-potential property (or properties) makes it intrinsically wrong to destroy something, and does so independently of whether the entity possesses intrinsic value? The second is an empirical question: At what point in its development does a human acquire the property (or properties) in question? Philosophers, not unnaturally, have been somewhat reluctant to grapple with the second question—falling as it does within science rather than within philosophy itself. But if I am right, the question of the morality of abortion can never be satisfactorily resolved until one comes to terms with the second question. Any serious philosopher working in this area needs, then, to have a sound and thorough understanding of the relevant scientific information.

The second reason why a detailed account is needed is this. As we consider carefully the scientific evidence it will become very clear, I think, that if one accepts any of the more plausible views of what it is that makes something a person, and if one thinks that there is nothing intrinsically wrong with destroying potential persons, one is led, very naturally, to a somewhat radical view on the morality of abortion and infanticide. Suppose, however, that one were offered only a summary of the relevant scientific evidence—but one which pointed toward the same, rather radical view of the matter. It seems clear that many readers would, as a result, have serious doubts about the accuracy of the summary offered. If the relevant information were readily accessible, this would not be such a serious matter. Those with doubts would, it might be hoped, simply examine detailed accounts of the relevant evidence available elsewhere. It turns out, however, that the material in question is really quite inaccessible, especially for those without any background in the scientific areas in question. It is crucial, therefore, that an account be offered which is sufficiently detailed to enable readers to decide, without an enormous expenditure of time and energy, whether the conclusions that I shall be advancing are reasonable in the light of the relevant scientific data concerning human development.

Let us begin by considering, then, the psychological

development of human infants. In doing this, we need to keep firmly in mind those characteristics whose acquisition may be morally significant. There are, as we have seen, different views as to precisely what properties make something a person. In section 5.3 I defended the view that it is being a subject of non-momentary interests that makes something a person. If this is right, there are a number of conditions whose satisfaction is necessary if something is to be a person: (1) the entity must be capable of having desires, where desires are construed as states that can be represented in consciousness, rather than merely as states that causally underlie behaviour in a certain way; (2) the entity must be capable of having thoughts about times other than the present; (3) it must possess, and have exercised in relevant ways, the concept of a self as a continuing subject of mental states. It would seem misguided, however, to predicate the present discussion upon the assumption that this view of the matter must be correct. In the absence of widespread agreement about what exactly it is that makes something a person, the reasonable approach is surely to keep in mind all the accounts that are at least minimally plausible. This means that in addition to the characteristics already mentioned, we should also be interested in when humans become capable of rational thinking and problem-solving behaviour of various types, and when they become agents in a sense that involves deliberation.

Let us turn, then, to what is presently known about the psychological development of humans. Perhaps the first point that needs to be made is that beliefs about this have undergone some substantial revision in recent years. Well into the 1960s, for example, it was fairly widely held that while new-born babies had a sense of pain, and responded to touch and pressure, their capacities for visual and auditory discrimination were very limited indeed. Gross variations in visual or auditory stimulation could evoke a response, but it was thought that new-born babies were incapable of form or pattern discrimination. Similarly, it was quite widely believed that the behaviour of new-borns was totally a matter of reflexes, unmediated by processes in the cerebral cortex. Recent experimental work has shown, however, that these beliefs are incorrect, and has led to a rather different view of the human infant, from birth onward, as 'an active, perceiving, learning, and information-organizing individual'.[38]

These characteristics do not, of course, provide any reason for viewing neonates as persons, unless one is prepared to defend an account of person-making characteristics that diverges radically from those canvassed in section 5.3. What would be required would be an account from which it followed that virtually all animals are persons, since all vertebrates, and most invertebrates, are certainly active, perceiving, learning, and information-organizing individuals.

Of what sort of learning is a new-born human capable? The type of learning normally regarded as simplest is *habituation*. A rough characterization of habituation is that an animal exhibits habituation if, when repeatedly exposed to a given sort of stimulus, its natural response to the stimulus gradually diminishes. But it is important, especially in the present context, to distinguish between the non-cognitive phenomenon of fatigue or sensory adaptation, on the one hand, and the cognitive phenomenon of habituation on the other. Where it is habituation, rather than sensory fatigue, that is occurring, one would expect that decrement in response will increase with exposures to the stimulus that are separated by a substantial interval, and will last over relatively lengthy periods of time without further stimulation.[39]

At what point do humans exhibit habituation? This question is considerably more difficult to answer than one might expect. On the one hand, there are studies that some believe show the existence of habituation in new-born babies. On the other, there are studies indicating that habituation is not even found in three-month-old infants, let alone in neonates.[40] There are, however, noteworthy differences in design among these experiments that may point toward an interpretation that enables one to make sense of these apparently

---

[38] L. Joseph Stone, Henrietta T. Smith, and Lois B. Murphy (eds.), *The Competent Infant*, 1973, p. 4. This collection of over 200 articles together with extensive editorial commentary and accompanying bibliographies provides very useful information about many aspects of early human development.

[39] V. G. Dethier and Eliot Stellar, *Animal Behavior*, 3rd edition, 1970, p. 110.

[40] For references to some of the more important studies, see Stone, Smith, and Murphy, op. cit., pp. 248 and 455.

conflicting results. In the first place, most of the neonatal work involves auditory or olfactory stimulation; the studies of three-month-old infants involve visual stimulation. Second, the neonatal studies generally involved sleeping infants, whereas in the studies of three-month-old infants, the babies were awake and alert. There is, however, a study by Friedman, Carpenter, and Nagy, involving visual stimulation of new-born infants, that demonstrates that response decrement is present.[41] Again, however, there are significant differences between the design of this study and, for example, the study by Lewis, Goldberg, and Campbell in which no response decrement was found even in three-month-old infants.[42] The former study involved the presentation of a constant stimulus for a number of sixty-second intervals; the latter involved repeated, brief presentations of a stimulus.

The fact that no response decrement is found in three-month-old infants when repeated, brief presentations are used, rather than longer presentations, suggests that what some of the neonatal studies may be detecting is sensory adaptation rather than habituation. Friedman, Carpenter, and Nagy attempted to determine, however, whether the decrement was attributable to sensory fatigue or to habituation, by seeing whether the response increased when a novel visual stimulus was presented after the response had declined. They found an increased response in approximately three-quarters of the cases. As a result, they were led to the tentative conclusion that 'the response recovery in visual fixation as indicated by the data reported here suggests that some central habituatory process may be involved'; they also indicate that they are undertaking 'further investigation of the nature of the apparent recovery phenomenon'.[43]

A very interesting discussion of the discrepancies between studies of neonates and three-month-old infants is found in

[41] Steven Friedman, Genevieve C. Carpenter, and Alice N. Nagy, 'Decrement and Recovery of Response to Visual Stimuli in the Newborn Human', in Stone, Smith, and Murphy, op. cit., pp. 361-5.

[42] M. Lewis, S. Goldberg, and H. Campbell, 'A Developmental Study of Information Processing within the First Three Years of Life: Response Decrement to a Redundant Signal', in *Monographs of the Society for Research in Child Development*, 1969, Volume 34, (9, Serial No. 133).

[43] Op. cit., p. 364.

an article by Michael Lewis.[44] He mentions a number of factors that may be relevant. One possible explanation of the discrepancies, for example, suggested by some Russian studies, is that 'the attending response in the newborn is sub-cortical and becomes cortical as the infant ages'.[45] Lewis feels, however, that more investigation is needed before a completely satisfactory account will be forthcoming.

Even in the absence of an explanation of the discrepancies, however, the mere fact that response decrement is not found, even in three-month-old infants, when repeated, brief presenta-tions of a stimulus are employed, may very well have impor-tant implications, given certain views of what it is that makes something a person. For it seems very plausible that suscepti-bility to habituation in response to brief presentations of a stimulus will be present only in individuals possessing at least some rudimentary capacity for storing and retrieving 'informa-tion'—though they need not, of course, possess memory in the full sense that involves a capacity for thought episodes that encapsulate stored information: 'Where repeated, rather than continuous, presentation is used it clearly implies memory. The course of development of habituation during the first year is an index of the ability to recognize, to discriminate, to process information; in short, boredom becomes a measure of cognition, of recognition of the "old-hat" stimulus.'[46]

If this is right, and one does not have anything that can be labelled 'memory', even in a very attenuated sense, until the individual exhibits habituation in response to repeated, brief presentations of a stimulus, then on any account of what it is that makes something a person that assigns a crucial role to the possession of the capacity to remember, there will be a very strong reason for thinking that three-month-old humans are not persons.

A number of other experimental results also point to the conclusion that there is very little that can be labelled 'memory' before the age of about three months. Jerome

---

[44] Michael Lewis, 'Individual Differences in the Measurement of Early Cog-nitive Growth', in *Exceptional Infant: Studies in Abnormalities*, edited by Jerome Hellmuth, 1971, pp. 172–210.

[45] Ibid., p. 195.   [46] Stone, Smith, and Murphy, op. cit., p. 457.

Kagan, for example, in his article, 'The Determinants of Attention in the Infant', points out that while four-month-old infants spend more time attending to a three-dimensional model of a human head than to an abstract three-dimensional form, two-month-old infants look equally long at either.[47] Kagan's explanation of this difference involves the notion of a schema: 'A schema is defined as an abstraction of a sensory event that preserves the spatial or temporal pattern of the distinctive elements of the event. A schema is to be regarded as a functional property of mind that permits an organism to recognize and retrieve information.'[48] Kagan advances what he calls the 'discrepancy hypothesis', which states that duration of sustained attention is a function of the degree of discrepancy between an object and a related schema, and he cites a number of findings that confirm this hypothesis. If the hypothesis is sound, it suggests that the difference between two-month-old infants and four-month-old infants, mentioned above, is to be explained in terms of the latter having acquired, and the former not, a schema of the human face.[49]

Let us now turn to another very simple type of learning: classical, or Pavlovian, conditioning. A dog responds by salivating when it smells meat. It does not salivate when a bell is rung. But if the bell is rung a number of times when the dog is presented with the smell of meat, the dog will in time come to salivate when the bell is rung unaccompanied by any presentation of meat. And in general, an organism is susceptible of classical conditioning if the presenting together of two types of stimuli, S and T—the former of which evokes a response of type R, while the latter does not—has the effect, if done sufficiently often, of bringing it about that a stimulus of type T also evokes a response of type R.

Before the 1960s there was considerable scepticism concerning the susceptibility of new-born humans to classical conditioning. Studies that had been done had generally led to quite equivocal results. Subsequent work has provided better support for the claim that classical conditioning is

---

[47] Jerome Kagan, 'The Determinants of Attention in the Infant', in Stone, Smith, and Murphy, op. cit., pp. 675–83. See pp. 677–8.

[48] Ibid., pp. 675–6. [49] Ibid., p. 677–8.

possible,[50] although the issue is by no means settled. Sostek, Sameroff, and Sostek have criticized the procedures employed in the more recent studies, and Sameroff's view is that classical conditioning of new-born humans is not possible.[51]

Another relatively simple type of learning is what is known as operant, or instrumental, conditioning. A hungry cat presses a bar, and is rewarded by the appearance of food. The more that this occurs, the more likely it is that the cat will respond to hunger by pressing a bar of the sort in question. And in general, an individual is susceptible to operant conditioning if the rewarding of a response of type R that it makes in the presence of a stimulus of type S has the result that, in the future, it is more likely to exhibit behaviour of type R in the presence of a stimulus of type S.

Operant conditioning of neonates was considered dubious by many well into the 1960s. More recent work, however, seems to have removed all grounds for doubt, and to have established quite firmly that newborn humans are susceptible to operant conditioning.[52]

The fact that new-born humans are susceptible to operant, and possibly also classical, conditioning, would not seem to provide any reason for holding that they are persons. For neither operant nor classical conditioning requires the postulation of psychological states or capacities of a sort that, according to the most plausible accounts, make something a person. If it were otherwise, our moral attitudes would stand in need of massive revision, since all vertebrates, and most invertebrates, are susceptible to both operant and classical conditioning.

What of more advanced types of learning? One important type is learning by *imitation*. Very few non-human animals are capable of this. It is true that birds, for example, often appear to be imitating one another. It turns out, however,

---

[50] For references to some of the more important studies, see p. 249 of Stone, Smith, and Murphy, op. cit.

[51] A.-M. Sostek, A. J. Sameroff, and A. J. Sostek, 'Evidence for the Unconditionability of the Babkin Reflex in Newborns', *Child Development*, Volume 43, 1972, pp. 509–19. A. J. Sameroff, 'Can Conditioned Responses Be Established in the New-born Infant: 1971?', *Developmental Psychology*, Volume 5, 1971, pp. 1–12.

[52] *The Competent Infant*, p. 250.

that what is happening might more accurately be 'described as "contagious behaviour," where the performance of a more or less instinctive pattern of behaviour by one will tend to act as a releaser for the same behaviour in another . . .'[53] When such behaviour is excluded, and the term 'imitation' is restricted to the copying of acts for which there is no instinctive tendency, 'it becomes doubtful whether (except possibly in cats) we can find any certain examples of such behaviour anywhere in the animal kingdom below the Primates'.[54]

This is a striking fact. But what is its significance? What does the capacity to learn by imitation indicate about an individual's underlying mental life? The general view seems to be that the capacity to learn by imitation is evidence of the presence of thought[55]—here construed as involving at least the occurrence of inner representations that are not tied to corresponding perceptual states, and that can be transformed in certain ways. Thorpe, in his discussion, suggests that the capacity to learn by imitation is also evidence of self-consciousness.[56] If either of these claims is correct, the capacity to learn by imitation points to a very important fact about an individual's mental life. Both claims seem to me quite plausible, though the claim that the capacity to learn by imitation presupposes self-consciousness is certainly more open to doubt than the claim that it presupposes thought. It is worth noting, however, that a view which is at least very close to Thorpe's has been advanced by a person who has studied imitation in children very closely and carefully. Thus Ina C. Uzgiris, in her article, 'Patterns of Vocal and Gestural Imitation in Infants', says: 'The present study implies the importance of self–other differentiation. Not only did the infants' reaction change when they began to differentiate between their own and the experimenter's acts, but at a later age as well when they began to treat an act as one performed by an actor rather than just occurring by itself.'[57]

[53] W. H. Thorpe, *Learning and Instinct in Animals*, 2nd edition, 1963, p. 133.
[54] Ibid., p. 135.
[55] Edwin G. Boring, *A History of Experimental Psychology*, 2nd edition, 1957, p. 629.
[56] Op. cit., p. 135.
[57] Ina C. Uzgiris, 'Patterns of Vocal and Gestural Imitation in Infants', in Stone, Smith, and Murphy, op. cit., pp. 599-604. See p. 604.

At what point in their development do humans become capable of learning by imitation? The studies that have been done appear to confirm views that Piaget advanced, about stages of imitation, on the basis of observations of his own children. Stone, Smith, and Murphy refer, for example, to the work of Uzgiris, mentioned above, and they summarize her findings as follows:

The first stage, during the first three or four months, appeared to involve the setting off of familiar acts, contagiously, so to speak; the second, about the middle of the first year, seems to be a stage of spectator sports and a 'pattern of acting in turn with the experimenter', whereas the third, toward the end of the first year, involves deliberate attempts to approximate the experimenter's act. Accurate imitation of unfamiliar acts appear to be a function of development in the second year.[58]

Let us now consider some experimental situations that have been developed to detect the presence of higher cognitive processes in animals, such as thought or ideation, reasoning, and problem solving. One problem situation often appealed to is that of the *delayed response*, described by Boring as follows:

In 1913 W. S. Hunter hit on the scheme of letting an animal subject see, by means of a signal, in which of a set of boxes food was placed without allowing it to go immediately to the box and get it. Could it 'remember' where the food was in order to go to it after an interval? Early results indicated that many animals could 'remember' the correct box only by maintaining a bodily orientation toward it, but later experiments showed that delayed responses in many species from rats to man are possible over periods which are fairly long—as long as four hours in one experiment with rats.[59]

What is the significance of ability to cope with the delayed response situation? The answer is not entirely uncontroversial. It has been widely held that this test is an indicator of ideational ability:

With odor controlled, the animal has no discriminative cue at the time of choice between two identical cups other than its memory of which

---

[58] Op. cit., p. 452.
[59] Op. cit., pp. 629-30. For Hunter's own description and discussion of his experiments, see Walter S. Hunter, 'The Delayed Reaction in Animals and Children', pp. 1–81 in *Behavior Monographs*, Volume 2, edited by John B. Watson, 1913-15.

one was baited. To be used effectively, this memory must be carried over the period of delay, and it has been suggested that to do this the animal must be capable of some 'symbolic process', akin to language, which it can use to represent the missing discriminative cue at the time of choice.[60]

The view that the ability to respond correctly after a delay points to the presence of inner representations seems plausible enough, though this view has certainly been challenged. Denny and Ratner, for example, maintain that an explanation can be given for delayed response behaviour, which does not postulate any underlying symbolic process, and which better fits the data.[61] This contention is part of a general view that they defend, to the effect that complex learning behaviour exhibited by infra-human animals can be adequately understood as a matter of responding to complex stimuli or cues. There appears, however, to be good reason to reject this general view. There was a vigorous debate between cognitive psychologists such as Tolman, and stimulus–response psychologists such as Hull. The former maintained that when a rat learned to run a maze, it acquired a cognitive map of the layout. The latter held that all that was involved was the acquisition of a chain of stimulus–response pairs in which each response gave rise to the stimulus for the next response. When attempts were made to determine experimentally which view was correct, the results supported the cognitive approach.[62]

It may be reasonable, then, to attribute inner representations to an animal that can cope successfully with the delayed response situation. What is much less clear, however, is whether failure provides good evidence that something lacks the capacity for inner representations. The reason for questioning whether it does is that the experiment involves two cups that are qualitatively identical, and it might well be the case that some animals that are unsuccessful here can choose the cup under which an object has been placed, after a

[60] Dethier and Stellar, op. cit., p. 128.
[61] M. Ray Denny and Stanley C. Ratner *Comparative Psychology*, 2nd edition, 1970, p. 722.
[62] For a lucid account of the issues and the relevant experiments see pp. 179–86 of Wayne A. Wickelgren's book, *Learning and Memory*, 1977.

delay, if the cups are of different shapes or different colours. And if they can, there is a good reason for attributing some inner representations to them. By itself, then, failure in the delayed response experiment would seem to show only that an individual cannot form a stable representation of situations such as: food in a red cup to the right of another red cup. Still, this in itself is quite a significant limitation.

How do humans fare when confronted with the delayed response problem? In general, it seems that human infants cannot cope with this task until they are about a year old.[63] If failure to handle the delayed response problem were indicative of an inability to form inner representations, there would be very serious reason for doubting whether human infants are persons much before the age of about twelve months. For all of the views that we considered earlier, of what it is that makes something a person, seem to imply that to be a person one must either be capable, or have been capable, of having at least some thoughts. But as I have indicated, it is not clear that an inability to cope with the delayed response situation provides good evidence for the absence of all inner representations.

Another important problem situation, developed by Harry F. Harlow,[64] is this. An animal is confronted with two objects between which it can discriminate perceptually. Every time the animal chooses one of the objects, it will be rewarded, whereas it will never be rewarded for choosing the other object. After a number of trials with the two objects, the animal is confronted with two other objects where, again, choice of one will always be rewarded, and choice of the other never rewarded. The question is whether a given animal will form what Harlow called 'learning sets', that is, whether the animal will, by being exposed to a sequence of situations, all of this type, eventually learn to choose in accordance with the following principle: if the choice of one object is rewarded, always choose that object; if it is not rewarded, never choose it.

[63] Alison Jolly, 'The Study of Primate Infancy', in *The Growth of Competence*, edited by Kevin Connolly and Jerome Bruner, 1974, pp. 49-74. See p. 60.

[64] H. F. Harlow, 'The Formation of Learning Sets', *Psychological Review*, Volume 56, 1949, pp. 51-65.

What animals are capable of forming learning sets? It was thought at one time that only very few could do so: 'Only primates have any degree of success in this type of problem. Rats fail miserably and must learn each new problem by trial and error, never carrying over the general principle from problem to problem.'[65] This view has, however, been shown to be incorrect:

Learning sets have been investigated most extensively in primates, but they have also been demonstrated in other mammals, including rats, cats, raccoons, and dolphins. Demonstrations of learning set phenomena in species below mammals, however, have not been terribly impressive. The formation of learning sets has been demonstrated in birds, and to a lesser extent in amphibians and fish, but there have been many many failures in working with such species. Species with more highly developed cerebral cortices tend to show more rapid development of learning sets, and ablations of the cerebral cortex diminish the capacity to form learning sets (more seriously than they diminish the capacity to master individual problems).

There has been very little work on learning sets in invertebrates, partly because of the difficulty of demonstrating learning sets in lower vertebrate species. The little work that has been done has yielded mostly negative results, though there is a successful demonstration by Mackintosh and Mackintosh of the development of a limited degree of reversal learning set in octopuses.[66]

What is involved when an organism forms a learning set? Wickelgren suggests that 'it seems reasonable to assume that they have not just suppressed error tendencies but have actually acquired some concepts or "hypotheses" about the regularities that underlie the learning situation'.[67] This suggestion seems to be supported, moreover, by Harlow's 'striking discovery', based upon a careful study of the formation of learning sets in monkeys, that 'a great *maturational* gulf exists between efficient individual-problem learning and efficient learning-set formation'.[68]

When do humans become capable of forming learning sets? The answer is not entirely clear, partly because the process is a gradual one, and partly because humans have not, apparently,

[65] Dethier and Stellar, op. cit., p. 127.
[66] Wickelgren, op. cit., p. 176. [67] Loc. cit.
[68] Harry F. Harlow, 'Infant Learning: The First Year', in *The Competent Infant*, pp. 605–13. Emphasis has been added in the quotation, taken from p. 612.

been as carefully studied as some other species. However Alison Jolly expresses the view that it is some time beyond the age of eighteen months before humans become capable of forming learning sets[69]—presumably at anything approaching the 100-per-cent level of competence. If this is the case, the ability of human infants to formulate generalizations appears to be very limited.

Another standard test of higher cognitive capacities involves what are called *oddity problems*. An individual is confronted with a sequence of choice situations. Each involves three objects, two the same, one different. The types of objects vary from trial to trial, but in each case one is rewarded if and only if one selects the object that differs from the other two.

This test is rather similar to that of the learning set: here too one must generalize from initial problems to those that follow. It is, however, more difficult. Rats, apparently, have no success in coping with this task.[70] And in the case of humans, it is once again only some time beyond about the age of 18 months that they become capable of solving oddity problems of a simple sort.[71]

Another psychological test which deserves mention is that of *double and triple alternation*, which Boring describes as follows:

Hunter invented what he called a temporal maze (1920), a maze in which partitions are shifted so as to cause a rat to run twice around a rectangle at one side and then reverse to run twice around a similar rectangular block on the other side, and so on, two right, two left, two right. It was a way of seeing whether the rat could count to *two*, or, with triple alternation, to *three*. The rats did badly with double alternation. Raccoons succeeded with double alternation, but failed with triple. Monkeys succeeded with triple. Rats can learn, however, to push a lever twice quickly to the left and then twice quickly to the right. In other words, rats have difficulty in learning to 'count' slowly to *two*, but can learn to count rapidly to *four*. The problem is one of 'memory'

[69] Op. cit., pp. 60–1. Harlow, in the article just cited, does not discuss the capabilities of normal human infants, but he does refer in passing to the difficulties of mentally defective humans in forming learning sets: '. . . discrimination learning-set formation taxes the prowess of the human imbecile and apparently exceeds the capacity of the human idiot.' (Op. cit., p. 613.)

[70] Dethier and Stellar, op. cit., p. 128.

[71] Alison Jolly, op. cit., p. 61.

or, in less mentalistic terms, of temporal integration—like the problem of the range of attention and memory span in man.[72]

Success in coping with this sort of situation appears, then, to be evidence for the presence of a certain memory span, together with the capacity for representative processes involving simple numerical concepts. Unfortunately, precise experimental data concerning the performance of humans at different ages in double and triple alternation tests seems not to be presently available.

A number of other interesting experimental situations have been developed for studying the psychological capacities of individuals that lack language. However the above survey should serve to drive home the great gulf that exists between the psychological capabilities of human infants, especially during the first few months, and those of normal adults. A good deal of work admittedly remains to be done, both on the basic capacities that underlie successful performance of various tasks, and on more precise dating of the times at which humans typically become capable of coping with various experimental problems. Until these two tasks are carried out, I do not believe that one can offer anything like a precise estimate of when human individuals typically become persons. Our concern here, however, is only with whether new-born humans are persons, and with regard to that question, I believe that what is presently known is quite decisive. New-born humans apparently are susceptible to conditioning, both instrumental and classical, contrary to what was once widely believed. But this capacity is possessed by all vertebrates, and most invertebrates. Higher psychological capacities emerge only later—and in many cases much later— in the development of a human infant. The upshot is that, as regards cognitive capacities, in contrast to potentialities, a new-born human is at best on a par with most other animals, vertebrate and invertebrate, and is inferior to adult members of many mammalian species.

[72] Op. cit., p. 630.

11.54 The Scientific Evidence: Human Neurophysiological Development

The other area of scientific investigation that is crucial in the present context is neurophysiology. Kluge and Blumenfeld, as we saw earlier, appeal to facts from this field in support of their views on abortion. In doing so, however, they are notable exceptions to the general rule. Remarkably few philosophers seem to be aware of the possibly decisive importance of information about the development of the human brain with respect to the morality of abortion and infanticide. In this section I shall attempt to provide a summary of the relevant material.

The central nervous system involves two types of cells. There are neuroglial cells, which play an important role in controlling development and metabolism, and neurons, or nerve cells, which are responsible for the transmission of information. Neurons exhibit a variety of sizes and shapes, but they always consist of a *soma*, or cell body, which contains the cell nucleus, together with branch-like structures running out from the soma. The latter can be divided into *axons*, which act as transmitters for the nerve cell, and *dendrites*, which, together with the soma, function as receiving areas. All nerve cells involve at least one axon, and usually several dendrites.

The transmission of information by a network of nerve cells is carried out by electrochemical processes within individual neurons which have appropriate points of interaction, called synapses. The process within an individual neuron is described by E. G. Gray as follows:

The neuron has a resting potential of about −70mV across the surface membrane which bounds the neuron throughout. This is achieved by an active transport mechanism, which maintains a high concentration of potassium ions and low concentration of sodium and chloride ions inside the neuron, resulting in an electrochemical gradient so that the neuron is polarized, being electronegative inside. When the neuron is sufficiently excited (depolarized) an action potential is generated usually near the beginning of the axon. Sodium ions flow through the membrane, reversing the resting potential; at this point the inner surface of the membrane is electropositive, the outside electronegative. . . . The action potential spreads along the membrane down the axon, which may branch many times, to a final knob-shaped terminal, which lies in contact with the dendrite or soma of the next neuron in the circuit.[73]

Synapses are classified into different types on the basis of the nature of the presynaptic membrane of the transmitting neuron and of the postsynaptic membrane of the receiving neuron. An axodendritic synapse, for example, is one where the presynaptic membrane lies on an axon, and the postsynaptic membrane on a dendrite. Similarly for axosomatic synapses and dendrodendritic synapses.

The presynaptic and postsynaptic membranes are not in contact at a synapse. They are separated by a fluid-filled, intercellular space, and transmission across the synapse usually involves the release of one of a number of chemical substances, although some special synapses do employ electrical transmission.[74]

Two further facts about neurons are important in the present context. The first is that many axons are ensheathed by a lipid-protein mixture called *myelin*. Whether an axon is myelinated depends upon its diameter: larger axons are myelinated; smaller ones are not. The presence of myelin alters, in a number of ways, the properties of a neuron. Thus, for example, the myelin sheath acts as an insulating layer that greatly increases the resistance of the nerve fibre membrane. This increase in resistance results, in turn, in a conduction velocity that is much higher in myelinated fibres than in unmyelinated ones.[75]

The other relevant fact is that the dendrites of many neurons, and in particular, those in the cerebral cortex, are covered by minute protruberances called *dendritic spines*. These structures are important because they are the main sites of synaptic contact in the cortex.[76]

A feature found in dendritic spines in mammalian cerebral cortex, and which may be very important, is what Gray calls the *spine apparatus*. This appears to consist of two or more membrane-bound sacs separated by wide, dense bands. It has been suggested that the spine apparatus may play a role in

---

[73] E. G. Gray, *The Synapse*, 1973, pp. 2-3. [74] Ibid., p. 6.
[75] *Fundamentals of Neurophysiology*, edited by Robert F. Schmidt, 1978, pp. 8-10 and 66-7.
[76] Gray, op. cit., p. 9.

the learning process. An evaluation of this suggestion must, however, await further studies correlating behaviour and ultra-structure.[77]

The part of the central nervous system that will be of primary interest here is the cerebral cortex, since it provides the physical basis for higher mental functions. It is made up, in humans and in the primates, of two cast, convoluted sheets of grey matter, called neuropil, consisting of immense networks of nerve cells. The number of neurons in the human cerebral cortex is very large indeed—something of the order of 10^9 to 10^{10}—and each neuron, in turn, may be involved in several thousand synaptic connections.[78] The resulting circuitry in the human brain is thus incredibly complex—far more so than that of any computer so far constructed—and it is this astronomical connectivity that makes possible complex brain functions.[79]

It should be possible in principle, then, to determine whether an organism possesses certain psychological capacities by considering the extent to which it has developed the necessary neuronal networks, or circuitry, in the relevant parts of the brain. This will involve taking a close look at the development of individual neurons, and at the establishment of synaptic connections among them.

There is, however, other evidence that may also be very helpful—namely, that provided by various electrical parameters, such as those measured by electroencephalograms. Our knowledge of the dependence of higher mental functions upon the brain is still in an early stage of development, and it is not always possible to state how mature individual neurons need to be, or how complex a given neuronal network needs to be, in order to make possible a certain function. Electrical measurements of individual neurons, or of regions of the brain, may provide considerable help in answering such questions.

[77] Gray, op. cit., p. 15; D. G. Jones, *Synapses and Synaptosomes*, 1975, pp. 15-16.

[78] There are serious limitations in the accuracy of the methods employed for estimating the number of neurons, and different methods lead to somewhat different results. See Marcus Jacobson, *Developmental Neurobiology*, 2nd edition, 1978, pp. 106-7.

[79] Gray, op. cit., p. 14.

The best place to begin, I think, will be with an overview of the development of the human cerebral cortex. The important details can then be much more easily grasped. The first part of the cerebral cortex to develop is called the ventricular zone. It contains the ventricular germinal cells, and gives rise to the other three zones: the marginal, the intermediate, and the subventricular. It then disappears.

The zones that interest us are those which contain neurons: the marginal, and the intermediate. Of these, the marginal is the first to be produced. Initially, it contains only processes from neurons whose nuclei are located at deeper levels. Later it comes to contain a sparse population of neurons. It constitutes the outermost part of the cerebral cortex, referred to as layer I.

The intermediate zone develops as a result of two processes: the growth of afferent axons from below, together with the migration of neurons from the ventricular zone. These form what is known as the cortical plate. As these two processes continue, the cortical plate gradually differentiates to form layers II through VI of the mature cerebral cortex.[80]

Next, there are a number of principles that apply quite generally to the development of the cerebral cortex. Of these principles, three are especially relevant. The first is that in many areas, such as the cerebral cortex, there is an inside-out pattern of assembly. This means that 'the neurons that originate at successively later times migrate past those formed earlier and take up successively more external positions, that is, successively farther from the ventricular germinal zone from which they originate'.[81] Thus, within the cortical plate, neurons of layer VI originate first, followed by those of layers V, IV, III, and II respectively. We shall see later that these differences in time of origin are reflected in later differences in the degree of development of various layers of the cerebral cortex.

The second principle is that there is a temporal gradient with respect to the time of origin of different types of neurons: in any region of the central nervous system, large neurons are produced first, and the small local circuit neurons,

---

[80] Jacobson, op. cit., pp. 62-3.   [81] Ibid., p. 58.

such as Golgi type II neurons and granule neurons, are produced last.

The third principle is that the ontogeny of the brain tends to recapitulate its phylogeny: 'It is the general rule that parts of the nervous system that appeared first in phylogeny have a tendency to appear early in ontogeny, and structures that arose later in evolution also often arise late in ontogeny.'[82] This principle will prove very useful for organizing facts about the relative development both of different layers of the cerebral cortex, and of different regions within a single layer.

Next, let us consider the approximate times of arrival of various types of neurons in different layers of the cerebral cortex. The first type to appear are the large, stellate, Cajal-Retzius cells, which are found in the marginal zone of the cortex. Their appearance, during the second month of gestation, takes place at the same time as the origin of the intermediate zone.[83] The function of these large cells is not yet known. Some investigators believe that they atrophy and disappear. Others believe that they merely undergo some alteration of position and shape.[84]

The next neurons to originate and migrate are the large pyramidal cells of layers VI and V. They can be found at a gestational age of five months. These are followed by, at around the seventh month, the cortical basket cells of layer IV. Next there are the pyramidal cells of layer III, followed, at around seven and a half months, by those of layer II. Finally, during the late prenatal period, Golgi type II neurons, and other types of small neurons, appear in all layers of the cerebral cortex.[85]

The neurons, however, are in a very immature state when they have completed the process of migration, and they must, in general, undergo considerable development before they will be capable of conducting impulses at all, let alone of functioning in the way that fully mature neurons do. This

---

[82] Ibid., p. 60.

[83] G. I. Poliakov, 'Some Results of Research into the Development of the Neuronal Structure of the Cortical Ends of the Analyzers in Man', *Journal of Comparative Neurology*, Volume 117, 1965, pp. 197-212. See p. 198.

[84] Jacobson, op. cit., pp. 64-5.   [85] Ibid., p. 66.

process of development involves a number of changes. At the ultrastructural level there is the development of the Nissl substance, of neurofilaments and microfilaments, and of neurotubules and microtubules. However, given our interests here, we can ignore these ultrastructural developments, and concentrate on changes, occurring at a grosser level, whose functional significance is more readily apparent.

There are two changes in neurons that are especially important. First, the myelination of axons. Second, the growth and differentiation of neural processes. The latter includes the growth of axons and the development of collaterals, together with the elaborate development of dendritic branches and their spines.

There is, of course, another crucial change that we shall need to consider: the development of synaptic connections. Synaptogenesis begins quite early—indeed, before the generation of neurons by the ventricular zone is completed.[86] But on the other hand, the process of synaptogenesis, as we shall see, also takes place over an extended period of time. This is so because the differentiation of neuronal processes occurs over an extended period, and these two developments are, of course, intimately related: 'Development of the dendrites occurs at the same time as the development of axodendritic and dendrodendritic synapses, and it will have become clear from the previous discussion that synaptogenesis and dendritic growth are interdependent processes.'[87]

We are now in a position to take a detailed look at the more important developmental processes. First, the myelination of axons. There is some disagreement as to precisely how important myelination is. One person who feels that it is less significant than sometimes thought is R. J. Robinson: 'The optic nerve and tract are incompletely myelinated at term, but we know perfectly well that the optic nerve is functioning by 28 weeks' gestation. A newborn opossum is quite good at finding its way into the mother's pouch and then finding the nipple, although it has no myelin in the central nervous system at all at the time of birth.'[88]

---

[86] Ibid., p. 196. [87] Ibid., p. 187.
[88] *Brain and Early Behaviour*, edited by R. J. Robinson, 1969, p. 348.

The view that Robinson is criticizing here is, however, an extreme one. Given that the axons of many neurons never have a myelin sheath, it does not seem very likely that neurons that will eventually be myelinated cannot function at all until this happens. The interesting issues, then, would seem to be these. First, what difference does myelination make to the functioning of individual neurons? Second, to what extent does the functioning of a network of neurons depend upon how far myelination of the neurons composing the network has proceeded?

As regards the second issue, it is true that the dependence has been overestimated in some respects in the past. Thus, as Lewis P. Lipsitt points out, one reason it was widely held that newborn humans could not be conditioned was that 'people assumed that myelination was insufficiently advanced to permit learning in the newborn'.[89]

How significant, then, is myelination? More research is needed before there can be a definitive answer to this question. Nevertheless many researchers, such as R. M. Bergstrom, do believe, for a variety of reasons, that myelination may be 'a very important factor'.[90] F. J. Schulte, for example, says: 'Myelination of axons and arborization of dendrites are the two basic structural changes which occur in the course of development of the nervous system. Both the thickness of the myelin sheath and the quantity of dendrites have important implications for nervous activity.'[91] Similarly, Paul I. Yakovlev says that myelination is 'a morphological criterion of the functional maturity of a conduction path',[92] and he and Andre-Roch Lecours, in their much-cited article, 'The Myelogenetic Cycles of Regional Maturation of the Brain', say:

A fibre system or a region may begin to myelinate either early or late in foetal life or even only after birth; however, in either case it may attain the relative term of myelination either rapidly or slowly. In other words, the *cycle* of myelogenesis is an important parameter of regional

[89] Ibid., p. 347.   [90] Ibid., p. 348.
[91] F. J. Schulte, 'Structure–function Relationships in the Spinal Cord', in R. J. Robinson, op. cit., p. 337.
[92] In *Regional Development of the Brain in Early Life*, edited by Alexandre Minkowski, 1967, p. 68.

maturation. One may reasonably assume that the cycle reflects and, in a sense, defines the position of a fibre system or region in the hierarchy of functional organization of the developing nervous system.[93]

But what reasons are there for accepting these claims that myelination is functionally significant? There are, I think, at least three sorts of considerations that deserve mention. In the first place, there are facts concerning the difference that myelination makes in the behaviour of individual neurons. Thus, as F. J. Schulte points out: 'Axonal myelination is positively related to impulse conduction velocity, to the amplitude of the action potential, to membrane excitability, and sometimes to the maximal frequency of impulses.'[94] Of these factors, Schulte believes that the second and third are particularly important. For on the one hand, 'the amplitude of the action potential determines the amount of transmitter which is secreted at the nerve endings', which may, in turn, 'have a tremendous effect on synaptic activity'.[95] And on the other hand, an increase in membrane excitability means that less depolarization is needed, and hence fewer excitatory postsynaptic potentials, in order to produce a certain number of action potentials.[96]

Another very important feature is pointed out by Peter Huttenlocher:

For some time after the onset of electrical excitability the immature central nervous system continues to differ markedly from the adult in its functional properties. One such difference lies in the ability to maintain sustained activity. A rapid decrease in amplitude of evoked potentials to repetitive sensory or electrical stimuli has often been demonstrated in immature cerebral cortex. On the efferent side, movements elicited by electrical stimulation of immature motor cortex decrease in amplitude and then cease entirely when the stimulus is applied repeatedly.[97]

Huttenlocher discusses experiments with cats in which there is found to be a positive correlation between conduction

---

[93] Paul I. Yakovlev and Andre-Roch Lecours, 'The Myelogenetic Cycles of Regional Maturation of the Brain', in Minkowski, op. cit., pp. 3–65. See p. 6.
[94] Op cit., p. 337.   [95] Ibid.   [96] Ibid.
[97] Peter R. Huttenlocher, 'Myelination and the Development of Function in Immature Pyramidal Tract', *Experimental Neurology*, Volume 29, 1970, pp. 405–15. See p. 405.

block in the axon, involving a progressive lengthening of conduction time, and conduction velocity of fibres in the pyramidal tract. Since the latter factor is related to myelination, these experiments suggest that 'myelination increases .the ability of central axons to fire repetitively'.[98]

Huttenlocher goes on to indicate why this feature may be very significant indeed:

The inability of developing axons to maintain repetitive activity may be of functional importance in the immature brain. In the adult, rapid repetitive firing of cortical neurons is commonly seen during normal activity. As early as 1939 Adrian and Moruzzi found that motor activity of an animal is correlated with high-frequency discharges in pyramidal tract fibers. . . . More recent studies in the monkey by Evarts have shown a correlation between bursts of rapid discharges in pyramidal tract units and voluntary contraction of small muscle groups. Firing rates of 50–100/sec were seen in pyramidal tract neurons during voluntary contraction of hand and forearm muscles. The inability of immature axons to maintain such rapid rates of activity may provide an explanation for the correlations that have been observed between myelination and the appearance of function in the immature brain. On the other hand, it is clear that some functions, primarily those of simple reflex type, develop prior to and quite independent of myelination.[99]

The second point is that the individual's acquisition of behavioural and psychological capacities appears to correlate very well with myelination of the regions of the brain thought to constitute the physical basis of those capacities. This point is stressed by Yakovlev and Lecours, and in the following passage they mention some of those correlations:

The protracted cycle of myelination of the median zone of the forebrain appears to correlate with the protracted ontogenetic development of the reflex and behavioural patterns in the sphere of visceral motility and metabolic, enzymatic and hormonal processes, which change slowly through the years of reproductive life. In contrast, the somatic motility of the outward expression of the internal states and movements of the body on the body itself such as mimicry, gestures, postural habitus, mannerisms and vocalizations become definitive of the individual 'makeup' by the end of the second decade and change little thereafter. The shorter cycle of myelination of the paramedian zone appears to correlate with the more rapid maturation of the reflex and behavioural patterns in the sphere of 'innate' or 'instinctive' movements conventionally assigned to basal ganglia and the 'extrapyramidal' system.[100]

[98] Ibid.   [99] Ibid., p. 414.   [100] Op. cit., p. 63.

Third, there are facts concerning the impairment of an animal's capacities when there is a deficiency of myelin. Such a deficiency may be brought about in a number of ways. In the case of mice it may be due to a single gene mutation. Alternatively, a deficiency may be produced by thyroidectomy at birth, or by nutritional deprivation during the period of myelination. Such deficiency is always associated with abnormal or impaired behaviour.[101] Moreover, there are several metabolic diseases, such as phenylketonuria, and inherited disorders of amino acid metabolism, that give rise to abnormal behaviour and mental retardation, and where deficiencies in the formation of myelin have been observed.[102] Finally, there are diseases that attack the myelin sheaths of mature neurons. Multiple sclerosis is such a disease:

A chronic disease of the central nervous system in which small, scattered areas of the brain and spinal cord degenerate and nerve fibres lose their insulating myelin sheaths and their ability to conduct impulses. The sclerosis resembles scarring after a virus infection such as poliomyelitis; but there is no evidence of infection or any other cause.

The symptoms depend entirely on where the patches of sclerosis appear, and they can therefore mimic those of almost any disorder of the nervous system.[103]

Let us now consider the timing of myelination in different parts of the human central nervous system. The classic study is 'The Myelogenetic Cycles of Regional Maturation in the Brain', by Paul I. Yakovlev and Andre-Róch Lecours. Two of the more important conclusions of their study are these. First, they found that there is considerable variation with respect to when myelination commences in different systems of neurons. The first neurons to exhibit any myelination are in the spinal cord. Myelin sheaths can be found in the motor root fibres from about the end of the fourth foetal month, and in the sensory root fibres from about the end of the fifth foetal month. On the other hand, of the twenty-five systems that Yakovlev and Lecours[104] examined, forty per cent exhibit no myelination at all until after birth.

---

[101] Jacobson, op. cit., pp. 178-9.   [102] Ibid., p. 179.
[103] Peter Wingate, *The Penguin Medical Encyclopedia*, 1972, p. 280.
[104] Paul I. Yakovlev and Andre-Roch Lecours, 'The Myelogenetic Cycles of Regional Maturation in the Brain', in Minkowski, op. cit., pp. 3-70.

Second, the time required for the development of the degree of myelination found in the adult human varies greatly from one system to another. The motor roots have a relatively short cycle, myelination generally being complete by term. Myelination of the sensory roots proceeds somewhat more slowly, and is not completed until four months or so after term. And in some systems the process is an extraordinarily protracted one—particularly in the reticular formation, the non-specific thalamic radiations, the great cerebral commissures, and the intra-cortical neuropil areas, where myelination is not complete even by the age of six years.

It will be useful, however, to go beyond these general points, and to take at least a brief look at some particular systems. One that is of interest consists of the middle cerebellar peduncles. Their function is to mediate the integrative activities of the cerebral hemispheres to the cerebellum.[105] It is one of the fibre systems that begins myelination only postnatally, and the process extends through about three years. Second, there is the reticular formation: 'Phylogenetically and embryologically this reticulate assembly of nerve cells and the feltwork of thin fibres represents the primordial core of the neuraxis. Rudimentary in the brain stem of the submammalian vertebrates, the reticular formation undergoes profound modifications and elaboration in primates and man.'[106] The reticular formation involves, among other things, collaterals from the ascending sensory systems, and it is generally thought that these collaterals make some sort of essential contribution to behaviour that is indicative of 'various degrees of consciousness, wakefulness and alertness'.[107] The precise relation is not, however, clear. At one time it was widely thought that the reticular formation was the crucial centre for wakefulness, but this hypothesis has proved untenable in the light of recent findings. It has been shown, for example, that 'even a chronically isolated brain lacking a reticular formation exhibits a sleeping–waking rhythm . . .'[108]

---

[105] Ibid., p. 62. [106] Ibid., p. 21.
[107] R. J. Lemire, J. D. Loeser, R. W. Leech, and E. C. Alvord, *Normal and Abnormal Development of the Human Nervous System*, 1975, pp. 29–30.
[108] Schmidt, op. cit., p. 288.

Myelination of the reticular system involves two aspects: on the one hand, the myelination of the collaterals of the long fibre systems passing through it; and on the other, myelination of the fibres that are intrinsic to it. Before birth, the reticular system is 'almost devoid of myelinated fibres', the only exception being the fibre systems that pass through it.[109] Moreover, myelination both of collaterals and of intrinsic fibres takes place over an unusually long period of time: 'The two processes may be assumed to continue beyond puberty and possibly go on until the age of senium is reached. However, in some brains from the eighth and ninth decades of life the reticular formation shrinks, again becomes lighter staining and contains fewer myelinated fibres.'[110]

Third, there are the commissural fibre systems found in the corpus callosum. These serve to connect the two hemispheres, and they have an important role to play in the unification of consciousness, as is shown by 'split-brain' cases.[111] Again, the commissural fibres do not begin to myelinate until after birth—at about the fourth postnatal month—and the process is a protracted one, perhaps continuing beyond the first decade.[112]

Finally, there are the association areas of the outermost (or supralimbic) zones of the cerebral hemispheres. These areas, which Yakovlev and Lecours characterize as 'specifically human',[113] are thought to provide the physical basis for higher mental functions such as thought and the use of language. Myelination of fibres in these areas is a very protracted process, and one that does not begin until about the end of the third postnatal month.

The phenomenon of myelination, then, illustrates the general principle that ontogeny recapitulates phylogeny. Those regions of the brain that were the last to emerge in the development of species leading up to man, and that provide the physical basis of those capacities that are often regarded as characteristically human, are also the areas that myelinate last

---

[109] Yakovlev and Lecours, op. cit., p. 21.

[110] Ibid., p. 23.

[111] For a description of the effects of transection of the corpus callosum, see Schmidt, op. cit., pp. 291 ff.

[112] Yakovlev and Lecours, op. cit., p. 61.   [113] Ibid.

in the development of the individual—and indeed, only post-natally.

Let us now turn to the growth of neuronal processes and the formation of synaptic connections. It will be convenient to treat these together, since, as was noted above, these processes go hand in hand.

The development of neuronal processes begins with the outgrowth of the axon. This is followed by the outgrowth of dendrites. The axon continues to grow both in length and diameter, and the dendrites develop a more and more elaborate branched structure. This branching is very important, because it 'results in a great increase in the surface area of the dendrites, which form more than 90 per cent of the postsynaptic surface of the neuron'.[114] And as we shall see shortly, this branching takes place over an extended period of time: 'Thus, after the neurons have migrated to their final positions, there is a long delay before full differentiation of the dendrites occurs.'[115]

There are some regularities of dendritic development that are relevant here. The first is that just as, in any region of the brain, neurons with short axons originate later than neurons with long axons, so too in any region of the brain 'the dendrites of neurons with short axons (Golgi type II) differentiate later than dendrites of the principal neurons, which have long axons'.[116] Similarly, just as neurogenesis tends to follow an inside-out sequence, so does the maturation of neurons. Thus 'the dendrites of the cortex of the brain mature later than the dendrites of the central nuclei projecting to the cortex; and within the cortex the dendrites of deeper layers tend to develop before those in more superficial layers.'[117] There are also extremely important regularities concerning the maturation of neurons within different regions of the cerebral cortex, which we shall consider later. These facts about dendritic differentiation will be reflected in corresponding facts about the formation of synapses.

There have been a number of studies of synaptogenesis itself, but very few of these have been quantitative.[118] And in

---

[114] Jacobson, op. cit., p. 183.   [115] Ibid.
[116] Ibid.   [117] Ibid., pp. 183-4.
[118] D. G. Jones, *Synapses and Synaptosomes*, 1975, pp. 36-7.

the case of human infants, there have, apparently, been no quantitative studies of synaptogenesis at all, due to the fact that a reasonably accurate count of synapses involves examining, by means of an electron microscope, sections that have been stained with ethanolic phosphotungstic acid, and this method, to be usable at all, requires material from the brain of an animal that has been dead less than two hours. In the case of human infants such material is obviously very difficult to obtain.

What about quantitative studies of non-human animals? Perhaps the most important result of such studies is that all attempts to estimate the number of synapses present have shown 'a very dramatic increase in the connectivity of the mammalian cerebral cortex during the early postnatal period of development'.[119] Thus it has been shown, for example, that in the molecular layer of the dendrite gyrus of the rat, the number of synapses present four days after birth is less than one per cent of the adult number, and that from day four through day eleven, the number more or less doubles each day. By day thirty the number of synapses is more than ninety per cent of the adult number.[120] Similarly, in the case of the cat visual cortex, Brian Cragg has observed that at eight days after birth the number of synapses is only about 1.5 per cent of the adult number, but this increases very rapidly, reaching a peak at about thirty-six days.[121]

Given the interdependence of dendritic differentiation and synaptogenesis, together with the fact that neurons in the cortex mature in an inside-out sequence, one should find the number of synapses increasing earlier at deeper levels than at more superficial levels. Cragg found this to be so in the case of the cat visual cortex. In the deeper layers, there is a large increase in the number of synapses between days one and eight postnatally, while in the superficial layers it is between days eight and twenty-seven that a large increase is observed.[122]

[119] Jacobson, op. cit., p. 193.
[120] B. Crain, C. Cotman, D. Taylor, and G. Lynch, 'A Quantitative Electron Microscope Study of Synaptogenesis in the Dendrite Gyrus of the Rat', *Brain Research*, Volume 65, 1973, pp. 195-204.
[121] B. G. Cragg, 'The Development of Synapses in Cat Visual Cortex', *Investigative Ophthalmology*, Volume 11, Number 5, 1972, pp. 377-85.
[122] Ibid., p. 381.

Let us now consider the case of humans. Perhaps the first point that should be made is that there is a difference between primates and subprimates with respect to the amount of synaptogenesis that occurs prenatally. Before birth, the cerebral cortex of subprimates contains very few synapses, whereas in the case of primates the formation of synapses is considerably more advanced at that time.[123] For the formation of synapses commences a long time before birth. Mark Molliver, Ivica Kostovic, and Hendrik Van der Loos report that in the case of humans, synapses can be found within the cortex at about eight weeks gestational age.[124] These early synapses, however, occur above and below the cortical plate. It was only in a foetus of twenty-three weeks that Molliver *et al.* found synapses within the cortical plate itself. It is possible that there may be synapses within the cortical plate slightly earlier, however, since Molliver *et al.* were unable to study any foetuses ranging from nineteen weeks to twenty-two weeks in age.[125]

The region examined in their study was chosen because, among other reasons, 'it is the first neocortical area to develop'.[126] Accordingly, the onset of synaptogenesis will take place later in other regions of the human cerebral cortex. It would be interesting to know how much variation in time there is between different regions. However comparative data on the time of onset of synaptogenesis in different regions of the human cerebral cortex are not presently available.

Fortunately, such data are not crucial in the present context. What matters here is how far synaptogenesis has proceeded in different regions of the cerebral cortex of the new-born human. And while it is true, as noted earlier, that no quantitative studies of postnatal synaptogenesis in different regions of the human cerebral cortex have been carried out, it is possible to approach the question less directly by considering something that has been studied in detail, namely,

---

[123] Jacobson, op. cit., p. 73.
[124] Mark E. Molliver, Ivica Kostovic, and Hendrick Van der Loos, 'The Development of Synapses in Cerebral Cortex of the Human Fetus', *Brain Research*, Volume 50, 1973, pp. 403–7. See p. 404.
[125] Ibid.
[126] Ibid., p. 406.

the postnatal development of neurons in different regions of the human cerebral cortex.

The classic study of the development of the human cerebral cortex after birth is J. LeRoy Conel's seven volume work, *The Postnatal Development of the Human Cerebral Cortex.*[127] Conel's observations concerning the maturation of neurons—and in particular concerning the development of dendritic processes—will, in conjunction with certain other considerations and studies, enable us to arrive at conclusions about how far synaptogenesis has proceeded in different parts of the new-born human's cerebral cortex.

The place to begin is by considering which regions of the new-born human's cerebral cortex are most developed. Conel's study shows that the region that is most advanced in the full-term human baby immediately after birth is the region which, following the cerebral localization charts of von Economo,[128] he refers to as region FAγ. This area is the motor cortex, and it is located in the anterior central gyrus—the most posterior part of the frontal lobe. The next most developed regions are PB and PC, in the posterior central gyrus—the most forward part of the parietal lobe. Their development is only slightly behind that of region FAγ. PB is the primary somesthetic area of the cortex. Next in degree of development is region OC, which is the primary visual cortex, and which is located in the occipital lobe, at the back of the brain.[129]

Within different lobes, the degree of development decreases as one moves away from those regions that are most highly developed. Thus, in the parietal lobe, differentiation decreases as one proceeds posteriorly from regions PB and PC, while in the frontal lobe, development falls off as one moves forward from area FAγ. The change is particularly striking in the latter case: 'Anterior to the gyrus centralis anterior there is a rapid decrease in the degree of development; the cortex in the anterior one-half of each of the three frontal gyri is

---

[127] J. LeRoy Conel, *The Postnatal Development of the Human Cerebral Cortex*, Volumes 1-7, 1939-63.

[128] C. von Economo, *The Cytoarchitectonics of the Human Cerebral Cortex*, 1929.

[129] Conel, op. cit., volume 1, pp. 103-4.

considerably less advanced in differentiation than in any other region of the cerebral cortex.'[130] The great significance, in the present context, of the retarded development of the anterior part of the frontal lobe will emerge in what follows.

During the first month after birth, it is the primary motor cortex—area FAγ—which exhibits the greatest advance in development, followed by the primary sensory regions. Of the latter, the most advanced is the somesthetic area—PB—followed by the primary visual and acoustic centres—areas OC and TC respectively.[131]

In the neonatal stage, then, the most developed regions of the cortex are the primary motor area and the primary receptive areas. The next task is to determine how developed these areas are. I shall concentrate on the motor cortex, partly because it is the most developed region, but mainly because much more useful information is available about it than about the primary sensory areas.

In the case of the primary visual cortex, however, there is an article that deserves to be mentioned, namely, 'Morphogenesis of Visual Cortex in the Preterm Infant',[132] by Dominick P. Purpura. Purpura studied a number of infants that were born prematurely, had survived for varying lengths of time, and had gestational ages ranging from twenty-five weeks through thirty-three weeks. In the case of the two thirty-three week-old infants he found that the neuronal development in the primary visual cortex was significantly more advanced than that described by T. Rabinowicz in an earlier study, 'The Cerebral Cortex of the Premature Infant of the 8th Month'.[133] The reasons for the divergent results are unclear. A possible factor is that Purpura employed the rapid Golgi method for metallic impregnation of neurons, while Rabinowicz employed the Golgi-Cox method. The former method is better for detecting the finest dendritic branches and dendritic spines. But whatever the explanation, Purpura observed a greater degree of dendritic differentiation,

[130] Ibid., p. 104.   [131] Conel, op. cit., volume 2, p. 134.
[132] In *Growth and Development of the Brain*, edited by Mary A. B. Brazier, 1975, pp. 33–49.
[133] In *Growth and Maturation of the Brain*, edited by D. P. Purpura and J. P. Schade, 1964, pp. 39–86.

especially in the case of the large pyramidal neurons and the giant stellate cells. He also detected, in the two thirty-three-week-old infants, the presence of dendritic spines: 'A consistent finding in the rapid Golgi preparations examined in this study is the presence of well-developed dendritic spines on pyramidal neurons in the premature infant of 8 months.'[134] Purpura believes that this latter aspect of dendritic differentiation is particularly important: 'The significance of this developmental event is attested to by the fact that dendritic spines in the mature brain are the postsynaptic targets for the vast majority of extrinsic and intrinsic afferents to cortical pyramidal neurons and spiny stellate cells.'[135]

The material in Purpura's study is, unfortunately, not very useful given our present purposes. What we need to know is the extent to which neuronal networks have developed in different layers of the cortex. The articles on the motor cortex to which I shall turn shortly attempt to deal with this question; Purpura's article does not.

In lieu of such information, it would be helpful to know at least *how far* dendritic differentiation has proceeded, for different types of neurons, in different layers of the visual cortex. Purpura concentrates his attention on the large neurons, which, as noted above, develop earlier than small neurons, and even in the case of large neurons he provides no data on how far dendritic differentiation has proceeded in comparison with that found in the fully developed neuron.

The same problem arises in connection with his discussion of dendritic spines. One needs to know not only when dendritic spines can first be found, but how many there are in comparison with the number present when the neuron is fully mature. One also needs to know to what extent the dendritic spines that are present are involved in axospino-dendritic synapses. Purpura's article provides no information of this sort.

There is also a serious question concerning the design of Purpura's study that deserves mention. Of the two thirty-three-week-old babies studied by Purpura, one was born at thirty-two weeks and survived a few days, while the other, on

[134] Op. cit., p. 45.   [135] Ibid., p. 46.

which the camera lucida drawings and photomicrographs in his text are based, was born at twenty-nine weeks and survived for four weeks. Purpura assumes that his findings in these two cases can be transferred to thirty-three-week-old foetuses. But this is justified only if there is reason to believe that development of the visual cortex is unaffected by visual stimulation. It appears that this condition is not satisfied:

Recent evidence has indicated that the mammalian visual system contains three functional projections to the visual centers originating from three classes of retinal ganglion cells, named X, Y, and W. These projections are affected differently by visual stimulation during development. Development of Y cells and their central projections is sensitive to visual stimulation during a critical period shortly after birth, while the development of X and W cells and their projections may not require visual stimulation.[136]

Jacobson goes on to point out that the 'dendritic spines of pyramidal cells in the striate cortex are particularly vulnerable to visual deprivation,' and that there is evidence that these pyramidal cells are the complex cortical cells that receive input from the retinal Y cells.[137] In the light of these points, it is clear that conclusions about the degree of development of the visual cortex of pre-term infants, particularly facts concerning the development of pyramidal neurons, cannot be simply transferred to foetuses of the same gestational age.

Let us turn, then, to the primary motor cortex—the most developed area in the new-born human's cerebral cortex. Two articles are especially helpful in understanding its development: G. I. Poliakov's 'Some Results of Research into the Development of the Neuronal Structure of the Cortical Ends of the Analyzers in Man',[138] and Miguel Marin-Padilla's two-part article, 'Prenatal and Early Postnatal Ontogenesis of the Human Motor Cortex: A Golgi Study'.[139]

Poliakov, in his article, describes the types of neuronal networks found in the motor cortex at different stages of the

---

[136] Jacobson, op. cit., p. 422.   [137] Ibid., p. 425.
[138] *Journal of Comparative Neurology*, Volume 117, 1961, pp. 197-212.
[139] *Brain Research*, Volume 23, 1970, pp. 167-91. Part I deals with the sequential development of the cortical layers (pp. 167-83), while part II is concerned with the basket-pyramidal system (pp. 185-91).

individual's development, and discusses their functional significance. He distinguishes three main types of systems, which
he refers to as the cortical projectional system, the cortical
projectional-associative system, and the system of associative
cortical connections proper. These involve, as we shall see,
neurons in different layers of the cortex, and they develop at
different times.

The central development during the prenatal period involves the cortical projectional system. It consists of a 'complex of neurons which are specialized in establishing two-way
cortico-subcortical projectional connections coupled on the
level of layer V'.[140] The important neurons in this complex
are the large pyramidal cells of layer V, together with the
stellate cells which function to switch incoming impulses over
to them, and which are found in layers IV and V. Pathways
originating in this zone lead, in turn, to the lower reflex
centres. It is this system of interneuronal connections that
'develops and matures earliest in ontogenesis, being in the
main formed at birth.'[141]

The development of the other two types of systems takes
place after birth. First, there is the projectional–associative
system of connections, which are coupled on the lower level
of layer III. The establishment of this system depends upon
the rapid postnatal growth of the bodies and dendritic
branches of large pyramidal cells located in sublayer III_3.
Commenting on these cells, Poliakov says:

> ... these cells originate cortico-cortical connections which are particu-
> larly developed in man and which form the foundation of the entire
> edifice of the cortical associative activity and of the functional connec-
> tions between the analyzers and within the cortical zones of the analyzers.
> The growth of these neurons is accompanied by the intensive develop-
> ment of the dendrite and especially axonal branchings of the star cells
> which are linked up with them; these cells are grouped in layer IV and
> sublayer III_3 ...[142]

Poliakov also emphasizes the difference in the time of development of these first two systems: 'The system of cortical
projectional-associative connections develop and mature
much later than the system of the cortical projectional

---

[140] Poliakov, op. cit., p. 200.   [141] Ibid., p. 202.   [142] Ibid.

connections. Apparently, it becomes sufficiently mature only by the beginning of the second year of life.'[143]

The final system to develop is that of associative cortical connections proper. The coupling here occurs on layer II and on the middle and upper sublayers of layer III. Poliakov points out that the neurons on these levels—particularly the multiform star neurons with short axons—are, in general, 'obviously immature' at the time of birth, and that they undergo, during postnatal ontogenesis, 'a gradual and greatly protracted maturation.'[144]

What is the significance of this final system of neuronal connections? Poliakov, on the basis of investigations carried out by others, says that this system of connections in the higher layers of the cortex, involving small neurons with a delicate structure, is 'one of the most characteristic specific features of the brain of primates, as distinct from all other mammals,' and that it presumably is of 'great significance' with respect to the development of higher mental functions.[145]

Let us now turn to the studies of the development of the human motor cortex carried out by Miguel Marin-Padilla. His description of the prenatal development of different layers may be summarized as follows. At a gestational age of five months, layers I, V, and VI can be identified, and possibly also the beginning of layer III.[146] Of these, layer I is the most advanced. By seven months, layer I has acquired mature characteristics, layer III is developing, layers II and IV are beginning to form, and layers V and VI are well established.[147] By seven and a half months, layer IV has undergone considerable development, and layer III has subdivided into upper and lower regions.[148]

To appreciate Marin-Padilla's description of the postnatal development of the motor cortex, one needs to know something about the basket-pyramidal system which he discusses in Part II of his article:

The existence in the human cortex of a cortical basket cell, a specific type of stellate interneuron with a short axon having terminal pericellular

---

[143] Ibid.   [144] Ibid.   [145] Ibid., p. 203.
[146] Op. cit., pp. 169–71.   [147] Ibid., pp. 171–3.   [148] Ibid., pp. 173–5.

baskets has been reported recently. The morphological characteristics of these neurons, their cortical distribution and the behavior of their axons suggests a functional interaction between them and pyramidal cells. These two types of neuron together form an intra-cortical basket-pyramidal system.[149]

This system involves several overlapping sets of horizontal connections between pyramidal cells and cortical basket cells, on different cortical layers. There are the giant basket cells of layer V; the large basket cells of lower layer III; the medium-sized ones of upper layer III; and finally, the small cortical basket cells of layer II. Each of these appears to form connections with the pyramidal cells on the same level, and also, where possible, with pyramidal cells on the layers or sub-layers immediately above or immediately below. The establishment of these synaptic contacts involves the formation of pericellular baskets around the bodies of the pyramidal cells. The formation of pericellular baskets is thus an indicator of the functional maturity of the relevant part of the basket-pyramidal system.[150]

Let us now consider Marin-Padilla's description of the postnatal development of the motor cortex. In the new-born infant, many pericellular baskets can be found at levels IV and V, and at lower level III, and Marin-Padilla says that the cortical cells at these levels can be considered mature. This is not the case with upper level III or with level II. Here the basket cells are immature, and no pericellular baskets are to be found.[151]

By two and a half months after birth, the pericellular baskets of layer V and lower layer III have increased both in number and complexity. A few pericellular baskets are also found in upper level III, so that the cortical basket cells of this sublayer may also be regarded as having reached maturity. In contrast, no pericellular baskets are to be found in layer II, where the basket cells are still immature.[152]

Between two and a half and eight months there is a considerable increase in the number of neuronal processes.[153] However the motor cortex is not fully mature even at eight months after birth. In particular, the cortical basket cells of

---

[149] Ibid., p. 185.   [150] Ibid., pp. 189-90.   [151] Ibid., pp. 175-6.
[152] Ibid., pp. 177-8 and 187.   [153] Ibid., p. 178.

layer II are still immature, and no pericellular baskets are to be found at this level in the cortex.[154]

The result is this. Of the four horizontal strata of connections between pyramidal cells and cortical basket cells involved in the basket-pyramidal system, two appear to be functional at least to some extent at birth: that involving the giant cortical basket cells of layer V, and that involving the large basket cells of the lower part of level III. The strata involving medium-sized cortical basket cells on the upper part of layer III apparently does not begin to be functional until around two and a half months, and even then it can be at most only partially so, since both the number of pericellular baskets on that level, and the number of processes, increases considerably in the following months. Finally, there is the horizontal system of connections involving small basket cells on layer II. The synaptic connections here have not even begun to be established at eight months after birth.

The general picture that emerges from the accounts of Poliakov and Marin-Padilla, put very simply, is this. The motor cortex is the region of the human cerebral cortex that is most developed at birth. However even its development is very far from complete. Functioning systems of neuronal connections are confined to the lower levels of the motor cortex. According to Poliakov, these are cortico-subcortical projectional systems. The cortical projectional-associative systems and the associative systems proper involve neuronal connections on the upper layers of the cortex, and these develop only postnatally, and over an extended period of time.

This picture of the development of the motor cortex agrees very well with the observations made by Conel, and the conclusions drawn by him, in his general study of the postnatal development of the human cerebral cortex. In his study of one-month-old infants Conel found that layer III is much less advanced than layers V and VI, and layer II the least developed of all, throughout the entire isocortex.[155] His conclusions in the case of three-month-old infants were as follows:

---

[154] Ibid., p. 187.   [155] Conel, op. cit., volume 2, p. 134.

On the basis of development it would seem that any function which the cerebral cortex may have at the age of three months would be almost entirely confined to the cells in layers V and VI, with possibly a little function in the cells in layer IV and the lower part of layer III. In all parts of the isocortex the cells in layers V and VI are more advanced in development than those in any other layers. Proceeding externally from layer V all nine of the criteria gradually diminish in degree of development. Layer II is so poorly developed that the cells are probably not functioning in conducting nerve impulses, even in those areas of the cortex which are the most advanced in development. Layer I is also poorly developed.[156]

Given the preceding discussion as background, it is now possible to set out, in relatively brief fashion, a number of considerations, based upon facts about the differentiation of neuronal processes and the formation of synaptic connections, which make it extraordinarily unlikely that the cerebral cortex of a human within a week or so after birth contains the necessary physical basis of those psychological states and capacities that are essential if something is to be a person.

The first consideration rests upon a very general fact about the human brain. To wit, that there is a tremendous increase in connectivity during postnatal development. Jacobson, for example, points out that 'axodendritic synapses are formed over an extended period during postnatal growth of dendrites',[157] and he goes on, a little later, to talk about the 'stupendous increase in connectivity, which mainly consists of axodendritic synapses . . .'[158] It is possible, of course, that this great increase in synaptic connections is not required for the existence of the psychological capacities in question, but that seems very unlikely. Given the rather limited psychological capacities exhibited by most non-human animals, even when their brains are mature and the interconnections fully established, it would be rather surprising if humans were psychologically more advanced even at a time when only a small proportion of the neuronal connections had been established.

The second consideration turns upon a distinction between *radial* (or columnar) connectivity and *tangential* connectivity. The former serves to establish links among different layers of

---

[156] Ibid., volume 3, p. 148.
[157] Jacobson, op. cit., p. 187.   [158] Ibid., p. 192.

the cortex, and between cortical and subcortical areas of the brain. The latter involves connections that are, roughly, within a given cortical layer. It is clear that the complexity of the circuitry will increase radically with the presence of both types of connections. This situation, however, comes about only postnatally. For as Jacobson points out, the 'tangential organization of dendrites develops only during the postnatal period'.[159] And in the case of man in particular, during the first twenty-four months after birth.[160] So it would seem most unlikely that the connectivity found in the brain of a new-born human provides an adequate physical basis for higher mental functions.

This point is related to a hypothesis advanced by the great Spanish neurobiologist, Ramon y Cajal. In a paper discussing the function of short-axoned cells known as Golgi type II neurons, he offers reasons for thinking that these neurons are of 'great importance',[161] and that their probable significance is that they play a role in the higher mental functions of man.[162] The connection between these two points lies in the fact that 'an important part of this tangential connectivity of the cerebral cortex is provided by the Golgi type II neurons, whose dendrites develop much later than those of the pyramidal neurons'.[163]

The third consideration involves the time of development of different cortical layers. Poliakov, in his discussion of the neuronal development of the cerebral cortex, refers to studies which, he says, show that:

. . . the accumulation in the upper levels of the cortical cross-section of cellular elements having a small size and a delicate structure is, along with other morphological peculiarities, one of the most characteristic specific features of the brain of primates, as distinct from all other mammals. There is no doubt that this feature of the cortical organization bears a direct relation to the qualitative transformations which the systems of analyzers undergo in the course of transition from the brain of insectivora to the brain of the primate type.[164]

---

[159] Ibid., p. 74.   [160] Ibid.
[161] Santiago Ramon y Cajal, 'Significacion Probable de las Celulas Nerviosas de Cilindro-eje Corto', in *Trabajos del Instituto Cajal de Investigaciones Biologicas*, Volume 44, 1952, pp. 1–8. See p. 2.
[162] Ibid., p. 7–8.   [163] Jacobson, op. cit., p. 74.
[164] Op. cit., p. 203.

Because of this, Poliakov concludes that 'the groups of neurons of the superficial cortical layers are of particularly great significance for the development of the higher nervous activity of the child. . . .'[165]

This view is echoed by Conel, who in his discussion of the cerebral cortex of the month-old infant remarks that the 'inner layers of the cortex are quite generally assumed by investigators to subserve the more primitive movements, while layers II and III are more particularly involved in higher associational functions.'[166]

If this is right, and if it is also the case, as Conel maintains, that any functioning in the cerebral cortex at the age of three months is 'almost entirely confined to the cells in layers V and VI, with possibly a little function in the cells of layer IV and the lower part of layer III,'[167] then it is very unlikely that the cerebral cortex of a three-month-old human infant, let alone that of a new-born baby, contains the necessary physical basis of the higher mental functions.

The final consideration involves comparing other regions of the cerebral cortex with the primary motor region. Given that this is the most advanced region during the early stages of postnatal development, one can draw conclusions about other regions from information about the motor cortex. Two points seem especially significant. The first is based on the conclusions of the studies by Poliakov and Marin-Padilla summarized above, to the effect that, in the new-born human, functioning systems of neuronal connections are confined to the lower levels of the motor cortex, and take the form of cortico-subcortical projectional systems, while projectional-associative systems and associative systems proper, which involve higher levels of the cortex, develop only postnatally, over an extended period of time. In view of the further fact that the degree of neuronal development in the new-born cerebral cortex declines rapidly as one moves forward from the motor cortex, systems of the latter two sorts will certainly not be present in the more anterior regions of the frontal lobe.

The second point rests upon the disappearance of primitive

---

[165] Ibid.   [166] Op. cit., volume 2, p. 134.
[167] Op. cit., volume 3, p. 148.

reflexes, such as the grasping reflex and the Moro reflex. It has been suggested by Myrtle McGraw,[168] and this idea is now widely accepted, that the disappearance of primitive reflexes is due to the motor cortex's developing to the point where it can exercise control over the subcortical structures upon which the reflexes depend. Commenting upon this view, Conel says:

According to McGraw the infant at three months is just at the end of the inhibitory phase of the grasp reflex. The state of development of the cortex in the region of the hand in area FAγ suggests that some function is occurring, and supports her interpretation of this phenomenon of neuromuscular activity as an indication that the cortex is exercising an inhibitory influence upon subcortical function. Inhibition of muscular activity is probably the earliest function of the cortical efferent cells.[169]

It is of considerable interest, then, at what point primitive reflexes disappear. Consider the Moro reflex, where, in response to a sudden change of bodily position, or a loud noise, the baby's arms and legs stretch outwards, then draw inwards, with the fingers curled as if ready to clutch something. There will, of course, be individual differences in the time at which this reflex disappears, and the process is a gradual one. In general, however, one can say that the Moro reflex disappears at around ten to twelve weeks.[170]

As a consequence, even in the case of those systems of neuronal connections that are at least to some extent functional in the motor cortex at birth, viz., the systems of cortico-subcortical projectional connections, it is still several weeks before they have developed to the point where the cortex inhibits the primitive reflexes based upon subcortical structures. And given that the motor cortex is the most advanced part of the cerebral cortex at that time, it will only be at a somewhat later time that other areas of the cortex, particularly more anterior regions of the frontal lobe, have developed to the point where they play a comparable role in the individual's behaviour.

[168] Myrtle B. McGraw, *The Neuromuscular Maturation of the Human Infant*, 1943, especially pp. 10-12.

[169] Op. cit., volume 3, p. 146.

[170] Alison Jolly, op. cit., p. 64, gives the time as ten weeks. Many writers simply say 'around three months'.

In order to arrive at some conclusions about the development of the human brain I have considered, first, the myelination of axons, and second, the differentiation of neurons and the formation of synapses. This brings me to the final sort of evidence that needs to be considered, namely, that involving the measurement of certain electrical parameters.

A variety of electrical measurements can provide information about the functioning of the central nervous system. The most familiar technique is electroencephalography. There are voltage differences between different areas of the brain, and these change, usually with a frequency of between one and fifty fluctuations a second. These changes in potential differences can be picked up by electrodes attached to the head at different points, and the resulting recording is called an electroencephalogram (EEG).

Another technique involves the study of evoked electrical responses. Such responses are either specific or non-specific. Specific responses can be elicited only by stimulation belonging to a particular sensory modality, such as vision. Nonspecific responses can be elicited by stimuli belonging to different modalities. Specific responses take the form of transient voltage changes of definable form which are superimposed upon the background brain wave activity. Nonspecific responses either take the form of transient voltage changes of definable form, or they consist in an alteration of the type of background brain wave activity.

Still another technique involves measurement of electrical properties of individual neurons, such as the duration of action potentials, and changes in synaptic potentials. Several studies of this sort have been carried out on non-human animals after birth, such as cats and rabbits, and a number of significant findings have emerged, such as that there is a decline in the duration of the action potential as the animal matures. Commenting on these findings, Bergstrom says: 'These characteristics indicate a diminution in the random features of the spontaneously active brain cells during ontogenetic development; a connection is discernible between this finding and the capacity of the brain structures to mediate information. The results of the study indicate that the informative state of the brain becomes more effective with increasing age.'[171]

Such studies of unit cell activity have not, of course, been carried out with humans, so the discussion will have to be confined to studies of EEGs and evoked potentials. First, the development of EEGs. C. Dreyfus-Brisac offers the following summary of what is typically found in the case of premature infants with a gestational age of from five to seven months: 'The following are the common characteristic records made during this period: a discontinuous and occasionally paroxysmal tracing, no electroencephalographic reaction to various stimuli, and no difference between sleeping and waking tracings.'[172] A significant change takes place around a conceptional age of thirty-six to thirty-seven weeks, when a clear difference in the EEGs associated with wakefulness and with sleep is seen for the first time. Robert Ellingson, in a very useful article which summarizes the findings of a number of investigators, offers the following description of the EEG pattern typically found during periods of wakefulness from a conceptional age of eight months through the end of the first month after birth:

> During wakefulness the EEG consists of continuous semirhythmic and irregular activity, largely at 4–7/sec., with some low-voltage slower activity and occasional weak beta activity. This activity is diffusely distributed, and the beginning of bilateral synchrony may be seen, first in the rolandic region and later in the frontal areas. This continues to be the predominant picture during wakefulness through the end of the first month post-term.[173]

This pattern, in fact, undergoes little change—aside from a slight increase in the regularity of the semi-rhythmic activity —until three to four months after term. At that point a significant change takes place, with the emergence, in the occipital region, of a rhythm having a frequency of about four

[171] R. M. Bergstrom, 'Electrical Parameters of the Brain During Ontogeny', in R. J. Robinson, op. cit., pp. 15–37. See pp. 24–5.

[172] C. Dreyfus-Brisac, 'The Bioelectrical Development of the Central Nervous System During Early Life', in *Human Development*, edited by Frank Falkner, 1966, pp. 286–305. See p. 293.

[173] Robert J. Ellingson, 'The Study of Brain Electrical Activity in Infants', in *Advances in Child Development and Behavior*, edited by Lewis P. Lipsitt and Charles C. Spiker, Volume 3, 1967, pp. 53–97. See pp. 65–6.

per second. This later develops into what is called the alpha rhythm—a rhythm with a frequency of eight to thirteen per second, located in the posterior regions, more or less sinusoidal in form, present during relaxation with the eyes closed, and attenuated during attention:

Some investigators refuse to call the occipital rhythm in infants 'alpha', since it is less than 8/sec. in frequency. Lindsley (1939) and others have shown, however, that it has all of the other characteristics of the alpha rhythm, and further, it increases gradually in frequency until it reaches the alpha range (8-13/sec.). Whether the infantile occipital rhythm is called alpha or not is of little importance as long as it is clearly identified.[174]

By the end of the first year the frequency of the occipital rhythm usually increases to about six to seven per second, though it may be as high as ten per second.

What about the EEG patterns associated with sleeping states? Here it is necessary to distinguish between active sleep, which involves considerable rapid eye movement, irregular respiration and heart rate, and intermittent bodily movements, and quiet sleep, which involves little rapid eye movement or bodily movement, together with regular respiration and heart rate.

A clear distinction between these two types of sleep states emerges at the same time as a clear distinction between wakefulness and sleep, that is, at around thirty-six weeks. The EEG patterns associated with the two types of sleep are as follows:

During active sleep the EEG is dominated by more or less continuous irregular slow waves (0.5-3/sec.) mixed with some 4-6/sec. activity which tends to be more rhythmic, with low-voltage faster activity superimposed. The slowest components tend to be most prominent over the posterior regions of the brain. During quiet sleep the EEG is characterized by bursts of similar activity alternating with periods of relative inactivity lasting 2 or 3 to 10 seconds, rarely longer. This pattern is called *tracé alternant*.[175]

The two types of sleep alternate with each other. Initially, most sleep is of the active variety, but this changes as the organism matures, so that eventually eighty per-cent of sleep is quiet rather than active.

[174] Ibid., p. 67.   [175] Ibid., p. 69.

During postnatal development a number of significant changes take place in the EEG pattern associated with quiet sleep. One occurs at around four to six weeks, when the slow, continuous waves begin to develop 'sleep spindles'. These are intermittent bursts of waves of greater amplitude and higher frequencies—around ten to twelve per second. These sleep spindle bursts gradually become better formed, and by two months post-term they are quite prominent.[176]

A second major change in the EEG pattern is the emergence of spontaneous K-complexes: 'The K-complex is a specific brief series of waveforms, consisting of conspicuous deviations from the ongoing EEG tracing. K-complexes are similar to sensory evoked responses, and can probably be elicited by sensory stimulation at earlier ages, but they do not occur *spontaneously* during sleep until after five months.'[177]

The final point that needs to be considered concerning human EEG patterns involves their relation to the patterns found in other animals. Given the facts about brain development set out above, together with the fact that in so many aspects of brain development, ontogeny recapitulates phylogeny, one would tend to expect that the EEGs of many animals, at birth, would be quite similar to those of new-born humans, and that the postnatal development, at least initially, would be along rather similar lines. This is in fact the case. Thus the Scheibels, for example, in an article on the postnatal development of the cat brain, point out that: 'Records of electrocortical activity in the newborn kitten are generally similar to those reported for the human neonate, the rat, the rabbit, the dog, etc.'[178] They then go on to describe a number of changes in cat EEG patterns that parallel those found in the case of humans, such as 'progressive enhancement in resting frequency', 'the development of well-formed spindle bursts', and the onset of alpha rhythm.

[176] Ibid., pp. 70-1.
[177] Rene A. Spitz, Robert N. Emde, and David R. Metcalf, 'Further Prototypes of Ego Formation: A Working Paper from a Research Project on Early Development', in Stone, Smith, and Murphy, op. cit., pp. 558-66. See p. 561.
[178] Madge E. Scheibel and Arnold B. Scheibel, 'Selected Structural-Functional Correlations in Postnatal Brain', in *Brain Development and Behavior*, edited by M. B. Sterman, Dennis J. McGinty, and Anthony M. Adinolfi, 1971, pp. 1-21. See p. 10.

Let us now turn to the topic of evoked cortical responses, both specific and non-specific. In the case of the former we can confine our attention to responses to visual stimuli. The most important facts can be summarized quite briefly. To begin with, all normal, full-term human new-borns display visual evoked responses. However these responses differ in a number of respects from those found at later stages. In the first place, the wave-form of the evoked response is simpler in the case of the new-born. A more complex response, characteristic of adult humans, develops only later: 'By the end of the first year many subjects show a polyphasic response resembling that seen in the adult. Rarely, this pattern is seen as early as the first month post-term, but, on the other hand, it may not be seen until 2–3 years of age.'[179]

Secondly, evoked responses in new-born humans exhibit a latency roughly twice that found in adults—latency being defined as the time interval between the stimulus and the trough of the major positive wave of the evoked response. A rather striking feature of the change in latency is that the decline is rather gradual, and apparently linear, through about the third or fourth week post-term, at which point there is a sharp break in the curve, and a much steeper rate of decline.[180]

A third difference is with respect to fatigability:

A striking characteristic of visual evoked responses in the newborn is their fatigability, by which is meant relative inability to respond to stimuli arriving soon after a preceding stimulus. In some infants, especially prematures, 4–5 (or more) seconds must be allowed to elapse between stimuli lest the second and succeeding responses fail to occur. At 40 weeks conceptional age, one in ten infants will respond well at rates of 1/sec.; almost none will respond at 2/sec. . . . Ability to respond at higher rates of stimulation improves rapidly after birth.[181]

Next, non-specific, or as they are sometimes called, diffuse responses. These have received less attention than specific responses. The central point, given our interests here, is the difference between waking and sleeping states. During sleep, diffuse modifications of bioelectrical activity can be produced, from about the thirty-seventh week on, by a variety

---

[179] Ellingson, op. cit., p. 83.   [180] Ibid., p. 86.
[181] Ibid., pp. 86–7.

of stimuli.[182] The reaction usually takes the form of a flattening of the wave patterns. In waking states, in contrast, it is, as Dreyfus-Brisac points out, only considerably later that any diffuse response is present, and the form it takes is different from that found earlier in sleeping states: 'No diffuse electroencephalographic reactivity can be detected in newborn infants in waking states. The flattening of the sleeping EEG is different from the blocking reaction found in waking states after 3 months.'[183]

What is the significance of these findings? A precise answer is, unfortunately, not possible at present, since these bioelectrical phenomena are not yet fully understood. This is especially so as regards the genesis of EEG activity. However a number of significant interrelationships have been discovered. Some of these involve neurophysiological changes. Thus J. Scherrer, for example, notes that latency of evoked cortical response is closely related to myelination,[184] while Jacobson points out that: 'The growth of dendrites and the formation of axodendritic synapses in the cerebral cortex have been correlated with changes in the electroencephalogram and in evoked cortical electrical responses.'[185]

Most of the interrelationships, however, are with physiological and/or behavioural states, rather than with neurophysiological ones. Some of these correlations, such as those between EEG patterns and states of wakefulness, active sleep, and quiet sleep, have already been described. What needs to be emphasized, however, is the way in which behavioural and bioelectrical developments go hand in hand. Initially, it is very difficult to distinguish between active sleep and quiet sleep on the basis of the defining criteria such as presence of rapid eye movement, rate and regularity of respiration and heart beat. As the infant matures, the identification of these two sleep states becomes clearer, until by about three months of age, very clear differentiations can be made.[186] The EEG

[182] Dreyfus-Brisac, op. cit., pp. 296-7.
[183] Ibid., p. 298.
[184] J. Scherrer, in Minkowski, op. cit., p. 432.
[185] Op. cit., p. 188.
[186] Arthur H. Parmelee Jr., Waldemar H. Wenner, Yoshio Akiyama, Evelyn Stern, and Jenny Flescher, 'Electroencephalography and Brain Maturation' in Minkowski, op. cit., pp. 459-76. See p. 461.

patterns undergo a similar development: the differences between the EEGs associated with active sleep and quiet sleep are much greater at three months post-term than they are at term.

A number of other investigators have emphasized the relations between the development of sleeping states and changes in EEGs. An especially interesting discussion is found in the article by Rene A. Spitz, Robert N. Emde, and David R. Metcalf. They suggest that there are three crucial points in early EEG development, which they believe are of special significance with respect to the maturation of the central nervous system: 'The three points are aspects of quiet sleep development. They are the development of sleep spindles at four to six weeks, the development of Stage II sleep at about three months, and the development of spontaneous K-complexes at five to six months.'[187] Of these three 'nodal points', they consider the second the most significant: 'Thus it appears that the age of three months is a period of critical developmental importance. EEG and physiological patterns became more clearly organized and systematically integrated with certain behaviors such as drowsiness, sleep behaviors, and sleep cycles.'[188]

Another area of behaviour where there appear to be correlations with bioelectrical phenomena is motor development. Thus R. M. Bergstrom argues that the motor development of human individuals can be divided into seven stages, based upon the primitive reflexes and typical motor behaviour present at a given time, and that these seven stages can then be correlated with EEG maturation. Bergstrom refers to the last two stages as the 'lethargic active' and 'voluntary active' respectively. The former occupies the period from a gestational age of eight months through three months post-term, at about which time the final stage of development begins.[189]

It is interesting that Bergstrom, like Spitz, Emde, and Metcalf, thinks that a significant transition occurs at around the age of three months. This view is, in fact, very widely shared by investigators in this area, due to the clustering

---

[187] Op. cit., p. 562. [188] Ibid.
[189] R. M. Bergstrom, op. cit., pp. 28–30.

together of a number of significant changes at this time. Robert Ellingson, for example, remarks that

The end of the third month of life is a period especially to be noted. At this time the occipital rhythm appears, lending a distinct topographical organization to the EEG, and the response of blocking of the rhythm to sensory or psychic stimulation becomes established. The photic following response becomes more clear-cut than it has previously been, and the latency of visual evoked responses achieves almost the adult level. On the behavioral side, primitive reflexes disappear, oculomotor coordination improves strikingly, prehension is developing, and smiling in social situations is established.[190]

In a similar vein, Jerome Kagan points out that the 'onset of a special reaction to discrepancy between two and three months is paralleled by other physiological and behavioural changes in the infant',[191] and he refers to many of the features mentioned by Ellingson in the preceding passage. Kagan then goes on to suggest that: 'Perhaps the infant's capacity to react to discrepancy at this age reflects the fact that the brain has matured enough to permit the establishment of long-term memories and their activation by external events.'[192]

A final investigator who deserves to be mentioned in this connection is Michael Lewis. In addition to the facts cited by Ellingson, Lewis refers to his own findings on the development, from three months onward, of response decrement, and to a study of the DNA content of the brains of children that died before the age of six months: 'The DNA content in the brain showed a rapid increase reaching an asymptote at about three to four months of age.'[193] And Lewis suggests that this large, and growing body of facts about changes taking place around the age of three months, lends support to the hypothesis that a significant cerebral reorganization takes place at that time.

This cluster of changes occurring at around three months is certainly striking, and the suggestion that it reflects a significant underlying cerebral development is surely plausible. It is quite another question, however, whether any of these changes, or combination of them, is morally significant, let alone representing the point at which the individual becomes

---

[190] Op. cit., p. 68.
[192] Ibid.

[191] Op. cit., p. 680.
[193] Op. cit., p. 194.

a person. These issues will be touched upon, albeit briefly, in section 11.6. In this section the discussion is to be confined, as was indicated earlier, to the question of whether neonates are persons.

11.55 Conclusion

Are new-born humans persons? The considerations outlined above establish, I believe, that the answer must be no—unless one is prepared to defend an account of person-making characteristics that differs radically from those canvassed in chapter 5. For in the first place, the behaviour of new-born humans provides no ground for attributing higher mental capacities to them. In particular, it provides no reason at all for believing that new-born humans possess a capacity for thought, or for self-consciousness, or for rational deliberation. All the behavioural evidence indicates that such capacities emerge only much later in the individual's development.

The neurophysiological data point to the same conclusion. The neuronal circuitry in the human brain undergoes, in general, tremendous development during the postnatal period. What is crucial, however, is that those networks, located in the upper layers of the cerebral cortex, that are thought to underlie higher mental functions, are not present at birth; their emergence takes place only over an extended period of postnatal development.

Finally, there is the bioelectrical evidence. This evidence is less direct, and its significance not yet fully understood. The bioelectrical changes taking place postnatally do, however, cohere very well with the behavioural and neurophysiological data, and thus lend additional support to the conclusions based upon those data.

11.6 Infanticide Destroys Quasi-Persons

In discussing moderate positions on abortion in chapter 8, I mentioned the possibility of a person-making property that admits of degrees, and that, moreover, is morally significant even when present to a lesser extent than is required if something is to be a person. Let us say that an entity is a *quasi-person* if and only if there is such a property, which that entity possesses, but not to the extent required to make it a person. The question, then, is whether new-born humans are quasi-persons.

First, however, the prior issue of whether there is such a property. As mentioned earlier, I am *somewhat* inclined to think there is. My reason is that, first, the sort of unification of consciousness over time that makes something a subject of non-momentary interests does appear to admit of degrees, and second, it seems that the extent to which most individuals value their own continued existence depends upon the extent to which they are going to enjoy a consciousness that is unified over time.

Try to imagine, for example, what it would be like to be unable to conceive of one's own existence as extending backwards more than a day into the past. This exercise is rather more difficult than it might initially seem. For while there is no problem in imagining what it would be like for one's memory to be limited to a very short period of time, it is considerably more difficult to imagine one's ability even to conceive of the past as restricted in the same way. It is tempting to suppose that if one can form the concept of events that happened five minutes ago, and of events that happened five minutes before that, and so on, up to, say, events that happened twenty-four hours ago, then surely one can extend that process a step further, and conceive of events that happened twenty-four hours and five minutes ago. However, though I cannot argue the issue here, I believe there is nothing incoherent in the idea of a mind that suffers from precisely this sort of limitation.

Assume, for the sake of argument, that this is right, and imagine contracting a disease that makes it impossible either to envisage a future, or to imagine a past, extending more than some time period t beyond the present. An operation is possible, leading with probability p to a complete cure, and with probability $(1 - p)$ to death. I suggest that if t were quite large, say a billion years, very few people would choose the operation, even if p were very close to one, while if t were rather small, say five seconds, most people would choose the operation even if the likelihood of success were very low indeed. If so, the value that most people assign to their own continued existence is a function of their beliefs about the extent to which they will be able, in that continued existence, to envisage a future and conceive of a past.

This line of thought is tied to a particular view of what it is that makes something a person. Might it not be possible to advance an argument not so tied? Perhaps. One line of thought that seems to have tempted some philosophers turns upon the continuity exhibited by an individual's physiological development. The idea seems to be that, in view of this continuity, all changes will be by degrees, so that it will be impossible to draw sharp lines that are morally significant. This appears, for example, to be Jonathan Glover's view. For in a section in which he argues in support of 'the inadequacy of sharp boundaries' separating persons from non-persons, he appeals, among other things, to the fact that 'the transition from fertilized egg to adult, like many biological developments, can better be represented by a fairly steady upward curve than by a series of obviously discrete stages with abrupt transitions'.[194]

This line of thought would seem, however, to be unsound. The properties of a complex system often change in radical and discontinuous fashion, even when they depend entirely upon properties of parts of the system, and the latter are changing in a gradual, continuous fashion. Continuity of an individual's physiological development could, therefore, be accompanied by discontinuous changes in the individual's psychological capacities, and this could be so even if the mind turns out to be identical with the brain. Continuity at the physiological level provides no reason, then, for thinking that morally significant changes in the developing individual will necessarily be by degrees. So the present argument cannot be accepted. I suspect, moreover, that any argument for the general conclusion that, regardless of what it is that makes something a person, that property must admit of degrees, all of which are morally significant, will turn out to be defective. The issue can only be addressed, I suggest, given some specific account of what it is that makes something a person.

[194] Jonathan Glover, *Causing Death and Saving Lives*, 1977, pp. 126-7.

Some accounts will leave room for the category of quasi-persons; others will not. If, for example, the possession of any capacity for thought, however limited, suffices to make something a person, there would not seem to be any room for quasi-persons. On the other hand, if the morally relevant property is a capacity for rational thought, or a capacity for rational deliberation, it certainly seems possible to view these properties as ranging along a continuous spectrum. Indeed, given the gradual changes in cognitive capacities from one species to another, this is perhaps the most plausible view. So on these other accounts too, one might very well want to introduce the category of quasi-persons.

In any case, let us assume, for the sake of the present discussion, that there is such a property. Is the killing of new-born humans then open to the objection that it involves the destruction of quasi-persons? I do not believe that it is. On the view that I have advanced, something is a person if it is a subject of non-momentary interests. This in turn requires a unification of consciousness over time—a unification that involves, among other things, the having of thoughts. A quasi-person will differ from a person not in the complete absence of some of these properties, but in their possession to a lesser degree. A quasi-person will be a subject of non-momentary interests, but of a more restricted sort. It will enjoy a consciousness that is to some extent unified over time, but by means of thoughts limited in certain ways. Something that enjoys no thoughts at all is not only not a person: it is not a quasi-person either. Therefore, since there is no reason for believing that new-born humans enjoy any thought-episodes, neither is there any reason for believing that they are quasi-persons.

The situation is essentially the same given other accounts. For although some accounts do not require that something has enjoyed thought-episodes in order to be a person, all of the plausible accounts require that something possess, or have possessed, the capacity for thought. Given that there is excellent reason for holding that new-born humans do not possess any capacity for thought, these alternative accounts also lead to the conclusion that new-born humans are not quasi-persons.

When, then, do humans become quasi-persons? Much more scientific research and philosophical reflection is needed if a well-founded answer is to be offered. If forced to speculate, the age of three months might be as reasonable a guess as any. In part because of the number of striking changes clustering together at around that time, and in part because some of those changes appear to be related in important ways to cognitive developments. Particularly noteworthy in this respect is the development of response decrement. In his article, 'Individual Differences in the Measurement of Early Cognitive Growth', Michael Lewis points out that there is 'a large and impressive quantity of literature' linking dysfunction of the central nervous system with response decrement in non-human animals, as well as in human infants and adults.[195] He also notes that the rate of response decrement varies across species in a systematic way, namely, 'as a function of higher nervous activity as seen in different animals along the phylogenetic scale'.[196] And finally, Lewis points out that there are significant relations between rate of response decrement, and various tests and measures of cognitive capacity: 'Moreover there was a positive relationship between amount of response decrement and other learning tasks—two-choice discrimination and concept formation. Finally IQ at 4 was related to response decrement at one year. The data strongly support the view that response decrement . . . is a sensitive predictor of individual differences in a wide range of cognitive tasks and reflects efficient CNS functioning.'[197]

There is some reason, then, for thinking that the emergence of at least a limited capacity for thought-episodes may take place at about the age of three months. Therefore, if the property that makes something a person does admit of degrees, and is morally significant to whatever degree it is present, there will also be some reason for thinking that humans become quasi-persons at about three months of age.

The general picture that emerges is as follows. New-born humans are neither persons nor even quasi-persons, and their destruction is in no way intrinsically wrong. At about the age

---

[195] Op. cit., p. 201.   [196] Ibid.   [197] Ibid., p. 205.

of three months, however, they probably acquire properties that are morally significant, and that make it to some extent intrinsically wrong to destroy them. As they develop further, their destruction becomes more and more seriously wrong, until eventually it is comparable in seriousness to the destruction of a normal adult human being.

Acceptance of this 'moderate' view of infanticide would need to be accompanied by a position on the killing of non-human animals that falls between the view commonly accepted by most vegetarians—to the effect that the killing of all animals is seriously wrong—and the standard assumption of present-day Western society—that animals are fair game, and may be destroyed for quite trivial reasons. The wrongness of killing non-human animals would have to be seen as varying from one species to another. Members of some species would not even be quasi-persons, and hence their destruction would be in no way intrinsically wrong. Members of other species would be quasi-persons, and their destruction therefore wrong to a greater or lesser degree. Finally, normal adult members of some species—such as, perhaps, chimpanzees, whales, and dolphins—might be persons, so that their destruction would be comparable to the destruction of normal adult human beings.

Though I find this general outlook on the morality of killing attractive, it is far from clear to me whether it will turn out to be correct. I do believe that it is a view that is eminently worth considering. The crucial point in the present context, however, is that even if it is right, it does not provide any reason for holding that infanticide, in the case of new-born humans, is morally wrong.

11.7 The Consequences of Accepting Infanticide

The six arguments considered in the preceding sections of this chapter all attempted to establish the conclusion that the killing of new-born humans is seriously wrong in itself, independently of its consequences. This final argument, in contrast, attempts to show that the practice of infanticide, even if not intrinsically wrong, is nevertheless morally unacceptable, because it is likely to have quite disastrous consequences.

Different suggestions have been advanced as to the undesirable consequences of admitting the practice of infanticide. The two most important are these. First, it has been contended that acceptance of infanticide will result in diminished respect for the lives of other human beings. A society that has no qualms about destroying human infants, when it is socially useful to do so, will rapidly come to accept the view that it is morally permissible to destroy other human beings, such as the weak, the handicapped, and the elderly, when that is socially useful.[198]

Second, it has been suggested that acceptance of infanticide will lead to a weakening of parental feeling. People will come to have less concern for those offspring they do not destroy, and treat them more harshly than they would in a society where infanticide was rejected. Besides being undesirable in itself, such a reduction in tenderness and consideration cannot but have an adverse effect upon the personality development of the children so treated.

If acceptance of infanticide did have either of these consequences, there would be a serious reason for prohibiting it, even if it is not wrong in itself. The crucial issue, then, is whether there is good reason to believe that acceptance of the practice of infanticide will, as a matter of empirical fact, have either of these consequences.

The train of thought underlying the claim that acceptance of infanticide will lead to a weakening of respect for the lives of other human beings seems to be this. If one accepts infanticide, one is willing in some cases to accept violations of the principle that one ought not kill innocent human beings, and doing this will surely make one more willing to countenance violations of that principle in other cases, especially when it is socially useful to do so.

The preceding discussion makes it clear that this argument rests upon an untenable assumption, namely, that it is membership in a particular biological species, *Homo sapiens*, that makes it at least prima facie wrong to kill certain individuals. The argument crumbles once it is realized that the

---

[198] R. J. Gerber advances an argument of this sort, albeit directed against abortion rather than infanticide, in his rather emotional article, 'Abortion: Parameters for Decision', *Ethics*, Volume 82, 1972, pp. 137–54. See pp. 151–4.

basic moral principles dealing with killing will contain no reference to particular species. If it is persons (and perhaps quasi-persons) that it is wrong to destroy, and if new-born humans are not persons (nor quasi-persons), then to accept infanticide in the case of new-born humans is not to accept the violation of a moral principle. And so there is no reason for concluding that people will thereby become more prone to violate the relevant moral principles when it is socially useful to do so.

Still, it might be argued that even if the basic moral principles involved here are to be formulated in terms of persons (and perhaps quasi-persons), rather than in terms of human beings, the vast majority of people do think in terms of human beings. So acceptance of infanticide will tend to lessen the sense that most people have of the wrongness of killing human beings who are persons.

This line of argument is not without *some* force. But in response it may be urged, first, that the force is considerably less than proponents are wont to believe, and second, that there are more important counterbalancing considerations.

In the first place, then, the above argument appears to overestimate radically the extent to which people hold, as a *basic* moral principle, that the killing of human beings is wrong. The willingness of most people to accept termination of life in cases of irreparable brain damage, and in abortions performed early in pregnancy, suggests that most people recognize, even if not in a very clear or explicit fashion, that what ultimately matters is not membership in a particular species, but whether one enjoys, or is capable of enjoying, a certain sort of mental life. This means that the moral change being envisaged here is not a matter of adopting a radically new position. It is simply a matter of formulating a clear and explicit moral perspective congruent with the underlying intuitions that people already have concerning basic moral principles.

At the same time, it is clear that there will be some people for whom the change in moral outlook will be a substantial one, and it seems likely that for some of these there will be a weakening of their sense of the sanctity of human life which may not be immediately replaced by a heightened sense of the sanctity of persons. But against this possibility, there are important gains to be weighed. In the first place, there is the general point that it is always desirable for society's moral principles to be ones that accurately capture right-making and wrong-making characteristics, provided that the more accurate principles are not significantly more complicated—a condition that is certainly satisfied in the present case. Second, there are specific features of choice situations involving abortion which mean that the difference to society between sound moral principles and unsound ones can be very great indeed. As long as one continues to think in terms of the principle that it is prima facie seriously wrong to kill any member of the species *Homo sapiens*, one must prohibit abortions in all but a very few circumstances. Adopting unsound principles means, then, that large numbers of women will be compelled either to bear children they do not wish to bear, or to seek criminal abortions. The cost of this in terms of human suffering is obviously very great.

The other important consequence which some have thought will follow from acceptance of the practice of infanticide is that parents will behave with less tenderness toward their offspring. At least three considerations tell against this contention. First, in spite of the fact that people do not usually regard non-human animals as persons, they still believe that it is morally wrong to treat them cruelly. Why should it be different with human infants if people come to view them as sentient beings that are only potential persons? Second, most people are deeply attached to their children simply because they are their children. Third, there is the evidence provided by societies in which infanticide was an accepted practice. As was noted in section 10.2, the testimony of anthropologists indicates that the tenderness with which parents treated those children that were allowed to live, and the concern they exhibited for the well-being of them, were by no means inferior to what is typical in our own society.

In conclusion, then, there do not appear to be strong consequentialist grounds for rejecting infanticide. For while it is not implausible to think that there may be some negative consequences associated with acceptance of infanticide, for some people, there would also seem to be excellent reason for thinking that these effects will be short term ones, and that they will be significantly outweighed by the positive consequences that will flow from the adoption of sound moral principles in this area.

PART IV

12

Summary and Conclusions

If the line of thought pursued above is correct, neither abortion, nor infanticide, at least during the first few weeks after birth, is morally wrong. This conclusion rests upon a number of claims, some normative, some purely factual. In this chapter I shall offer a brief synopsis which focuses upon the central issues, and upon some of the more important considerations of method which have guided the discussion.

The central normative questions that were considered, and which seem crucial for an understanding of the moral issues raised by abortion and infanticide, were these. First, is membership in a biological species morally significant in itself? Second, what properties are necessary and/or sufficient for a an entity to be a person? Third, do any of the properties which suffice to make something a person admit of degrees? If so, are they morally significant even when not present to the extent required to make something a person? Fourth, is it morally wrong to destroy potential persons? Fifth, is it wrong to refrain from producing additional persons, or additional persons whose lives will be happy, or satisfying, or desirable in other respects?

With regard to the first issue, I argued that basic moral principles should involve neither terms referring to particular biological species, nor the general concept of membership in a biological species. It follows that the fact that abortion and infanticide result in the destruction of innocent human beings cannot, in itself, be a reason for viewing such actions as wrong.

A number of answers to the question what makes something a person were surveyed. It was argued that the most plausible view is that it is being a subject of non-momentary interests that makes something a person. If this is right, there are a number of necessary conditions that something must satisfy if it is to be a person, including the possession, either now or at some time in the past, of a sense of time, of a concept of a continuing subject of mental states, and of a capacity for thought episodes.

The property of being a subject of non-momentary interests appears, I suggested, to admit of degrees, and to be significant to whatever extent it is present. If so, and if it is indeed this property that makes something a person, one needs to introduce another moral category—that of quasi-persons—to cover those individuals who possess that property to some extent, but not to the extent characteristic of full-fledged persons, such as normal adult human beings.

Is the destruction of potential persons wrong in itself? Several arguments bearing upon this question were canvassed. Some were directed toward the conclusion that there is nothing wrong with the destruction of potential persons. The more important arguments, however, established at best a more modest, conditional conclusion. To wit, that it is wrong to destroy potential persons only if it is equally wrong to refrain from producing additional persons.

Is it wrong to refrain from producing additional persons? Or at least, additional persons with certain characteristics? This is, I believe, quite a difficult issue. Some very interesting arguments have recently been advanced in support either of the contention that there is a prima-facie obligation to produce additional people if it can be known that they will lead satisfying lives, or of the contention that it is at least an intrinsically good thing to produce such people. In my discussion, I attempted to show that none of these arguments is ultimately sound. I also attempted to suggest quite a general moral perspective that seems antecedently plausible, and that entails the conclusion that there cannot be a prima-facie obligation to produce additional people, even ones who will be very happy, or who will lead lives that are in themselves especially satisfactory in some respect.

These were the central normative issues. If the views advanced above on these normative issues are roughly correct, the moral status of abortion and infanticide turns upon a crucial question of a purely factual sort. At what time does a human being become a person? Or a quasi-person, if the latter concept is a morally sound one? In approaching these factual questions, I began by considering a metaphysical attempt to demonstrate that humans are persons from conception onwards. After indicating why such a line of argument is unsatisfactory, I turned to a relatively detailed examination of the relevant empirical evidence concerning the psychological and neurophysiological development of human beings. The conclusion of that survey was that the empirical evidence makes it most unlikely that new-born humans are quasi-persons, let alone persons.

There is an important point concerning this conclusion that probably needs to be emphasized very strongly, namely, that it does *not* rest upon the view that I advanced as to the properties that make something a person. For one point appears to be common to all plausible accounts of what it is that makes something a person: an entity cannot be a person unless it possesses, or has previously possessed, the capacity for thought. And the psychological and neurophysiological evidence makes it most unlikely that humans, in the first few weeks after birth, possess this capacity.

No attempt was made to determine the precise time at which humans in general become persons or quasi-persons. I did suggest that in view of a number of quite significant developments clustering together at around ten to twelve weeks, it may be that humans become quasi-persons at about that time. This suggestion was, however, a highly tentative one. Any serious attempt to determine the point at which a human being becomes a person, or a quasi-person, would require scientific information not presently available, together with a rather more precise account of the properties that make something a person.

These, then, are the main steps in the line of thought that justifies, I believe, a liberal position on abortion, and a somewhat radical view of infanticide. In setting out this line of thought, I have had two main objectives in mind. In the first place, the issues of the morality of abortion and infanticide are of grave practical import, and I have tried to offer a circumspect and explicit statement of the view of the matter that I believe to be the most plausible, together with a cogent defence of that view. Second, I have tried to make it clear why certain issues are crucial ones. This I believe to be an important undertaking, given that the issues on which the discussion has focused here are ones that are rarely even touched upon in public discussions of abortion in the press and other media, in political forums, and within vocal lobby groups on both sides of the abortion 'debate'. There is, I feel, little hope for anything remotely resembling a consensus on the abortion issue until a significant number of people begin to think about the issues in a philosophically informed way.

Philosophical discussions, of course, can themselves go astray in a variety of ways. I should like to conclude by pointing to some possible dangers, and by drawing attention to some methodological points that have guided the present discussion. The first point is that a satisfactory account of the morality of abortion is, in my opinion, unlikely to be forthcoming if one attempts to approach the question of abortion in isolation from that of the morality of infanticide. I realize that this observation will not commend itself to many defenders of a liberal view of abortion. They would like very much to embrace abortion without having to take infanticide on board as well. But this attitude is generally based, I believe, upon the unjustified belief that we just know that infanticide is wrong. This view, in turn, usually rests upon the assumptions that intuitions can provide, in general, a satisfactory basis for moral beliefs, and that, in particular, they can do so in the case of beliefs about the morality of infanticide. One objection to this approach concerns the question, discussed briefly in chapter 1, of whether one is ever justified in ascribing epistemic status to moral feelings. The crucial point, however, is the one developed in chapter 10—namely, that even if epistemic value is to be ascribed to moral feelings in many cases, there are excellent reasons for holding that the issue of infanticide is not one that can be decided by any appeal to moral feelings that are widely shared today.

There is a second way in which discussions of the morality of abortion can, and very often do, go astray. This is by treating the question of abortion in isolation from the question of the morality of killing non-human animals. It is very difficult indeed to arrive at a coherent moral outlook when this is done.

This point may be illustrated by considering the following set of views, which many people currently accept. Abortion is not morally wrong, at least when carried out sufficiently early in pregnancy. Infanticide is seriously wrong. The killing of non-human animals, even adult ones, on the other hand, is not wrong, or at least not seriously so. How is one to make sense of this combination of positions? If species membership were morally significant in itself, there would be no problem. But once that is set aside as irrelevant, it is very hard to see how all of these claims can be defended at the same time. One might, for example, try to justify the claim that infanticide is seriously wrong, while the killing of non-human animals is not, by appealing to the superior potentialities possessed by human infants. But this line of argument would force one to abandon the view that abortion is not morally wrong provided that it is performed sufficiently early. Alternatively, one might contend that the reason infanticide is seriously wrong, while the killing of non-human animals is not, is that the psychological capacities of human infants generally surpass those of adult members of non-human species. However this is simply not the case.

There are a number of morals to be drawn here. First, there is a grave danger that, if one discusses the question of the morality of abortion in isolation from the questions of the morality of infanticide and of the killing of nonhuman animals, one will wind up with a combination of views that is not rationally tenable.

Second, the interrelationships among these three questions provide another reason why the liberal on abortion should not dismiss infanticide on the ground that it conflicts with his or her moral feelings. The juxtaposition of abortion, infanticide, and the killing of non-human animals strongly suggests that the liberal on abortion is going to have to undertake serious revision of his or her moral views in one area or another. Either abortion is morally suspect, or infanticide is morally permissible, or the killing of at least some non-human animals is seriously wrong.

Third, when the questions of abortion, infanticide, and the killing of non-human animals are considered together, it becomes clear that unless potentialities are morally relevant, or unless there is a serious obligation to produce additional people, it is quite likely that the view of the morality of killing non-human animals that is so widely shared in present-day Western society stands in need of serious revision. How serious will depend upon a number of issues, of which the most relevant is whether the category of quasi-persons turns out to be a sound one. If it is not, and if it also turns out that humans do not become persons until, say, about the age of one, then it may be that revision of our moral views will be required only with respect to a few non-human species. But if, as seems to me more likely, the category of quasi-persons is a sound one, and humans become quasi-persons at around three months, then quite massive revision would seem to be called for.

When one does discuss the question of the morality of abortion without isolating it artificially from the questions of the morality of infanticide and of the killing of non-human animals, one is naturally led to the framework that has structured the present discussion. In particular, one is more or less forced to grapple with the question of the properties that make it seriously wrong to destroy something. The centrality of categories such as that of persons, potential persons, and possibly also, quasi-persons, then emerges very clearly. This happens much less frequently when the discussion is narrowly focused upon the issue of abortion.

I should like to conclude by suggesting that much more philosophical energy needs to be directed toward answering some of the questions considered here. There are, for example, a number of relatively plausible proposals as to the non-potential properties that make it intrinsically wrong to destroy something—independently of its value—and there is a dearth of arguments bearing upon the choice among these alternatives. Much more work needs to be done in this area, both with regard to the formulation of more precise alternatives, and especially with regard to the problem of justifying the choice of one alternative over another. One also needs to know whether the properties in question admit of degrees, and if so, whether they are morally significant to whatever extent they are present.

A second area that is, if anything, even more problematic,

concerns the question of whether there are any prima-facie obligations to produce additional people, or additional people with certain characteristics. In this area, at least, interesting arguments are being generated. The issues are, however, possibly as difficult as any in normative ethics, and they are very far from being settled.

Finally, it is important for philosophers working in this area to pay *much* more attention to scientific evidence bearing upon human development, and upon the relative psychological capacities of humans and non-humans. But it must also be said that the scientific information currently available is often deficient in precisely those respects that would be of most interest to philosophers, and of most assistance to them in their attempts to grapple with the questions of the moral status of humans and non-humans at various stages of development. What is needed, then, is much closer co-operation between, on the one hand, philosophers working in this area of ethics, and, on the other, scientists working in areas such as psychology and neurophysiology. There is, unfortunately, a tradition of splendid isolation that has grown up between philosophy and the sciences. While that endures, there is little hope that these issues can be completely resolved.

Bibliography

Anglin, William, 'The Repugnant Conclusion', *Canadian Journal of Philosophy*, Volume 7, 1977, pp. 745-55.

Aquinas, St. Thomas, *Summa Contra Gentiles*, Garden City, New York, 1955.

— *Summa Theologica*, New York, 1945.

Arey, Leslie Brainerd, *Developmental Anatomy*, 7th edition, Philadelphia, 1974.

Aristotle, *Politics*.

Armstrong, David M., *Nominalism and Realism—Universals and Scientific Realism*, Volume 1, Cambridge, 1978.

Ayer, A. J., *Language, Truth and Logic*, London, 1936.

Bayles, Michael (ed.), *Ethics and Population*, Cambridge, Massachusetts, 1976.

Benn, S. I., and Peters, R. S., *The Principles of Political Thought*, New York, 1965.

Benn, Stanley, 'Abortion, Infanticide, and Respect for Persons', in *The Problem of Abortion*, edited by Joel Feinberg, Belmont, California, 1973.

— 'Personal Freedom and Environmental Ethics: The Moral Inequality of Species', in *Equality and Freedom: International Comparative Jurisprudence*, Volume II, edited by Dorsey Grey, New York and Leiden, 1977, pp. 401-24.

Bennett, Jonathan, *Rationality*, London, 1964.

— 'Whatever the Consequences', *Analysis*, Volume 26, 1965, pp. 83-102.

— 'On Maximizing Happiness', in *Obligations to Future Generations*, edited by R. I. Sikora and Brian Barry, Philadelphia, 1978, pp. 61-73.

Bergstrom, R. M., 'Electrical Parameters of the Brain During Ontogeny', in *Brain and Early Behaviour*, edited by R. J. Robinson, London, 1969, pp. 15-37.

Bishop, John, 'More Thought on Thought and Talk', *Mind*, Volume 89, Number 353, 1980, pp. 1-16.

Blumenfeld, Jean Beer, 'Abortion and the Human Brain', *Philosophical Studies*, Volume 32, 1977, pp. 251-68.

Brandt, Richard B., *Ethical Theory*, Englewood Cliffs, New Jersey, 1959.

— 'The Morality of Abortion', the *Monist*, Volume 56, Number 4, 1972, pp. 503-26.

Brazier, Mary A. B. (ed.), *Growth and Development of the Brain*, New York, 1975.

Brody, Baruch A., 'Abortion and the Law', *Journal of Philosophy*, Volume 68, Number 12, 1971, pp. 357-69.
— 'Morality and Religion Reconsidered', pp. 592-603 in *Readings in the Philosophy of Religion: The Analytic Approach*, edited by Baruch A. Brody, Englewood Cliffs, New Jersey, 1974.
— *Abortion and the Sanctity of Human Life: A Philosophical View*, Cambridge, Massachusetts, 1975.
Cajal, Santiago Ramon y, 'Significacion Probable de las Celulas Nerviosas de Cilindro-eje Corto', in *Trabajos del Instituto Cajal de Investigaciones Biologicas*, Volume 44, Madrid, 1952, pp. 1-8.
Carrier, Leonard S., 'Abortion and the Right to Life', *Social Theory and Practice*, Volume 3, Number 4, 1975, pp. 381-401.
Clarke, Francis P., 'St. Thomas on "Universals"', *Journal of Philosophy*, Volume 59, 1962, pp, 720-5.
Conel, J. LeRoy, *The Postnatal Development of the Human Cerebral Cortex*, Cambridge, Massachusetts, Volumes 1-7, 1939-63.
Connolly, Kevin, and Bruner, Jerome (ed.), *The Growth of Competence*, London, 1974.
Copleston, F. C., *Aquinas*, Harmondsworth, Middlesex, 1955.
Cragg, B. G., 'The Development of Synapses in Cat Visual Cortex', *Investigative Ophthalmology*, Volume 11, Number 5, 1972, pp. 377-85.
Crain, B., Cotman, C., Taylor, D., and Lynch, G., 'A Quantitative Electron Microscope Study of Synaptogenesis in the Dendrite Gyrus of the Rat', *Brain Research*, Volume 65, 1973, pp. 195-204.
Davidson, Donald, 'Thought and Talk', in *Mind and Language*, edited by S. Guttenplan, Oxford, 1975.
Davis, Lawrence H., 'Could Fetuses and Infants Have a Right to Life?'.
Denny, M. Ray, and Ratner, Stanley C., *Comparative Psychology*, 2nd edition, Homewood, Illinois, 1970.
Dethier, V. G., and Stellar, Eliot, *Animal Behavior*, 3rd edition, Englewood Cliffs, New Jersey, 1970.
Devine, Philip, 'Tooley on Infanticide', a paper read at the Eastern Meetings of the American Philosophical Association, December 1973.
— *The Ethics of Homicide*, Ithaca, 1978.
Dinello, Daniel, 'Killing and Letting Die', *Analysis*, Volume 31, 1971, pp. 85-6.
Donagan, Alan, *The Theory of Morality*, Chicago, 1977.
Donceel, Joseph F., *Philosophical Psychology*, 3rd edition, New York, 1955.
— 'Immediate Animation and Delayed Hominization', *Theological Studies*, Volume 31, 1970, pp. 76-105.
Dreyfus-Brisac, C., 'The Bioelectrical Development of the Central Nervous System During Early Life', in *Human Development*, edited by Frank Falkner, Philadelphia, 1966, pp. 286-305.
Economo, C. Von, *The Cytoarchitectonics of the Human Cerebral Cortex*, London, 1929.

Ellingson, Robert J., 'The Study of Brain Electrical Activity in Infants', in *Advances in Child Development and Behavior*, edited by Lewis P. Lipsitt and Charles C. Spiker, Volume 3, 1967, pp. 53-97.

Engelhardt, H. T., 'The Ontology of Abortion', *Ethics*, Volume 84, 1974, pp. 217-34.

English, Jane, 'Abortion and the Concept of a Person', *Canadian Journal of Philosophy*, Volume 5, Number 2, 1975, pp. 233-43.

Feinberg, Joel (ed.), *The Problem of Abortion*, Belmont, California, 1973.

—— 'The Rights of Animals and Unborn Generations', in *Philosophy and Environmental Crisis*, edited by William T. Blackstone, Athens, Georgia, 1974, pp. 43-68.

—— 'Abortion', in *Matters of Life and Death*, edited by Tom Regan, Philadelphia, 1980, pp. 183-217.

Finnis, John, 'The Rights and Wrongs of Abortion: A Reply to Judith Thomson', *Philosophy & Public Affairs*, Volume 2, Number 2, 1973, pp. 117-45.

Foot, Philippa, 'The Problem of Abortion and the Doctrine of the Double Effect', *The Oxford Review*, Number 5, 1967, pp. 5-15.

Friedman, Steven, Carpenter, Genevieve C., and Nagy, Alice C., 'Decrement and Recovery of Response to Visual Stimuli in the Newborn Human', in *The Competent Infant*, edited by L. Joseph Stone, Henrietta T. Smith, and Lois B. Murphy, New York, 1973, pp. 361-5.

Gerber, R. J., 'Abortion: Parameters for Decision', *Ethics*, Volume 82, 1972, pp. 127-54.

Gillespie, Norman C., 'Abortion and Human Rights', *Ethics*, Volume 87, Number 3, 1977, pp. 237-43.

Glover, Jonathan (ed.), *The Philosophy of Mind*, Oxford, 1976.

—— *Causing Deaths and Saving Lives*, Harmondsworth, England, 1977.

Godlovitch, Stanley and Roslind, *Animals, Men, and Morals*, London, 1972.

——, Roslind, 'Animals and Morals', in *Animals, Men, and Morals*, edited by Stanley and Roslind Godlovitch, London, 1972.

Gorovitz, Samuel, *et al.* (ed), *Moral Problems in Medicine*, Englewood Cliffs, New Jersey, 1976.

Gray, E. G., *The Synapse*, London, 1973.

Grisez, Germain C., *Abortion: The Myths, the Realities, and the Arguments*, Washington, 1969.

Hare, R. M., *The Language of Morals*, Oxford, 1952.

—— 'Rawls' Theory of Justice—I and II', *Philosophical Quarterly*, Volume 23, 1973, pp. 144-55 and 241-52.

—— 'Abortion and the Golden Rule', *Philosophy & Public Affairs*, Volume 4, Number 3, 1975, pp. 201-22.

—— 'Survival of the Weakest', in *Moral Problems in Medicine*, edited by Samuel Gorovitz *et al.*, Englewood Cliffs, New Jersey, 1976, pp. 364-9.

Harlow, Harry F., 'The Formation of Learning Sets', *Psychological Review*, Volume 56, 1949, pp. 51-65.
— 'Infant Learning: The First Year', in *The Competent Infant*, edited by L. Joseph Stone, Henrietta T. Smith, and Lois B. Murphy, New York, 1973, pp. 605-13.
Howell, Robert, 'Correspondence', *Philosophy & Public Affairs*, Volume 2, Number 4, pp. 407-10.
Humber, James M., 'Abortion: The Avoidable Moral Dilemma', *Journal of Value Inquiry*, Volume 9, Number 4, 1975, pp. 282-302.
Hunter, Walter S., 'The Delayed Reaction in Animals and Children', in *Behavior Monographs*, Volume 2, edited by John B. Watson, New York: 1913-1915, pp. 1-81.
Huttenlocher, Peter R., 'Myelination and the Development of Function in Immature Pyramidal Tract', *Experimental Neurology*, Volume 29, 1970, pp. 405-15.
Jacobson, Marcus, *Developmental Neurobiology*, 2nd edition, New York, 1978.
Jolly, Alison, 'The Study of Primate Infancy', in *The Growth of Competence*, edited by Kevin Connolly and Jerome Bruner, London, 1974, pp. 49-74.
Jones, D. G., *Synapses and Synaptosomes*, London, 1975.
Kagan, Jerome, 'The Determinants of Attention in the Infant', in *The Competent Infant*, edited by L. Joseph Stone, Henrietta T. Smith, and Lois B. Murphy, New York, 1973, pp. 675-83.
Kant, Immanuel, *Groundwork of the Metaphysics of Morals*, translation by H. J. Paton, *The Moral Law*, 3rd edition, London, 1956.
Kluge, Eike-Henner W., *The Practice of Death*, New Haven and London, 1975.
— 'Infanticide as the Murder of Persons', in *Infanticide and the Value of Life*, edited by Marvin Kohl, Buffalo, 1978, pp. 32-45.
Kohl, Marvin (ed.), *Infanticide and the Value of Life*, Buffalo, 1978.
Langer, William L., 'Infanticide: A Historical Survey', *History of Childhood Quarterly*, Volume 1, Number 3, 1974, pp. 353-65.
Langerak, Edward, 'Correspondence', *Philosophy & Public Affairs*, Volume 2, Number 4, 1973, pp. 410-16.
Lecky, W. E. H., *History of European Morals*, 3rd edition, London, 1910.
Lemire, R. J., Loeser, J. D., Leech, R. W., and Alvord, E. C., *Normal and Abnormal Development of the Human Nervous System*, Hagerstown, Maryland, 1975.
Lewis, M., Goldberg, S., and Campbell, H., 'A Developmental Study of Information Processing within the First Three Years of Life: Response Decrement to a Redundant Signal', in *Monographs of the Society for Research in Child Development*, 1969, Volume 34 (9, Serial No. 133).
Lewis, Michael, 'Individual Differences in the Measurement of Early Cognitive Growth', in *Exceptional Infant: Studies in Abnormalities*, edited by Jerome Hellmuth, New York, 1971, pp. 172-210.

McCloskey, H. J., 'The Right to Life', *Mind*, Volume 84, Number 335, 1975, pp. 403-25.

McGraw, Myrtle B., *The Neuromuscular Maturation of the Human Infant*, New York, 1943.

McKeown, Thomas, *The Modern Rise of Population*, London, 1976.

Mackie, John, 'A Refutation of Morals', *Australasian Journal of Philosophy*, Volume 24, 1946, pp. 77-90.

—— *Ethics—Inventing Right and Wrong*, Harmondsworth, England, 1977.

McMahan, Jefferson, 'Problems of Population Theory', *Ethics*, Volume 92, 1981, pp. 96-127.

Marin-Padilla, Miguel, 'Prenatal and Early Postnatal Ontogenesis of the Human Motor Cortex: A Golgi Study', *Brain Research*, Volume 23, 1970, pp. 167-91.

May, William E., 'Abortion and Man's Moral Being', in *Abortion: Pro and Con*, edited by Robert L. Perkins, Cambridge, Massachusetts, 1974, pp. 13-35.

Minkowski, Alexander (ed.), *Regional Development of the Brain in Early Life*, Philadelphia, 1967.

Molliver, Mark E., Kostovic, Ivica, and Van der Loos, Hendrik, 'The Development of Synapses in Cerebral Cortex of the Human Fetus', *Brain Research*, Volume 50, 1973, pp. 403-7.

Morillo, Carolyn R., 'Doing, Refraining, and the Strenuousness of Morality', *American Philosophical Quarterly*, Volume 14, Number 1, 1977, pp. 29-39.

Murphy, Jeffrie G., 'The Killing of the Innocent', *Monist*, Volume 57, Number 4, 1973, pp. 527-50.

Nagel, Thomas, 'Brain Bisection and the Unity of Consciousness', in *The Philosophy of Mind*, edited by Jonathan Glover, Oxford, 1976, pp. 111-25.

Narveson, Jan, 'Future People and Us', in *Obligations to Future Generations*, edited by R. I. Sikora and Brian Barry, Philadelphia, 1978, pp. 38-60.

Nelson, Leonard, 'Duties to Animals', in *Animals, Men, and Morals*, edited by Stanley and Roslind Godlovitch, London, 1972.

Noonan, John T., Jr., 'An Almost Absolute Value in History', in *The Morality of Abortion*, edited by John T. Noonan, Jr., Cambridge, Massachusetts, 1970, pp. 1-59.

Parfit, Derek, 'Overpopulation' (1973 Draft).

—— 'Rights, Interests, and Possible People' in *Moral Problems in Medicine*, edited by Samuel Gorovitz, *et al.*, Englewood Cliffs, New Jersey, 1976, pp. 369-75.

—— 'On Doing the Best for Our Children', *Ethics and Population* edited by Michael Bayles, Cambridge, Massachusetts, 1976, pp. 100-15.

Parmelee, Arthur H., Jr., Wenner, Waldemar H., Akiyama, Yoshio, Stern, Evelyn, and Flescher, Jenny, 'Electroencephalography and Brain Maturation', in *Regional Development of the Brain in Early Life*, edited by Alexandre Minkowski, Philadelphia, 1967, pp. 459-76.

Penfield, W., and Rasmussen, T., *The Cerebral Cortex of Man: A Clinical Study of Localization of Function*, New York, 1957.

Plato, *Republic*.

Poliakov, G. I., 'Some Results of Research into the Development of the Neuronal Structure of the Cortical Ends of the Analyzers in Man', *Journal of Comparative Neurology*, Volume 117, 1965, pp. 197–212.

Postow, B. C., 'Rights and Obligations', *Philosophical Studies*, Volume 32, 1977, pp. 217–32.

Purpura, D. P., 'Morphogenesis of Visual Cortex in the Preterm Infant', in *Growth and Development of the Brain*, edited by M. A. B. Brazier, New York, 1975, pp. 33–49.

—, and Schade, J. P. (eds.), *Growth and Maturation of the Brain*, Amsterdam, 1964.

Regan, Tom (ed.), *Matters of Life and Death*, Philadelphia, 1980.

Robinson, R. J. (ed.), *Brain and Early Behaviour*, London, 1969.

Roupas, T. G., 'The Value of Life', *Philosophy & Public Affairs*, Volume 7, Number 2, 1978, pp. 154–83.

Russell, Bruce, 'On the Relative Strictness of Negative and Positive Duties', *American Philosophical Quarterly*, Volume 14, Number 2, 1977, pp. 87–97.

Sameroff, A. J., 'Can Conditioned Responses be Established in the Newborn Infant?', *Developmental Psychology*, 1971, Volume 5, pp. 1–12.

Scheibel, Madge E., and Scheibel, Arnold B., 'Selected Structural Functional Correlations in Postnatal Brain', in *Brain Development and Behavior*, edited by N. B. Sterman, Dennis J. McGinty, and Anthony M. Adinolfi, New York, 1971, pp. 1–21.

Schmidt, Robert F. (ed.), *Fundamentals of Neurophysiology*, New York, 1978.

Schulte, F. J., 'Structure–function Relationships in the Spinal Cord', in *Brain and Early Behaviour*, edited by R. J. Robinson, London, 1969, pp. 337–42.

Schwartz, Thomas, 'Obligations to Posterity', in *Obligations to Future Generations*, edited by R. I. Sikora and Brian Barry, Philadelphia, 1978, pp. 3–13.

Scriven, Michael, *Primary Philosophy*, New York, 1966.

Sen, Amartya K., 'The Nature and Classes of Prescriptive Judgments', *Philosophical Quarterly*, Volume 17, Number 66, 1967, pp. 46–62.

Sikora, R. I., 'Utilitarianism: the Classical Principle and the Average Principle', *Canadian Journal of Philosophy*, Volume 5, Number 3, 1975, pp. 409–19.

— 'Is it Wrong to Prevent the Existence of Future Generations?' in *Obligations to Future Generations*, edited by R. I. Sikora and Brian Barry, Philadelphia, 1978, pp. 112–56.

—, and Barry, Brian, *Obligations to Future Generations*, Philadelphia, 1978.

Singer, Peter, 'Anglin on the Obligation to Create Extra People', *Canadian Journal of Philosophy*, Volume 8, Number 3, 1978, pp. 583–5.

Singer, Peter, 'Animals and the Value of Life', in *Matters of Life and Death*, edited by Tom Regan, Philadelphia, 1980, pp. 218-59.

Sostek, A. M., Sameroff, A. J., and Sostek, A. J., 'Evidence for the Unconditionability of the Babkin Reflex in Newborns', *Child Development*, 1972, Volume 43, pp. 509-19.

Spitz, Rene A., Emde, Robert N., and Metcalf, David R., 'Further Prototypes of Ego Formation: A Working Paper from a Research Project on Early Development', in *The Competent Infant*, edited by L. Joseph Stone, Henrietta T. Smith, and Lois B. Murphy, New York, 1973, pp. 558-66.

St. John-Stevas, Norman, *The Right to Life*, New York, 1964.

Stevenson, Charles, L., *Ethics and Language*, Yale, 1944.

Stich, S. P., 'Do Animals Have Beliefs?', *Australasian Journal of Philosophy*, Volume 57, 1979, pp. 15-28.

Stone, L. Joseph, Smith, Henrietta T., and Murphy, Lois B. (eds.), *The Competent Infant*, New York, 1973.

Strawson, P. F., *Individuals*, London, 1959.

Sumner, L. W., 'Toward a Credible View of Abortion', *Canadian Journal of Philosophy*, Volume 4, Number 1, 1974, pp. 163-81.

— *Abortion and Moral Theory*, Princeton, 1981.

Thomas, Larry L., 'Human Potentiality: Its Moral Relevance', *The Personalist*, Volume 59, 1978, pp. 266-72.

Thomson, Judith Jarvis, 'A Defense of Abortion', *Philosophy & Public Affairs*, Volume 1, Number 1, 1971, pp. 47-66.

— 'Rights and Deaths', *Philosophy & Public Affairs*, Volume 2, Number 2, 1973, pp. 146-59.

— 'Killing, Letting Die, and the Trolley Problem', *Monist*, Volume 59, Number 2, 1975, pp. 204-17.

Thomson, W. A. R. (ed.), *Black's Medical Dictionary*, 31st edition, London, 1976.

Thorpe, W. H., *Learning and Instinct in Animals*, 2nd edition, London, 1963.

Tooley, Michael, 'Abortion and Infanticide', *Philosophy & Public Affairs*, Volume 2, Number 1, 1972, pp. 37-65.

— 'Critical Notice of Kluge's *The Practice of Death*', *Canadian Journal of Philosophy*, Volume 6, Number 2, 1976, pp. 339-57.

Trammell, Richard L., 'Tooley's Moral Symmetry Principle', *Philosophy & Public Affairs*, Volume 5, Number 3, 1976, pp. 305-13.

— 'Saving Life and Taking Life', *Journal of Philosophy*, Volume 72, Number 5, 1975, pp. 131-7.

Uzgiris, Ina C., 'Patterns of Vocal and Gestural Imitation in Infants', in *The Competent Infant*, edited by L. Joseph Stone, Henrietta T. Smith, and Lois B. Murphy, New York, 1973, pp. 599-604.

Van de Veer, Donald, 'Justifying "Wholesale Slaughter"', in the *Canadian Journal of Philosophy*, Volume 5, Number 2, 1975, pp. 245-58.

Wade, Francis, C., 'Potentiality in the Abortion Discussion', *Review of Metaphysics*, Volume 29, Number 2, 1975, pp. 239-55.

Warren, Mary Anne, 'On the Moral and Legal Status of Abortion', *Monist*, Volume 57, Number 1, 1973, pp. 43-61.

— 'Do Potential People Have Moral Rights?', *Canadian Journal of Philosophy*, Volume 7, Number 2, 1977, pp. 275-89.

Wertheimer, Roger, 'Understanding the Abortion Argument', *Philosophy & Public Affairs*, Volume 1, Number 1, 1971, pp. 67-95.

— 'Philosophy on Humanity', in *Abortion Pro and Con*, edited by Robert L. Perkins, Cambridge, Massachusetts, 1974, pp. 107-28.

Werner, Richard, 'Abortion: The Moral Status of the Unborn', *Social Theory and Practice*, Volume 3, Number 2, 1974, pp. 201-22.

Westermarck, E. A., *The Origin and Development of Moral Ideas*, London, 1906-8.

Wickelgren, Wayne A., *Learning and Memory*, Englewood Cliffs, New Jersey, 1977.

Williams, Bernard, 'The Self and the Future', in *The Philosophy of Mind*, edited by Jonathan Glover, Oxford, 1976, pp. 126-41.

Williams, Glanville, 'The Legal Evaluation of Infanticide', in *Infanticide and the Value of Life*, edited by Marvin Kohl, Buffalo, 1978, pp. 115-29.

Williamson, Laila, 'Infanticide: An Anthropological Analysis', in *Infanticide and the Value of Life*, edited by Marvin Kohl, Buffalo, 1978, pp. 61-75.

Wingate, Peter, *The Penguin Medical Encyclopedia*, Harmondsworth, England, 1972.

Yakovlev, Paul I., and Lecours, Andre-Roch, 'The Myelogenetic Cycles of Regional Maturation of the Brain', in *Regional Development of the Brain in Early Life*, edited by Alexandre Minkowski, Philadelphia, 1967, pp. 3-65.

Young, Wayland, *Eros Denied*, New York, 1964.

Index